DAILY LIFE DURING

THE BLACK DEATH

Recent titles in
The Greenwood Press "Daily Life Through History" Series

The Medieval Islamic World
James E. Lindsay

Jews in the Middle Ages
Norman Roth

Science and Technology in Colonial America
William E. Burns

Science and Technology in Nineteenth-Century America
Todd Timmons

The Mongol Empire
George Lane

The Byzantine Empire
Marcus Rautman

Nature and the Environment in Twentieth-Century American Life
Brian Black

Nature and the Environment in Nineteenth-Century American Life
Brian Black

Native Americans in the Twentieth Century
Donald Fixico

Native Americans from Post-Columbian through Nineteenth-Century America
Alice Nash and Christoph Strobel

Cooking in Europe: 1250–1650
Ken Albala

DAILY LIFE DURING

THE BLACK DEATH

JOSEPH P. BYRNE

The Greenwood Press "Daily Life Through History" Series

GREENWOOD PRESS
Westport, Connecticut • London

Library of Congress Cataloging-in-Publication Data

Byrne, Joseph Patrick.
  Daily life during the Black Death / Joseph P. Byrne.
      p.   cm.—(The Greenwood Press "Daily life through history" series,
  ISSN 1080–4749)
  Includes bibliographical references and index.
  ISBN 0–313–33297–5
  1. Black death—History.   2. Black death—Social conditions—History.
  3. Black Death.   4. Civilization, Medieval.   I. Title.   II. Series.
  RC172.B97   2006
  614.5'732—dc22   2006012033

British Library Cataloguing in Publication Data is available.

Library of Congress Catalog Card Number: 2006012033
ISBN: 0–313–33297–5
ISSN: 1080–4749

First published in 2006

Greenwood Press, 88 Post Road West, Westport, CT 06881
An imprint of Greenwood Publishing Group, Inc.
www.greenwood.com

Printed in the United States of America

The paper used in this book complies with the
Permanent Paper Standard issued by the National
Information Standards Organization (Z39.48–1984).

10 9 8 7 6 5 4 3 2 1

CONTENTS

ACKNOWLEDGMENTS

My thanks to Greenwood Press for presenting me with the challenge of writing this work, and to Mike Hermann for his guidance and enthusiasm along the way. I would also like to express my gratitude to Meaghan Minnick, whose editorial work greatly improved my original effort, and to Paige Carter at Belmont University, whose patience and creativity gave me access to a wide range of rare sources. I would also like to acknowledge the opportunity presented by the National Endowment for the Humanities and Marshall Poe to conduct research at Harvard's many libraries, and to the university for its hospitality.

Most images are courtesy of the National Library of Medicine. Others were taken from *Devils, Demons, and Witchcraft* and *The Dance of Death: 41 Woodcuts by Hans Holbein the Younger* (designated Dover), both published in 1971 by Dover Books.

Chronology

c. 460–380 B.C.E.	Life of Hippocrates, Greek physician who pioneered rational medicine and established practical rules for good health.
c. 130–201	Life of Galen, Greco-Roman physician who wrote important works on humoral medicine and pestilence.
541–c. 760	The Plague of Justinian (First Pandemic); epidemic throughout Mediterranean—probably bubonic plague.
980–1037	Life of Avicenna, great Arab philosopher and medical writer (*Kanon*) who had great influence on Muslim and Christian medicine.
1211	Earliest known civic physician appointed in Reggio, Italy.
1260	Earliest organization of flagellants, in Perugia, Italy.
1330s	Probable outbreak of bubonic plague as epidemic in area of Gobi Desert or Central Asia.
1347	Incident at Kaffa: Warriors of Djanibeg's Golden Horde supposedly infect Genoese colony with pestilence; Genoese (and plague) escape to Constantinople.
Fall, 1347	The Black Death (Second Pandemic) begins; Constantinople, Alexandria, and Messina on Sicily are struck by pestilence; it begins to move outward in Middle East, Africa, and Europe.

Winter, 1347/1348	Italian ports of Genoa, Pisa, and Venice struck, along with Ragusa, Marseille, and the French Riviera. Venice develops first board of sanitation.
Spring, 1348	Naples, Florence, Siena, and Perugia in Italy; Avignon in France; the Balearic Islands, Barcelona, and Valencia in Aragon; Damascus, Aleppo, Jerusalem, and Cairo struck. First attacks on Jews in southern France and Aragon.
Summer, 1348	Rome; Paris, Lyon, Bordeaux, Burgundy, Normandy, and Brittany struck. Pestilence first appears in England and Germany. Flagellant movement begins.
Fall, 1348	London and Ireland struck; Italian and southern French cities begin recovery. Flagellant movement gains momentum. University of Paris medical faculty publishes its *consilium* on the pestilence.
Winter, 1349	Pestilence moves northward through England; Switzerland struck.
Spring and Summer, 1349	Vienna and upper Rhine, Flanders, and Holland struck. England's Ordinance of Laborers promulgated.
Fall, 1349	Bergen, Norway, Cologne, and middle Rhine region struck; Pope Clement condemns flagellant movement. Black Death ends in Islamic regions.
1350	Scotland and Sweden struck. Flagellant movement fades away.
1351	Poland, Baltic region, and western Russia (Pskov) struck. England's Statute of Laborers reinforces Ordinance of Laborers.
1352	Russia (Novgorod) struck.
1358	Boccaccio finishes the *Decameron;* French peasant uprising (*Jacquerie*).
1360–1363	Second Epidemic in France, Catalonia, Italy, Britain, Sweden, Norway, Pskov, and Egypt; later in Germany and Poland.
1370–1374	Third Epidemic in France, Barcelona, northern Italy, Ireland and southern England, Germany, and Hainaut.
1378	Ciompi Revolt in Florence.
1381	Peasants' Revolt in England.

1382–1384	Epidemics in France, Catalonia, Seville, Portugal, northern Italy, London, Kent, Ireland, central Europe, the Baltic region, the Rhineland, and Poland.
1385	Florence begins registry of all burials.
1390–1391	Epidemics in Burgundy, Lorraine, northern England and Scotland, and northern Italy.
c. 1395	First pest house established in Ragusa (Dubrovnik).
1399–1400	General epidemic in Italy, northern Europe, and Seville.
1410–1412	General epidemic in western Europe, Silesia and Lithuania, and Egypt.
1422–1424	General epidemic in Italy, Flanders, and Portugal.
1429–1430	Widespread epidemic in Italy and Haute Auvergne; major epidemic in Mamluk lands.
1438–1439	General epidemic in Italy, France, Portugal, northern Britain, Germany, Switzerland, the Netherlands, Poland, Cairo, and Syria.
1448–1450	General epidemic in northern Italy, France, northern and western Germany, Holland, and Egypt.
1454	Johann Gutenberg develops the printing press in Mainz, Germany.
1456–1457	General epidemics in northern France, Barcelona, and Italy.
1480–1484	Plague in France, Portugal, central Italy, London, Germany, and Poland.
1486	Venice establishes first permanent Commission of Public Health.
1494–1499	Epidemics in southern France, Italy, Aragon, Scotland, Luxembourg, central Germany, Austria, Bohemia, and Poland.
1518	The practice of shutting in victims and their family begins in London, England.
1537	Henry VIII requires registry of all deaths and burials in England.
1560s	London regularizes the recording and issuance of bills of mortality.
1593	Major plague in London; theaters shut down.
1603	Queen Elizabeth of England dies, James I is crowned, and London suffers major plague.

1630–1631   Major plague in Tuscany, Italy.

1653   Major plague in Spain.

1656   Last major plague in Rome and Italy.

1665–1666   Major plague in Amsterdam; Great Plague in London. End of pestilence reports in England.

1712   Last major plague in Austria (Vienna).

1720–1722   Last pestilence in Marseille, France, and mainland western Europe; said to have been imported from Syria. Daniel Defoe writes *Journal of the Plague Year.*

1720s   Austrians establish cordon sanitaire along borders with Ottoman Empire.

1743   Last major plague in Messina, Sicily.

1771–1772   Last major pestilential outbreak in Russia kills 100,000 in Moscow.

1830s   Last epidemics of Second Pandemic occur in North Africa and the Middle East.

1894   Third Pandemic of bubonic plague in China, Southeast Asia, and Hong Kong; Yersin and Kitasato conduct research, identifying *Y. pestis;* serum against the bubonic plague proven successful in following years.

1896–1914   Continued research identifies full epidemiology of bubonic plague bacillus.

INTRODUCTION

As the twenty-first century unfolds we find ourselves in a world in which most people feel threatened by disease. In relatively underdeveloped states in Africa, AIDS, malaria, and the more exotic Ebola virus are taking a vicious death toll, and few seem entirely immune. In far richer and more technologically advanced America and Europe, people rightly fear heart disease, diabetes, and cancer. Across the globe new strains of influenza, HIV-AIDS, and recently SARS have appeared, and everyone seems vulnerable to terrorist attacks with biological agents such as anthrax and smallpox. A whole host of microbes and physiological conditions pose threats to human health, as they have done since people first appeared on earth. When William Shakespeare has Hamlet reflect on "The thousand natural shocks that flesh is heir to," he no doubt had illness in mind: as he wrote, the "English sweating sickness" was running rampant in London, and the plague had claimed his son Hamnet only a few short years before.

As the Bard knew so well, there were times in history when disease struck a mighty blow—the root meaning of the word "plague." We know of many epidemics in history, when a particular disease spread through a large population for a limited time. But relatively few outbreaks have reached the level of pandemics, in which huge geographic areas are affected, often for decades or even centuries. Fortunately for modern humanity, people's ability to travel far and swiftly, and thus spread disease rapidly and widely, began at the same time we began to understand what disease really is, how it affects the human body and spreads through populations, and how it might be treated effectively. Prior to the late nineteenth century, people were largely ignorant of these matters and thus remained at the mercy of disease; but since the average person traveled little, and when he did so he traveled slowly, pandemics were rather rare. The greatest exceptions in Europe and North Africa were the two pandemics of what most believe was the bubonic plague, a bacterial disease passed from rodent fleas to humans. The First Pandemic, also known as the Plague of Justinian, raced across the Mediterranean world, killing millions, and recurred sporadically between the mid-sixth and mid-eighth centuries. The Second Pandemic originated somewhere in Central Asia and appeared in the West in 1347.

The Second Pandemic—the Black Death with which this book is concerned—mauled the Muslim and Christian worlds for over three centuries, receding from Europe in the late seventeenth century and lingering in North Africa and the Near East well into the nineteenth. For much

The Plague Demon afflicts biblical Job; his wife advises "Bless God and Die." From H. von Gersdorf's *Feltbuch der Wundarzney*, Strasbourg, 1540. Dover.

of this period, any given region experienced the horrors of plague about once a decade. While epidemics usually rose in the spring, raged across the summer, and waned in the fall and winter, perhaps reappearing lightly the following spring, they could lay siege to a population for several years at a time. No generation was spared, and those who avoided contracting the disease or survived its ravages, as many did, were nonetheless subjected to the tribulations of stricken friends and loved ones. In addition, during plague time all had to endure a range of trials, from legal restrictions to local economic collapse, from the assault on the senses of the sick and dying who littered the streets to the palpable fear that they were next.

DAILY LIFE AMID DAILY DEATH

The very term "daily life" implies some level of normalcy, of routine, consistency, typicality, stability. But in plague time, this "daily life" was suspended for virtually everyone. For some it meant abandoning everything and fleeing to a safe place, for others shutting themselves up in their own homes to wait the epidemic out. Special diets and medicines that promised good health replaced regular fare at the table, and travel restrictions—formal and informal, official and self-imposed—severely limited communication and even simple shopping. In cities, schools let out, churches closed, shops were abandoned, neighbors moved, construction halted, and the streets were emptied of crowds and theaters of paying audiences. It was like some long, ghastly holiday.

Daily life, such as it had become, was balanced by daily death. Acquaintances disappeared and dreadful signs appeared on front doors, warning visitors away. The shouts of street vendors hawking their wares were replaced by the coarse calls of "Bring out the dead!" Two-wheeled tumbrels piled high with corpses and the dying creaked along the streets in the place of carts brimming with fresh groceries and other merchandise. Fires burned not to cook food or warm bodies, but to incinerate victims' belongings, punish criminals, or fumigate the supposedly "poisonous" atmosphere. In the face of pestilence people's faith in doctors and Catholic priests waned, and for many it shifted to self-help medical books and Protestantism.

Yet despite the reign of "King Death" life did go on, as people altered their habits, assumptions, concerns, and routines to adapt to the extraordinary times. Despite their transformation by corpses, searchers, corpse-bearers, fumigators, plague-doctors, charlatans, gravediggers, and other denizens of plague time, churches, houses, streets and roads, monasteries, city halls, hospitals, and other scenes of "daily life" retained some level of vitality. These "places" are the main points of interest along our tour of the plague-ravaged West. Chapters are organized around the activities associated with them and the manners in which these activities were transformed by the plague and its recurrences. They explore daily life during plague time by

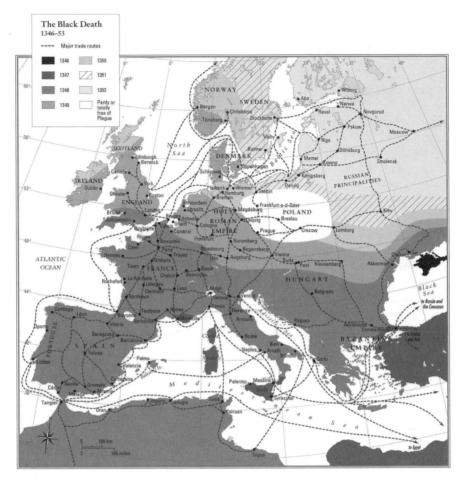

Map of major European medieval trade routes and the spread of the Black Death.

wandering across its landscape and echoing the voices of those who inhabited it, from physicians to bureaucrats, playwrights to theologians, from an emperor to a common tanner. Theirs was a world not merely threatened by disease, but forever altered by it.

THE MEDIEVAL BLACK DEATH

Sometime in the 1330s plague slipped out of its isolated homelands in the vast expanses of Central Asia. While it may well have spread eastward into China and south into the Indian subcontinent, records from these regions tell us little. The disease certainly migrated westward, appearing in the eastern reaches of the Muslim world by the mid-1340s. It swept southwestward around or across the Black Sea, striking Constantinople and the eastern

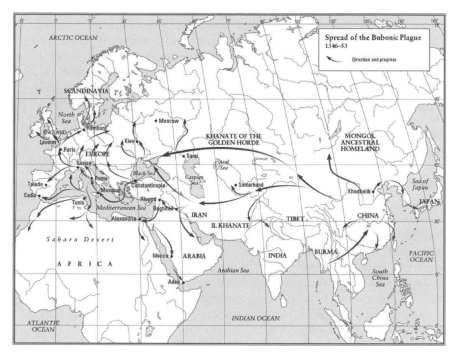

Map of the spread of the Black Death across Asia, the Middle East, Europe, and Africa.

fringes of the Mediterranean in late 1347. At this point Muslims and Christians begin recording what they understood of the plague's origins and early path and the horrors to which they became unwilling witnesses.

The pestilence traveled with merchants, caravans, armies, pilgrims, and diplomatic missions, and on ships loaded with goods and passenger from plague-struck ports. Plague broke out in Sicily, Marseille, Pisa, Genoa, and Alexandria. It coursed inland on boats and barges, along waterways and down roads and horse-paths in carts and on pack animals. It crossed the Alps and Pyrenees, the Apennines and Balkans, the English Channel and North Sea. Eventually it made its way across the great plains of eastern Europe and struck the Russian cities of the Don Basin and Moscow itself. Eyewitnesses described the course of the disease in people and communities, the suffering of victims and survivors alike, and the terrible economic and social wreckage the plague left in its wake. Muslim travelers, physicians, and bureaucrats recorded its devastation in Islamic cities from Baghdad across the Middle East and North Africa to southern Spain (Andalusia). Only a few isolated pockets appear to have been spared, and in the end perhaps as many as four of every ten people were struck down. Others contracted the disease but lived, perhaps gaining some immunity in

the process. In the end, the Western world lost something in the neighborhood of 35 million people, most of them in the span of two years.

Holy men and women prayed, priests and doctors ministered to the
sick and dying, and bishops thundered against the people's sins that had
angered God and brought down his wrath in the form of the pestilence.
After its passing some repented, others took pitiless advantage of the
weak, and all sighed in relief that the scourge had ended. But the horrors of 1347–1352 were only the beginning. Though never again would
the plague be as widespread or as lethal, it nonetheless broke out time
and again as the Middle Ages lurched to a close throughout the West.
Where the records are reliable it seems that plague struck roughly every
ten years, with regional death tolls in the range of 10 to 20 percent rather
than 40 or 50 percent. The young seemed to die more readily than the more
mature, and women more than men, though none could count on immunity. This pattern kept populations from rebounding for a century and a
half, but also prompted many changes in public policy that were meant
to mitigate—or even prevent—the plague's raging. From better sanitation
and health care to quarantining and early warning, local and royal governments adapted to the new regime of recurring pestilence. The medical
profession, too, attempted to deal with the disease, but its theories and
therapies were literally ancient and proved fruitless. Yet each generation
continued to place its trust in doctors and their diets, medicines, and regimens for living. Despite the failure of clergy to placate an obviously angry
God, people also continued to place their faith in the religions of Islam and
Christianity. The Reformation, which fragmented the Catholic tradition in
the early sixteenth century, had deep roots in postplague disaffection, but
developed only a century and a half after the plague's initial outbreak.
Indeed, early Protestants initially sought to purify the venerable religion
and its church, not replace it.

PLAGUE IN EARLY MODERN TIMES

As the Middle Ages gave way before the shifts and innovations of the
Renaissance and Catholicism wrestled with the Protestant challenge, plague
continued to raise its head time and again. As the early modern period
unfolded, however, people noticed that the disease became increasingly
limited to urban areas. As these centers of trade, government administration, education, industry, and culture grew in size and complexity, bureaucrats and magistrates continued to take action against epidemic disease,
increasing both the scope and severity of their activities. City governments
developed health boards and magistracies to create and oversee stricter
sanitation and quarantine regulations both in the cities and in the territories
they administered. They funded plague hospitals and pest houses to isolate
the sick and blockaded ports and rivers to stop potentially deadly maritime

traffic. They established policies and mechanisms for isolating—really imprisoning—the sick and their families in their own homes. Deciding that local plague outbreaks seemed to have their origins in poor neighborhoods, they readily sealed these off at the first sign of the disease, condemning their inhabitants to stay and suffer while ostensibly protecting the city at large. Governments large and small exchanged ideas and learned from one another as all came to realize that none could work alone to stanch the movement of the pestilence that recognized no political boundaries.

At the same time, plague-ridden international armies crisscrossed central Europe with abandon, contracting the pestilence and spreading it as they did rapine, destruction, and slaughter by the sword. Even in peacetime busy trade routes continued to facilitate the dissemination of plague, and increasingly sophisticated smugglers found it easy to avoid the well-intentioned obstacles the authorities provided. It should not be surprising that the last major western European cities to suffer were commercial ports such as Amsterdam, London, Naples, and Marseille, or that plague continued to visit Ottoman harbors in the Mediterranean long after it vanished from Europe.

When a plague epidemic struck northern Europe for the last time, at Marseille in 1720, the medical profession was no more capable of dealing with the disease than it had been in 1350. Despite the Renaissance and the Scientific Revolution, medical education and practice were still mired in the models and practices of the ancient Greeks Hippocrates and Galen. The medieval procedure of bloodletting to reduce harmful "humors," and timing these sessions according to astrological charts, remained common practice through the end of the Second Pandemic. One is hard-pressed to point to a single breakthrough in medical knowledge or treatment related to the plague, even though very bright men had wrestled with it for almost three centuries. In Isaac Newton's England, physicians no less than clerics advised prayer and repentance above any other prophylaxis or treatment for plague. When Muslim physicians began importing supposedly superior European medicine in the sixteenth century, they were getting no bargain.

WHAT WAS THE PLAGUE?

The great breakthroughs in understanding and treating plague came as a result of the mid-nineteenth-century developments of germ theory by the French Louis Pasteur and the German Robert Koch. When the Third Pandemic broke out in East and Southeast **Bubonic Plague** Asia in the 1890s, their students raced to discover its secrets. In Hong Kong the Swiss Pasteurite Alexandre Yersin and Koch's Japanese student Shibasaburo Kitasato vied to isolate the bacillus and prepare a vaccine, and Yersin won. This disease was now bubonic plague—so named for the distinctive swellings, or buboes, in the victims' lymph nodes—that was caused in the human body by the bacillus *Pasteurella* (later *Yersinia*) *pestis*. Further research determined that the *Y. pestis* germ was carried in the gut and the blood-siphoning feeding tube of the flea known as *Xenopsylla cheopis* and was transmitted to victims when the flea punctured their skin and regurgitated the mass of bacteria. Normally *X. cheopis* lived on the scalp of the black rat (*Rattus rattus*), a rodent that lived either in isolated colonies or in close proximity to humans, but when the rat hosts developed the disease and died off, fleas sought new, human hosts, and an epidemic began.

Once in the human body the bacillus multiplies rapidly, evading the natural defensive mechanisms that would normally isolate and neutralize disease germs in the lymphatic ducts and bloodstream. The result is blood poisoning that induces a high fever and other predictable symptoms. Much of the matter created in the bloodstream as the body struggles with the germs, and masses of the germs themselves, are deposited in the lymph glands located in the groin region, under the armpits, or on the neck behind the ears. These therefore swell into the characteristic lumps, or buboes. If enough of the toxic material is diverted to these regions and is drained off naturally or by a physician, the patient may live. If not, the fever persists, with attendant delirium, weakness, and loss of appetite. Ultimately the body suffers toxic shock, organs shut down, and the person dies. Depending on the health of the victim and the course of the disease, death will occur—if it does—within 7 to 10 days after the initial fleabite, and perhaps three days after symptoms first occur. Normally bubonic plague victims are not contagious, though one might be exposed to the bacillus in a victim's blood or in the pus and other material ejected from a lanced or burst bubo.

Septicemic and Pneumonic Plague   In some cases the amount of injected bacteria is so large and enters the bloodstream so rapidly that little is sloughed off to the lymphatic system, and the rapidly multiplying toxin quickly overcomes the body's defenses. In these cases of septicemic plague the victim is stricken and dies very quickly, and almost certainly, without having developed the characteristic buboes. A third variant is pneumonic plague, which occurs when the plague bacillus is lodged and multiplies in a victim's lungs. This may occur in the course of a normal case of bubonic plague, but is more likely when the victim inhales the bacteria-laden, bloody sputum coughed from the mouth of someone who has developed pneumonic plague. As with septicemic plague, the onset of symptoms is rapid and the victim is quickly immobilized with pain, weakness, and high fever. Though it is very lethal and theoretically highly contagious, modern studies have shown that pneumonic plague does not usually spread rapidly or far. In part this is because the victim is usually bedridden or otherwise prostrate shortly after becoming contagious, thus having little opportunity to spread the disease beyond attending family members or medical workers.

Shortly after the discoveries about plague in the early twentieth century, historians began to look at the Black Death in light of them. Those familiar with the historical descriptions of the disease immediately recognized the characteristic buboes readily found in verbal and artistic depictions throughout the Second Pandemic. More subtle analyses of the records over the

Bubonic Plague and the Black Death

twentieth century convinced most historians and medical researchers that indeed the *Y. pestis* bacillus was the culprit in the historical plagues. Victims who were described as dying without developing buboes or while spitting up blood clearly suffered from septicemic or pneumonic plague. Living and sanitary conditions in both the medieval and early modern West and contemporary plague-struck Asia were similar, and the requisite rats lived closely with people in both cultures. Just as contemporaries did, modern historians noted the existence of other, distinct diseases at work alongside plague, further confirming the belief that earlier "pestilence" or "plague" was indeed the same disease as that of the Third Pandemic. When descriptions of plague symptoms did not match the modern profile, they could be easily credited to simultaneously occurring maladies other than bubonic plague.

Even the stories of the origins and spread of the Second Pandemic seemed to fit the model of bubonic plague. Modern scholars theorize that isolated reservoirs of plague-immune or resistant rats or other rodents lived in Central Asia apart from people until the aggressive Mongol expansion disturbed them. Plague-carrying rodents mixed with susceptible rodents, perhaps including those who lived "commensally" with humans. As the susceptible rats were infected and died off, the fleas found human hosts, and the disease took off. Historians easily imagined flea-infested rats inhabiting traveling carts filled with Asiatic grain or the saddlebags of Mongol horsemen. Eventually ships and barges filled with grain transported the deadly living cargo from the Black Sea into the broad Mediterranean, up the Nile, the Rhône, the Tiber and Arno, the Rhine and Thames Rivers. European carts then carried the rats with their deadly parasites to urban palaces and rural huts. The fleas infested existing colonies of rats throughout the Mediterranean and northern Europe, and immune or resistant colonies emerged as new reservoirs from which the disease would reappear decade after decade. Eventually these began to die off, restricting the pestilence to new infusions of plague rats from outside. European efforts at better sanitation and isolation, however, were credited with stemming these infusions or interfering with their effects, bringing the reign of King Death to an end. The pieces seemed to fit nicely and satisfied—and still satisfy—most students of the Second Pandemic. Most, but not all.

In 1970 English scientist J. F. Shrewsbury published a book on the plague in England in which he explored the clear disconnect between the plague death rates during modern epidemics and those reported in the Middle Ages. He correctly noted that—even in the absence of modern medicines—no modern epidemic has killed anywhere near

The Black Death Was Not the Bubonic Plague?

the 40 or 50 percent of local populations that the historical records claim for the first outbreak of the Black Death. Of course he was not the first to notice this, but he was among the earliest to challenge openly the "authorized" picture. Either the witnesses lied or were mistaken, or the Black Death was not the modern "plague." Shrewsbury chose to dismiss the high death rates claimed by medieval witnesses, establishing that bubonic plague could not have killed more than around 5 percent of England's population, not the one-third or more usually reported. In 1985 and since, biologist Graham Twigg has argued that the Black Death was not the bubonic plague at all, since the dynamics of the historical transmission and spread—its speed and breadth—were utterly inconsistent with the biology and behavior of rats and fleas.[1] More recently other biologists, social scientists, and historians have expanded the challenge to the "Black Death = bubonic plague" paradigm.

Critics' arguments revolve around seven major problems. First, the reported symptoms of the Black Death fit the profile of many potentially epidemic diseases other than modern plague. Second, the Black Death was far more infectious than bubonic plague should be. Third, even with water-borne transportation, the historical pestilence spread far too rapidly when compared with modern outbreaks. Fourth, medieval records are not consistent with the known ecological characteristics of rats and fleas, especially insofar as plague occurred in very cold or very dry places, or during very cold seasons that could not support the survival of *X. cheopis*. Fifth, some scholars question whether there was an adequate density of black rats in medieval Europe, concluding that assumptions rather than research support their role in the Black Death. Sixth, modern plagues persist locally for several years at a time, but most reported historical epidemics lasted a single year and then died out. And seventh, the lethality of the disease—the percentage of a local population that dies of a disease—clearly dropped over time for no discernible reason, and then the disease inexplicably disappeared completely from Europe. Thus rejecting bubonic plague, some critics have suggested alternative diseases, ranging from anthrax to an as yet unidentified viral hemorrhagic fever similar to Ebola.

Defenders of the paradigm have responded vigorously, countering most of the critical charges, if not entirely convincingly. The first they can ignore since evidence fails to point to any specific alternative. As for very high rates of infection, some defenders of bubonic plague point out that the human flea (*pulex irritans*) can also contract and pass along the plague bacilli, while others claim that pneumonic plague probably accounts for cases of very rapid transmission. This also addresses the third and fourth criticisms, since it omits the need for fleas. The critics reply, however, that fleas and bubonic plague are necessary to sustain pneumonic plague. The fifth criticism is difficult to prove one way or the other, since there is scant archeological evidence of the rats' presence. Proponents of *Y. pestis* also point out that many species of mammals can host the *X. cheopis* flea, making rat populations less necessary. The final two criticisms seem to hinge on the nature and effects of the plague bacillus. If one assumes that the virulence of *Y. pestis,* its ability to kill its host, has not changed over the centuries, then the problem remains. Scientists, however, have found several strains or variations of *Y. pestis* and note that earlier forms may have simply been more deadly than those active today. Indeed, the theory of natural selection and evolution suggests that species will lose their virulence over time since killing off hosts is counterproductive to a species' survival. The strains that thrive will, in the long run, have the least adverse effect on the organisms—in this case fleas, rats, or people—on which they depend for survival. If plague-infected fleas stopped killing off their rat hosts, then they had no need to seek and infect humans, and the epidemics predictably disappeared. And so the debate continues to simmer.

Around the year 2000 geneticists began studying the tooth pulp of likely plague victims for DNA evidence of the presence of *Y. pestis.* Though early reports from France were positive, critics have challenged the labs and their findings, and research will probably continue. Yet nothing that modern science might discover regarding the nature of the disease will change the facts of daily life during medieval and early modern plague times. For those who suffered, both those who died and those who survived, it mattered little whether the disease was bacterial or viral, rat-borne or passed among people, or, as they believed, in the air they breathed. Whatever its natural causes, they explained, plague ultimately came from God: a punishment unleashed on a sinful and unrepentant humanity.

NOTE

1. J. F. Shrewsbury, *History of Bubonic Plague in the British Isles* (New York: Cambridge University Press, 1970); Graham Twigg, *The Black Death: A Biological Reappraisal* (New York: Schocken Books, 1985).

1

AT MEDICAL SCHOOL

During the Second Pandemic many people strove to prevent or reduce the effects of the Black Death: civic leaders with their legislation, kings with their edicts, and clergy with their prayers. None, however, had as direct a role in confronting the plague as the era's medical practitioners. Europe had a wide variety of these, including apothecaries who dispensed herbs and medicines; barber-surgeons who set broken bones, tended wounds, and performed bloodlettings; midwives who helped women give birth; so-called empirics who used herbs and various nonprofessional healing techniques as their experience taught them; quacksalvers, or quacks, whose elixirs and pills promised amazing cures at low, low prices; and, at the top of the hierarchy, university-trained physicians. The physician reigned supreme as the master of theory and practice, the heir to Greek, Roman, and Arabic medical traditions. Medieval and early modern Europeans entrusted these men with their very lives and afforded them a status just beneath the priests whose services could gain one eternal life.

The theories of health and sickness that guided physicians had deep roots in classical notions of physiology and medicine. These theories were passed on formally through the European medical schools that emerged in the late eleventh century in Sicily and southern Italy, where Arabic and Byzantine cultures reinvigorated the western European mind. At the time of the Black Death, medical science was essentially where it had been a millennium and a half earlier, with some additional overlays from Arabic medicine, such as astrology, and some new instruments and techniques.

Europe's Renaissance polished the luster of the ancients, embedding them even deeper in the Western psyche. It also privileged human experience in a way that eventually led to an overthrow of Aristotle's physiology and the medical practice of the ancient Greek medical giants Galen and Hippocrates. This shift was, however, long in coming. In the early eighteenth century Galen still ruled, while rival theories based on the emerging sciences of biology, human anatomy, and chemistry merely chewed away at the edges. The real revolution in medicine—like the discovery of what plague really was—would not occur until the nineteenth century. Meanwhile, young men in medical schools studied the ancient paradigms, taught people the nature of plague, and worked very hard to prevent and control it. This chapter outlines the basic theories of health and sickness on which medical education was based, the course of this education itself, and the theories of plague that physicians developed during the period from 1348 to the early eighteenth century. Chapter Two discusses more fully the range of medical practitioners, the place of physicians in society, and the ways practitioners dealt with the Second Pandemic given their (mis)understanding of the causes and nature of pestilence.

MEDIEVAL THEORIES OF HEALTH AND SICKNESS

The Greco-Roman Roots   The foundations of what modern people would consider a scientific approach to medicine were laid by three major figures of the ancient Greek world: Hippocrates of Cos, Aristotle, and Galen of Pergamum. The historical Hippocrates (460–380 B.C.E), to whose oath of duty every doctor pledges, is buried under tradition and some 70 books both correctly and falsely attributed to him, known collectively as the Hippocratic Corpus. A product of his age's interest in the processes of nature, or natural philosophy, he rejected the various religious and magical explanations of health and disease, instead basing his key ideas on rational conclusions drawn from an acute observation of nature. Good health followed from living in a healthy environment, developing proper habits of diet and exercise, and avoiding things proven detrimental to one's health. The Corpus is divided by various types of health problems—fractures, epidemics, fevers, and so on—and each section is organized around specific case studies that record in great detail every natural aspect of the patient and his or her illness, from local environmental conditions to the onset of the problem through its course to its conclusion. Hippocratic physicians followed changes in a patient's temperature, skin coloring, urine and feces qualities, breathing, appearance of the eyes, behavior, and other indicators of deterioration or recovery. They also closely watched and recorded the effects of various treatments—such as baths, purgatives,[1] foods, rest, or exercise—for their effects, whether good or ill. Generalizations about diseases or their treatments were to be developed only upon the bases of such observations. Hippocratic medicine concluded that disease is natural and understandable and its course predictable; therefore, the proper treatment is likewise natural and based on a doctor's experience or an authority made trustworthy by experience or reputation.

In the Hippocratic *Nature of Man*, however, the author elaborates upon a theory of the earlier Greek natural philosopher Empedocles, who believed that everything in the material world consists of one or a combination of four elements: air, water, fire, and earth. The Hippocratic author claimed that these corresponded to four distinct "humors," generally understood as fluids, in the human body; and these in turn corresponded to four major organs and four sets of "qualities" that combined "dryness"

Seventeenth-century portraits of Galen and Hippocrates. Note that Hippocrates's side of the rose bush is flowering while Galen's is all thorns. The title page of *De morbo attonito* by Justus Cortnumm, Saxony, 1677. National Library of Medicine.

and "moistness" with "cold" and "heat." Maintaining good health, then, came to be a matter of maintaining the proper balance of humors, and thus the body's "heat" and "humidity."

THE FOUR HUMORS AND THEIR CORRESPONDENCES

Humors:	Blood	Phlegm	Yellow Bile	Black Bile
Element:	air	water	fire	earth
Organ:	liver	brain/lungs	gallbladder	spleen
Season:	spring	winter	summer	fall
Qualities:	warm/moist	cold/moist	warm/dry	cold/dry
Character (dominant mood):	sanguine	phlegmatic	choleric	melancholic
Planet:	Jupiter	Moon/Venus	Sun/Mars	Saturn

Medieval scholars recognized Aristotle (384–322 B.C.E) as the "master of those who would know." Like many of the works of Hippocrates, many of the 150 works attributed to Aristotle were not really his but were penned by his students or assistants. Like Hippocrates, Aristotle was heavily influenced by Greek natural philosophy, and he was educated to be a physician. His fascination with animal anatomy and physiology extended to that of the human animal, but his interests were far more with how the body works than with what to do when it fails to do so. Most of his work on human anatomy has been lost, and modern science has refuted most of that which survives. Aristotle further applied and developed humoral theory, passing it on to the Western world as unquestionable fact that held sway until the nineteenth century. He also developed a highly rational and systematic approach—not necessarily based upon observation or experience—to answering questions regarding just about anything. When medieval western Europeans revived knowledge of this logical method, they, too, applied it to just about everything, from theology to law to medicine. This developed into medieval scholasticism, socalled because of its association with early universities. This system of thinking, arguing, and teaching favored rational argument and previous authorities over personal experience and even common sense. When it came to matters of nature, the greatest of the authorities was Aristotle, whose surviving books often proved terribly convincing and influential—and wrong.

Galen of Pergamum (130–201 C.E.), a trained physician who worked in the Roman Empire but wrote in Greek, was a kind of intellectual watershed into which Hippocratic medicine and Aristotelian natural philosophy flowed. Galen, too, wrote a huge number of books on medicine, largely based on a combination of the theories he had received and his own experience with patients. In dealing with disease, he developed a matrix of medical factors that he placed in three categories: naturals, contra-naturals, and non-naturals. The naturals constituted the state of the human body at any given time: the humors, elements, and qualities, and their balance or imbalance that resulted in health or sickness. When ill, the body had too much or too little of one or more of these, and, of course, all of these were linked by correspondence. Contra-naturals were the causes of imbalance, the symptoms the patient displayed, and, ultimately, the disease itself. If the symptoms were high temperature and sweating, for example, then the disease was a fever whose cause was an excess of "hot and moist" blood. The six non-naturals were factors external to the person but controllable by him or her: air, motion/rest, food and water, sleep/waking, evacuating waste or humors (or not), and what Galenic physicians called "affections of the soul," essentially mood. Disease—humoral imbalance—could be caused by these non-naturals, and thus cured, or at least treated, by them as well. Bad air, the wrong type of food, lack of sleep, too much blood, or fright could affect the balance of humors and cause disease. Relocation to a place with good air, a diet of the right food, sound sleep, phlebotomy (controlled bleeding), or soothing music could heal. This matrix was the heart of Galenic medicine, which served as the model for Arabic, Byzantine, and western European medical theory and practice over nearly two millennia. Shortly before 1300 Catalan physician Arnauvde Vilanova summarized why Hippocrates and Galen remained so influential in his day:

[T]hey were the ones really responsible for a rational form of medicine, of which they were in possession of the technique, and of which they also transmitted the way of finding the true method of applying it when putting remedies into practice.

Despite advances in knowledge of anatomy and physiology and the development of several competing medical theories, Hippocratic and Galenic medicine retained their dominance throughout the Second Pandemic.[2]

While it is incorrect to claim that the medieval Arab/ Islamic civilization rescued the Greek scientific tradition from oblivion, it is true that important Arab and Persian thinkers absorbed the tradition and developed it in ways important to themselves and the Christian West. Ninth- **Arab Variations and Contributions**
and tenth-century Arab physicians like Hunayn ibn Ishaq (809–873 C.E.) were translating, commenting on, and composing new medical works based upon the Greeks at a time when Christian western Europe had few scholars at all, and virtually none who could even read Greek. The watershed of Muslim medical knowledge was the Persian scholar and physician known to the West as Avicenna (Abu Ali al-Husayn ibn Abdallah Ibn Sina, 980–1037 C.E.). His enormous *Kanon* [Encyclopedia] *of Medicine* contained the full range of Islamic medical knowledge and laid out the elements of medical practice based on them. Once translated into Latin it remained the principal medical textbook of the Christian West from the twelfth to the sixteenth century.

One of the most influential—if dubious—contributions of Islamic medicine to the medieval West was the firm linkage of astrology to medicine, a connection originally found in the writings of the Roman Egyptian astronomer Ptolemy (85–165 C.E.). Medical astrology supposed that each celestial body, especially the sun, moon, and planets, had a distinct effect on human bodies. This belief was based on the correspondences among these heavenly bodies and the elements, humors, and qualities of the human body. Just as being born under certain celestial conditions was thought to have an impact on a person, so certain times of the year or month associated with particular arrangements of heavenly bodies were better or worse for performing certain operations, taking particular drugs, or pursuing a specific diet. The Muslim and Christian physicians and public who accepted medical astrology did not see its practice as threatening to their religious culture, but rather as an extension of natural influences, or better, as another nonnatural. They believed the influence of the skies was hidden from direct sight, and thus "occult," but with effects no less real or physical. In fact, epidemic disease—including the Black Death—that potentially affected everyone was considered the result of certain astrological configurations, as many physicians explained in 1348 and for centuries afterward.

MEDIEVAL MEDICAL EDUCATION

Medical Schools and Universities   Medieval western European medical education began at the medical school in Salerno, southern Italy, where the Latin, Byzantine, and Arab cultures met. Here European Christian students and teachers benefited from the presence of Muslim medical scholars and their translations of Greek and Islamic texts into Latin. Constantine the African (1020–1087 C.E.), a Muslim who converted to Christianity and became a monk, began the process of translation while teaching what he had learned as a student and practitioner in Baghdad and Africa. Other translators worked in places like Sicily, Constantinople, Syria, and Toledo, Spain, and together they created a library of medical texts that would form the backbone of medieval and early modern medical education. The early establishment of medical schools at Salerno and elsewhere in southern Europe served to break the clergy's virtual monopoly on medical education that had been a minor part of monastic life. Physicians would no longer be exclusively monks and priests, and soon monks and priests were excluded from formal medical education.

In 1180 Count William VII founded the medical school in Montpellier and opened it to Jews and Muslims as well as Christians. During this early period many schools, such as those at Chartres and Rheims in France and Padua in Italy, taught medicine in the arts program as an offshoot of natural philosophy, or sometimes as a branch of theology. At Bologna, Italy, famed for its law school, physician Taddeo Alderotti founded the faculty of medicine in the school of arts about 1260. The University of Paris obtained its medical faculty in 1253, and Avignon in 1303. Northern European universities and medical schools were later in arriving. The Holy Roman Emperor founded the University of Vienna in 1365, but its medical school appeared only in 1399. Cambridge very tentatively added medical study in 1423.

The medical curriculum varied by school, but all relied almost exclusively on the classical and Islamic inheritance. **The Medical** Typically the student prepared for advanced study by **Curriculum** attending a Latin or grammar school in his—women were not allowed in universities and medical schools—hometown. Here he would learn to read, write, speak, and understand spoken Latin, vital skills since all higher education was conducted in Latin. Around age 14 he would be off to the university to study the seven liberal arts[3] in the arts faculty, earning a bachelor's and perhaps a master's degree after four or five years. Medical school lasted another four or five years, and consisted of a steady diet of Hippocrates, Galen, and Avicenna, peppered with other Islamic works in Latin translation. Professors would read directly from the texts, commenting as they saw fit, and students wrote down what they said. What students received was considered the last word on medical science, and it was presented in a very systematic fashion. What they did not receive was new knowledge or the means of dealing with new medical phenomena, such as plague.

OFFICIAL UNIVERSITY RUBRICS ON DISSECTION AT BOLOGNA, 1405

Since the performance of dissection regards and pertains to the industry and advantage of scholars, and quarrels and rumors have often been customary in finding or searching for bodies from which or of which dissection should be made, they decreed and ordained that any doctor or scholar or anyone else shall not dare to presume or dare to acquire for himself any dead body for such purpose of dissection, unless he has first obtained permission from the rector then in office. The rector, moreover, is held and required in giving permission to doctors and scholars to observe quality and order, when the said license is requested. Also, that not more than twenty persons may attend the dissection of a male; and not over thirty the dissection of the corpse of a woman. And that no one may attend a dissection unless he has been a student of medicine for two whole years and is in his third year, even if he has attended classes for a forbidden [*sic*] time. And he who has once seen a dissection of a man cannot attend another the same year. He who has attended twice cannot attend again in Bologna except the dissection of a woman, which he may see once and no more. . . .

From Lynn Thorndike, *University Records and Life in the Middle Ages* (New York: Norton, 1972), p. 283.

They also received precious little in the way of practical experience, unless they attended one of the few universities in which students followed a professor on his rounds in a hospital. Since only surgeons, who were usually trained as apprentices rather than in universities, worked with surgical and other tools, medical students had no need of instruction in their use. Students generally studied anatomy from schematic drawings, though human dissections slowly appeared in European medical schools. The earliest seem to have been Bologna in the mid-thirteenth century. Here the impetus may have been its use in forensic pathology—dissecting corpses to determine cause of death—stemming from the university's law school. At Montpellier dissections began about a century later, and the Duke of Anjou soon ordered his judicial officers to provide a criminal's corpse every year. One of the main objections to public dissections, a practice begun just before the Black Death, was that a viewer's relative could end up as the corpse on the cutting table. Many schools came to require that cadavers be brought from neighboring towns to avoid this embarrassment. The dissection itself was conducted by a physician/professor who read from a text as a surgeon made the incisions and removed and displayed the organs. True to scholastic form, the text was often a Galenic work on anatomy describing ape organs, often the only corpses allowed the old Roman.

Astrology, a branch of the astronomy the student learned in his arts courses, became a major feature of Western Christian medical instruction from the thirteenth century. Each part of the body was supposed to be governed by one of the 12 zodiac signs, and knowing these relationships would help the physician diagnose illnesses or determine the best treatments or times for treatment. In many ways this was an extension of the humors/planets theory, and it had a long life. The doctor without astrology, one scholar said, "is a blind man; he is unable to serve his patients with skill." In 1405, Bologna required its medical students to study astrology during all four years, and considered them students of "physica (medicine) et astrologica."[4] The same came to be true in northern universities such as Erfurt, Vienna, Kraków, and Leipzig. Paris became a major center of astrological medicine, only rejecting it in 1537. Significantly, opposition to astrological medicine in later years came from clergy and philosophers, not the physicians themselves.

Upon graduation with a doctorate from the medical school at the University of Perugia, Italy, the student underwent a public oral examination by his teachers and then presented a public speech in which he displayed his eloquence in Latin. After a brief presentation by his mentor, the new doctor received a book, ring, and beret as signs of his new status, and the Christian kiss of peace from the faculty. He then hosted a banquet for his teachers and colleagues and handed out small pouches with coins as tokens. Though some guilds or other professional organizations of physicians required a new doctor to perform a term of practice prior to membership, for most purposes the young man of 25 or so was now one of society's most sought-after professionals.

The anatomy professor lectures from a textbook while his assistant pulls back the ribs on the cadaver; note the knife on the table. From the early-fourteenth-century *Anatomia corporis humani* of Mondino dei Luzzi, Martin Landsberg's printed edition, Leipzig, c. 1493. National Library of Medicine.

MEDIEVAL THEORIES OF PLAGUE

As one might expect, the medieval theories of disease and its treatment as formulated and taught in the medical schools shaped the way medieval physicians understood and battled the Black Death. Aristotle had taught the West to think in terms of a hierarchy of causes for any phenomenon. In making a chair, for example, one needed a reason to do so, materials, a plan or schema, and the effort or labor of assembling it. Absent any one of these: no chair. Medieval and early modern physicians believed that the Black Death, too, had a hierarchy of causes, and this notion remained remarkably consistent across the Second Pandemic.

Despite the rational nature of medieval Galenic medicine,
Divine few if any physicians were arrogant enough to deny that God
Causation could and did play a role in the health and sickness of individuals and entire societies. The Bible is full of examples of
God visiting illness or other disasters on people, from the near destruction
of humanity with the Flood to the sores and boils of innocent Job. God
softened the Egyptian Pharaoh's hard heart with "plagues," used epidemics to weaken Israel's enemies, and employed disease and other punish-
ments to chasten the wayward Hebrews. Any outbreak of disease on the
scale of the Black Death had to have its source in divine anger. And such a
display of wrath had to be related to the sinfulness of the Christian people.
Archbishop William Zouche of York, England, made this connection in a
letter to his diocese in the summer of 1349:

. . . who does not know what great death, pestilence and infection of the air hangs
about various parts of the world and especially England these days. This indeed
is caused by the sins of people who, caught up in the delights of their prosperity,
neglect to remember the gifts of the Supreme Giver.

While one might expect this from a religious leader, it may be a bit surprising to hear it from the King of Sweden: "God for the sins of man has struck
this great punishment of sudden death. By it most of our countrymen are
dead." Yet even physicians, such as the German Henry Lamm, could write
in the early fifteenth century, "[I]t is better to say that the epidemic comes
from God than to repeat all the opinions one hears." Poets, philosophers,
merchants, and notaries echo the notion of Gabriele de' Mussis of Piacenza
that the plague was a punishment on

the entire human race wallowing in the mire of manifold wickedness, enmeshed in
wrong-doing, pursuing numberless vices, drowning in a sea of depravity because
of a limitless capacity for evil, bereft of all goodness, not fearing the judgments of
God, and chasing after every evil.[5]

When confronted with the agony and deaths of apparently innocent
infants and children, Christians could take some consolation in the
innocence of suffering Job, or the doctrine that due to original sin all are
worthy of chastisement, or that punishment for the "sins of the father"
may be visited on the children.

The Planets After three major outbreaks of plague, Thomas Brinton,
and Stars Bishop of Rochester, wrote to his flock in 1373:

Since the corruption of lust and the designs of wickedness are greater today than in
Noah's time—for a thousand forms of vice are practiced today which did not exist
then—let us not impute the scourges of God to planets, but rather to our sins.

According to many physicians and otherwise educated people, God used
the planets as a mechanism for visiting plague on humanity. Brinton's point

is that one should not blame the instrument, but the deeper cause: one's own failings. Even so, celestial bodies were a divine instrument, as the German natural philosopher Albert the Great of Cologne had claimed a century before the Black Death. Building on the Muslim Albumasar (who in turn had borrowed from Aristotle), Albert taught in his "Causes and Properties of Elements" that the conjunction of Mars and Jupiter provokes "a great pestilence in the air, particularly when it happens in a warm and humid sign of the zodiac." For him, this process was very natural, if occult: moist Jupiter attracts vapors from the earth and warm/dry Mars "ignites the elevated vapors thus causing the multiplication in the air of lightnings, sparks, pestiferous vapors and fires."[6] Here we have a perfect scholastic explanation, logical and based on Aristotle's authority—and wrong.

As plague raged in October 1348, King Philip VI required the medical faculty of the University of Paris to provide an explanation of the plague and its origins. Echoing Albert they responded in the *Paris Consilium* that the plague was "caused by a conjunction of the planets Saturn, Jupiter, and Mars at precisely 1:00 P.M. on March 20, 1345." Thanks to the reputation of the source, this analysis had long life and found its way into several surviving poems and many medical tracts. Comets, too, came under suspicion. In his *Meteorologia* Aristotle had claimed that the passage of comets creates hot and dry conditions, and some medieval physicians, like Raymond de Viviers of Avignon, argued that "in times of plague, comets are seen, whose burning shapes fly through the air, which they vitiate. In turn, the humors of our bodies are corrupted and the plague is induced." In 1482 Hans Folz wrote in his plague verses, "[C]omets with fiery tails are known in Germany as drying stars because they withdraw all moisture over which they fly. This may be seen by the great plague and this too is a cause of corrupt atmosphere."[7]

Once the role of divine and celestial forces, sometimes called the "remote causes," was made clear, Avicenna's *Kanon* provided the immediate cause: **Corruption of the Air**

[V]apors and fumes rise into the air, and provoke its putrefaction by means of soft warmth. When the air that has undergone such putrefaction arrives at the heart, it rots the complexion of its spirit and then, after surrounding the heart, rots it. An unnatural warmth then spreads all around the body, as a result of which a pestilential fever will appear. It will spread to any human who is susceptible to it.

Galen and Hippocrates had warned against the ill effects of miasma, or bad air. People had long associated stench with this bad air, and stench had many sources, including swamps, piles of corpses after a battle, decaying animals and vegetation, human and animal waste, and stagnant air. Medieval towns had long legislated against things that stunk, believing that stink kills. Thomas Burton of Meaux Abbey in England noted a great earthquake on March 27, 1349, and wrote, "The earthquake was quickly followed in this part of the country by the pestilence."[8] Others causally connected earthquakes with the plague, and some physicians decided that tremors broke the earth's surface and released pent-up noxious vapors that corrupted the air, a theory that lasted well into the nineteenth century.

With the plague came death on a huge scale, death that rolled across the countryside from one place to another. So many fell ill and so many died that it had to be due to the air that all breathed. Yet all did not fall ill, and not all who fell ill died. Physicians concluded that some people were more susceptible to the poisonous, corrupt air than others. Since plague was associated with "warmth" and "moisture," people who were naturally "warm and moist," such as young women and children, were considered most susceptible. Fat people and those who ate largely "warm and moist" diets were also at risk. But what of the deceased victims who had been apparently "cool and dry," such as healthy mature men and older women? In explaining their deaths some fell back on divine will, others claimed that cause of death was not the pestilence, and still others that these people's true state of health was more perilous than known, such that they only seemed healthy to begin with. Of course, certain behaviors could also make one more susceptible: exercising, having sex, and bathing in hot water all increased respiration and opened the skin's pores, drawing in the corrupted air even more rapidly.

The Effect on the Body

To the medieval physician the effect of the pestilence was to introduce corrupted air through the lungs or pores of the skin, which in turn generated a poison inside the body. Once this poison built up around the heart, as Avicenna and a host of Western physicians agreed, the victim is as good as dead. Before affecting the heart, though, the poison circulated in the body, and it is during this period that treatment might be successful. Physicians recognized that the human body has natural mechanisms for discharging poison, and if the amount is small or the mechanisms in good shape, the poison will be moved away from the heart. Depending on its weight, they believed, the poison would move toward and collect in one of three areas associated with major organs and naturally suited for removing poison: behind the ears (brain), the armpits (heart), and the groin (liver). Not coincidently, these were in fact the three areas that usually developed the characteristic lumps or buboes, which physicians rightly associated with the discharge of the pathogen. Buboes were thus considered good things, and if they "ripened" properly and burst, then recovery seemed imminent. If they hardened, or never appeared at all, then the prognosis was quite poor.

Contagion

However, the most virulent moment of this *epidemia*, which causes an almost sudden death, is when the air spirit emitted from the sick person's eyes, particularly when he is dying, strikes the eye of a healthy man nearby who looks closely at him; then the poisonous nature of this member [the eye] passes from one to another, killing the healthy individual.[9]

The "Anonymous" physician of Montpellier described a phenomenon that modern physicians would associate with pneumonic plague, but explains it in a fashion we find bizarre. Yet many others agreed with him about the deadly gaze, such as papal doctor Guy de Chauliac and Matteo Villani, a Florentine chronicler who wrote that "it seems that this pestiferous infection is caught by the sight and by the touch." Avicenna had admitted that some diseases pass from one person to another, but that this process was really a transmission of corrupted air. Even so, this phenomenon complicated matters greatly, in terms of both explaining and treating the plague: it was not just a matter of "bad air," but of people spreading this "bad air" well beyond its environmental source.

Physician Gentile da Foligno observed in 1348 that "communication of the evil disease happens principally from contagious conversation with other people who have been infected," and Mariano di Ser Jacopo noted that "it happens often that men die of plague in healthy air simply through contagion."[10] But if Villani, and many others, were correct in saying that plague could be passed through touch, then what was the role of corrupted air? Perhaps it was a matter of the poison moving directly from the pores of the infected to those of the healthy. But then what of contagion from things, such as cloth or furniture or even coins? From the outset people believed they observed humans and animals dying from having handled "infected" items, and not just from the air or other people. These matters remained unresolved among premodern physicians, but the implications of both theory and observation were clear: avoid corrupted air and anyone who has the plague.

EARLY MODERN MEDICAL EDUCATION

During the sixteenth and seventeenth centuries medical schools and the doctors they produced multiplied. Around 1500 **Medical** Oxford and Cambridge together created only five or six new **Schools** doctors per decade. After closing down many of his realm's hospitals as part of his reformation in the 1540s, Henry VIII created a Regius (King's) professorship in medicine at each university. In France, Paris was producing an average of 2.2 new physicians each year between 1390 and 1500; but by the 1660s 9 French medical schools graduated an average of 68.4 physicians per year. France had 2 medical schools in 1500 (Paris and Montpellier) and 19 in 1700. Scholars have decided, however, that both academic rigor and standards for admission and graduation fell over time at all these schools except Paris.

Neither the medieval nor early modern medical schools taught a course on "plague." In an age noted for scientific **Curricula** advancement and discovery, the medical schools, like much of university life, remained frustratingly stagnant. Classical scholars known as humanists produced superior printed versions of Galen, Aristotle, and

Hippocrates in their Greek originals, but these works remained key medical teaching texts instead of being relegated to the libraries of collectors and students. This project did, however, eliminate much in the way of medieval commentary and other scholastic rubbish, whether Christian or Arab in origin. Students now commonly studied Greek, and the printing press made not only the classics, but the handful of new texts much cheaper and more readily available. These trends had their earliest effects in Italy and slowly affected the rest of Europe.

Thanks to impulses related to the Renaissance, schools added courses in pharmacy and medicinal botany, and theaters for anatomical dissections became much more common. The "discovery" of the Western Hemisphere forced botanists to abandon the ancient Greek botanist Dioscorides and the mere 600 plant species he discussed and illustrated in the first century; by 1623 Europeans had 6,000 to deal with. Public dissections became even more popular, as illustrated in Rembrandt's famous *Anatomy Lesson of Dr. Tulp* (1632). Felix Platter, a German student at Montpellier's medical school in the 1550s, describes several in his journal. One was

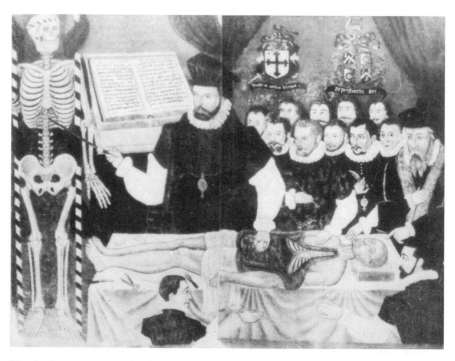

The barber-surgeon John Banister delivering an anatomy lecture at the Barber-Surgeons' Hall in London, 1581. Note that he is the one handling the cadaver, not an assistant. From a contemporary painting. National Library of Medicine.

conducted in the old theater on the corpse of a boy who had died of an abscess in the stomach . . . Doctor Guichard presided at this autopsy, and a barber did the operation. Besides the students, the audience contained many people of the nobility and the bourgeoisie, and even young girls, notwithstanding that the subject was a male. There were even some monks present.[11]

Of course, these procedures required fresh corpses, which were not always obtained in the most legitimate of ways.

A MEDICAL STUDENT AND DEATH, 1550s

Like most others of his day, the German medical student Felix Platter was no stranger to death and dead bodies. In his journal he recalls several encounters in France: While riding in a dense fog he bumped into a corpse suspended by a rope from a tree and later on the same trip rode past a place of execution where "pieces of human flesh hung from the olive trees." He later witnessed brutal executions, which were far from uncommon during this age of civil and religious strife. In one case he describes the decapitation of the local baker's son, after which the young man's arms and legs were severed ("as is the usage in this country"). The limbs and head were soon hanging in the gruesome olive grove. Nor was plague foreign to him: it appeared in Basle just as the young man was leaving for medical school in Montpellier, laying low a family servant who eventually recovered. When he arrived in Montpellier he purposely hid the fact that he had come from a plague-infested place lest his landlord, an apothecary, deny him a room.

Platter also describes how he and friends, wishing to carry out secret dissections, stole corpses at night from the local cemetery of St. Denis. "We had spies to tell us of burials and to lead us by night to the graves," he wrote. Late one night he joined an Augustinian friar and a bachelor of medicine and together "in complete silence, swords in hand, we made our way to the cemetery of St. Denis. There we dug up a corpse with our hands, the earth being still loose, because the burial had taken place that day." The body of a woman was wrapped in their cloaks, and carried on poles to the bachelor's house, where the trio carried out their surreptitious dissection. Five days later they repeated their adventure, snatching the fresh corpses of a male child and a student they had known when alive. To dissuade further ghoulish acts, the monks that ran the cemetery began guarding its gate armed with crossbows.

Adapted from Seán Jennett, trans., *Beloved Son Felix: The Journal of Felix Platter, a Medical Student at Montpellier in the Sixteenth Century* (London: F. Muller, 1961).

Despite the opposition of physicians' guilds, surgery entered the curricula at many medical schools in the sixteenth century. It was as a professor of surgery at the University of Padua that Andreas Vesalius developed his monumental and highly accurate illustrated work on human anatomy, *On the Structure of the Human Body*, published in 1543. One of the most important advances in medical education was the introduction of systematic clinical teaching, in which the students were taught at patients' bedsides. Padua's Giambattista da Monte began this method in the 1540s at the hospital of

San Francesco, and his students carried the practice to the Netherlands and beyond. Experience gained a toehold as a source of authority among medical professors, as a few began to question the classical authorities in light of what they actually observed. One of the most famous physicians of the early seventeenth century was Daniel Sennert, who taught at Wittenberg's university and whose books went through 125 editions. He believed that "experience is the teacher of all things," and that it needed to trump not only classical authors but even human reason as the final authority for the physician.[12] Ironically, both Hippocrates and Galen would have agreed. Yet Sennert's remained a minority opinion: Vesalius visited Bologna in 1544 and presented a dissection of and lecture on the venous system, which caused a great uproar among the audience. But rather than confronting what Vesalius had done or said, the crowd vociferously debated the relative merits of Galen and Aristotle. Bored, Vesalius left in a huff.

Alternative Medicine: Paracelsus

The most interesting challenge in the sixteenth century to academic Galenic medicine came from the students of the German physician Theophrastus Bombastus von Hohenheim, known as Paracelsus. Though trained in Galenism, he rejected it as a valid paradigm for understanding and treating illness, and his followers often attacked its adherents for their antiquated, pagan, and ineffective approach to medicine. Paracelsus understood and treated illnesses not as imbalances of humors, but as disorders of specific organs in the body. He attempted cures by using chemical medicines that were meant to address the three chemical "principles" that he claimed regulated health: sulfur, mercury, and salt. By connecting inorganic cures with organic ailments, Paracelsus was a key figure in developing iatrochemistry, or "medical chemistry." In many ways his ideas were linked to alchemy, which also supposed there to be certain occult "life forces" in inorganic matter (think of a magnet). Of course, his theory of three principles was no more accurate than his contemporaries' notion of four humors. But Paracelsus strayed further still from medical orthodoxy by linking his biochemical ideas to both Christian and Neo-Platonic mysticism, and to the Protestant Reformation, declaring that his reform of medicine was an integral part of divine reform in the world. Though he gained a number of adherents and affected the history of biochemistry, he and his followers were often dismissed as "magicians" or "conjurers," and their ideas had little effect on understanding or battling the plague effectively.

AN ENGLISH PARACELSIAN ATTACKS THE MEDICAL ESTABLISHMENT: THE LAWYER RICHARD BOSTOCKE, 1585

And, O most merciful God, because the heathenish physic (medicine) of Galen doth depend upon that heathenish philosophy of Aristotle, therefore is that physic as false and injurious to thine honor and glory, as is the philosophy.

For, that heathenish physic, O God, doth not acknowledge the creation of man, whereby it doth not rightly know why he is Microcosmus, or little world: which is the cause why they neither know his diseases rightly, neither provide medicines for him aptly, nor prepare it fitly, neither minister it accordingly. This heathenish philosophy and physic doth attribute thy works to heat, cold, and such causes, which it calleth falsely natural . . . and whereby seeking for like cure in such defects, their physic must needs err, in not seeking help at thy hands, nor praying to thee, nor giving thanks to thee. . . . And because they understand not that diseases do proceed of the mechanical spirits and tinctures of impure seeds joined to the pure [seeds] by thy curse, O just God, therefore they seek not their medicines in the pure seeds [salt, mercury, sulfur].

From his *The Difference Between the Ancient Physick . . . and the Latter Physick*, in *Health, Disease, and Society in Europe, 1500–1800: A Source Book,* ed. Peter Elmer and Ole P. Grell (New York: Manchester University Press, 2004), pp. 111–12.

EARLY MODERN PLAGUE THEORIES

Because it is God who has given us disease, He could, when the time were proper and the limit of our purgatory[13] had come, take **Divine and** it away from us, even without the physician. If he fails to do so, it **Celestial** is only because he does not want this to be accomplished without **Causation** the help of man. If he works a miracle He does it only in the human way and through man.

Living in the midst of the Protestant Reformation, even the unorthodox Paracelsus felt keenly the need to attribute the condition of people to their Creator. This strain of thinking continued throughout the sixteenth and seventeenth centuries, though physicians tended to find it less and less useful. In reformed England, however, many physicians were also clergymen, such as Thomas Brasbridge, author of *The Poor Man's Jewel* (1578). He railed against astrology as the "idolatry of the heathen," but repeatedly blamed plague on human sinfulness and emphasized that repentance was the only sure cure. A few decades later the Utrecht professor of medicine Isbrandus van Diemerbroeck described pestilence as a venom specially created by God that propagates itself like "a ferment [yeast] in leaven." In his book *Loimologia* (Study of Plague), which was reprinted in 1721, physician Nathaniel Hodges wrote of London's Great Plague in 1665:

The Sacred Pages [Bible] clearly and demonstratively prove that the Almighty, by his authority, and at his pleasure, may draw the sword, bend the bow, or shoot the arrows of death . . . and in this contagion before us the footsteps of an over-ruling power are very legible.[14]

About the same time the physicians of Rouen, France, were writing that God's wrath was the cause of plague. But with what was God now angry? Most commentators listed the usual human failings, but the Reformation added a new dimension: In Geneva Catholics attributed God's anger to Calvinist heresy, and Calvinists to Catholic blasphemy. One could always blame one's religious enemy for bringing on or prolonging the plague.

THEOLOGIAN MARTIN LUTHER ON ILLNESS AND MEDICINE, WITTENBERG, 1532

Unlike most Christian theorists, whether Catholic or Protestant, Martin Luther saw devilish forces rather than divine behind the plague and other diseases, which validated the physician in a special way:

> I believe that in all grave illnesses the devil is present as the author and cause. First, he is the author of death. Second, [St.] Peter says in Acts [10:38] that those who were oppressed by the devil were healed by Christ. Moreover, Christ cured not only the oppressed but also the paralytics, the blind, etc. Generally speaking, therefore, I think that all dangerous diseases are blows of the devil. For this, however, he employs the instruments of nature. So a thief dies by the sword, Satan corrupts the qualities and humors of the body, etc. God also employs means for the preservation of health, such as sleep, food, and drink, for he does nothing except through instruments. So the devil also injures through appropriate means. When a fence leans over a little, he knocks it all the way to the ground. Accordingly, a physician is our Lord God's mender of the body, as we theologians are his healers of the spirit; we are to restore what the devil has damaged.

From Luther's *Table Talk,* vol. 54 of *Luther's Works,* ed. and trans. Theodore G. Tappert (Philadelphia: Fortress Press, 1967), p. 53.

And one could still blame the stars and planets as God's instruments, as did numerous Spanish physicians, including the Sevillians Gaspar Caldera de Heredia and Alonso de Burgos, and the head of the Jesuit College in Huesca in 1652. In 1629 the French physician and royal councilor Antoine Davin claimed the plague of the previous year had been brought on by "evil constellations, celestial conjunctions, and an eclipse of the moon, which happened on the twentieth of January."[15] During the same plague the French physician Antoine Mizaud published his *Certain and Well-proven Remedies against the Plague* with a cover illustration of three physicians searching the starry night sky, astrological treatise in hand. Two years later a Milanese doctor wrote that since "Saturn rules the ears," naturally buboes would appear on the back of the neck. In 1679 the Austrian court's principal physician, Paul de Sorbait, blamed a conjunction of Mars and Saturn, and French doctors considered the moon a factor as late as 1785. It may be the case that among physicians astrological theories tended to be associated more with Roman Catholic scholasticism, thus retaining less traction among Protestants.

Though many scientists and physicians retained the cor-
rupted air theory, others rejected it in favor of more specific and   **Contagion**
explanatory—though equally wrong—mechanisms, especially   **Revisited**
for contagion. The Italian physician Girolamo Fracastoro got
the ball rolling with his *De contagion*. Published in Venice in 1546 and with
10 editions by 1600, it contained his theory that plague was not mere putrefaction, but a matter of "seedlets" or "tinder" that floated through the air,
entered the human body, and caused "putrefaction" and disease. The original seeds were created in the stars and fell to earth, but infected people also
created more in their bodies, passing them along to others. Robert Boyle, of
"Boyle's Law," theorized that tiny "poisoned corpuscles" in the air, in differ-
ing concentrations, formed a poisonous dust that accounted for the plague
and its varying effects. The German Jesuit Athanasius Kirchner, sometimes
called the "Father of Bacteriology," using a 32X microscope, found what he
called "worms" in the blood of plague victims. In his *Investigation of Plague*
(1658) he blamed these for the disease, an observation very close to being
accurate.

Many of the current theories, however, remained tied to humoralism,
with an increasing emphasis on the conditions and behaviors of poorer
people in growing early modern cities. In 1577 Dr. Girolamo Donzellini
of Verona wrote that the causes of plague were malnutrition, overcrowd-
ing, pollution, carelessness, and food poisoning. The last was a matter
of "internal corruption" brought on by eating the leftovers found in
market garbage bins: herbs, fruits, roots, old fish and meat and internal
organs, and badly cooked bread made of poor flour. The London College of Physicians' list of purported causes might have been compiled in
1348: slaughterhouses, inadequate burials, drainage from outhouses and
vaults in which corpses were buried, musty grain, unwholesome bread,
unsound cattle, and tainted fish. They did, however, add more "modern"
factors, including increased building in cities and grossly overcrowded
living conditions. A pamphlet published in London in 1636 listed over
seventy "causes," including drinking beer in an overheated room and
eating foods like cherries, mutton loin, cucumbers, cream and gooseberry
custard, or eels.

Despite a few attempts to shift the paradigm of health and disease away
from ancient humoralism, the hierarchy of causes from God to eels remained
dominant throughout the Second Pandemic. Despite the Renaissance, Reformation, and Scientific Revolution, medical education remained mired in
antiquated theories and practices that retarded the advance of medical science. As long as physicians were the products of such a system, and were
dissuaded from looking outside of the box, they would remain ineffective
in the face of the plague. And the broader culture, despite many advances,
did not help these matters: at least Hippocrates had moved beyond divine
and celestial models of health and disease that muddied the waters in
which medieval and early modern physicians swam.

NOTES

1. Medicines that helped the body purge itself of bodily wastes like sweat, urine, feces, or stomach contents.

2. Luis Garcia-Ballester, "The 'New Galen,'" in *Text and Tradition*, ed. Klaus-Dietrich Fischer (Leiden: Brill, 1998), p. 63.

3. Grammar, logic, rhetoric, arithmetic, geometry, music, and astronomy.

4. Carole Rawcliffe, *Medicine and Society in Later Medieval England* (Stroud, Gloucs., England: Sutton, 1997), p. 83; R. Lemay, "The Teaching of Astronomy at the Medieval University of Paris," *Manuscripta* 20 (1976), pp. 198–99.

5. Zouche in William J. Dohar, *The Black Death and Pastoral Leadership* (Philadelphia: University of Pennsylvania Press, 1995), p. 4; Magnus in William G. Naphy and Andrew Spicer, *The Black Death and the History of Plagues, 1345–1730* (Stroud, Gloucs., England: Sutton, 2001), p. 32; Lamm in Sèraphine Guerchberg, "The Controversy over the Alleged Sowers of the Black Death in the Contemporary Treatises on Plague," in *Change in Medieval Society*, ed. Sylvia Thrupp (New York: Appleton-Century-Crofts, 1965), p. 213; Gabriele in John Aberth, *From the Brink of the Apocalypse* (New York: Routledge, 2000), p. 114.

6. Brinton in John Friedman, "Henryson's *Testament of Cresseid* and the *Judicio Solis in Conviviis Saturni* of Simon de Couvin," *Modern Philology* 82 (1985), p. 14; Albert in Jon Arrizabalaga, "Facing the Black Death: Perceptions and Reactions of University Medical Practitioners," in *Practical Medicine from Salerno to the Black Death*, ed. Luis Garcia-Ballester et al. (New York and Cambridge: Cambridge University Press, 1994), p. 253.

7. Faculty in Aberth, *From the Brink*, p. 115; De Viviers and Folz in John Friedman, "He hath a thousand slayn this pestilence," in *Social Unrest in the Late Middle Ages*, ed. Francis X. Newman (Binghamton, NY: Medieval and Renaissance Texts and Studies, 1986), pp. 83–84.

8. Arrizabalaga, "Facing," p. 251; Byron Lee Grigsby, *Pestilence in Medieval and Early Modern English Literature* (New York: Routledge, 2004), p. 106.

9. Arrizabalaga, "Facing," p. 263.

10. John Henderson, "The Black Death in Florence," in *Death in Towns*, ed. Steven Bassett (New York: Leicester University Press, 1992), pp. 140–41.

11. *Beloved Son Felix: The Journal of Felix Platter, a Medical Student in Montpellier in the Sixteenth Century*, trans. Seán Jennett (London: F. Muller, 1961), pp. 43, 47, 89.

12. Wolfgang Eckart, "'Auctoritas' vs. 'Veritas' or: Classical Authority and its Role for the Perception of Truth in the Work of Daniel Sennert (1572–1637)," *Clio medica* 18 (1983), pp. 132–33.

13. Suffering that brings salvation.

14. Jolande Jacobi, ed., *Paracelsus, Selected Writings* (Princeton: Princeton University Press, 1988), p. 81; on Diemerbroeck see William Boghurst, *Loimographia* (New York: AMS Press, 1976), p. 14; Nathaniel Hodges, *Loimologia* (New York: AMS Press, 1994).

15. Raymonde Elise Doise, *La Peste en Bretagne* (La Poiré-sur Vie: Sol'air, 1998), pp. 32–33.

2

AT THE DOCTOR'S OFFICE

We have seen how classical precedents and the nature of medieval and early modern medical education shaped medical theory in general and theories about the plague in particular. This education also heavily influenced the ways physicians practiced, especially during plague time. Theory and practice changed remarkably little during the nearly four centuries of the Second Pandemic: people continued to blame God, the stars, and bad air; and doctors continued to fight sources of evil odors and unbalanced humors and bleed their patients to balance them. Despite such epoch-marking phenomena as the Renaissance and the Scientific Revolution, the most common medical advice in the eighteenth century was still to flee. Although the number of university-trained doctors in Europe increased greatly, their ability to prevent or treat the plague effectively was no greater in 1720 than it had been in 1348. But physicians were not alone in battling the plague. They had allies among surgeons and apothecaries and faced competition from empirics, Paracelsians, quacks, and "wise women," whose alternative medicines both challenged and complemented that of the medical establishment.

A VARIETY OF MEDICAL PRACTITIONERS

Medical education in the medieval universities was almost exclusively a matter of book-learning and theory, both of which reflected and reinforced the intellectual nature of the physician. The heaviest physical labor a physician might expect to perform was lifting a glass jar of urine to examine it or taking a patient's pulse. Following the initial outbreak of plague in Paris, physicians agreed to take an oath to avoid

The Surgeon

doing "manual surgery," and other guilds followed their lead. The heavy lifting, so to speak, was carried out by the men—and sometimes women— known as surgeons or barber-surgeons. These professionals received their education and training within the guild system of masters and apprentices. Surgeons learned on the job, and their knowledge was largely based upon experience rather than theory and reading. Some European communities distinguished between the surgeons who also shaved men's beards *(barba)* and those who dealt exclusively with medical matters. Surgeons' responsibilities included dentistry, bone setting, wound dressing, limb amputation, surgery on all parts of the body, and phlebotomy, or bleeding to reduce the humor in a body. When practicing as barbers their tasks included shaving, styling, and cutting hair, washing people's upper bodies, cleaning teeth, paring nails, and picking off nits and lice. They were vital adjuncts to the physicians who essentially practiced internal medicine.

The interior of a barber-surgeon's shop. The patient is having blood let. Pans for blood and jars of leeches hang from the ceiling. From Malachias Geiger's *Microcosmus hypochondriacus,* Monaco, 1652. National Library of Medicine.

Though surgeons regularly visited patients—especially wealthy ones—in their homes, they also found it useful to have a shop to which customers would come for service. They attracted customers with the sign of a bowl of blood—a real bowl with real blood early on, though some places later adopted the more familiar barber pole wrapped in white bandages with spiral stripes of red and blue representing veins and arteries. Not unlike modern styling facilities, these shops were centers of community, with music, food, drink, conversation, and gambling, all of which drew in customers and distracted the people being bled. In seventeenth-century Amsterdam these shops were located in the surgeons' houses. Here one would find the surgeon's various tools and a stool for the patient. A skull might serve both as decoration and as a teaching device, and his guild's license would be posted on the wall. Various jars and phials would litter the place, but nowhere any anesthetic, since none was known or used. The surgeon relied on booze and a sturdy apprentice to keep the patient still.

Because of their lack of university education and generally lower income and status, surgeons often were second-class citizens within physicians' guilds. Florentine and Venetian physicians and surgeons enjoyed rather similar status within their guilds until the fifteenth century, when physicians began to assert their higher social standing. In some cities, the

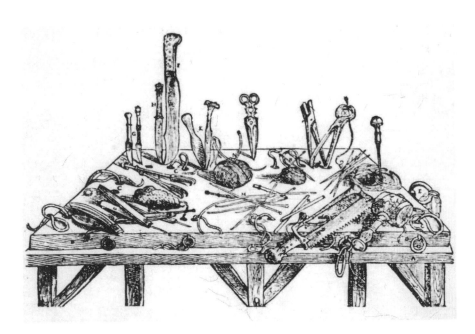

An operating table with various surgical tools. From a 1606 edition of Vesalius's *Fabrica corpore.* National Library of Medicine.

master surgeons broke away and organized their own guilds, as at Paris in the thirteenth century and Amsterdam in 1635. Shortly after the Black Death first appeared, surgeons in Paris arranged to have a formally recognized and guild-directed education ladder from bachelor to licensed practitioner to master surgeon. This was clearly separate from the university, but students and masters were required nonetheless to know Latin, a step toward achieving higher social status. Paris's barbers had traditionally been separate from surgeons and of lower status, but in 1506 they were raised to the level of surgeons and in 1656 united with them in a single guild. London surgeons organized the Fellowship of Surgeons shortly after the Black Death started, and by 1368 the group capped membership at seventeen. In the mid-sixteenth century there were nearly 200 independent surgeons, who were united with barbers into a guild in 1540; by 1641 there were almost 300. Because of the need to treat female bodies, women surgeons were far from unknown in the medieval period, though they became less plentiful during and after the sixteenth century. This trend was no doubt due in part to the greater professionalization—and thus masculinization—of surgeons, and coincided with the advent of the witch-craze in parts of Europe, which often mistook feminine healing for malevolent power. Naples and Venice licensed female surgeons in the fourteenth century, and York, Dublin, Lincoln, and even London allowed women to practice in the fifteenth.

Lacking a university education did not mean that surgeons were ignorant of the medical theories of the day; quite the contrary. In London in 1424 a man sued a surgeon for botching an operation on his thumb. Three other surgeons testified on their colleague's behalf that since the surgery occurred on January 31, it was when "the moon was consumed with a bloody sign, to wit, Aquarius, under a very malevolent constellation!"[1] The man, the surgeons insisted, was in fact lucky to live. The patient lost his case. In fact, the surgeon should have taken the stars into account, since successful bloodletting was clearly linked to time of day and of the year, and these also determined from where the blood should be drained. To help them remember, surgeons had "vein man" and "zodiac man" charts of the body drawn on stiff paper to be carried around in their belts. Surgeons recognized as many as 39 specific bleedable points on the body, each associated with a particular ailment. They opened veins with special tools called lancets or placed leeches on the proper spot to suck out the prescribed amount. Leeches, considered a second-rate tool, were also used to suck out matter from open wounds, ulcers, hemorrhoids, and boils. Women, children, and the very old tended to be "cupped" instead of having a vein opened. Over skin that had been cut open a surgeon placed a glass cup and then heated it to create suction and draw the blood out. Cupping uncut skin was thought to draw poisons out through the pores. As time went on, bleeding fell out of favor with some physicians; for example in the seventeenth century Jan Baptiste van Helmont believed one could never have too much blood since it is a "treasure" and very close to a person's "vital strength." Even so, as late as 1771, by which time bleeding was considered "the refuge of the ignorant doctor," prominent British physician Patrick Russell was prescribing it during a plague in Aleppo, Syria.

During epidemics surgeons were key players, especially in bleeding both the healthy and the sick. They accompanied doctors and were hired by towns and cities to serve the poor and in general hospitals and plague hospitals called pest houses. They knew enough of "higher" medical practice to fill in for physicians who had died or fled, and they died in numbers that indicate the great risks they took.

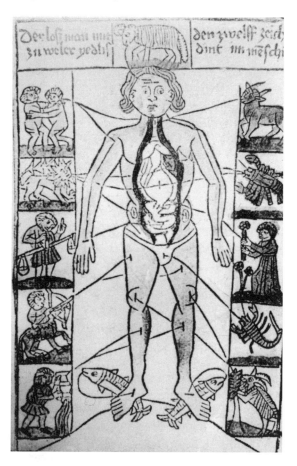

The "zodiac man": a medical chart that displays the relationship of each zodiac sign (symbolized in the margins) to its specific body part. From the *Calendar of Regiomontanus*, German, c. 1475. National Library of Medicine.

**The
Apothecary**

Long before modern, mass-produced drugs and gleaming pharmacies, the apothecaries kept communities healthy by preparing their medicines—or so everyone thought. With mortar and pestle they ground down the roots, flowers, herbs, and minerals they made into powders or pills; mixed the powders, fruit extracts, and other liquids into syrups and potions; and blended the salves and oils for ointments and plasters to be applied to wounds and boils. Yet fifteenth-century English schoolchildren read in one of their textbooks:

The apothecary's craft is fullest of deceit of all the crafts in the world, for these apothecaries lack no deceit in weighing their spice, for either the balance be not like [even] or else the beam is not equal or else they will hold the tongue of the balance still in the hollow with their finger when they are weighing. They care nothing for the wealth of their soul so they may be rich.[2]

The craft was also one of those most filled with secrets, since only the apothecary knew what went into the musky or cloying concoctions or gritty pills for which the townspeople paid good money. Thief, fraud, sorcerer, and healer—the medieval pharmacist drew as much criticism and praise as any medical practitioner.

The word apothecary was derived from the Greek word for "storehouse," and the profession first developed in Islamic cities of the ninth century. The natural philosopher Abu Rayhan al-Biruni wrote around the year 1000 that the job of the apothecary is to "collect the best and purest of drugs—both simples and compounded—and prepare them as best prescribed by eminent physicians."[3] By the time of the Black Death, European apothecaries gathered ingredients and compounds from out in the local fields and from the far corners of Europe's trading network, offering their wares for sale in shops scattered about the city. Along walls lined with sturdy shelves ranged scores of colorful, heavy crockery jars with spices from the Indian Ocean, dried fruits from the Mediterranean, sugar from Egypt, honey from local beehives, and dried toads, snakes, and scorpions. When placed in the window the jars themselves advertised the shop, but in seventeenth-century Amsterdam a stuffed crocodile announced the apothecary.

The shop masters were organized into their own guilds or shared affiliation with spice merchants, grocers, or even painters (who used ground-up mineral powders for pigments). In Toulouse, France, they studied alongside medical students and later joined their guild, but in most places apothecaries were simply trained by practicing masters. In seventeenth-century Montpellier, apothecaries had to have completed at least ten years of training as an apprentice and journeyman and passed a public oral examination. Because drugs could kill as well as heal, and because of the opportunity for fraud, apothecaries tended to be carefully watched and regulated by guild and civic officials. In Renaissance France the apothecary had to maintain careful and public records and keep in the shop medical textbooks, including

The interior of a sixteenth-century Dutch or north German apothecary's shop. Note the stuffed crocodile hanging from the ceiling. A woodcut from H. Braunschweig's *Thesaurus pauperum*, Frankfurt, 1537. National Library of Medicine.

a book of antidotes for poisons and one that listed accepted medicinal substitutes for both single ingredients (simples) and compounds.

One of the most commonly prescribed drugs for preventing and curing the plague was theriac or treacle, an ancient Greek concoction with many variations and some 64 ingredients that took 40 days to process. The key component was roasted viper flesh. A similar, simpler drug known as "oil against poison" was developed at the court of the Grand Duke of Tuscany; its active ingredient was boiled scorpions. The most trusted theriac came from Venice. Each year all of the Venetian apothecaries met in a large square at public tables to prepare ingredients for the new year's supply. Actually, it was the supply for a dozen years hence, since theriac had to age 12 years. Many, including Paracelsus, believed that the best antidote to a poison was another, controlled poison that would drive it out. In 1639 John Woodall, a surgeon with the East India Company, wrote recommending theriac since it acts by "provoking sweat . . . and thereby opening obstructions, and by evaporation expunging venom, and refreshing nature, and so by consequent, curing the plague." Galenists considered theriac "warm and dry" and thus effective for eliminating moist phlegmatic and melancholic humors. It was also used against other types of swellings, fevers, heart trouble, dropsy, epilepsy, and palsy, and to induce sleep, restore lost speech, counteract other poisons, heal wounds, and induce menstrual flow. One drank a bit of it dissolved in wine, ale, or rose water. As Arabs first discovered, the wretched flavor of many drugs could be masked with boiled sugar water known as julep and taken in the form of flavored syrup. "Every syrup is a combination of a julep and the juice of the fruit named with it, extract of the flower, or what you include of herbs and drugs,"[4] intoned a fourteenth-century Islamic text. It went on to list 70 different syrup flavors, from peach to silk cocoon.

GENERIC TYPES OF GALENIC DRUGS

Type	Effect
Calefactives	add heat
Infrigidatives	cool
Humefactives	add moisture
Desicatives	dry
Mollifactives	soften
Purgatives	purge
Laxatives	aid defecation
Lubricatives	lubricate
Stupefactives	produce a stupor

Source: Carole Rawcliffe, *Medicine and Society in Later Medieval England* (Stroud, Gloucs., England: Sutton, 1997), p. 59.

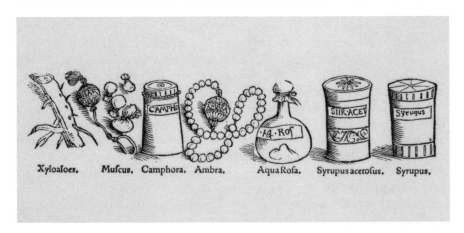

Xyloaloes.   Mufcus. Camphora. Ambra.   AquaRofa. Syrupus acetofus. Syrupus.

A variety of sixteenth-century apothecary's wares, some in traditional containers: from left, aloe wood, musk, camphor, an amber ball or pomamber, rose water, syrup of vinegar, and syrup. From the *Tacuini sanitatis,* a Latin version of Ibn Butlan's eleventh-century medical treatise, Argenteuil, c. 1531. National Library of Medicine.

The main function of any medicine during this period was purely Galenic: to help rebalance unbalanced humors. Only the body could produce blood, bile, or phlegm, so medicines could only purge these. As long as the body was urinating, sweating, defecating, menstruating, vomiting, expectorating, oozing, or otherwise draining—and the more often the better—there was hope. John of Gaddesden wrote *The English Rose* in Latin about 1314, and nearly two centuries later (1491) it became the first printed medical text by an English author. John wrote that

> during pestilence everyone over seven should be made to vomit daily from an empty stomach, and twice a week, or more if necessary; he should lie well wrapped up in a warm bed and drink warm ale with ginger so that he sweats copiously . . . And as soon as he feels an itch or prickling in his flesh he must use a goblet or cupping horn to let blood and draw down the blood from the heart.

Aiding evacuation was the heart of the apothecary's art: laxatives, purgatives, diuretics, and suppositories were literally his stock in trade. And it could be a stinky trade at that. In his fictional dialogue on plague time William Bullein has his greedy apothecary lie to keep a visitor away from his rich patient's house: "[H]e hath taken a purgation, which has cast such an air abroad that I was not able to abide in the chamber. I had forgotten my perfumes to make all well against your coming."[5]

Medieval and early modern societies considered apothecaries to be vital, however absurd many of their medicines appeared to be. In plague time people clamored for their preventatives, cures, diagnoses, and advice. Apothecaries tended to survive at rather higher rates than other medical practitioners and even the public at large, which added to their aura of competence. During the Great Plague of 1665, London lost at least 50 apothecaries, as we know from their wills, of some 225 who were in the city for some part of the horror.

Association with a guild—physicians', surgeons', apothecaries'—gave a medical practitioner "professional" status, but there was a host of nonprofessionals working beside them. Above all one has to mention the women of Europe **Women as Practitioners** who learned the healing arts at their mothers' knees and dealt with a wide range of maladies. Since the urban professional guilds policed such activities rather closely, female practitioners who served those outside their own families were most common in the countryside. At one end of the social scale were wealthy women, often landladies responsible for several villages. They tended the needs of villagers and others as a form of Christian charity or noblesse oblige.[6] During the Renaissance, literacy among noblewomen rose, as did their access to medical literature, especially the increasing percentage written in the vernacular or translated from Latin. Lady Grace Mildmay, daughter-in-law of Queen Elizabeth's chancellor, had a personal library of 250 books on diseases and cures, and *Utopia*'s author Thomas More wanted his daughter to study "physic" right alongside the Scripture. During and after the Reformation, Protestant pastors' wives replaced nuns and monks as local healers, especially of the rural and urban poor.

At the other end of the scale were the various women "folk-healers" scattered across Europe's countryside. Their brand of medicine tended to be a mixture of common sense, personal experience, an often profound understanding of natural processes, and superstitious gobbledygook passed down through the generations or made up on the spot. While both church and medical officials ridiculed these illiterate and supposedly ignorant women as frauds who pandered to the worst tendencies of the equally ignorant poor, the vast majority of Europeans trusted and depended upon them, from birth to final illness, including plague. As products of the local communities, they shared the customs, beliefs, and languages of the people, something most urban professionals did not. Dr. Ludovico Pucci, sent to inspect the condition of health care in rural Tuscany in 1608, reported that "peasants treat themselves and hardly ever consult the doctor, either because they are too poor to pay for the treatment or because they have little faith in medicine, as is usual among country people."[7] Even during plague time physicians complained that the rural folk wanted nothing to do with them, preferring their "healers," "root-wives," "cunning women," conjurers, seers, prophetesses, diviners, and other specialists in the esoteric. England and other countries tried to crack down on these women and their practices: Parliament passed laws in 1542, 1563, and 1604. Not coincidently, these were all plague years. Though not singling out healers, the acts specified all those who took

upon him or them by witchcraft, enchantment, charm, or sorcery, to tell or declare in what place any treasure of gold or silver should or might be found or had in the earth, or other secret place; or where goods, or things lost or stolen should be found or be come; or shall use or practice any sorcery, enchantment, charm or witchcraft to the intent to provoke any person to unlawful love.[8]

The penalty was death. In the eyes of the authorities the line between a folk-healer and a witch was a thin one. And, of course, a woman who could heal naturally could also injure naturally, perhaps even bring on the plague by foul means. Contemporary physicians and natural philosophers certainly believed this and wrote about the threat such people posed, though at least one modern study says that there is no clear evidence that any "witches" were executed for spreading plague.

The most common and accepted female health specialist was the midwife. The English term derives from the German for "with-wife," the woman responsible for seeing a woman through labor and birth. In times of plague both healthy women and those with the plague gave birth and required the services of the midwife. Plague was especially hard on pregnant women and newborn babies, as anecdotal evidence, medical literature, and comments from pest houses attest. Babies who survived birth were washed thoroughly to protect them against the corrupt air, and, if their mothers were victims, to counteract the poison in the blood and placenta. The tanner Miquel Parets wrote of his own child's experience in seventeenth-century Barcelona: the infant was "stripped naked and washed in vinegar and rubbed with lavender and other soothing herbs and passed over the flames in the fireplace"[9] before being wrapped in new cloth. In northeast France and the Netherlands in the sixteenth and seventeenth centuries communities hired "plague midwives" to serve only victims, lest a midwife spread plague from the sick to the healthy. The Dutch city of Leiden originally hired in 1524 a "civic midwife" who would simply serve rich and poor alike in normal and plague times. In 1538 the city council responded to the complaints of wealthier clients who feared contamination and hired several plague midwives. The city fathers received a steady stream of applicants who agreed to stay in town during plague outbreaks; to work only with plague victims; to do everything possible for each mother and child with no discrimination for social or health condition; to share her experiences so that all might be more effective; and to do diligently all that a midwife normally does.

The statutes of the Florentine physicians' guild complained in the wake of the plague that even people "who previously worked as smiths or in other mechanical trades have begun to practice medicine."[10]

Empirics, Quacks, and Charlatans

The repeated waves of pestilence that washed over Europe proved two things incontrovertibly: the medical establishment was powerless to stop it, and there was money to be made as a medical practitioner, licensed or not. Yet long before 1348 universities and guilds fought to prohibit the unregulated practice of quacks, empirics, charlatans, and any other self-appointed medical men and women. These folk often differed little from physicians and surgeons in theory and practice, but they did not share other key characteristics: education, literacy in Latin, stability and accountability, social status, and reputation. And often their methods did differ, as in the case of one Roger Clerk, who placed a charm around the neck of Johanna atte Hache, wife of the Lord Mayor of London. Tried and convicted of being an illiterate (idiotus) quack, he was paraded through the city on a horse, with blank parchment and a whetstone[11] hung round his own neck as a sign of his lies, and an empty uroscopy flask—used by physicians to inspect urine—as a sign of what he was usurping.

During plague time civic authorities were often of two minds concerning the unlicensed, since they desired to limit illicit activities but usually needed anyone they could get to alleviate the people's suffering. The University of Paris, already in charge of licensing the city's physicians, gained the right to prosecute the unlicensed early in the thirteenth century. They argued successfully to the church that unlicensed practitioners threatened the welfare of the populace, and the faculty convinced the Archbishop to allow them to threaten excommunication. From early fourteenth-century trials we learn that typical infractions included the provision of herbs, massages, and medicinal baths. One female empiric, Jacqueline Félicie, argued in 1322 that no man should be allowed to handle a sick woman's body and that many women died rather than allowing themselves to be groped and prodded by a male physician. She cited her own effectiveness in treating female patients, but the male court proved unsympathetic and fined her. Both papal and royal power was brought to bear on regulating medical practice in Paris, and a king's decree of 1336 forbade practice by rustics, monks, old women, medical students, or herbalists. One did not have to be an educated physician, but one needed to be licensed by them. In 1500 the provost of Paris asked the university's medical faculty to help battle the plague; the faculty agreed, but only if the provost would help them combat quackery. The magistrates of Antwerp in 1625—a plague year—merely began registering and tracking these folk, noting their names, residences, and duration of practice. Those who left town either because of the plague or after it had subsided were not allowed to return.

Civic authorities were most concerned with the sale of drugs, plague-remedies and preventives, and cure-alls. As in the case of apothecaries, they wanted to ensure that no one sold medicines that were either worthless or dangerous. Both "quack" and "charlatan" derive from the "chattering" of the sellers of pills, elixirs, powders, amulets, recipes,

"Monsieur Probatum," a dentist and charlatan, hawks his wares from the kind of bench that gave its name to the "mountebank," while a sickly "patient" approaches for a cure. A seventeenth-century engraving. National Library of Medicine.

lozenges, and other remedies that were guaranteed to be effective. With the clear failure of the medical establishment, many people, often desperate, fell for the colorful huckstering on which the charlatan relied.

Salesmen mounted makeshift benches accompanied by music, eloquent testimonials, and on-the-spot miracle cures. In an effort to curb this kind of street theatre, Roman authorities in 1672 forbade these sellers "to swallow poisons of any sort, nor have themselves bitten by snakes or other poisonous animals, nor to cut or burn their own flesh . . . without our permission."[12] Florentines were entertained by the likes of Battista Oliva, a Turkish convert to Catholicism who sold medicinal ointments and "wrestled a bear." In Holland, France, and England books like John Primrose's *Popular Errors* (1638 in Latin for doctors; translated in 1651 for "gentlewomen") and Thomas Browne's *Pseudodoxia Epidemica* (1646 in English) were written to undermine people's faith in charlatanry and steer them back to the professionals. For example, Browne attacked the use of "unicorn horn" in expensive patent medicines, proving that the horns many used really came from numerous normal animals. But did this mean that there is no such thing as unicorn horn, or just that much of it was phony? As early as the sixteenth century popular theater like the Italian commedia dell'arte used the colorfully clothed and often "foreign" quack as a stock comic figure who fleeced the gullible.

THE PHYSICIAN IN SOCIETY

One may gauge the access people had to physicians at any given time and place in a number of ways. The rawest statistics are those of the number of physicians per thousand or ten thousand people. The following chart provides some of this raw data.

The Availability of Physicians

Scholars have estimated that in rural areas of Tuscany, France, and England there was about one physician for every 10,000 people in the first half of the seventeenth century; this figure rose in England to one for every 6,000 by 1675. In Elizabethan England only 415 of some 9,000 parishes had resident physicians, and in 1643 Cumberland County had only one. In all of France the number rose from about 400 in the 1530s to four times that a century later, though it dropped by a few hundred by the end of the seventeenth century despite a rising population. In 1571, Lyon, a city of about 50,000 people, had 14 physicians, 28 surgeons, and 42 apothecaries. Generally speaking, the further east one went the fewer physicians one found: seventeenth-century Russia only had around a hundred at any one time, and all of these were foreign-trained.

Availability was also a function of location and class. Most men became physicians in part because it was a lucrative profession, and the people with money to pay generally lived in towns at least part of the year. Many urban physicians developed a set clientele among wealthy merchants,

URBAN PHYSICIANS PER 10,000 POPULATION

City	Year(s)	Number per 10,000 pop
Milan	c.1325	1.8
Florence	1339	0.6
Paris	1340s	4.0
Milan	1517	7.6
Mantua	1539	5.8
Cremona	1548	3.4
Lyon	1550s	1.4
Brescia	1552	4.2
Basel	1555	17.0
Venice	1564	9.5
London	1590	2.5
Barcelona	1599	6.9
Florence	1630	4.3
Edinburgh	1700	11.3

Sources: Lawrence Brockliss and Colin Jones, *The Medical World of Early Modern France* (New York: Oxford University Press, 1997), pp. 200–205; Vivian Nutton, "Continuity or Rediscovery? The City Physician in Classical Antiquity and Medieval Italy," in *The Town and State Physician in Europe from the Middle Ages to the Enlightenment,* ed. A.W. Russell (Wolfenbüttel: Herzog August Bibliothek, 1981), p.33; Carlo Cipolla, *Fighting the Plague in Seventeenth-Century Italy* (Madison: University of Wisconsin Press, 1981), p. 79; Jean-Noël Biraben, "L'hygeine, la maladie, la mort," in *Histoire de la population Français,* ed. Jacques Dupâquier (Paris: Presses Universitaires de France, 1988), p. 433.

bankers, and nobles, while others exclusively served great households of kings, dukes, bishops, or the pope. During plague time doctors often fled with their wealthy clients, sometimes stripping a town of qualified medical help. When plague hit southern and central France in 1399 and 1400 civic authorities had to hire a physician from Nevers—130 miles away—since all of theirs had fled. At Poitiers and Orange officials fined and banished physicians and other care-givers who fled during plague time. Fourteenth-century papal physician Guy de Chauliac wrote "And I, in order to avoid infamy, did not dare to go. But being afraid continually, I protected myself as much as I could." Yet even those who stayed might do their best to avoid the plague-struck and the risks they posed. Guy's contemporary Chalin de Vinavio noted, "Since there is a real and certain danger of approaching the sick, few doctors, unless promised great remuneration, face such a great peril."[13]

The Status and Organization of Physicians   Dr. Filippo Ingrassia of Palermo, Sicily, was fully aware of his place in society. In his book on the plague of 1576 he boasted that he was "never called by low people of this sort," that is, the poverty-stricken among whom the pestilence first spread. He was decidedly not one of the "base physicians who attend people of this kind," those "poor, sickly-looking people full to overwhelming with the coarsest and filthiest humors."[14] As among merchants, nobles, clergy, and other occupational groups, physicians ranged along a social and economic spectrum, in their case defined largely by clientele and income. At one end were those like Ingrassia, who worked among the rich and powerful, perhaps for a single client, perhaps on retainer for several important families or other groups, being paid whether needed or not. At about the same level were physicians who served on medical faculties and saw prosperous and important clients on the side. Somewhat lower were those who served a variety of clients, including the wealthy and those who were less well-off but could still afford professional services. These independent professionals were the heart of physicians' guilds and worked out of offices in their homes, or in apothecaries' or surgeons' shops. The less well-off journeyed to these offices, while the wealthy received house calls. Yet lower were those physicians, generally young and inexperienced, who served as civic physicians, hired by civic authorities to treat the poor for free and get what payment they could from others. Specially hired "plague physicians" helped or replaced civic physicians during epidemics. Charged with treating all plague victims in a given town or city, these men ranged from the dregs of the profession to those of the highest caliber and reputation. Sometimes they served alongside others in the pest houses, picking their way through a sea of dead and dying. If indeed these were Ingrassia's "base physicians," they were also the saints and heroes of plague time, overcoming fear and revulsion to live up to the Hippocratic Oath.

The earliest organizations of professional physicians in European cities were the guilds, which consisted of those practitioners, generally with university diplomas, recognized and licensed to practice by existing guild members. Guilds of physicians operated like guilds of all types, members meeting together to set policies for practice and pay, to hear legal cases and discipline members when necessary, to organize charitable activities, and to ensure that only members were practicing. Various committees and from two to six elected consuls administered the guilds. In Florence, according to the guild statutes of 1314, prospective members were examined in Latin by six consuls and four friars, who presumably had to vouch for the candidate's good morals and judgment. In the second year of the Black Death six doctors—two of whom had to be consuls—did the examining, and by 1353 there were only four examiners, one of whom was a surgeon. Florence was not a university town, but it and many other cities borrowed this process from the universities, whose faculties did the examining. In cities with and without medical schools, these examining boards evolved into medical "colleges" whose power and authority in the civic arena came to supersede those of either guild or faculty. As territorial rulers like kings and dukes gained power, they came to rely on these institutions to regulate medical matters. The colleges were distinct, however, from health boards that created and directed public policies regarding issues of sanitation and plague prevention; these boards were made up of important citizens representing just about everyone but the doctors. Medical colleges oversaw the medical profession itself, especially education and enrollment. In 1560 Grand Duke Cosimo I of Tuscany made the positions on his 12-man board lifetime appointments. In Milan not just any physicians could serve, only those of the patrician class; and in Pavia, thanks to the special favor of the emperor, in 1667 all members of the college were given the noble rank of count palatine.

Thomas Linacre, who studied in Bologna and Florence, brought the idea of a medical college to London, where he established the London (later Royal) College of Physicians in 1518. The physicians had been organized briefly in the 1420s, but since most worked for private parties and many were clerics or foreigners—mostly French and Italians—the movement had died after only two years. Linacre's London College was the first successful attempt to govern medical practice in England. Like other medical colleges across Europe, London's imposed strict Galenic and resisted both empirical and Paracelsian medicine. In France similar boards worked between 1500 and 1700 to make education and requirements uniform across the country. This effort was especially important after the religious inroads of Calvinism among the Huguenots, who gained control of some cities and even medical schools. Among Catholics the broader issue was maintaining peace and coordination between physicians and clergy, both of whom were "healers" and very necessary in plague time. Whatever judgments modern scholars may make, medieval and early modern physicians appeared to heal people and told the public they did, and indeed death tolls from plague fell over time, all of which allowed the physicians to retain their status, trappings, and even arrogance.

MEDICAL PROPHYLAXIS (PREVENTION)

General Principles   In plague time the physician had three principal tasks: to prevent a patient from getting the disease; to diagnose it properly if it appeared a patient had it; and to treat the diseased patient in such as way as to effect a cure. Given the dominance of Galenic theory in both the medical profession and among the people generally, in all three cases the patient and physician supposed they were working with a poison that had affected the humoral system. The poison was the result of "corrupted air" or "miasma" introduced through the human body's nose or mouth or through open skin pores. Once a human body had produced the poison, it could be excreted through the skin or breath or even eyes. The poison could pass along to materials such as cloth or pass directly to another person through touch or respiration or even sight. From Dr. Gentile and poet Giovanni Boccaccio in 1348 to Dr. Bertrand and novelist Daniel Defoe in 1720 this model remained dominant and guided university-trained physicians as they sought to prevent, diagnose, and cure the plague.

Hippocratic and Galenic medicine stressed the impor-
tance of "good air" for healthy living. When applying   **Environmental**
this teaching in the fourteenth century, physicians like   **Adjustments**
Gentile da Foligno emphasized two strategies: Avoid
bad air or, if one's air becomes corrupted, correct it. In normal times one
should avoid stagnant water bodies, including swamps and marshes, and
sources of stench, including rotting plant or animal matter. Houses should
be well ventilated with air from the north, or at least not from the south,
which was considered a source of generally bad air. In pestilential times,
however, even the best air could be corrupted. Gentile suggests that people should flee the corrupted area for one with better air, flee low ground
for high, humid air for dry, a pest-wracked city for the open countryside.
His Spanish contemporary Jacme d'Agramont, however, suggested fleeing high ground for lower, since the source of corruption was the stars,
and the further one was from them, the better—underground if possible.
If one had to stay, then windows and doors should remain sealed tightly,
with only northern windows opened for short times each morning.

Altering the corrupted air was a complementary tactic, and this could be
done, Jacme believed, by fumigating—from *fumare*, to smoke—with aromatic materials that would balance the corruption. Gentile and most doctors
suggested burning pleasant-smelling materials like ash, pine, juniper, mar-
joram, mint, savory, aloe wood, and ambergris or musk for the wealthy. The
Spanish physician Alfonso de Cordoba came up with a very complex recipe
for a fumigating briquette that would be thrown onto a brazier or fire:

One and a half drams each of powder of red roses, spikenard, wood of aloes, testi
marini, mastic, sandalwood, bedellium root, ladanum, olibane [frankincense],
saffron, rind of colocynth, and liquid storax; three drams each of harnanae [?], or
else of pepper, saffron, and selanum; a sufficient amount of greater cardamom,
cubebe,[15] and camphor; and six grains of barley. This is all ground together and
shaped [into a briquette] with the best rose water.[16]

In fact, the fumes may not have purified "corrupted air," but they would
have acted as a stimulant and made a patient feel better. Others believed
in battling stink with stink, a variation on the poison-versus-poison tactic
advocated by later Paracelsians. This distinctly minority view advocated
the use of nasty-smelling matter, including buckets of human waste, or
the burning of foul-smelling materials like sulfur, leather, gunpowder, or
human hair. Fire alone was also considered effective in purifying the air,
whether in or out of doors. In 1348 papal physician Guy de Chauliac had
Clement VI sit between two great fires in the main hall of his palace in
Avignon for this very purpose. Fire's natural drying effect counteracted the
vile humidity that, he believed, sustained the corruption.

Perfume and cologne first appeared in the West as personal air purifiers.
Amber apples, or pomanders (*pomum ambrae* in Latin), also emerged during
the Second Pandemic as a means of affecting the air one breathed. The

author of *The Surgeon's Mate* (1639) recommends "a good Seville orange stuck with cloves" as a simple pomander. A variation used by Henry VIII's chancellor Cardinal Wolsey consisted of a whole orange rind hollowed out and filled with a vinegar-soaked sponge. The point was to create and use a hand-held, aromatic ball that one kept at the ready to sniff and smell to "purify" the immediate air one breathed. More typical than oranges were artificial balls of ambergris, camphor, aloes, musk, and other odiferous stuff bound with rose water, with cheaper options for poorer folks. In 1607 the Earl of Northumberland spent 10 shillings, a goodly sum, on a pomander—but then, what price to put on one's health?

Tobacco, which arrived in Europe from the Western Hemisphere, was also quickly adopted as a personal fumigant during the sixteenth century. Paintings and illustrations of plague scenes feature minor figures puffing away on pipes as they carry corpses or read lists of dead at the pest-house gate. The Dutch physician Isbrandus van Diemerbroeck preached the use of tobacco during the 1630s. During the epidemic of 1635–1636 he routinely smoked two or three bowls after breakfast, three after lunch, and "always in the presence of infected corpses." In London during the Great Plague of 1665 rumor had it that tobacconists never caught the plague. In early June the naval administrator and diarist Samuel Pepys came across the first houses he had seen marked with the red X indicating plague victims: "It put me into an ill conception of myself and my smell, so that I was forced to buy some roll tobacco to smell and chaw—which took away the apprehension."[17] At the famed boys' school in nearby Eton, all students had to smoke or risk flogging.

Materials that may have been "infected" by a sick person or the air itself also needed to be purified. Vinegar and other "drying" astringents such as warm wine, rose water, or sage were used to launder clothes and bedding, to soak items such as coins, and to wash down the walls of a room in which a victim stayed. For the first time in the West people regularly laundered clothing, though washing the body was considered unhealthy since it opened pores to corrupt airs or poisons.

While many of these measures may seem silly today, in fact they may have played a part in reducing the incidence of plague. Burning sulfur would have killed or run off rats; fleas and the *Y. pestis* bacteria were averse to very dry air; and laundering clothing would have reduced flea populations somewhat.

Diet, Affect, and Behavior Humoral theory also relied heavily on proper diet for good health and for avoiding plague. The foods one ate were naturally warming or cooling, humidifying or drying. People themselves were considered "warm and dry," "cold and moist," and so on according to their age, sex, physical condition, and general disposition. Since plague was considered "warm and moist," the best prevention was to avoid warm/moist foods and make one's humors as well balanced toward the cold and dry as possible. One should also avoid foods that are not easily digested and that lay long in the body and naturally "corrupt" it. Fatty or boiled meats, dairy products, and fish generally fit the pattern, as did juicy fruits and vegetables, fried foods, and pastries. Physicians continually disagreed over specific foods and their qualities: Plums, for example, were sweet and juicy (bad), but they also acted as a laxative (good); hot spices opened pores (bad) but let the sweat out (good). Every doctor had his own variation, with only his apparent success to recommend him. Nonetheless, the theory remained intact, and all prescribed the classical virtue of eating and drinking in moderation.

Moderation in mood or temper was also a key to remaining healthy. Beginning with Gentile da Foligno in 1348, doctors warned against giving in to feelings that heated the body, such as anxiety, fear, or anger. Sadness and what we would call depression cooled the body too much and deadened the spirit that helped fight the poison. When Boccaccio in his *Decameron* has his young people escape Florence, they are following the recommendations of the best doctors: not only are they fleeing bad air, they are leaving behind the sights, sounds, and smells that created horror, fear, and the intense sadness that weakened one's constitution. When they relax listening to fine music and tell gentle tales and eat delicate foods, they are following the very prescriptions left to us. About the same time Dr. Jobus Lincelius of Zwickau in Germany linked the physical and the affective:

All physical exertions and emotions of the mind should be avoided, such as running, jumping, jealousy, anger, hatred, sadness, horror or fear, licentiousness and the like; and those who, by the grace of God, are in a position to do so, may spend their time in relating tales and stories and with good music to delight their hearts, as music was given to man by God to praise God and give pleasure to mankind.[18]

Three centuries later the advice remained current.

Most physicians also prescribed regular bleedings and purgations as a good way to maintain humoral balance and thus lessen one's chance of getting the plague. They also recommended against hot baths, sexual activity, and strenuous exercise. All of these activities opened pores, heated the body, and made respiration rise, each of which invited the pestilence.

In sources on the plague one occasionally runs across the bizarre in prophylaxis. For example, in sixteenth-century Geneva one of the city's plague-house cleansers prepared for the day's risks by eating a "burnt nut" washed down with a glass of his own urine. Robert Boyle, in his famous scientific work **Prophylactic "Medicines"** *The Sceptical Chymist* attested to the effectiveness of drinking an extract of horse dung and rotted ivy berries. For others the trick was equally simple and more palatable. A late-seventeenth-century announcement in London declared "one Doctor Stephanus Chrisolitus, a famous physician, lately arrived at these parts, having traveled in several countries which have been affected with the plague hath found by experience" that the answer was raisins in the morning and raisins, specifically from Malaga, baked or boiled, in the afternoon.[19] By the eighteenth century, when the idea that the "corruption" might actually be tiny animals was current, one doctor suggested chewing garlic to keep these "insects" out of mouth and nose. Others touted coffee, newly available in London shops, as a prophylactic; a pamphlet published in London during the French plague of 1721 advertised in its title "The Virtue and Use of Coffee with Regard to the Plague and Contagious Distempers."

Some who were influenced by Paracelsianism or alchemy recommended metals thought to absorb airborne poison: "[Get] a piece of angel[20] gold, if you can of Elizabeth's coin (it is the best), which is philosophical gold and keep it always in your mouth when you walk out or any sick persons come to you," advised John Allin in a letter written during London's Great Plague of 1665. His friend was to keep it between cheek and gum, turning it from time to time.[21] Presumably the gold absorbed the poison, as did powdered gold included in many prophylactic and curative potions. By the sixteenth century apothecaries and physicians (and quacks and empirics) were marketing pills, potions, and powders with claims of prophylactic powers. Some were little more than placebos, while others had strong effects, often purgative, that convinced customers of their value. Theriac, or treacle, was certainly one of these. In England, the Statute of Monopolies (1624) protected the maker's rights to these "over-the-counter" medications with a patent that ran for fourteen years and was renewable. Anderson's Scots Pills, a purgative, appeared in the 1630s and was still being sold nearly three centuries later. Apothecaries sold their own concoctions, while others peddled them from inns and taverns. In the face of the high fees charged by doctors and their relative unavailability, self-medication had a real appeal.

Amulets or talismans, defined by one modern scholar as "visible symbols of invisible power,"[22] were very popular during the Second **Amulets** Pandemic. All ancient Western cultures had used them, and even Christianity folded them into its generous spiritual toolkit as sacramentals (rosaries, crucifixes, and holy water) and relics worn to ward off the devil and attract divine favor. By the fourteenth century amulets included special Bible verses copied and worn on the body in a locket and certain gems supposed to have special power against poison. The diamond engagement ring was originally associated with the talismanic effect of counteracting poison in the beloved's body. Though such objects sometimes were associated with sorcery or witchcraft, Renaissance Neo-Platonism and the Scientific Revolution that followed gave credibility to the hidden powers of inanimate objects. Gems tended to be associated with celestial effects, drawing down the power of the stars; religious items relied on divine aid; and organic materials were generally seen to work "sympathetically" on other organic matter, including poisons.

The mechanisms were occult, or hidden, but few doubted their effects. For the scientist Robert Boyle amulets indeed counteracted poison in the body, and only "fools" doubted their success. For some people, they simply worked or did not. Samuel Pepys purchased a rabbit's foot as a cure for gas ("wind") in 1665; his health immediately improved and he wrote in his diary, "[T]ruly I cannot but impute it to my fresh hare's-foot." Rather later he was also taking another medication, however, and he wrote of his good health, "Now I am at a loss to know whether it be my hare's-foot which is my preservative against wind . . . or whether it be my taking a pill of Turpentine every morning." Physicians, too, praised the effects of certain kinds of amulets. Galenists preferred organic toad: "I likewise hung about my neck a large toad dried . . . sewed up in a linen cloth . . . placed about the region of my stomach," wrote Dr. George Thompson in his plague tract of 1666. He claimed that the dried toad absorbed the poison from the body and bloated up, something, he wrote, that he would not believe had he not seen it. Amulets were especially useful when working around plague victims. In his 1659 book *On Fevers,* Thomas Willis gave a mechanical explanation for toad efficacy and that of other poisons used in amulets such as mercury and arsenic: "atomical" particles emerge from the material in the amulet and "allured the pestilential particles out of the patient's body, into their embraces."[23]

Empirics, cunning women, and Paracelsians also trafficked in amulets. The cheaper amulets of the Paracelsian Oswald Croll, the imperial physician of Rudolf II, contained inorganic mercury, sulfuric acid (vitriol), salt, and verdigris cooked into a paste, dried, and cut into "coins." According to his *Basilica chymica* the coins were stamped with an alchemical "seal of the stars" and wrapped in red silk. The silk turned blue in plaguey air . . . or so he said. For peasants he recommended some mercury placed in the shell of a filbert nut. Croll and others sought Paracelsus' own famed "zenexton," a plague amulet whose materials he never specified but whose success he trumpeted in his *De peste* plague tract, which was translated from Latin into French in 1570. His followers experimented with various combinations of arsenic, arsenic trisulfide (orpiment), mercury, silver, pearls, and even toads and spiders. One of Croll's wilder recipes called for the powder of 18 dried toads, the first menstrual blood of young girls, white arsenic, orpiment, dittany roots, pearls, corals, and oriental emeralds. During the proper phase of the moon one made these into a paste and shaped it into a cake. The cake was to be stamped with a small metal case engraved with a scorpion and snake, and then placed inside the case and worn near the heart where poisons collect. For the really wealthy he created pure gold cases with a sapphire, a hyacinth, and four stones from toads or spiders. Inside the case Croll sealed a small, perforated gold pipe smeared with a paste of toad and vinegar and stuffed with linen rags wetted with menstrual blood. Jan Baptiste van Helmont's zenexton had as its active ingredient the worms that lived in the eyes of toads and the vomit of toads suspended upside down, all obtained during July's waning moon. Johannes Irmbler, personal physician to the ruler of Moravia, tried to copy a recipe of Van Helmont but could not get the suspended toads to vomit, so—ever the resourceful one—he used their feces instead, and to full effect. Van Helmont explained that the toads' natural fear of humans imprinted itself on the "active force" of the disease and eliminated it.

In the sixteenth and seventeenth centuries these antics were the cutting edge of plague research. Yet there were skeptics. Athanasius Kircher, the Jesuit "father of bacteriology," considered religious amulets effective but evil because their power came from the "devil's impious cooperation with the engraver and the misplaced faith of the wearer." Kircher, who believed in airborne "worms" as the cause of plague, accepted toad therapy for three reasons: (1) their skin was bumpy like a plague victim's; (2) they eat worms like those in the plague victim's belly; and (3) the toads' hatred of humans caused an exuding of poison that itself drew poison from the air around, ironically protecting the hated human. Van Helmont, though influenced by Paracelsus, attacked the usefulness of metallic poisons based on his observation in Brussels of hundreds of dead victims with these amulets around their necks. Others noted the ineffectiveness of any amulets; Francis Herring, a member of the Royal College of Physicians, offered this criticism in his book *Opinion Concerning Amulets or Plague Cakes* of 1603. This work infuriated his elite colleagues, who responded in *A Modest Defense of the Impact* published the following year. They also shunned him personally, as he complained in 1604: "[T]hey have shut me off, and slandered me. I have been discourteously and hardly intreated [sic], rejected and shut out from conference."[24] Even so, the debate continued among the greatest minds of the era, and amulet defenders virtually always won. As late as 1692 Dr. Jacob Wolf of Frankfurt would publish a book of 400 standard pages cataloging diseases that are curable with the use of amulets. And he did so in Latin for the use of his colleagues across the continent.

DIAGNOSING THE PLAGUE

Signs of Plague Since the plague was a celestially caused corruption of the air that all animals breathed, physicians and natural philosophers fell back on three main types of evidence that plague was in the area: celestial, atmospheric, and animal behavior. Though others looked to earthquakes or large deposits of corpses after battle, most followed some version of these litanies. The medical faculty at the University of Paris in 1348 listed change of season, "flying" stars, change in the color of the air, lightning and other aerial lights, winds and thunder, dead animals, and an increase in frogs and reptiles as signs of the plague. In 1350 the physician and poet Simon de Covino listed heavy mists, clouds, lightning, and falling stars. Modern historian Dominick Palazatto studied dozens of plague tracts by physicians and others written between 1348 and 1350 and found the following portents: comets, lightning, and "fiery drakes" (meteors?) in the sky; storms and rains of snakes or frogs; floods, famine, earthquakes, and locusts; strangely deformed snakes, worms, toads, and badgers; animal deaths and human spontaneous abortions; fungi and crop failures; changes in animal behavior; fish die-offs; withering of trees; and in general seasons not being what they should be. Marsilio Ficino, son of a physician and Neo-Platonic philosopher at the Florentine court of Lorenzo de Medici, described the portents of plague, which the physician Thomas Coghan translated in his *Haven of Health* a century later (1584):

Where the air of that place varies from [its] natural temperature, declining to heat and moisture, when it seems cloudy and dusty; when the winds are gross and hot; when the fields smoke and smell; and the fishes are ill both in savor and taste; when many worms breed of putrefaction of the earth; toad stools and rotten herbs abound; the fruits and beasts of the earth are unsavory; the wines become muddy; many birds and beasts fly from that place; strange agues arise, raging, continual burning, frantic, when the small pox are rife, and worms abound in children and old folks.[25]

To a subtle ear this may sound like a passage right out of Shakespeare, describing a place abandoned by God, a witches' lair perhaps or a land cursed for the evil that men once did there. And yet this is the medical science of the Elizabethan Age: a blend of poetic rhetoric and ancient misconceptions.

DR. INGRASSIA ON PLAGUE IN VENICE IN 1535 AND 1555

In 1535, while I was a student in Padua, a pestilence broke out in Venice and the doctors were unable to identify it. . . . In Venice again, in 1555, there prevailed a great diversity of opinions among doctors, some maintaining it was the plague, others denying it. This happened in a great city such as Venice where there are so many and excellent physicians.

From Carlo Cipolla, *Fighting the Plague in Seventeenth-Century Italy* (Madison: University of Wisconsin Press, 1981), p. 91.

The Tools of the Trade

With plague in the neighborhood, doctors had to be especially careful about correctly diagnosing patients' ailments. In general the physician relied on four of his five senses—normally he would not taste anything—because he had little in the way of quantitative data such as white blood cell counts or blood pressure. Yet the late medieval and early modern physician depended on a number of indicators, including pulse rate; quality of urine, blood, and feces; body temperature; visual examination of the skin and external organs; the body's smells, including breath and skin; uncontrolled actions of the body such as hemorrhaging, diarrhea, vomiting, labored breathing, and insomnia; and observable qualities such as attitude, energy level, restlessness, and mental sharpness. Trained by scholastic method to categorize everything, physicians developed complex scales of qualities for fluids like urine and blood and other indicators such as pulse rate and attitude. For example, physicians examined blood visually for color, viscosity, and foreign matter; by agreeability of smell and sometimes taste; and by touch for smoothness, greasiness, grittiness, and warmth. They checked feces for color, texture, smell, firmness or liquidity, and presence of blood or parasites.

Urine was placed in a bulbous glass jar called a jordan or uroscopy flask and swirled about while being held up to the light by the examining physician. This action became symbolic of the doctor's trade and appears scores of times in prints and manuscripts. He judged the sample's clarity, color, and texture, and let it sit to precipitate sediments. We still have late medieval charts that link urine colors—up to 20—to associated physical conditions, and in 1379 the English Dominican physician Henry Daniel published a book that laid the entire scheme out. In a similar document from the same time we read

Heat is the cause of red color, dryness is the cause of thin substance; moistness is the cause of thick substance. As thus: if the urine of the patient be red and thick it signifies that the blood is hot and moist. If it be red and thin, it shows that choler is dominant, because choler is hot and dry. If the urine appear white and thick, it betokens phlegm, for phlegm is cold and moist. . . .[26]

Doctors took the pulse with four fingers placed on the radial artery of the patient's wrist. Physicians were said to be able to distinguish up to 40 different pulse rates, all of which were expressed qualitatively, from "antlike" to "sluggish." As the beating of the heart was little understood, this rhythmic action was—at least in theory and until Copernicus' ideas caught on—related directly to the "music of the heavenly spheres," created by the rotation of the heavens around the earth. This explanation serves as a reminder that the well-educated physician also had his astrological toolkit by which he could diagnose illness related to seasons and signs.

Tokens and Symptoms   At the end of the sixteenth century Italian physician Dr. Pietro Parisi named seven contemporary medical writers on plague and noted that they each listed between 15 and 52 symptoms of plague. From the beginning the most obvious signs of the plague were the buboes, or swelling in the lymph nodes of the groin, armpits, and behind the ears. Nonetheless, French and Italian doctors immediately recognized cases of pneumonic plague as being a form of plague without the buboes. Around 1400, the Italian physician Jacopo di Coluccino wrote in his diary about a woman who "died of the worst and most contagious kind of plague, that with blood spitting."[27] Physicians noted that this type killed more quickly

In his office, a physician examines a "jordan" of urine while a student or assistant consults a text. Two others point to other flasks that may contain either color samples to which a patient's urine is compared or the sample belonging to the man at left. A couple arrives with their samples in flasks protected by baskets, as does a woman at bottom left, while two boys or young men scuffle while waiting. From the *Hortus sanitatis* published by Jacob Meydenbach, Mainz, 1491. National Library of Medicine.

and surely than the bubonic variety. Around 1410 Johannes Aygel of Korneuburg, a member of the Viennese medical faculty, listed the following plague symptoms: sleeplessness, vomiting, loss of appetite, restlessness, shortness of breath, weakness, and diarrhea. But how could such a list indicate plague without either the spitting of blood or buboes? And Dr. Aygel left out fever, which was always associated with plague.

Medical literature from the mid-fourteenth century on also listed various combinations of swellings, blisters, boils, blotches, pustules, pimples, scabs, and other marks that indicated the buboes and probably the points of infection and the associated necrosis (destruction of cells). The variety of these blemishes, often referred to as "tokens" in English, as well as the vast range of other symptoms have led modern scholars to doubt that all cases described were only bubonic plague—or were even plague at all.

MEDICAL TREATMENTS

General Principles   Once the physician was certain the patient had plague, the Galenic assumptions came into play and dictated a fairly predictable course of treatment. The victim had to rest and regain physical strength by reducing moisture and warmth in the body. The poison that would eventually destroy the heart had to be counteracted, either internally with medicines or externally with salves and poultices and treatments such as bloodletting and opening the buboes. Essentially, the principles of prevention shaped the attempts at cure.

External Treatments   Since stopping the infected blood from reaching the heart was a prime consideration, seventeenth-century Tuscan doctors tried to use tourniquets, though exactly how and where on the body is not entirely clear. In 1348 both Gentile da Foligno and the Paris faculty prescribed bloodletting—also known as phlebotomy or venesection—to remove as much of the problem as possible. Both suggested draining blood until the patient lost consciousness. Gentile, following classical principles, instructs the surgeon: "If the bubo is located on the neck or head, then open in succession the cephalic vein in the two thumbs. If under the armpit or in the right arm, then open the pulmonary vein, which one can find in the middle finger and ring finger of the right hand . . ." and so on. At about the same time Dionysius Colle, a physician of Belluno, Italy, reflected in his *De pestilentia,*

With the young I abstained from venesection, because all those who were abundant in blood who used this practice [and] who died displayed burnt, black blood, flowing thickly with some greenness, and very watery with some yellow color and waxy. . . .[28]

But his was a minority view, and phlebotomy, cupping, and the use of leeches remained important tools.

Many physicians experimented with directly attacking the bubo in an attempt to make it divulge its pus without causing further infection and death. Some recommended various ointments and salves meant to draw out the poison. One remedy, included in an English *Leechbook*, or medical handbook, of the 1440s includes honey, duckgrease, turpentine, soot, treacle, egg yolks, and "scorpion oil." Another, in *The Secrets of the*

A woman applies leeches from a jar to draw blood from her arm. From Guillaume van den Bossche, *Historia medica*, Brussels, 1639. National Library of Medicine.

Revered Master Aleris of Piedmont (1568), instructs one to "take bay salt well beaten into powder and sifted, incorporate with the yolk of an egg, and lay it upon the sore and . . . it will draw to itself all the venom of the plague or sore."[29] A seventeenth-century Dutch recipe says to soap the skull of an executed man, or one who otherwise died violently, and mix this soap with two ounces of human blood, lard, linseed oil, and some spices. Less-scientific approaches included applying a simple onion poultice or pressing the plucked anus of a live chicken up against the bubo. The chicken will absorb the poison, choke, and die; continue until a chicken lives. Popular nonsense perhaps, but it was prescribed by both the physician Jacme d'Agramont of the medical faculty at Lérida in northern Spain (1348) and the Royal College of Physicians in their "Certain Necessary Directions as Well for the Cure of the Plague and for the Prevention of Infection" near the end of the Second Pandemic.

Jacme was among many who also recommended lancing the bubo to release the pus, then cauterizing the wound with a hot iron to seal it. Gentile advised the same thing, adding the use of cupping to draw out the "venom." Three centuries later William Bullein recommended incising the bubo, draining it, then covering it with lint soaked in this mixture: three drams each of quince seed and oak "tanner's bark"; two and a half drams each of myrrh, frankincense, and aloe; two drams of alum; one and a half drams of calamint; the round roots of aristolochia;[30] and a "scruple" of sulfuric acid. A treatment from Italy had the surgeon cut the bubo open to drain, then cover the opening with a pigeon, rooster, or dog—preferably all three—cut open at the chest. Francis Bacon, sometimes called the "father of experimental science," heard about this procedure and declared it disgusting—not ineffective, but disgusting.[31]

Internal Remedies   Doctors recommended a host of antidotes to the poison of the plague, most of them designed to eject it (purgatives, laxatives, emetics) or absorb it and pass it out (gold powder).

In his *Historie of Plants* of 1583, English botanist John Gerard lists 188 plants, of which only 2 have curative power against the plague: valerian and rue. He also says that verbena is often prescribed by doctors and apothecaries, but "these men are deceived . . . for it is reported, that the Devil did reveal it as a secret and divine medicine."[32] Unicorn horn, or "alicorn," which was probably powdered narwhal[33] horn—or some fraudulent substitute—was touted by many as a miracle cure. In his 1672 *Loimologia,* Nathaniel Hodges debunked the use of both alicorn and powdered bezoar stone (small crystals formed in the bodies of plants and animals, like human kidney stones or gallstones), but accepted the use of "sprit of hartshorn" (ammonium bicarbonate, an agent used today to leaven cookies). The Jesuit Athanasius Kircher was also skeptical of many of the "cures" of his day, so he went back to what he believed to be Hippocrates' own secret recipe for plague cure: powdered viper sweetened with honey.

Literally hundreds of recipes for plague antidotes survive. They range from simple pills or lozenges of aloe, myrrh, or saffron to complex concoctions mixing animal horns, hooves, flesh, brains, lungs, livers, urine, and dung with vegetable matter such as rue, valerian, chicory, and saw thistle. Naturally physicians recommended theriac, but also mithradatum, a standard formula that was said to date back to the first century B.C.E. Many concoctions also utilized powdered clays called *bol armeniac* and *terra sigillata,* which have genuine absorptive powers. A number of healers suggested cordials made of pearls, gems, and especially gold. Gold was thought to possess the powers of the sun and serve as a natural purifier. The problem was keeping it in suspension in a liquid. One answer was to drink fluids like barley water or rose water in which gold had been soaked. Distilled water and alcohol (known as *aqua vitae,* or the "water of life") were solvents developed by early alchemists, including monks, in which powdered gemstones and gold were thought to be soluble.

For almost four centuries millions of people facing the onslaught of plague believed in and trusted the knowledge, expertise, theories, and treatments of Europe's medical professionals. But such faith was misplaced and the trust betrayed. However conscientious and well meaning

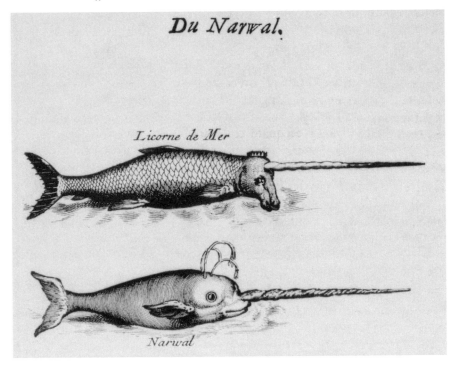

Du Narwal.

Licorne de Mer

Narwal

Engravings of two narwhals, "unicorns of the sea." From Pierre Pomet's *Histoire generale des drogues,* Paris, 1694. National Library of Medicine.

these healers were, they were trapped by an educational and professional system that stifled creativity and continued to bless fraudulent and ineffective models of the disease, its prevention, and its treatment. Some historians have blamed the Catholic Church or Christianity more broadly for standing in the way of medical progress, but it is hard to see where, by even 1600, either the institution or the religion had effective roadblocks in place. Paracelsians began an important shift away from the Galenic trap, but the immediate effects were minimal. Europe was very fortunate that the Second Pandemic ended—for reasons still hotly disputed—when it did. Heroic dedication and the best intentions in the world were no match for bad theory.

NOTES

1. Carole Rawcliffe, *Medicine and Society in Later Medieval England* (Stroud, Gloucs., England: Sutton, 1997), p. 89.

2. Rawcliffe, *Medicine,* p. 148.

3. Sami Hamarneh, "Medical Education and Practice in Medieval Islam," in *The History of Medical Education,* ed. C. D. O'Malley (Berkeley: University of California Press, 1970), p. 60.

4. Woodall in B. K. Holland, "Treatments for Bubonic Plague," *Journal of the Royal Society of Medicine* 93 (2000), p. 322; Martin Levey, "Fourteenth-century Muslim Medicine and the Hisba," *Medical History* 7 (1963), p. 181.

5. Maria Kelly, *The Great Dying* (Stroud, Gloucs., England: Tempus, 2003), pp. 115–16; William Bullein, *A dialogue against the fever pestilence* (Millwood, NY: Kraus Reprint, 1987), p. 20.

6. An obligation or expectation of a noble person.

7. Carlo Cipolla, *Miasmas and Disease,* trans. Elizabeth Potter (New Haven: Yale University Press, 1992), p. 34.

8. Owen Davies, *Cunning-Folk* (London: Hambledon and London, 2003), p. 4.

9. Miquel Parets, *A Journal of the Plague Year: The Diary of the Barcelona Tanner Miquel Parets, 1651,* trans. James S. Amelang (New York: Oxford University Press, 1995), p. 61.

10. Katherine Park, "Healing the Poor: Hospitals and Medical Assistance in Renaissance Florence," in *Medicine and Charity before the Welfare State,* ed. Jonathan Barry and Colin Jones (New York: Routledge, 1991), p. 36.

11. Used to sharpen a penknife with which one scratched out or erased writing on parchment.

12. David Gentilcore, "All That Pertains to Medicine," *Medical History* 38 (1994), p. 133.

13. Yves Ferroul, "The Doctor and Death in the Middle Ages and Renaissance," in *Death and Dying in the Middle Ages,* ed. Edelgard DuBruck and Barbara I. Gusick (New York: Peter Lang, 1999), p. 46.

14. Carlo Cipolla, *Public Health and the Medical Profession in the Renaissance* (New York: Cambridge University Press, 1976), p. 77.

15. Spikenard: aromatic plant from India related to valerian; testi marini: oysters?; ladanum: a tropical plant juice; colocynth: type of cucumber used as purgative; storax: oil derived from tree of same name; selanum: a plant related to nightshade; cubebe: a pepper.

16. Dominick Palazzatto, "The Black Death and Medicine: A Report and Analysis of the Tractates Written between 1348 and 1350" (Ph.D. dissertation, University of Kansas, 1974), p. 180.

17. Simon Schama, *The Embarrassment of Riches* (New York: Vintage, 1997), p. 197; Robert Latham and Williams Matthews, eds., *The Diary of Samuel Pepys,* vol. VI (Berkeley: University of California Press, 2000), p. 120.

18. Johannes Nohl, *The Black Death,* trans. C. H. Clarke (New York: Ballantine Books, 1960), p. 91.

19. Watson Nicholson, *Historical Sources of De Foe's Journal of the Plague Years* (Boston: The Stratford Co., 1919), p. 55.

20. An English gold coin.

21. Cooper, W. D. "Notices of the Last Great Plague," *Archaeologia* 37 (1857), p. 15.

22. Henri Mollaret and Jacqueline Brossollet, "La peste, source meconnue d'inspiration artistique," *Koninklijk Museum voor schone Kunsten, Jaarboek* (1965), p. 32.

23. Latham and Matthews, *Diary,* VI, p. 17–18, 67; Nicholson, *Historical Sources,* p. 59; Martha Baldwin, "Toads and Plague: Amulet Therapy in Seventeenth-century Medicine," *Bulletin of the History of Medicine* 67 (1993), p. 241.

24. Baldwin, "Toads," p. 242.

25. Palazzotto, "Black Death," pp. 84 ff; F. P. Wilson, *Plague in Shakespeare's London* (New York: Oxford University Press, 1999), p. 5.

26. Rawcliffe, *Medicine,* p. 48.

27. Cipolla, *Public Health,* p. 24.

28. Palazzotto, "Black Death," pp. 218, 221.

29. Charles F. Mullett, *The Bubonic Plague and England* (Lexington: University of Kentucky Press, 1956), p. 76.

30. Alum: aluminum sulphate; calamint: a common European mint-scented herb; aristolochia: a woody vine of the Birthwort family.

31. Palazzotto, "Black Death," p. 224; Bullein, *Dialogue,* p. 47.

32. Marcus Woodward, ed., *Gerard's Herbal* (Twickenham: Senate, 1998), p. 162.

33. Narwhal: A small northern whale with a single long, straight, spirally twisted tusk.

3

AT HOME WITH THE PLAGUE

All too often, pestilence destroyed family. It swept away its members, twisted its structure, and negated its functions. Rituals associated with death had evolved from a desire to provide order at a time of relative chaos. Customs dictated functions and tasks, etiquette defined proper emotional reactions and displays, and community involvement from the deathbed to the requiem Mass or funeral banquet reintegrated the suffering family into the larger social body. In plague time, every element of this comforting regularity disintegrated: slowly at first, but with increasing rapidity the ceremonial fell away, leaving only the barbaric work of the corpse-hauler.

THE HOUSEHOLD: STRUCTURE AND FUNCTION

The Extended Family

The term family today conjures images of many types of arrangements, from three-generational households in which grandpa or grandma reside, to childless gay couples and single parents with several children. Currently Western society is evolving away from the so-called nuclear family of mom, dad, and around two children all living in one house. In the age of the Second Pandemic families were also evolving, but toward the nuclear pattern. The majority probably had some elements of the extended family: older children from the father's previous marriage, the parents' elderly parent(s) or uncles or aunts, or younger brothers or sisters or cousins.

Family might also include servants, apprentices, foster children, slaves, orphaned nieces or nephews, or godchildren. Wealthier families with the room and resources to support additional members tended to be larger than poorer ones, but even peasant households had to harbor widowed or orphaned family members, those unable to work because of age or condition, travelers, refugees, and fugitives. When plague threatened or attacked "family," then, it threatened or struck a much larger number of people than one might think.

The Ancestors When a woman married she left her birth family and joined that of her husband. Taking his surname, she birthed into that family children who would carry his name. Whether the name was notorious, praise-worthy, or little known may have been a matter of her husband's activities, but it was as likely due to the reputation of his ancestors. Family names often reflected the first name, occupation, or birthplace of the first notable family member, or traditional connections to occupations like those of the miller, smith, carter, or weaver. Among the lower classes that had neither property nor wide reputation to consider, family lore blended with village or neighborhood traditions and resulted in family stories told around winter fires. Upper-class families that needed to protect property and reputation recorded significant events and family tales in books. Family crests or heraldic shields displayed one's nobility and specific pedigree as heraldic elements were recombined each generation to reflect new unions of bloodlines in marriage. By the fourteenth century rich nonnobles could purchase coats of arms to provide the appearance of good blood, something especially useful for a commoner marrying a young noblewoman. Nobles also produced genealogies to trace family connections over the generations and placed memorials with family heraldry over the graves of family members in churches that sometimes came to resemble family burial chapels. In family chronicles, genealogies, heraldry, and family burial sites the generations came together and created an identity that transcended the individual and time itself. One's wealth, honor, sense of self-worth, social acceptance, and even marriageability were bound up with the ancestors.

Husband and Wife At the heart of the European family were the husband and wife. They were themselves children whose parents were often still living when they wed. Their union and new life together, blessed by the Catholic Church in the sacrament of matrimony and by most Protestant denominations in formal ceremonies, were meant to be fruitful in producing the next generation, who would in turn continue the cycle of life. At marriage women tended to be younger than their spouses—sometimes by decades—and brought with them to the marriage a dowry, their portion of their generation's inheritance. While one cannot say that no one ever married for love, it is true that among all classes marriage constituted a union of families and property, and not just of two lovers. The generally accepted expectation was that the pair would grow into lovers with the passage of time. Loving one's spouse was like the Christian virtue of loving one's neighbor—not necessarily natural, but expected by society.

Society imposed an order on the family, some of the effects of which we still feel today. Modern scholars recognize two "spheres" of activity and responsibility, the husband's and the wife's. The world within the walls of the house and garden belonged to women and girls. Their focus was on the biological success of the family: they cared for infants and children, cooked meals, nursed the sick and dying, and prepared the dead for burial. During pregnancy and wet-nursing their bodies defined their functions. In higher-class homes they directed the domestic servants or slaves and ensured that the structure and furnishings of the house were maintained. As primary caregivers to and educators of the next generation, women were also the family's spiritual core, though Luther and other Protestants tried to shift this role to the father. Mothers taught their children the essentials of Christianity, from Bible stories to prayers and hymns, and generally saw to it that they attended the appropriate church services. An old German phrase neatly sums up the typical married woman's world at the time of the Second Pandemic: *kinder, küche, und kirche* (children, kitchen, and church). But typical is not absolute, and many women had either greater relative freedom or greater responsibilities than outlined here. The older widow had several options and often resources of her own, and the bourgeois wife might also help in her husband's business or even run her own.

The husband's "sphere" was usually an extension of what he had been doing before marriage. Though responsible to and for his family, his most significant activities took place in the broader arena of village, city, or even world. Men dominated the social, political, cultural, and economic realms of the late medieval and early modern world. Where the wife tended most needs of the family, the husband provided many of the means for her to do so. He also represented the family in the political community. Communities across Europe excluded women from virtually all political activities and service. They were barred from the clergy, military, and most guilds, from civic offices, university education, and in some places and times even ownership of property. Within a family the husband, perhaps in consultation with his wife, made all of the major decisions: where to live; which servants to hire (even which wet-nurse); how his sons would be educated and whom his daughters might marry; how to spend or invest the family's resources, including his wife's dowry; what to do with his own illegitimate children; and during the Reformation which denomination to adopt.

If no one in a given generation of the family had children, the family would die. However people might have felt about their **Children** own children, having children was an obligation for married men and women. A childless marriage was often seen as cursed by God;

a large family considered itself blessed. Scholars argue over whether medieval and early modern parents cherished their children in the ways modern parents are expected to. Some contend that because of high infant mortality and the fact that many families—especially of the upper classes—sent their babies to be nourished by wet-nurses in the countryside, parents avoided bonding with their children early in life and remained emotionally distant as they grew. Others dismiss this notion, pointing to letters and diaries that express terrible grief at the deaths of children as clear evidence of close attachments. Among both Catholics and Protestants one found a strand of stoicism that accepted children as gifts from God to be returned as he willed. In Elizabethan England, a time of population growth periodically assaulted by plague, only about half of the children born lived to see their fifth birthday, and a little over half of these lived to marriageable age. Childhood and epidemic diseases, accidents, poor nutrition and bad water, and even infanticide all took their toll. Children are traditionally underrepresented in medieval demographic data, and plague data on children's deaths are especially hard to come by. Both modern models of bubonic plague and anecdotal evidence in later medieval sources, however, lead one to expect high mortality among infants and children.

While modern cultures tend to view childhood as a stage of life with value in its own right, medieval and early modern cultures tended to consider it merely a stage preliminary to adulthood. Children were treated as small adults who were just less capable of physical and intellectual labor. At the first signs of usefulness they were put to work in the fields or shop, with boys as young as eight being contracted out to tradesmen or craftsmen for training. These boys would develop into apprentices in the household of the master, living with his family while learning the trade or craft and helping the master make money. While some girls learned useful crafts from their mothers (and sometimes fathers), others were put out as servants in wealthy families, or simply married off young. Marriage at the onset of adolescence for Renaissance-era girls was far from uncommon, as Shakespeare's Juliet reminds us, but the age at marriage for both men and women rose over the period, with the men always older on average.

The Family and the Threat of Plague The family operated within a communal matrix from which it drew a great deal of information and according to whose rules it had to function. Relatives, fellow guildsmen, friends, physicians, the church, the traditional legal system, and civic, village, or manorial authorities all might have influenced how a family learned about and reacted to the approach of plague. Family traditions, social and economic resources, and personal experiences also played their parts. One wealthy family might use its money and network of friends in other cities to flee, leaving all else behind; another with the same resources might choose to stay to protect its assets; and a third might have its head remain in town while his dependents were relocated for their protection. In the case of flight, a family's servants, apprentices, and hangers-on were likely to be left to shift for themselves. Sometimes trusted servants were left behind to look after the house and other assets: the City of London was said to have become a city of servants during plague time in the seventeenth century. A husband who sent his family away lived with the constant fear that he would never see them again, and, no doubt, his family feared the same; yet business or other duties proved more compelling than fear.

DIRECTIONS FOR CLEANSING

Being some few experimentals gained in the Time of Infection (sixteenth-century Yorkshire)

1. All wooden vessels or ware, as likewise metals, such as plate, pewter, tin, lead, brass and iron etc. must be washed in hot, scalding water.
2. Linen must be washed in hot water and thoroughly dried, but not to be used of a good while later.
3. Woolen clothes to be scalded in hot water and so dried. Woolen cloth, carsay pieces [coarse woolens] etc., to be put in a running stream two days at least, then dried on the ground or on tenters [racks]. Wool is to be opened and washed in a running water; dry it on the ground or on stakes, with sun, wind or fire.
4. Featherbeds or flock beds are to be opened, the feathers, flocks and cloth ticks scalded and well dried before they be made up.
5. Such house is to be cleansed in every part both abovehead and below. The wainscot, posts, bedstocks, tables, etc. to be washed in scalding water as before is directed.
6. All straw, dust, rags or other rubbish (not worth the cleansing) are to be burnt, or, much rather, to be buried deep in the ground, that swine root it not, nor others dig it up.
7. Make fires [in rooms] with green broom, green hay or both. Slake lime in vinegar. Burn much tar, pitch, resin, frankincense, turpentine, etc.

From S. J. Chadwick, "Some Papers Relating to the Plague in Yorkshire," *Yorkshire Archaeological Journal* 15 (1900), pp. 459–60.

When a family decided to stay, its head had to provide the very best in prophylaxis to prevent any members from contracting the disease. Drugs, amulets, pomanders, and recipes for cures had to be purchased, as well as disinfectants such as vinegar to be washed with and fumigants to be burned. Windows and other exterior openings might be sealed up to keep the corrupted air at bay. Social activities were curtailed. Servants and others who would have uncontrolled contact with the world outside were often given rooms in the house away from the family proper. Indeed, servants were often the first members of a large household to fall ill. In places like London and Italy, where authorities shut whole families up in their houses when a member fell ill of plague, householders had great incentive to keep a plague victim a secret from the authorities. Stricken family members might be nursed, but servants and others could well find themselves relegated to an outbuilding or a country residence and provided a minimum of attention.

A DEATH IN THE FAMILY

Commonness of Death

In the Western industrialized world death usually takes place in rest homes, hospices, and hospitals, isolated from everyday life. Under normal circumstances in the era of the Second Pandemic the elderly, terminally ill, and victims of accidents or violence died in their homes among their friends and family. Households experienced deaths in every age group: infants and mothers died in childbirth; toddlers died of accidents with water, fire, and animals; adults were victims of domestic violence fueled by alcohol and poverty; the elderly usually died in their own beds; and war, famine, and disease swept through towns and villages, killing indiscriminately. In normal times families visited the dying and attended showings of the dead, along with their funerals and burials. Church sermons and religious art trumpeted the message that life was merely a vestibule or prelude to death. Families literally stood by as members suffered fevers, delirium, gastrointestinal problems, broken limbs, poisonings, the pox, venereal disease, dementia, and debilitating chronic illness. Doctors, surgeons, and apothecaries[1] were rarely of any help, even in dulling pain. Each parish had its graveyard that every parishioner passed each Sunday; urban cemeteries were often playgrounds for the young. Death and its often-terrible precursors were no strangers even to the wealthy household: Lady Fanshawe, an English ambassador's wife, provided the following litany in her memoires:

Richard my third [son]; Henry my fourth; and Richard my fifth, are all dead; my second lies buried in the Protestant Church-yard in Paris, by the father of the Earl of Bristol; my eldest daughter, Anne, lies buried in the parish church of Tankersley, in Yorkshire, where she died; Elizabeth lies in the chapel of the French Hospital at Madrid, where she died of a fever at ten days old; my next daughter, of her name, lies buried in the parish of Foot's Cray in Kent . . . and my daughter Mary lies in my father's vault in Hertford, with my first son, Henry.[2]

Medical Care at Bedside: The Physician and Surgeon

Most doctors had few delusions about their power over death. There were even those who argued that a physician should not waste his time or the family's resources treating someone clearly destined to die. It was often the physician who tore away the last veil of hope, who declared the prognosis was "terminal." Yet in towns and cities the appearance of the physician was heartening. He arrived on horseback, or in later years in a litter or carriage. He carefully cultivated his demeanor, fancy clothing, and use of sophisticated and confusing language to provide reassurance of his professional competence. He might clear the sickroom grandly or invite onlookers to observe the mysteries of medicine. Rarely was the patient a complete stranger, so rapport was simple. In the case of a long illness, doctor and patient were quite familiar; if time was short, then the doctor's work was all but done. Typically he would discuss the patient's symptoms and the progress of the illness, and whether any previously ingested medicines had had an effect. Of special interest were fevers and evacuations, including phlegm, pus, sputum, blood, sweat, feces, and urine. The last was examined in a bulbous glass jar for color, sediment, viscosity, smell, and other qualities. The physician took the patient's pulse, but without quantitatively measuring it; rather he determined its strength and rapidity qualitatively. He did the same with the patient's body temperature. If there were external "tokens" on the body, such as lesions or pustules, he would examine them for changes in hardness, appearance, or discharge. Based on his findings he might prescribe the good offices of a surgeon or apothecary. Second opinions and consultations with colleagues were not at all unusual, especially with wealthier patients. Nonetheless, one French author, whose works printing pioneer William Caxton translated into English, warned against contentious consultations:

And when many masters and physicians are assembled in the presence of the patient or sick man, they ought not there to argue and dispute one against the other. But they ought to make good and simple collation together, in such a way that they do not seem to be disputing one another, in order to encroach and get more glory of the world to themselves than to treat the well-being and health of the sick man.[3]

In cases of fevers the surgeon would bleed the patient to reduce the amount of "hot" blood in the patient's system. Surgeons would also carry out other manual procedures such as lancing boils, smearing ointments, and applying or changing dressings. The apothecary, or pharmacist, sold medicinal remedies that ranged from simple herbs to complex potions, powders, and pills. If the determination was that the patient's condition was terminal, then the honest doctor offered his last good-byes and condolences; the unscrupulous one continued expensive treatments in full knowledge they were of no value.

The "Good Death": Catholic and Protestant

Based on its doctrine of "life everlasting"—whether in heaven or hell—Catholicism taught its followers that death was a transition between life in this world and life in the next. Because the character of one's life in this world determined one's place in the next (unless one believed in predestination), a person's beliefs and actions right up to the end had eternal consequences. The sacrament of last anointing (extreme unction) or last rites allowed the dying person one final chance to "get it

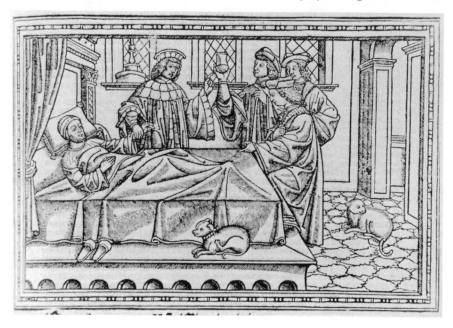

Four medical men attend a wealthy, bedridden patient. One takes his pulse, another examines his urine, and a third, by his gesture, appears to be conversing with him. A late fifteenth-century woodcut. National Library of Medicine.

right" through a fervent and honest confession and reception of communion. The victim's own final prayers, those of family members, and the blessing of the priest were a vital part of the Christian's send-off.

To help guide the Catholic through this process, theologians and pastors developed a genre of moral literature known as the Art of Dying (*Ars moriendi*). These handbooks were originally in Latin for the use of clergy and monks, but were translated into the vernaculars for an increasingly literate lay public. They were meant to be read and absorbed by the hale and hearty, so that they would be prepared both for their own deaths and to assist others in dying well. A typical English example from the fifteenth century, *The Craft of Dying,* had five sections. In the first the reader is reminded of the terrors of spiritual death and damnation. The second warns against typical temptations of the dying, such as impatience, unbelief, or spiritual despair. The third consists of questions regarding one's spiritual fitness: belief in Christian doctrine; matters of conscience left unsettled; how one might live differently if he or she recovers. The fourth is a meditation on the power of Christ and the Crucifixion in allowing for salvation, and the fifth instructs bystanders on how best to help the dying person pass, with prayers, readings from Scripture, and presentation of pictures of Christ or the saints. The

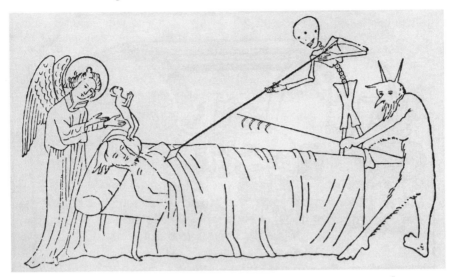

While Death torments a man's body, the Devil tries to capture the soul (in the form of a "little man" floating away) that appears to be well guarded by the angel at left. From a fourteenth-century English manuscript. Dover.

handbooks featured illustrations of the deathbed with devils waiting to take the soul of the person who did not die well. Because of the Catholic teaching that even the firmest believer did not have absolute certainty of salvation, the deathbed was always a tense and fearful place. Faith and hope provided comfort, however, as did the belief in the power of saintly intercession and purgatory.

A FLORENTINE EXILE DIES A GOOD DEATH IN BOLOGNA, 1374

During the plague of 1374, the surviving members of Giovanni's [Morelli] family and the entire family of Paolo [Morelli] fled to Bologna and lived together in one house, dividing the expenses equally. . . . [Giovanni's rather young son] Gualberto was in charge of providing the necessities and supervising expenditures, and he was responsible for keeping records and maintaining an account of the money that was given to him. . . . Finally, realizing that he had been stricken by the plague and aware that he was dying, he provided for the salvation of his soul with the same care, requesting all of the Holy Sacraments, and receiving them with the greatest devotion. With good and holy Psalms, he devoutly recommended his soul to God. Then, with good and gentle words, he begged the pardon of all members of that household, recommending his soul to everyone, having no more regard for the great than for the small. Then, in the presence of everyone, he accused himself of having spent some ten or twelve lire from the fund for his own affairs, and, as I said, denouncing himself in the presence of all, he returned the money to the cash box. Then he departed from this life, being in full possession of his faculties to the final moment. Together with the priest, he said the prayers with a loud voice so everyone heard him. Then, sensing that he was at the point of death, he urged the priest to recite more rapidly. And, by God's grace, having completed the prayers, he and the priest together spoke the last words, "Thanks be to God, amen." He closed his eyes and rendered his soul to God at that precise moment.

From the *Cronica* of Giovanni Morelli, in Gene Brucker, *The Society of Renaissance Florence* (New York: Harper, 1971), pp. 46–47.

Protestants continued the "Art of Dying" tradition, modifying it according to their own beliefs. Because of their emphasis on faith rather than ceremony or works, most if not all outward signs of a religious nature, other than a Bible or prayer book, were stripped away. Early English examples specifically warn against "papist" practices and the use of sacramentals such as candles, rosaries, holy water, or, in some cases, even a crucifix. While good Catholics were to obey the priest and church and faithfully undergo the last sacrament, Protestants were to suffer as stoically as possible and leave their witnesses with whatever faith-filled wisdom and advice they could and a fine example of the Christian way to die. Because only God knows the dying person's fate, friends and family (unless they were predestinarians) might pray that the victim hold fast to her faith, but not that God might save her. They also might pray for their own good deaths and for the consolation of one another.

Legal Affairs at the Bedside: The Notary and the Will   The medieval and early modern notary played a vital part in Europe's legal system. To men and women contemplating death he was the officially licensed legal practitioner who drew up their last wills and testaments, the contractual arrangement between the deceased and the community that stipulated exactly how the property and dependents of the deceased would be handled. In this document the head of the household, for example, would return his wife's dowry to her; arrange for his children's wardship or education; distribute his cash and property among family, friends, and charities; provide for his daughters' dowries; pay off debts; dissolve business partnerships; free slaves; reward servants; specify details about his funeral and burial; and appoint executors to see that all his wishes were carried out properly. Widows, wives, and mothers who controlled property were also encouraged to make wills. The practice was deemed so important by the church that dying intestate—without a will—was declared a sin that relegated the thoughtless soul to no better than purgatory. Thoughtful people with property and dependents made wills during times of trouble and before traveling, when death might suddenly and unexpectedly overcome them. But, as the church insisted, death might occur at any time, so the good Christian always had a valid will. Even with an existing will, a dying person might well want to make changes that, for example, rewarded his last caregivers, increased contributions to the church or the poor that might help save his soul (if a Catholic), or eliminated executors or benefactors who had died. A testator could alter his will by adding or changing terms through amendments (codicils) or by tearing up the old one and making a new one from scratch.

EXCERPT FROM THE WILL OF FRANCIS PYNNER, GENTLEMAN OF BURY ST. EDMUNDS, ENGLAND, 1639

Item, whereas my late wife's kinsman Francis Potter, of Bury St. Edmunds, baker, at the late heavy visitation [of plague] did take great pains about me in the time of my trouble, in regard I could get no body to help me; and that all my household fled from me and left me both comfortless (in respect that at that time I had my man die of the sickness) when my self and my wife were both lame; in consideration whereof I have enfeoffed the said Francis Potter and his heirs forever in two messuages or tenements in Bury St. Edmunds. . . .

Item, whereas Elizabeth Pell, wife of William Pell the elder, and John Pell their son, did take like pains about me, as is before mentioned, in the time of my great calamity and heavy visitation, as is above specified, I do give and bequeath unto the said William and John Pell all and singular such sum and sums of money as the said William and John do owe unto me either by bonds, bills, or any ways or means whatsoever.

Item, in consideration that John Newgate, malster, divers and sundry times hath come and resorted to comfort and confer with me in the time of my sorrow and heaviness, I do give and bequeath unto him the said John Newgate the sum of four pounds of lawful money of England.

From Samuel Tymms, ed., *Wills and Inventories from the Registers of the Commissary of Bury St. Edmunds* (New York: AMS Press, 1968), pp. 172–73.

Like the physician, the notary was often a man with whom the family had done business for years. They had to feel that they could trust him for financial and legal advice, and he had to be careful to avoid conflicts of interest. Often he worked in tandem with a lawyer, who was better educated and better able to sort out difficult legal issues. Since wills embodied emotional and spiritual elements as well as financial and social ones, the legal professionals who helped the testator shape the document took on a unique responsibility to their client.

Renaissance Florentine mother Alessandra Strozzi left a large body of correspondence from which we learn a great deal about the importance of the rituals of dying. In a letter to her son Filippo regarding the death of his brother Matteo, who died while away on family business, she wrote:

Spiritual Care at Bedside: The Priest and Last Rites

I am certain he was provided with doctors and medicine, and that everything possible was done for his health, and that nothing was spared. Yet, it was all to no avail; such was God's will. I have also been comforted by the knowledge that

A priest prays with outstretched arms over a sick man, who is also attended by a physician. From Lorenz Fries's *Spiegl der Artzny*, Strasbourg, 1519. National Library of Medicine.

when he was dying, God granted him the opportunity to confess, to receive communion and extreme unction . . . God has prepared a place for him.[4]

Having benefited as much as possible from the services of notary, surgeon, and physician, the dying Catholic's last and most important ministrations would be by the priest. Depending on the circumstances, the visiting cleric might appear for only the last rites, or spend hours with the dying person, providing spiritual comfort to the entire family. Generally the family's parish priest, or a favorite friar, he was the church's representative at a time of great stress and sorrow. He appeared formally, wearing signs of his clerical office, carrying holy water and a small container lined with gold (pyx) in which the Eucharist was kept. A clerk who carried a candle, handbell, and the book with the ritual text accompanied him.

The priest greeted the household with a blessing and sprinkled holy water around the sickroom as a prophylactic against the demons illustrated in the *Ars moriendi*. He asked about the person's will and presented a crucifix for the dying person to kiss. The priest anointed the dying person with special olive oil blessed each Easter morning, dabbing it on the person's eyelids, nostrils, ears, hands, lips, feet, and back. If the person was cogent, he or she would make a final confession and receive absolution from the priest. Having prepared the patient for communion, the priest offered the Eucharist. If appropriate, he would remain to pray well-known prayers for the soul of the soon-to-be departed, asking for God's mercy on a sinner and for the saints to pray on his or her behalf. The bell tolled at the moment of a person's passing to make the death known to all; this practice, with its origins in monastic tradition, continued even in Protestant countries.

Just as mother, midwife, and their female attendants brought people into the world, the family's women took charge of the physical aspects of sending them on their way out of it. The older girls and women of the family acted as **Women and Death** nurses throughout illnesses, caring for the patient's various physical needs. Traditionally, preparing the dead for burial was one portion of the woman's sphere. The women of the household would undress and wash the corpse, trying to place it in a fitting position before rigor mortis set in. They shaved the men's faces and pared the nails of those of both sexes, and perhaps rubbed down the body with an odiferous ointment to offset the stench of putrefaction. If custom dictated the showing of the body in the home, then the women had to prepare the public room or rooms while the men dealt with the arrangements for the funeral and burial.

In the warm climate of central Italy, Renaissance Florentines gathered at the house of the deceased within a day after death. From here the cortege processed on a preplanned **The Family and the Funeral** route through the city to the burial church. Members of the immediate family wore jet-black gowns or capes; other mourners donned brownish-black ones. Wealthy families paid poorer folk to march in the procession and even paid for their garb. Mourners or special torchbearers carried candles, while the coffin and the horse that pulled its caisson were covered in rich cloth with family, guild, or confraternity heraldry. With the redistribution of wealth that accompanied the first outbreak of plague in 1348, many less-wealthy families began emulating their social betters, which from 1374 provoked sumptuary laws restricting lavish public display. In Florence, and later Bologna and Rome, female mourners—excepting close kin—were banned from corteges presumably because of their ostentatious wailing. (The ban did cut down on the cost of mourning apparel.) Powerful Florentine families got around these laws by petitioning for exemptions from the civic government, 233 of which were issued between 1384 and 1392. Funereal banquets were private affairs rather than public: the requiem Mass was the public display to which all interested parties were invited, and the size of attendance, like the number of candles in the cortege, was a sign of the family's prestige.

In seventeenth-century, Calvinist Holland the cleaned and re-dressed body was placed on its own bed in the house's entrance hall, which had been cleared of all other furniture. Inside the house all pictures and mirrors were turned toward the wall and all windows closed; cheap black cloth (crepe) was hung about as a sign of mourning. The corpse was shown for several days—Holland's cool weather generally being conducive to long exposure—during which time the family circulated a death notice, which might be in verse and even proclaimed orally by "public priors." After the procession to the graveyard, the family and close friends shared a lavish meal, sometimes presented in the street in front of the house, washed down with beer and wine. During plague time, when the Calvinist authorities forbade such displays, families provided guests with coins to spend at the local tavern or merely as mementos.

PLAGUE STRIKES THE FAMILY

As the pestilence wracked London in July of 1563, Anglican Bishop Edmund Grindal prescribed the following family ritual in his "Form of Meditation, very meet [appropriate] to be daily used by householders in their houses:"

The master, kneeling with his family in some convenient place of his house, perfumed before with frankincense, or some other wholesome thing, as juniper, rosemary, rosewater, and vinegar, shall with fervent heart say, or cause to be said, this that follows. The servants and family to every petition shall say "Amen."[5]

He follows this recommendation with a litany of prayers for forgiveness, mercy, and assistance from God. Such regular rituals helped to maintain the bonds that kept families and even societies together. As plague tore away at the fabric of the family and society, such short but highly meaningful ceremonies disappeared, leaving the living to bury the dead and face each new day in some mixture of hope and terror.

The Course of the Disease Medical historian Mary Lindemann recently warned that "plague . . . cannot be facilely equated with bubonic plague; plague was rather a catch-all term for a number of ailments, quite different afflictions . . . or generally awful conditions." Even so, there is a certain uniformity to the descriptions of symptoms of "plague" or "pest" across the Second Pandemic. Writers even seem to distinguish clearly between cases of bubonic plague (with buboes) and pneumonic (fever and coughing up of blood, symptoms that so swiftly overcame one that buboes did not develop). The Irish friar John Clynn, who died in the midst of the first outbreak in 1349, recorded that "many died of boils and abscesses and pustules which erupted on their shins or under their armpits; others died frantic with pain in their head, and others spitting blood." The Russian *Novgorod Chronicle* entry for 1417 includes a typical picture of the plague patient:

First of all it would hit one as if with a lance, choking, and then swelling would appear, or spitting of blood with shivering, and fire would burn one in all the joints of the body; and then the illness would overwhelm one, and many after lying in that illness died.

This passage is a layman's description rather than that of a physician, which would be far more typical. John of Fordun, a cleric in Aberdeen, Scotland, wrote in his chronicle under the year 1350, "By God's will this evil led to a strange and unwonted kind of death, in so much that the flesh of the sick was somehow puffed out and swollen, and they dragged out their earthly life for barely two days." Between 1367 and 1369 John VI Cantacuzenos, who had served as Byzantine emperor from 1341 to 1354, wrote a *History* of his reign in which he described in detail the course of the plague:

[N]o physician's art was sufficient; neither did the disease take the same course in all persons, but the others, unable to resist, died the same day, a few even within a few hours [of showing symptoms]. Those who could resist for two or three days had a very violent fever at first, the disease in such cases attacking the head; they suffered from speechlessness and insensibility to all happenings and then appeared as if sunken into a deep sleep. Then, if from time to time they came to themselves, they wanted to speak but the tongue was hard to move and they uttered inarticulate sounds because the nerves around the occiput [back of the head] were dead; and they died suddenly. In others the evil attacked not the head, but the lung, and forthwith there was inflammation inside which produced very sharp pains in the chest.

Sputum suffused with blood was brought up and disgusting and stinking breath from within. The throat and tongue, parched from the heat, were black and congested with blood. It made no difference if they drank much or little. Sleeplessness and weakness were established forever.

Abscesses formed on the upper and lower arms, in a few also in the jaw, and in others on other parts of the body . . . Black blisters appeared. Some people broke out with black spots all over their bodies; in some they were few and very manifest; in others they were obscure and dense.

Great abscesses were formed on the legs or the arms, from which, when cut, a large quantity of foul-smelling pus flowed. . . . Whenever people felt sick there was no hope left for recovery, but by turning to despair, adding to their prostration and severely aggravating their sickness, they died at once.[6]

This was the face of plague that millions of Europeans encountered under their own roofs; this was how their loved ones died.

The Family and the Victim   The first impulse of family members was to do all things possible to nurse the victim back to health. It became common knowledge that many who contracted the disease survived: modern figures and those from seventeenth-century pest houses suggest 40 to 50 percent. Tending to the sick and maintaining hope was thus no fool's errand. The evidence we have suggests that, as usual, the women of the household did most of the work, from preparing prescribed foods and medicines, to applying cool compresses to reduce the fever, to cleaning sweat-soaked or soiled bedclothes, to calming and praying with the often delirious patient. It is clear that many families were struck repeatedly with plague; at any one time several members might lay sick or dying, making the job of the nurse even more difficult. The Zurich printer Thomas Platter recalled how, when he was a boy, he went to stay at the house of a friend's mother: "And as she didn't have many beds, I had to sleep with two young girls who both caught the plague and died right next to me, although nothing happened to me."[7]

Of course, for some family nurses the job simply became too oppressive. Many fell ill themselves; others simply abandoned the sick, fleeing both the "bad air" and its victims. Florentine writer Giovanni Boccaccio, and many observers who followed him, recorded that

disaster had struck such fear into the hearts of men and women that brother abandoned brother, uncle abandoned nephew, sister left brother, and very often wife abandoned husband, and—even worse, almost unbelievable—fathers and mothers neglected to tend and care for their children as if they were not their own.

Thus for the multitude of men and women who fell sick, there remained no support except the charity of their friends (and these were few) or the greed of servants, who worked for inflated salaries without regard to the service they performed and who, in spite of this, were few and far between; and those few were men or women of little wit [knowledge] (most of them not trained for such service) who did little else but hand different things to the sick when requested to do so or watch over them while they died.[8]

The Barcelona tanner Miquel Parets, whose diary provides many important insights into the 1651 plague, tells us that his own wife fell ill and buboes appeared.

Although she had two sisters in Barcelona, neither was willing to come to nurse her, I mean not to nurse her, but even to see her for they could have seen her without having to come into my house, as they could do so from the house in front, where everyone was quite well and happy.[9]

In Italy, England, and the Netherlands old women, sometimes midwives, were hired or appointed by the family, parish, or city to care for victims in their homes. The women who survived this service usually had to undergo up to six weeks of quarantine once the plague had abated. But who among them would bother to call upon the physician, surgeon, notary, or priest? When the family survived intact its members certainly would try—often unsuccessfully—to provide for a normal deathbed, but when it had disintegrated all of the hopefulness and comfort dissipated with it. Priests fired up with Counter-Reformation piety often made great sacrifices to provide at least the last confession and the Eucharist to dying family members and even those dying alone in the streets. But, harried as they were, the clergyman could hardly linger to soften death's blow for either victim or family.

By the later sixteenth century many families were relieved of the burden when the sick were forcibly carted off (literally) **Removal of** to the pest house to recover or die. More than any other civic **the Victim** ordinance, this practice tore at the fabric of the community and family itself. It denied all the opportunity to participate in the victim's passing, and eliminated the victim's last moments of ritual comfort in the bosom of his or her family. Though as many as half of those taken to early modern pest houses survived to return to their families, no departure was looked on as anything other than a death sentence.

When the epidemic had settled in upon a community the mechanisms of mass corpse removal and burial went into motion. Postmortem rituals, showings, funeral corteges and funeral masses, graveside services, and funeral banquets were all banned or abandoned in the interest of public hygiene and safety. Upon the death of a loved one the terrible *becchini* or corpse-removers violated the sanctity of the home to carry the victim off to an anonymous grave. In the case of households in which families were "shut in" by authorities because of an incidence of plague, corpses were often dumped by family members from second-story windows onto carts already heaped with bodies. Not only were the survivors deeply affected by the death and disposal of a family member, whatever the relation, but each had to ponder the fact that he or she might very easily follow the same painful and identity-stripping course.

Rural areas were spared the great density of the dead and dying, but Death's scythe swept through no less cleanly. Rural Europeans also valued funeral rituals like the folks in the big city, and all sought burial in the consecrated ground of the churchyard. While these customs normally presented few problems thanks to the infrequency of deaths and burials, in plague time the sheer numbers complicated matters greatly. In an entry in the Bishop's Registry for York the writer noted that terrain and weather often made transporting corpses to the proper burial sites very difficult:

[S]o that they cannot bring such bodies of the dead that should be buried in the mother [parish] church aforesaid; and so, sometimes the bodies of the parishioners of the said chapel, when they died, were and are carried thither with cruel roughness, having their bones broken, and are very often left unburied in the waters and the woods.

No doubt many settled for burial as close to home as possible to simplify the process of burial and keep the survivors and their loved ones in proximity. In at least one case it served another purpose. In the parish register for Malpas, Cheshire, England, we read:

Richard Dawson, being sick of the plague and perceiving he must die at that time, arose out of his bed and made his grave, and caused his nephew John Dawson to cast some straw into the grave which was not far from the house, and went and laid down in the said grave, and caused clothes to be laid upon and so departed out of this world; this he did because he was a strong man and heavier than his said nephew and another wench were able to bury.

Of course certain rituals, such as showing the body for several days, served multiple purposes, in this case ensuring that the person was in fact dead, a nicety ignored in the time of *becchini* and mass graves. English poet William Austin wrote in his "Anatomy of the Pestilence" (1665),

> Wisely they leave graves open to the dead
> 'Cause some too early there are brought to bed . . .
> One out of trance returned, after much strife
> Among a troop of dead, exclaims for life![10]

The fear of live burial realized: those buried alive in 1348 rise again! From an untitled German engraving by A. Aubrey, 1604. Dover.

Stories, such as that of Ginevra degli Almieri of Tuscany, circulated widely: Having been carried off to the mass grave she revived, escaped, and returned home. Her husband, thinking her a ghost, chased her off with threats of violence. And from Cologne, Germany, came the famous story of Richmondis von Lyskirchen, the wife of a local knight. Having fallen into a coma she, too, was carried off, only to revive when a greedy gravedigger tried to pry off an expensive ring. When she returned home her incredulous husband swore that his horses would mount to the loft of the house before she would really return from the dead. At that his mounts entered the house and clopped up the stairs. Until the Second World War the knight's house on the Neumarkt featured two horses' heads protruding from the second story window. Traditions and customs die hard.

More than any other "place" in medieval and early modern society, the home and family bore the brunt of the plague. The home was a nexus where the biological realities met the physicians and their theories, which intersected religious beliefs and practices, which bumped up against civil ordinances that curtailed tradition and custom. Home was where most people lived and fell ill, recuperated and died. The walls of the house and the arms of the family embraced the plague and its shocks because they had to; in the long run they proved the more resilient.

NOTES

1. Producers and sellers of herbal mixtures and medicines.

2. Christina Hole, *The English Housewife in the Seventeenth Century* (London: Chatto and Windus, 1953), p. 86.

3. Carole Rawcliffe, *Medicine and Society in Later Medieval England* (Stroud, Gloucs., England: Sutton, 1997), p. 107.

4. Gene Brucker, *The Society of Renaissance Florence* (Toronto: University of Toronto Press, 1998).

5. Charles F. Mullett, *The Bubonic Plague and England* (Lexington: University of Kentucky Press, 1956), p. 82.

6. John T. Alexander, *Bubonic Plague in Early Modern Russia* (Baltimore: Johns Hopkins University Press, 1980), p. 15; D. Hamilton, *The Healers: A History of Medicine in Scotland* (Edinburgh: Canongate, 1981), p. 11; Christos Bartsocas, "Two Fourteenth-Century Greek Descriptions of the 'Black Death,'" *Journal of the History of Medicine* 21 (1966), p. 396.

7. Felix Platter, *Beloved Son Felix*, trans. Seán Jennett (London: F. Muller, 1961).

8. Giovanni Boccaccio, *The Decameron*, trans. Mark Musa and Peter Bondanella (New York: Mentor, 1982), p. 9.

9. Miquel Parets, *A Journal of the Plague Year*, trans. James S. Amelang (New York: Oxford University Press, 1995), p. 59.

10. A. Hamilton Thompson, "The Pestilences of the Fourteenth Century in the Diocese of York," *The Archaeological Journal* 71 (1914), p. 110; Clare Gittings, *Death, Burial and the Individual in Early Modern England* (London: Croom Helm, 1984), p. 9; Watson Nicholson, *Historical Sources of De Foe's Journal of the Plague Years* (Boston: The Stratford Co., 1919), p. 16.

4

AT THE CHURCH AND CHURCHYARD

Despite the presence of Jews, Muslims, and a sprinkling of freethinkers and atheists, Europe remained a Christian continent throughout the era of the Second Pandemic. While it is true that the Reformations of the sixteenth century ripped the Roman Catholic Church asunder, Christianity remained the foundation of European culture. Churches served as the centers of community in good times and bad and in most countries as the residence of the dead, thanks to customary funerary rites, burial practices, and memorialization. In plague times normal funeral and burial practices fell away as the sheer number of bodies and fear of contagion forced communities to resort to minimal rituals—if any—and burial in cemeteries specifically segregated from the community. But even if the church building and its rituals lost their centrality, Christian beliefs retained God as the principal source of pestilence and adherence to his will—variously interpreted—as a major means of prevention, avoidance, and cure.

CHURCH AND SOCIETY

Over nearly thirteen centuries the Catholic Church developed a complex structure of personnel, rituals, and **Basic Beliefs** beliefs that were all aimed at aiding the faithful in the pursuit of their salvation. At one level of society were the highly educated theologians and clergy who had absorbed over a millennium of church history and teaching. Friars preached, monks and nuns prayed to a God who promised in the Bible to answer prayers, and priests carried out the private and public rituals that were thought to bless the individual and community from baptism to the grave. These traditions filtered down to the common person through the preaching and writing of these men and women and their students. Even further removed from church teaching were those, usually living in rather remote rural areas, whose ideas of Christianity were very limited and often heavily influenced by local non-Christian traditions.

Late-medieval Catholic belief envisioned the world as having been created and still heavily influenced by God. The Christian God had certain expectations of all his followers, and those who obeyed the teachings of his church could expect to find salvation, a heavenly eternal afterlife. Those who ignored or disobeyed these teachings were sinners who faced eternal punishment in the flames of hell, a place whose horrors were vividly depicted in sermons, church decorations, and the *Divine Comedy* of the Florentine poet Dante Alighieri. But God and the church loved the repentant sinner, and all were called to repent and confess their sins to a priest and thereby wash away the guilt that condemned them. By Dante's time, around 1300, the church had also developed the teaching on purgatory: The soul of the sinner with minor sins left unconfessed at the point of death went to this place of punishment and separation from God in order to purge the guilt for sin. The punishment and separation were temporary, however, and the prayers of friends and family left behind could help shorten the time spent or lessen the agony of the departed.

Saints   Saints were also believed to be very active in human affairs. These men and women had lived exemplary lives and now stood before the throne of God acting as advocates for the weak and sinful—but faithful—people. According to the Bible, God (specifically Jesus) would judge each person justly and according to his or her spiritual merits. The saints served as spiritual intermediaries whose own prayers on behalf of the sinner invoked God's mercy. Saints also became key players in everyday life, helping people find lost objects, protecting women during childbirth, and even defending cities under siege. Parts of a saint's body or belongings were collected as relics, and these reportedly had powers of their own, not least of all the ability to heal. Communities dedicated churches to saints, pilgrims traveled to their shrines, and prayers and hymns praised them and asked for their advocacy with God. The saints, especially the Virgin Mary, mother of Jesus, had a vast following, and their aid was never more actively sought than in plague time.

The Parish   Christians grouped themselves in communities centered on a common house—literally in the earliest years—of worship, the church. These communities of believers, many of which existed in a single large city, were known as parishes, and ordained priests led them in worship. Parishes were grouped under the administration of a bishop, himself a priest, into a diocese, the earliest of which had been centered on Roman cities.

Most Christians lived their spiritual and social lives locally as members of urban and rural parishes. In the context of the parish one performed charitable acts that paved the way to salvation. In the church one heard the Gospel preached and was reminded of the joys of salvation and the pains of hell. One was baptized in its font, received the very Body of Christ at its railing, was betrothed at its door, had the spiritual penalty of sin removed in confession under its roof, and found eternal rest beneath its floor or in its yard, surrounded by family. The Christian community life of the parish was bound by its local traditions, the preaching of the priest, and the sacraments—baptism, penance, the Eucharist, confirmation, matrimony, and last rites—that it administered to the laity.[1] Through obedient participation in these rituals the believer gained grace from God that was necessary for salvation.

In the sixteenth century—midway through the Second Pandemic—a number of church leaders like Martin Luther, **Reformations** Huldrych Zwingli, and the bishops of England renounced **in Europe** many core beliefs and practices as well as the administrative system of the Roman Catholic Church. The Christian Church in the West was redefined in a series of Reformations, each of which has its own history and pattern. The Reformation was not a single movement, but a fragmentation that spawned literally dozens of variations on traditional Christianity, collectively and generically called Protestantism. Luther in Germany, Zwingli in Switzerland, Henry VIII and his bishops in England, and Calvin in France and Switzerland all rejected the central leadership of the Bishop of Rome, or pope, the concept of purgatory, and the power and influence of saints. The continental reformers, and Puritans and others in England influenced by Calvin, also rejected bishops, the ordained priesthood, and the spiritual benefits of the sacraments and any other "good works" that the church had traditionally taught as necessary for grace and salvation. Luther and the Calvinist traditions believed that God had "predestined" all people to heaven or hell, and that nothing, including prayer, could change God's decision. Protestants, left without an intermediating priesthood, sacraments, or saints, relied on an individual spiritual life centered on Scripture and preaching. In many places the old territorial parishes morphed into looser congregations centered on a charismatic preacher or minister rather than a residential community. Parishes remained in place where bishops continued to administer the churches, especially in England and parts of the Lutheran world.

Although the Reformations spawned many Protestant denominations and sects, for the sake of simplicity and clarity our discussion will only distinguish the Lutheran (Evangelical), primarily in northern Germany and Scandinavia; the Anglican, or official church of England; and the Calvinist (Reformed), with branches in Switzerland, France (Huguenots), the Low Countries (Dutch Reformed), Scotland (Presbyterian), and England (Puritan and other dissenters).

CHURCHES

Catholic Church Types
Christian places of worship, or churches, varied widely in size, decoration, and even function. In the Catholic world a church was defined as a specially consecrated space in which Christ was physically and spiritually present in the form of the Eucharist. The most vital furnishing was an altar on which the priest carried out the miraculous transubstantiation (change of substance) of simple bread and wine into the literal body and blood of Christ (the Eucharist) during the course of the ritual ceremony known as the Mass. The part of the church that the altar occupied was called the sanctuary, or holy place, and was architecturally set apart from the rest of the structure. Most of the remaining space was given over to the congregation that gathered for the Mass.

The largest churches usually belonged to the bishop and contained his symbolic chair, or "cathedra," from which we derive the name cathedral church, or simply cathedral. Each Catholic diocese, and Anglican and some Lutheran dioceses, had one cathedral, which was always located in the diocese's main city. This building was also likely to be the most ornate and richly decorated church—or even building—in the city, thanks to the power and wealth of the local bishops and church. Other large churches included shrines, sometimes called basilicas, which were dedicated to specific saints, like St. Peter's or Santa Maria Maggiore in Rome, or St. Francis in Assisi. Churches associated with the Franciscan and Dominican friars were also large; their spacious structures were meant for huge crowds that attended the special services and sermons for which the preachers were famous. Monks, too, often had huge churches attached to their monasteries, usually the gifts of generous benefactors that included nobles and royalty.

Chapels were generally small churches found in castles, palaces, and city halls; along roadways, at bridges, and over city gates; and in church-related buildings like hospitals, orphanages, and schools. Larger churches might also contain chapels, small rooms or alcoves with altars set aside for the special use of patrons such as wealthy families, guilds, or lay brotherhoods (confraternities), or for the veneration of certain saints or display of special relics. In the Renaissance, chapels often came in for special artistic treatment by the patron: examples are the pope's Sistine Chapel, the Brancacci family chapel frescoed by Masaccio in Florence, or Padua's Arena chapel, whose walls are still covered with Giotto's famous paintings.

Catholic Parish Churches
Parish churches were sometimes the pet projects of wealthy parishioners, and thus could be small or large, ornate or simple, fashionable or ancient. In every case the focal point was the sanctuary, while at the opposite end

stood the baptismal font: located near the door, it represented the importance of baptism to entering the life of God and the church. Symbolically, outside the church was, well, outside the church. Inside, candles represented Christ as the light of the world and the light to the world that each Christian was expected to be. High-medieval theologians influenced by Platonic philosophy made the explicit connection between the light that entered through the church's stained-glass windows and God's spiritual presence in the church. Stained glass stood for the transformation of that light in the world, and through its narrative decoration provided lessons on church tradition and teaching. These illustrations often included pictures of saints, who also appeared as statues or icons, or in frescoed narratives. The most important, indeed necessary, depiction was Christ on the Cross, or the Crucifixion. Whether sculpted or painted, this required image was positioned in direct relation to the altar and reinforced the teaching that the Mass was a re-presentation of not only the Last Supper but the Crucifixion itself, through which Christ made salvation possible.

Small pictures of saints and simple sculptures in wood, clay, or wax littered the side aisles and hung from columns. Many of these were "thank-yous" known as ex-votos that were placed by parishioners thankful for miracles or other saintly interventions. Important families, guilds, or brotherhoods donated larger paintings or sculptures of Christ, Mary, or saints that adorned chapels or the side walls of the church. Those seeking divine favor lit candles and prayed in front of the images as if petitioning in person. Less-sophisticated believers sometimes attributed miracles to certain images, and these became the object of pilgrimage from far and wide. During crises in the community they might be taken out of the church and paraded through the streets as a way of asking the saint to invoke God's mercy and lift the plague. Even the simplest village or parish church was thus a place of great mystery and miracle, truly a sacred space in which heaven and earth met.

Most Protestants appropriated Catholic churches but adapted them to their own styles of worship. While Protestants themselves argued over their understanding of the Eucharist, they all rejected the idea that it was a "re-presentation" of the **Protestant Churches** Crucifixion, so no altar (just a table, though sometimes called an altar) and no crucifix (though maybe just a cross). In many denominations the preaching of the Word, or Scripture, took center stage over the Eucharist, so pulpits from which the Bible would be proclaimed replaced even the tables that remained. Since God is everywhere, and not specially present in a church, these buildings tended to lose their sacredness. No saints, so no relics or pictures of them, and certainly no statues. Some Protestant churches removed all imagery, even going so far as to smash stained-glass windows and whitewash over frescoes. Without altars, there could be no chapels in the Catholic sense. Early Protestants also rejected the use of such "papist" (Catholic) trappings as gold communion vessels, incense, and even candles. To "worship the Father in spirit and in truth" (John 4:23) one needed nothing physical, just a gathering place.

Church Burials

Many of the earliest Christian churches were identified with the burial places of local saints, spawning a desire among many to be buried in the church and near the saint. As with many practices based upon medieval church teaching, this desire was not merely a symbolic matter, nor one of fondness for the holy person, but was directly related to the doctrine that on "the last day" of the world as we know it all dead bodies would rise to be rejoined with their souls and live again. One's proximity to a saint, according to the popular imagination, was itself almost enough to guarantee a happy resurrection. In addition, the saint's body or relics were generally buried in or beneath the altar on which the Eucharist was consecrated, an added incentive to be buried as close to the altar as possible. But if one could not find rest near the altar, one might at least be buried in the church—literally in the walls—or beneath the paving stones. Some corpses, clad only in a shroud, were buried in the earth, and others in vaults lined with dressed stones. Once the flesh had rotted away, the bones could be reburied elsewhere and the space could be used again, although coffins of stone or lead placed in the walls or floor were not reusable. The Fourth Lateran Council of the Catholic Church in 1215 opened the door to charging fees for burials in churches, and soon a real market developed. Even under Anglican management, in the 1620s the parish of All Hallows the Great in London had five "regions" within the church, from cheapest near the door to the highest next to the sanctuary. At about the same time English poet and cleric John Donne lampooned the scramble for prime burial places: "Ambitious men never made more shift for places in court, than dead men for graves in churches. . . ." One poorer parishioner laconically commented on the practice via his epitaph:

> Here lie I at the chancel door
> Here lie I because I'm poor;
> The further in the more you pay
> Here lie I as warm as they.[2]

Many family chapels in or attached to churches were really funerary chapels meant for burial of generations of the family, whose living members would gather in the sacred space for Mass and commemoration of the ancestors. The belief was also strong that a priest could say a Mass with a special "intention," that would, so to speak, direct God's attention to a special need, such as mercy for a deceased relative's soul languishing in purgatory. In fact, many late-medieval wills specify that Masses be said, sometimes by the hundreds, for the testator's soul, just in case no one else was praying on his behalf.

A Catholic priest presides over a burial beneath a church floor during plague time, while an acolyte with holy water and mourners stand behind him. The corpse is in a shroud rather than a coffin. While the skulls at upper left may be in a painting, they may also be real, gathered when previous corpses were dug up to make room for another generation. A woodcut from Renward Cystat and Lorenz Hager's *Nützlicher und kurtzer Bericht. Regiment und Ordnung, in pestilentzischen Zeiten*, Munich, 1611. National Library of Medicine.

At the very least, one expected to be buried in "sacred ground" that had been specially blessed by a priest or bishop and was generally located adjacent to the church itself. Walls around the churchyard protected the graves from scavengers and afforded visitors a bit of privacy. When space became scarce, bones might be dug up and relocated to a charnel or vault, usually beneath the church. Since the flesh had rotted away, there was little in the way of offensive smell. In this way generations of parishioners literally shared the same church building.

Christian Differences and Plague Whichever Christian path one followed, God remained in command of the world, and the plague remained his responsibility. For all, repentance, amendment of life, and the avoidance of sin were necessary to placate an angry God and avoid plague, but consensus on how to achieve this broke down. On one side, Catholics continued to count on the sacraments, prayer, the Mass, and good works. On the other, those who believed in predestination sometimes did absolutely nothing—not praying, or fleeing, or even medicating—since all was in God's hands and predestined by his unalterable will. In between, prayer and even fasting were considered useful for quelling divine wrath. Catholics continued invoking the saints, holding processions, and doing what they had done for generations, while Protestants eliminated most of the rituals and doctrines that had provided their ancestors with hope and solace. The Protestant elimination of purgatory also removed the need to pray for a dying or deceased person: neither saved nor damned could benefit. For Protestants even the deathbed scene was transformed. They eliminated the Catholic sacramental send-off with last rites, confession, and communion, replacing it with a stoical final good-bye in which the dying person exhibits faith in Christ and certainty of salvation as a model for friends and family.

FUNERALS

The Catholic Tradition By the fourteenth century the funeral rites conducted at monasteries had found their way into parishes, thanks in large part to the Franciscans' desire to share traditionally clerical spirituality with the laity. The rites began with the traditional cleaning and preparation of the body at the home, where death usually occurred. In some cultures the corpse was exhibited for a day or some part of it, not least to ensure that the person had indeed died. At an appointed time the church bell tolled a second time for the deceased and the corpse was carried to the church. The priest or deacon headed the procession, accompanied by candle-bearers (acolytes) and the mourners, some of whom may have been poor persons paid by the family to attend. The body would have been simply wrapped in a white shroud or placed in a coffin, depending on the person's preference, wealth, or status. Nobles and members of groups such as guilds or religious brotherhoods often had special painted or embroidered cloths (palls) decorated with heraldry or group symbols draped over their coffins, allowing the public to identify them by family or as a group member. In the case of guilds and confraternities, other members were expected to join friends and family to enhance the train of mourners; indeed, many of these groups began as organizations that guaranteed members proper burial. The Guild of St. George in Lynn, England, was founded in 1376 so that members could share the cost of the candles, pall, and other funeral equipment. They pledged to attend each others' funerals and have sixty Masses said on behalf of each deceased member.

At the church the body or coffin would be placed on a bier, a table-like stand, in the aisle before the main altar. The presiding priest blessed the body, led prayers for the soul of the deceased, and perhaps said a funeral or requiem Mass. Incense smoldered in a censer, masking the stench of the body and signaling God's presence in the congregation. Funeral services were somber, with black the dominant color. While modern Catholic services emphasize the joy of death as a passing into glory and resurrection with Christ, medieval and early modern services depicted death as punishment for sin and stressed the necessity of God's mercy to ensure delivery from hellfire. The prayers and hymns featured meditations on repentance, sorrow, and final judgment, while the joyful Hallelujahs and Glorias of a typical Mass were omitted. One of the most famous of these funeral prayers was the thirteenth-century *Dies irae,* attributed to the Franciscan Thomas of Celano. This driving poetic prayer dramatically portrays the final judgment of humanity as sketched in the biblical Apocalypse and by the Hebrew prophet Zephaniah. The prayer for a merciful judgment is the prayer of all present, all who share the mortality of the deceased and the hope that God may give merit to their good works and overlook their flaws.

AWAITING THE APOCALYPSE: THE DIES IRAE, C. 1250

Day of wrath, day that
Will dissolve the world into burning coals,
As David bore witness with the Sibyll.
How great a tremor is to be,
When the judge is to come
Briskly shattering every (grave).
A trumpet sounding an astonishing sound
Through the tombs of the region
Drives all (men) before the throne.
Death will be stunned and (so) will Nature,
When arises (man) the creature
Responding to the One judging.
The written book will be brought forth,
In which all (evidence) is contained
Whence the world is to be judged.
Therefore when the Judge shall sit,
Whatever lay hidden will appear;
Nothing unavenged will remain.
My prayers are not worthy,
But do Thou, Good (God), deal kindly
Lest I burn in perennial fire.
Among the sheep[3] offer (me) a place

And from the goats sequester me,
Placing (me) at (Thy) right hand.
After the accursed have been silenced,
Given up to the bitter flames,
Call me with the blest.
Kneeling and bowed down I pray,
My heart contrite as ashes:
Do Thou, my End, care for my end.

After the prayers or service the body and mourners proceeded to the open grave in the graveyard. The priest blessed the grave and the body was lowered. Final prayers reminded the bystanders that Christ said "I am the Resurrection and the Life" and asked God to have mercy and to grant eternal rest to the soul of the deceased. Upon returning to the church everyone who knew it recited Psalm 129/130 *(De profundis)*, which begins, "Out of the depths I cry to You, Lord hear my prayer." In some societies a funeral feast in front of the home of the deceased or a tavern or inn followed the church service.

Plague and Catholic Funerals   The notary Gabriele de' Mussis of Piacenza in northern Italy described the effect of the first outbreak of plague on funeral customs:

[I]t was often the mother who shrouded her son and placed him in the coffin, or the husband who did the same for his wife, for everybody else refused to touch the dead body. No prayer, trumpet or bell summoned friends and neighbors to the funeral, nor was Mass performed. Degraded and poverty-stricken wretches were paid to carry the great and noble to burial, for the social equals of the dead person dared not attend the funeral for fear of being struck down themselves. Men were borne to burial day and night, since needs must, and with only a short service.

These changes in custom are reflected in the chronicles of many cities. The abbot Gilles li Muisis of Tournai, Belgium, noting that church authorities did nothing to regulate behaviors during the pestilence, related the laws imposed by the city government regarding funerals. At first the authorities ordered that plague victims be buried in a coffin or box immediately upon dying, day or night, regardless of social status. Bell tolling and Masses were relegated to Sundays, when funeral Masses would include a bier covered with the customary pall and candles as desired by the deceased or her family. The law forbade the wearing of black by others than the immediate family in processions of mourners, or after-service gatherings in the home or street, "nor should other customary observances be performed." By September the city council had gotten far stricter. No black was to be worn at all; no bells tolled at all; no palls used at any funeral masses. Only two people, presumably family, were allowed to attend the service or burial.[4]

Across the era of the Second Pandemic the pattern was similar. On their own accord or pressed by the authorities, people trimmed back processions and services to the bare necessities of conveying the body to the church and grave, and praying as one might for the victim's soul. Authorities stepped in to limit the depressing effects of mourners in black and tolling bells, and prevented gatherings of people through which the disease might be spread. The times were extraordinary, and the death tolls often unbelievable. Gilles mentions that 25,000 died in his city alone; the processions would never have ended, no color other than black seen, no respite from tolling bells enjoyed. Without controlling—or outright banning—the traditional ceremonies, cities would have become true necropolises, cities of the dead.

For early Lutherans the proper funeral service occurred in the graveyard itself, minus the Mass, blessings, candles, and other trappings that they had grown up with. All prayers were in German rather than Latin, so all could participate. The prayers were also meant for the living, that they might be blessed by God. No one prayed on behalf of the deceased. A homily urging all to live righteously was typical and might draw upon the life of the deceased for a model to avoid or emulate. Later funerals adopted more traditional pomp, with a procession to the grave behind a large cross and the singing of Psalms, including the *De profundis,* in the vernacular. A church service followed, consisting of a sermon and half a dozen readings from Scripture. Though the importance of repentance remained, greater emphasis was placed on hope in Christ's promise of eternal life in the Gospel.

Protestant Funerals

The French reformer Jean Calvin returned to the early church for guidance in affirming acceptable Christian funeral rites. In his *Institutes of the Christian Religion* (III 25.5), he notes that Christian funerals could only be of use as evidence to pagans or unbelievers of the Christian belief in an afterlife: "For why the sacred and inviolable custom of burying, but that it might be the earnest of a new life?" According to Calvin's own service book, a few well-chosen words on the promise of the Resurrection and heaven should suffice. Calvin's Scots follower John Knox dictated to his fellow Presbyterians in his *Book of Discipline* of 1560 that a corpse was simply to be "conveyed to the place of burial with some honest company of the church, without either singing or reading, yea without all kind of ceremony heretofore used."[5] He believed that sermons should be left to Sunday mornings and the pulpit. In Scotland in 1638 the General Assembly of the church forbade funeral services altogether. English Puritans like Walter Travers in 1586 also believed in avoiding any ceremony: a silent procession from house to graveyard and immediate burial sufficed. Travers did note, however, that civil authorities had every right to sponsor fancy funerals for anyone they wanted to. Dutch Reformed families relied on the burial associations to which they belonged to handle most of the funeral arrangements. Six members carried the black pall-covered coffin to the gravesite on a bier as a bell tolled. The procession circled the grave several times while a preacher prayed. Mourners wearing long black rented coats stood silently and stoically by as the coffin was lowered.

In the Anglican Church funeral rites vacillated during the mid- and later sixteenth century. Under its founder Henry VIII, the church retained much of Catholic ceremony, including a full Eucharistic liturgy (though no longer called "Mass"). Under young Edward VI Lutheran tendencies prevailed: no Eucharist, no psalms, no commending the soul to God, just the relegation of the body to the earth. Under Queen Mary Catholic rites were reinstated, but Elizabeth I returned initially to Edward's model. By 1560 she brought back the funeral Eucharist and congregational prayers "to be raised with this our [departed] brother (sister)." Although the Anglican Church was under constant pressure to simplify its ritual along lines preferred by the Calvinist Puritans, the ruling bishops tended to hold the mark and ensure relative uniformity and conservatism.

Protestant Funeral Rites in Plague Time
Since Protestant funerary rituals had been reduced to a skeleton of what they were in Catholic communities, and the disbelief in purgatory removed any need to pray *for* the dead, one might think that typical adjustments in funeral services for plague would have been easily absorbed. Yet many modern scholars stress the psychological importance that people attached to allowing life to remain as normal as possible during plagues. Since these outbreaks manifested death on a massive scale and in ways that had an impact on everyone, the manner in which a society dealt with death and the dead was especially important. Protestant authorities, like catholic ones, tried to limit gatherings to reduce opportunities for contagion. In 1542 London's Anglican bishop forbade the entry of a corpse into a church during plague time unless it was necessary to gain access to the graveyard. A century later, the mayor of Sandwich forbade the preaching of sermons over corpses during the plague, though this change may have been driven as much by Puritans as by plague concerns. Civic authorities appointed specific men to act as pallbearers for all plague victims, and some complained that these were rough men of slovenly appearance, unworthy of carrying people of wealth and status to the grave.

One must believe that Protestants clung to their rituals as tenaciously as Catholics did, even if much of the spiritual element had been stripped away. When civil authorities forbade the comfort of gatherings at gravesites or at homes, or the chance to say one last good-bye as a loved one was lowered into her last resting place, Protestants and Catholics alike were stung and society's fabric torn. Yet how infinitely more unnerving were the horrors of mass graves, carts on which the dead of all classes were piled high, and the awful corpse-bearers who went about their grim business with a terrifying smugness.

GRAVES, GRAVEDIGGERS, AND BURIAL

The grave cries "give" . . . the grave is daily fed, and yet is daily hungry. The mouth thereof is opened, and it devours men; and yet for all that, it still cries for our "return to the dust" as we were.[6]

Early in any epidemic and throughout most of them the normal patterns of funeral rites and burials were little disturbed. Family members, burial associations, parish authorities, confraternities, and guilds continued burying the corpses for which they were responsible, and did so in the manners and places to which they were accustomed. But custom was set aside as death levels soared, people fled, and consecrated ground filled up. For example, during 1348–1349 spice sellers in London lost 12 of their 35 members to plague. Following tradition survivors all gathered for the first four funerals, but that was it. Even though 29 of them remained in town—presumably to protect their warehouses—custom fell away as the body count mounted. At Givry, France, whose register of burials is one of the most complete in Europe, the average number of burials in a normal year was about 23; in only four months of 1348 the town buried 626. In 1665 St. Olave's Parish in London lost 194 members, of whom 146 were buried in the small churchyard. The following January Samuel Pepys, a parishioner, visited the church for a service for the first time

Parish Graveyards

since I left London for the plague; and it frighted me indeed to go through the church, more than I thought it could have done, to see so [many] graves lie so high upon the churchyard, where people have been buried of the plague. I was much troubled at it, and do not think to go through it again [for] a good while.

Five days later, he noted, "it was a frost and had snowed last night, which covered the graves in the churchyard, so I was the less affeared for going through." The following year Londoner Thomas Vincent wrote in *God's Terrible Voice in the City,* "churchyards are now stuffed so full with dead corpses that they are in many places swelled two or three feet higher than before."[7] The Lord Mayor required that plenty of quick-lime be shoveled on top of the buried corpses to aid decomposition and discourage scavenging. Like many materials related to funerals and burial, however, lime quickly fell into short supply and became very scarce indeed. Here as in so many places the graves were so shallow that corpses could be easily unearthed. Formal churchyards and other burial grounds had walls built around them at least in part to keep dogs and other earthbound creatures out, but undaunted birds like crows and ravens covered the cemeteries when the gravediggers were away. Many parishes purchased additional burial space adjacent to their churchyard when possible. In July and August 1349, 11 parishes in York, England, added space after petitioning the bishop for permission. Before the Reformation, donating land for cemetery space, as the Earl of Huntingdon did in Sandwich in 1349, was considered a pious act beneficial to one's soul. Like other graveyards, plague cemeteries were usually walled in and blessed, and in normal times became the "second-class" cemeteries—often designated for paupers—because of their very newness and especially their association with plague.

"Public" Cemeteries   Many cities had extensive cemeteries that were not connected to specific parishes. In London one option was to send corpses to be buried at St. Paul's Cathedral cemetery. Normally only clergy and the odd vagabond found rest here, so there tended to be plenty of room. During the epidemic of 1593 St. Paul's was used intensively, to the consternation of its neighbors. In its midst lived author Gabriel Harvey, a fierce literary rival of popular playwright and wit Thomas Nashe. Nashe wrote of Harvey's plight, perhaps exaggerating for literary effect:

Three quarters of a year thus cloistered and immured[8] he remained, not being able almost to step out of doors, he was so barricadoed [sic] up with graves, which besieged and undermined his very threshold; nor to open his window evening or morning but a damp, like the smoke of a cannon, from the fat manured earth with contagion, being the burial place of five parishes, in thick, rolling clouds would strugglingly funnel up and with a full blast puff in at his casements [windows].[9]

The Cemetery of the Innocents in Paris had its origins in Roman times and by the fourteenth century belonged to three distinct religious bodies and the Hôtel Dieu (public hospital). Situated on the right bank of the Seine, next to the marketplace of Les Halles, its high, arcaded wall (built in 1186) enclosed a place of death, but also of surprising life: children and adolescents played, friars preached sermons, lovers strolled, and notaries and charlatans did business. According to tradition its soil contained dirt from the Holy Land that dissolved a body in an amazing nine days. As new space was needed, bones were exhumed and stored in the long, narrow "charnier" or charnel that ran above the wall under a gabled wooden roof.

Plague Cemeteries   In plague time new cemeteries, in Catholic regions usually associated with a church or religious order, sprung up around large cities. In papal Avignon, "There were not enough churches and burial grounds in the city to hold all the dead bodies, and the pope himself ordered a new burial ground to be consecrated for the burial of those killed in the pestilence." In France royal permission had to be granted before creating new cemeteries; dozens of letters of request survive in the French National Archives for towns like Amiens, Abbeville, Coincy, and Montreuil-sur-Mer. Because they were meant to hold plague victims whose corpses were considered corrupting of the air, plague-time cemeteries were often located outside of the town walls, isolated far from other habitations. In communities that traditionally treasured close connection of living and dead, this "alienation" of the dead disrupted a deeply seated cultural foundation, for every person now was threatened with depersonalization after death.

Large public cemeteries were often the earliest sites of mass pit-graves, but even these proved inadequate in years of severe plague. Since 500 people a day were being buried in Les Innocents, La Trinité hospital bought new cemetery space in 1350. Amounting to 4,500 square meters in area, the cemetery reportedly received 9,224 bodies from the Hôtel Dieu during the epidemic of 1416–1418. In late 1418 the anonymous "Bourgeois of Paris" wrote in his diary,

When it got so bad that no one could think where to bury them, huge pits were dug, five at Les Innocents, four at La Trinité, at the others according to their capacity, and each pit held about 600 people. The Paris cordwainers [leather shoemakers] on the day of St. Crispin and St. Crispian [October 25], which was their guild day, reckoned up how many of their trade had died in the town, both masters and men, and they found it came to at least 1,800 dead within these two months. The men belonging to the Hôtel Dieu, who dug the pits in Paris' cemeteries, affirmed that between the Nativity of Our Lady [September 8] and the Conception [March 25] they had buried more than 100,000 people in Paris.[10]

During the 1466 outbreak, workers excavated trenches designed to hold 700 corpses. In 1576, during the French Wars of Religion, Catholic authorities grudgingly agreed to grant Calvinist Huguenots burial space in Paris; they were given La Trinité. In the course of the great plague outbreak in Marseille in 1720 a typical trench measured 140 feet long, 52 feet wide, and 14 feet deep.

During severe outbreaks London, too, required extraordinary burial sites. "Ralph Stratford, Bishop of London, in the year 1348 bought a piece of land called No Man's Land, which he enclosed with a wall of brick and dedicated for burial of the dead, building thereupon a proper chapel." Later, Sir Walter de Manny, a Flemish knight, expanded the field to "thirteen acres and a rod," and arranged that he would be buried in the chapel. This cemetery, St. Mary Spital (for hospital), was located at Spital Cross outside of Aldersgate in West Smithfield. In 1371, Carthusian monks colonized the chapel, established a monastery called the Charterhouse, prayed for the souls of the dead, and tended the graveyard. Excavations of the site, now squarely in downtown London, had yielded the remains of 11,000 bodies by 2001. In 1348 clergyman John Corey bought a "toft of ground"[11] (probably a few acres) in East Smithfield near the Tower of London and on the current site of the Royal Mint. This plot, too, was surrounded by a stone wall, provided with a chapel, and dedicated by the bishop of London in 1349. Known as St. Mary Graces, it became the site of a Cistercian Abbey of the same name. In 1569 Bethlehem (Bedlam) Hospital received a cemetery, consisting of an acre donated by Lord Mayor Thomas Rowe. By Anglican custom it was walled but had a pulpit instead of a chapel. Besides plague victims, it received the poor, prisoners from

Newgate Prison, and religious dissenters who had no set church. Known as New Churchyard, in 1665 it received the 48 members of St. Olave's Parish who could not find rest near friends and family. During the Great plague of 1665 yet another cemetery was added, at Bunhill north of the City. This, too, became a famous dissenter cemetery.

Other early modern cities buried their dead in the earth of the broad, flat terraces atop city ramparts; the practice was common in port cities and among the Dutch, whose high water tables made other arrangements impracticable. Some utilized the leftover towers of long obsolete walls or other fortifications as temporary vaults for the dead, storing the bodies with the idea of reburying them in suitable soil once the plague had passed. Cities resorted to this practice only after death rates climbed astronomically and the numbers of corpse-carriers and gravediggers had dwindled.

Mass Burials   Mass burials in plague pits became common during major outbreaks of plague. At both the East and West Smithfield sites archeologists have found that long trenches had bodies buried very neatly stacked up to five deep with dirt deposited between layers. The rich and the poor, the sinner and the saint, the abandoned and the beloved—all were carted away to the same end. In his *Decameron* Florentine writer Giovanni Boccaccio was among the first to describe the practice:

So many corpses would arrive in front of a church every day and at every hour that the amount of holy ground for burials was certainly insufficient for the ancient custom of giving each body its individual place; when all the graves were full, huge trenches were dug in all of the cemeteries of the churches and into them the new arrivals were dumped by the hundreds; and they were packed in there with dirt, one on top of another, like a ship's cargo, until the trench was filled.

Elsewhere the procedure was not so neat. The description by the author of the *Chronicle of Rochester* (England, 1349) was far from atypical:

Alas, this mortality devoured such a multitude of both sexes that no one could be found to carry the bodies of the dead to burial, but men and women carried their own little ones to church on their shoulders and threw them into mass graves, from which arose such as stink that it was barely possible for anyone to go past a churchyard.

A 1349 entry in the *Chronicle* of the monastery of Neuburg, in Vienna, notes that

Because of the stench and horror of the corpses they were not allowed to be buried in churchyards, but as soon as life was extinct they had to be taken to a communal burial ground in God's Field outside the city, where in a short time five big pits were filled to the brim with bodies.

The practice of gathering the dead in lumbering carts and simply dumping them into yawning pits was horrifying in its seeming inhumanity. Nearly three centuries later the horrors had not abated. An anonymous Florentine clergyman wrote of the carnage in 1630 that bodies were thrown

[t]here haphazardly—some with legs akimbo, some with their kidneys toward the sun, some one way, some in another, without regard to who was rich and who was poor, who was noble, who ignoble—but everyone was stacked and piled haphazardly, thrown there as if they were mounds of hay or piles of wood, only, I say, if they had been hay or wood they would have been stacked more neatly; but they will be stacked there haphazardly, some half covered, some with an arm exposed, some with their head and some with their feet left as prey for the meals of dogs and other beasts.

Only two years earlier Englishman George Wither had written verses commemorating the gruesome spectacle of a London pit:

> Lord! what a sight was there? And what strong smells
> Ascended from among Death's loathsome cells . . .
> Yon lay a heap of skulls; another there;
> Here, half unburied, did a corpse appear . . .
> A lock of woman's hair; a dead man's face
> Uncovered; and a ghastly sight it was.[12]

The Gravediggers

Known by a variety of names, the corpse-carriers and gravediggers—often the same men—move through chronicles and descriptions like repulsive forces of nature. These men were chosen or forced to perform the most heartless of acts day in and day out, with an efficiency, inhuman lack of emotion, and even cruelty that nauseated and terrified the populace. They literally manhandled the dying, the dead, and the putrescent; for the living they had little use or apparent sympathy. They carried out their awful, yet necessary, duties while smoking and drinking and singing and laughing like carefree porters or longshoremen. In 1630 Florentine physician Francesco Rondinelli characterized the Tuscan *monatti:* "They believed that those who lived in fear would die. They chose to remain dauntless among the stricken by day, and then go out, drink, and gamble by night." In his description of a visit to a victim's house in 1630 the Archbishop of Milan, Federigo Borromeo, captured their bravado, but also the terrible nature of their tasks:

Naturally the disgust and horror aroused by the *becchini* was overcome by another disgust and horror . . . the putrefied bodies oozing with corruption and corrupted blood remaining before one's eyes within the room, often in the same bed. But with them [*becchini*] tears had no value, nor prayers: all it took was money to get them to come into the house. Once in, as I have said, they were unleashed and no longer recognized any law.

In Milan they dressed in red and carried bells to warn of their approach. Borromeo remarks that the worst died off early, but the best were spared for some time: One claimed to have buried 40,000 with his own hands. Having done his duty "courageously and honestly," he succumbed at last.[13]

In Florence before the Second Pandemic gravediggers belonged to the Physicians and Apothecary's Guild and had to remove only the occasional body of a murder victim or dead beggar from the streets. Traditionally they received a gift of the deceased's clothing as a tip to ensure quick and deep burial. But by 1375 municipal regulations required them to "clean the streets . . . prepare the wood tables [biers] for corpses . . . remove carpets and mattresses . . . shave and dress cadavers,"[14] and each carried a card on which these expectations were written. In plague time the only task was to move the bodies quickly and efficiently from where they lay to the grave. Taking advantage of the chaos, the corpse-carriers demanded money, rummaged through chests, and took what they wanted, acting like ransacking soldiers despoiling their enemies. They faced death at every turn; what greater risk could they run?

Callous toward the public, these men were often prosecuted by authorities. In Montelupo, Tuscany, during spring of 1631 the mayor ordered two gravediggers to bury a plague victim. Citing long overdue back pay they refused, using "arrogant words." These same men had mixed with the plague-free population despite a ban and now were threatened with forced labor in the duke's galleys. Uncowed, they then threatened to throw the dead body in front of the mayor's house. Later, they buried two plague victims next to the house of a local nobleman, claiming that the cemetery was too far away. As punishment they suffered torture, but lived to bury the mayor, who soon after died of the plague.

One reason for the insolence of the *becchini, monatti,* or *enterreurs* was that they were often members of a second generation called into service when the professionals had died off. In papal Avignon all of the original gravediggers died and were replaced by mountain men thought to have been immunized by the fresh alpine air. When all of them died, the pope turned to prisoners on death row. In port cities, galley slaves and prisoners were often called into duty, lorded over by equally coarse soldiers. But even under the best circumstances they were isolated with none other than themselves for company. In 1603, the Great Court at Ipswich, England, appointed John Cole and William Forsdyke as "buriers" for sixteen pence per day.

> They shall remain in the house builded for them, they shall have their victuals and things brought them, with their daily wages, and when they go abroad in town in pursuit of their duties they shall carry white wands or rods in their hands, so as to be known from other men.[15]

Theirs was indeed a ghastly, lonely, thankless, and deadly business.

RELIGIOUS ART AND RITUALS

Dancing skeletons, putrefying corpses, an angry God hurling arrows, a saint pointing out his bubo, a priest performing last rites; Masses, processions, fasts, sermons, prayers; memorial churches and columns and confraternities. While few argue that the Black Death transformed Christianity, Christianity clearly shaped the cultural response to pestilence, and plague had a clear and definable impact on religion.

\ Christianity explains death as a passage from mortal to immortal life, as the gateway to heaven or hell, a point of divine **Death and** judgment and the punishment for sin. Death was terrifying, but **Plague in** by participating in sacraments like penance and the last rites **Popular Art** the Catholic Christian could confront death and the next world with a clear conscience. Plague brought sudden death, death alone, death unprepared for, death without spiritual solace; ugly, painful, horrifying death, with the comfort of a proper funeral and burial stripped away. In light of Jesus' resurrection, St. Paul challenged, "O death, where is thy sting? O grave, where is thy victory?" But death and the grave seemed all too victorious. \

Death's inevitability took expression in a number of popular pictorial themes. In the *danse macabre* skeletons representing death are depicted taking as "partners" people from every walk of life, from peasants to popes. Stopped in the midst of their activities, each had to dance; none was immune. This scene appeared on cemetery walls, perhaps the earliest at Les Innocents in Paris in 1424, with the first German version at the Marienkirche in Lübeck (1463). Woodcuts provided popular illustrations for poetry that developed the theme first in Latin and later the vernaculars; one famous French example of an illustrated poem included only women among the partners, and another, more inclusive, was published by the great German artist Hans Holbein during the early Reformation.

Another popular theme is known as the "Three Living Meet the Three Dead." Depictions of this theme, which dates back to the twelfth century, show three young noble riders confronting three corpses rotting in their coffins. The corpses ominously warn, "We were once what you are now; what we are now you will soon be." The most famous surviving example dates from before the Black Death and is located at Pisa's Campo Santo cemetery; large fragments of others may still be seen for example at the parish churches of St. Andrew's in Wickhampton, Northamptonshire (c. 1380), and Hurstbourne Tarrant, Hampshire, England.

A third theme also has preplague roots but flourished during the medieval pestilence. The Triumph of Death shows death, often in the form of an army of gruesome corpses or skeletons, overcoming large groups of people, some of whom try to fight back in a futile attempt at escape. A fine example is in the Limbourg Brothers' *Tres Riches Heures*, a fifteenth-century prayer book for the French Duc du Berry; another is a large and famous canvas by Dutchman Pieter Brueghel the Elder from 1562.

The Three Living Meet the Three Dead at a roadway cross,
while a hermit passes on the cadavers' ominous warning,
"What we are now you will soon be!" From the opening
page of the vigil of the dead in a Book of Hours (*Horae*) by
Wynkyn de Worde, Westminster, 1494. Dover.

The skeleton or corpse had long signified death, but Western art had
no traditional "human" image for plague. Sometimes it appears as a girl
in a blue flame or a woman or witch armed with arrows or a scythe; both
images were derived from the popular imagination. Most often either the
dead or "Death" stood in for plague. As for depictions of people with
the plague, these are very rare until the mid-fifteenth century. The earliest are generally woodcut deathbed scenes often connected with medical literature. During the Renaissance and Baroque eras Catholic artists
depicted heroic saints or clergy at work providing solace and the last rites
in streetscapes littered with the dying. Such works were meant both to

Death, with plague arrow and clock with counterweights, strides triumphant in the streets of a Renaissance city. From the book of hours, *Horae in laudem beatissime virginis Marie,* by Geoffroy Tory, Paris, 1527. Dover.

commemorate the brave men of the cloth and to reassure viewers that the church was undaunted in providing care for the stricken. In the seventeenth century purely secular scenes of plague appeared in Italian, Dutch, and English printed broadsheets and histories that memorialized or chronicled an epidemic. Works in both of these genres are usually quite accurate and detailed in their depictions of the sights and even smells of plague time. People cover their noses or smoke heavily to avoid the bad air; the dying take positions that relieve pressure on the buboes in the groin, armpit, or neck regions; criminals who violated the plague laws hang from gibbets; and hungry dogs gnaw on unburied corpses.

Transi Tombs   A unique type of unburied corpse sculpted in stone
began to appear on some Catholic tombs in the 1390s in
France, Germany, Austria, and England. These large and
expensive monuments generally belonged to wealthy clergy or nobles and
dominate the side aisles or chapels in which they were installed. The transi
(as in "transition") tomb features two life-sized images of the deceased
lying down bunk-bed style. The top figure shows the fully clothed person
as if sleeping; beneath lies a rotting corpse undergoing decomposition.
Worms slither and toads perch on the exposed bones and liquefied skin,
mocking the beauty and power embodied in the figure above. The message was clear, and taken up in poems and sermons. On his tomb (1424)
Archbishop Henry Chichele of Canterbury had this epitaph written:

> I was a pauper born, then to Primate raised
> Now I am cut down and ready to be food for worms
> Behold My grave / Whoever you may be who passes by
> I ask you to remember / You will be like me after you die
> All horrible dust, worms, vile flesh.[16]

An Angry God   Priests and preachers, physicians and philosophers,
peasants and kings all agreed that God was the ultimate
source of the plague, and that the disease was the expression of his wrath provoked by humanity's sinfulness. Borrowing an image
with roots in both the Bible and Greek antiquity, medieval people imagined
plague as a shower of arrows falling from the sky, hitting many, wounding
some and killing others. In 590 Honorius of Autun wrote of "arrows falling from heaven"; eight hundred years later De' Mussis described plague
as "arrows [that] were raining down from heaven." For nearly 50 years
people in Luxembourg painted crossed arrows on their houses as a prophylactic talisman. The use of a group of three arrows by itself, perhaps
one for each member of the Trinity, had as its originator the founder of
the Dominican Order in the early 1200s. Painters showed God the Father
surrounded by angelic archers on clouds shooting their bows at horror-
stricken people; in a Carmelite monastery in Göttingen, Germany, a painting shows Christ firing arrows at people below, where 16 lie dead with
the missiles embedded in their heads, groins, or armpits. If the anger is
the Father's, then humanity has Christ as its perfect intercessor to seek his
Father's mercy. Indeed, some plague images show just such a scene. But if
Christ is the judge punishing wayward humanity, then another advocate
was needed.

Saintly   This is where the saints, beginning with the Virgin Mary,
Intercessors   come in, at least for Catholics. Christian invocation of the
aid of those "seated around the throne of God" was ancient
by the fourteenth century, and the Counter-Reformation
reinforced the practice. Indeed, how could the prayers of sinful people on
earth gain favor with a wrathful God? Traditionally, the most powerful

intercessor was Mary, Jesus' mother, to whom he could, theoretically, refuse nothing. She served as the patron—or especially protective—saint who aided parishes, confraternities, guild members, and even entire cities. "Lady" chapels in English cathedrals were dedicated to her; many cathedrals in France were named Notre Dame (Our Lady) in her honor; in the prayer "Hail Mary" believers ask that she might pray for them "now and at the hour of our death." Many plague-related images of Mary stress

"A Prayer to drive away the pestilence." A seventeenth-century Italian prayer sheet invoking the Virgin Mary's aid and depicting the major plague saints Sebastian (in Roman armor with bow and arrows, crushing Satan in the center) and Roche (in pilgrim's hat, with staff, dog, and tunic pulled up to show bubo at bottom right), along with local saints Adrian, Bennone, and Antonio. Published by Peter de Jode, undated. National Library of Medicine.

her relationship with her son and depict her pleading for those threatened by plague; others show her shielding her undersized followers with her broad mantle or cloak as arrows fall all about, killing those without her protection. Typically her "followers" would be identifiable by their garb as monks or confraternity members, or a city might be depicted to indicate a more general population. The earliest known image of the Madonna *Misericordia* (Mercy) was painted in Genoa, Italy, about 1372. At least in part because it seemed to imply that Mary could thwart the will of God, the Council of Trent (1545–1563) suppressed the image, but by no means the devotion to Mary as a protectress.

St. Sebastian and St. Roche   Other saints, too, played their roles as protectors. The author of one scholarly study has counted 110 different plague saints from across Europe, 53 in France alone. The most universal and popular of these were St. Sebastian and St. Roche (Roch, Rocco). Sebastian was an early Christian soldier executed for his faith. Roman soldiers shot him full of arrows, but he lived, recovered, and returned to preach to the pagan emperor. This enraged the authorities, who finished the job properly. The cult of devotion to Sebastian began during the First Pandemic and was revived during the Second. His appeal was his survival of the shower of arrows: By a kind of "associative property" he could pass that immunity to followers or at least plead before God on their behalf. As Gabriele de' Mussis put it in 1349, "For among the aforesaid martyrs, some, as stories relate, are said to have died from repeated blows, and it was thus the common opinion that they would be able to protect people against the arrows of death."[17] One image of him displays the horrors of plague below, and the saint, arrows all in place, kneeling before God and pleading for mercy. Later medieval and Renaissance pictures of him show a very young, handsome, and nearly nude man tied to a stake or column, with arrows—from a few to nearly a hundred—sticking out of his body. In Normandy alone 564 statues or paintings of St. Sebastian remain.

O BLESSED SEBASTIAN: MOTET SET BY GUILLAUME DUFAY, FIFTEENTH CENTURY

A motet could be a simple prayer set to music as in the first case, or a very complex composition in which three separate voices sang three separate texts (triplum, motetus, contra) at the same time to different tunes and rhythms, as in the second case. These are from a fifteenth-century music manuscript known as Bologna Q15.

1) O blessed Sebastian, great is thy faith.
Intercede for us with our Lord Jesus Christ that we may be freed from the plague and sickness of the epidemic.
Amen.
2) *Triplum*
O Saint Sebastian, always, evening and morning, at all hours and moments, while I am still of sound mind, protect and preserve me and, O martyr, break the power over me of the harmful sickness called epidemic.

Do thou defend and guard
from such plague
me and all my friends,
who confess ourselves guilty
to God and holy Mary
and thee, merciful martyr.
Thou, a citizen of Milan,
hast the power, if thou hast the will,
to cause this pestilence to cease
and obtain a boon from God,
for it is well known to many
that thou hast earned merit with Him.
Thou didst heal Zoe the dumb
and restore her healed
to her husband Nicostratus,
doing this in wondrous wise.
In the conflict thou didst console
the martyrs and promise them
life everlasting,
owed to martyrs.
Amen.
Motetus
O martyr Sebastian
do thou ever remain with us
and by thy merits guard,
heal, and govern us who are in this life,
and protect us from the plague,
presenting us before the
Trinity and the holy Virgin Mother.
And may we end our lives
in such manner that we have as reward
both in the company of martyrs
and the sight of God the merciful.
Contra
O with what wondrous grace
did Sebastian, the renowned martyr, shine,
who wearing the uniform of a soldier,
but concerned for his brethren's palm of
martyrdom comforted their bloodless hearts
with the word bestowed on him by heaven.

Translation by Christine Darby in the booklet notes to the recording "Guillaume Dufay: Sacred Music from Bologna Q15" (Perivale, Middlesex, UK: Signum Records, Ltd, 2002), pp. 12, 24, 26, 28.

St. Roche was contemporary to the first fourteenth-century plague outbreak and is believed to have survived it. He went on to nurse victims until his death. He is usually depicted as a standing pilgrim with one pant-leg hitched up to show a bubo and a small dog that was said to have brought him food as he recovered in the wilderness. The church's Council of Constance endorsed the cult of St. Roche in 1414.

Paintings of these men were usually ordered either by grateful surviving victims who had prayed to the saint or as a spiritual prophylaxis against ever getting the plague. Thus a Catholic church might have several of these images, large and small, simple and very artistic, hanging from walls or columns. Smaller versions also appeared in countless Catholic homes, often in the form of printed broadsheets with prayers beneath. On March 9, 1511, the uncle of the Venetian boy Zuan Francescho wrote the boy's absent father, a merchant, that Zuan "everyday says a lovely prayer to Our Lady for you, and the prayer to St. Sebastian to protect you from the plague; and he asks me to tell you this." Another type of prayer referencing St. Sebastian appears in the *House Book* of Michael de Leone of Würzburg, Germany, from around 1350:

Ever Almighty God, who because of the prayer of your most glorious martyr, St. Sebastian, called back a universal and lethal epidemic of plague, grant those asking you, that those who thus pray and bear this prayer about with them, and seek refuge in you because of their confidence that a wholly similar epidemic would be recalled [that] through his prayers and merits, they will be liberated from the plague or disease as well as from every danger and tribulation. Through our Lord Jesus Christ, Amen.[18]

Local saints, too, had their place as plague intercessors: St. Remegius, an early bishop of Rheims, France; St. Thomas Cantilupe (canonized 1320) at Hereford, England; St. Mark the evangelist in Venice; St. Adrian, who was beaten to death with a hammer, in northwestern France and who has 203 surviving monuments; Florence's own Blessed Domenica da Paradiso, founder of the Crocetta Order; Archbishop St. Carlo Borromeo, who battled the effects of the disease in his archdiocese of Milan in the later 1500s. The Counter-Reformation church urged devotion to many saints like Carlo, who also risked their lives in plague time helping the needful such as Francis Xavier, John of God, Aloyisius Gonzaga, and Francesco Romana. In the case of all these plague saints churches housed their relics, displayed ex-voto offerings and portraits, and echoed prayers to them as the faithful sought safety for themselves and their loved ones in the face of death by plague.

Communal Piety   In Catholic Europe special Masses and processions with the Eucharist or images or relics of saints had long been communal responses to wars, famines, and epidemics. During the first outbreak, Pope Clement had a special Mass written in which God's mercy and forgiveness are sought. In outdoor Masses and religious processions the entire community gathered together to show God or the saint how faithful they all were; to plead for mercy or aid; to promise repentance; to view the miracle-producing statue or painting or sacred relics. The bishops and other church authorities tightly controlled these well-attended ceremonies. With plague on the horizon, the bishop of Bath and Wells ordered his clergy to

arrange for processions and stations [stops] (in which you should lead the people) to be performed at least every Friday in every . . . church, so that, abasing themselves humbly before the eyes of divine mercy, they should be contrite and penitent for their sins, and should not omit to expiate them with devout prayers, so that the mercies of God may speedily prevent [sic] us and that he will, for his kindness sake, turn away from his people this pestilence . . . and send healthy air.[19]

A major problem for civil authorities, of course, was that during plague time such gatherings attracted many people from near and far, some of whom may have been contagious (as they understood it at the time). Though some civic leaders cancelled all such rituals, others tried various ways to limit them, while still others firmly believed that God simply would not allow plague to spread in such a pious setting.

Naturally, Protestant church leaders rejected the Catholic Masses, processions, saints, relics, and images. The Protestant Bible-centered approach to religion did, however, suggest two communal activities they felt might appease an angry God: fasting and sermons urging repentance. While fasting was, of course, a private affair, services might well be held on days dedicated to fasting as a means of strengthening the community spiritually. In Restoration England, communal fasting was also imposed by church authorities when England was faced with the naval might of the Dutch, as in April 1665.

When the pestilence had finally passed, the survivors in Catholic countries were sometimes faced with having to **Thanksgiving** fulfill vows they had taken during the epidemic, vows that **Memorials** often involved building a church or memorial. The most famous memorials are the Baroque *Pestsäule* (plague monuments) in former imperial cities such as Linz, Zwettl, and Kremnica. Unique to the old Empire, these are skyward-reaching, mixed-media works that celebrate the divine favor and triumph over horrible death. The most famous, finished in 1693, is in Vienna. Commissioned by Emperor Leopold I and designed by Johann Fischer von Erlach, the monument commemorates the devastating plague of 1679. Von Erlach also designed Vienna's Karlskirche, or Charles Church, which was promised in 1713 and completed in 1737. The "Karl" is the Milanese archbishop and plague saint Carlo Borromeo, who died in 1584. In Venice, churches dedicated to "St." Job, St. Roche (Rocco), and St. Sebastian were either built or remodeled as plague churches, all three between 1460 and 1510. Later, Venetians built two more churches in fulfillment of plague-time vows: Palladio's Redentore (Redeemer) of 1577 and Longhena's Santa Maria della Salute (Health) built after the plague of 1630. In Rome the church of Santa Maria in Campitelli, which held a

revered portrait of Mary, was remodeled by Carlo Rainaldi and rededi-
cated as a plague church after the terrible epidemic of 1656.

Churches and churchyards played extremely important roles as centers
of community in normal times. During plague time they became in turn
places of horror, spiritual refuge, hope, and commemoration. In their sacred
precincts the Eucharist was celebrated and consumed, sermons preached,
paintings hung, confessions heard, relics venerated, and loved ones visited. When plague necessitated the deritualized, anonymous dumping of
bodies in great pits, the whole community suffered: memory was shattered
and the generations disrupted.

NOTES

1. The ordination of a priest, or Holy Orders, is the seventh sacrament.

2. F. P. Wilson, *Plague in Shakespeare's London* (New York: Oxford University
Press, 1999), p. 43; Alec Clifton-Taylor, *English Parish Churches as Works of Art*
(London: Batsford, 1974), p. 212.

3. Sheep and goats: biblical distinction between saved and damned.

4. Rosemary Horrox, ed., *The Black Death* (New York: Manchester University
Press, 1994), pp. 23, 52–53.

5. Geoffrey Rowell, *The Liturgy of Christian Burial* (London: Alcuin Club/
S.P.C.K., 1977), pp. 80, 82.

6. John Fealty and Scott Rutherford, eds., *Tears Against the Plague* (Cambridge,
MA: Rhwymbooks, 2000), p. 7.

7. Robert Latham and William Matthews, eds., *The Diary of Samuel Pepys*,
vol. VII (Berkeley: University of California Press, 2000), pp. 30, 35; Justin A.I.
Champion, *London's Dreaded Visitation* (London: Historical Geography Research
Paper Series, 1995), p. 33.

8. Immured: walled up.

9. Katherine Duncan-Jones, *Shakespeare's Life and World* (London: Folio, 2004),
p. 104.

10. Horrox, *Black Death*, p. 82; Janet Shirley, *A Parisian Journal, 1405–1449*
(Oxford: Clarendon Press, 1968), p. 132.

11. Duncan Hawkins, "The Black Death and the New London Cemeteries of
1348," *Antiquity* 64 (1990), pp. 637–38.

12. Giovanni Boccaccio, *The Decameron*, trans. by Mark Musa and Peter Bondanella (New York: New American Library, 1982), p. 11; Horrox, *Black Death*, pp.
61, 70; Giulia Calvi, *Histories of a Plague Year* (Berkeley: University of California
Press, 1989), p. 153; Wilson, *Plague*, p. 44.

13. Calvi, *Histories*, p. 148; Federico Borromeo, *La peste di Milano* (Milan: Rusconi,
1987), pp. 75–76.

14. Calvi, *Histories*, p. 148.

15. A.G.E. Jones, "Plagues in Suffolk in the Seventeenth Century," *Notes and
Queries* 198 (1953), p. 384.

16. Kathleen Cohen, *Metamorphosis of a Death Symbol: The Transi Tomb in the Late
Middle Ages and the Renaissance* (Berkeley: University of California Press, 1973), p. 16.

17. Horrox, *Black Death*, p. 26.

18. David Chamber and Brian Pullan, *Venice: A Documentary History, 1450–1630* (New York: Blackwell, 1992), p. 276; Stuart Jenks, "The Black Death and Würzburg: Michael de Leone's Reaction in Context" (Ph.D. dissertation, Yale University, 1977), p. 215.

19. Horrox, *Black Death*, p. 113.

5

AT THE BISHOP'S PALACE AND THE MONASTERY

The Catholic Church was the most highly structured and influential organization in Europe at the time of the Black Death. Each local church where Christians worshipped was merely a part of a much larger and more complex organization. The elected bishop of Rome, or pope, headed up the Church, ruling as Vicar of Christ through local bishops responsible for the administration of the resources and personnel of their dioceses, the church's geographic administrative units. In England and Lutheran Germany during the sixteenth century bishops remained as administrative leaders, but they answered to the king or other territorial ruler, as the church was absorbed by the state. In the Orthodox world bishops were very nearly autonomous, especially after the fall of Constantinople in 1453. Because of the omnipresence of religion in the life of Christian Europe, these leaders played very important roles in shaping the Christian response to plague and maintaining the structure and discipline of the clergy. In the early years of the Black Death the tasks were nearly overwhelming.

Throughout the Second Pandemic monasteries remained centers of prayer and ritual, and early on they provided important chronicles of the epidemics. The effects of plague on Europe's monasteries were both immediate—great loss of life—and long lasting, as an evolving Christian religiosity marginalized the attraction and utility of the cloistered life.

BISHOPS AND THE PLAGUE

Like all other leaders Europe's bishops found themselves utterly incapable of directly affecting the course or impact of the Black Death. Some found themselves hampered by extraordinary circumstances. The most important church leader in England, Archbishop of Canterbury John Stratford, died in May 1348. His successor, King Edward's paralytic chancellor John Offord, died about a year later without ever having been formally installed as bishop by the pope in Avignon. At this time in history high church offices were effectively purchased from the pope. The archbishop's post cost a good deal of money, and Offord had borrowed much of what was required. His early death left many creditors bankrupt. His successor Thomas Bradwardine, the original choice of the cathedral canons themselves, died after only a few months. *His* successor, Simon Islip, inherited a diocese whose treasury had been looted by his predecessors to pay the pope and whose feudal and religious revenues had shriveled away.

Bishops were spiritual pastors, political hacks, and administrators of vast organizations rich in lands, personnel, and other resources. Drawn for the most part from the nobility, they tended to rise to the occasion as leaders and decision makers. Apart from their responsibility to train, ordain, and assign priests to parishes, bishops oversaw all institutions and facilities that had any religious element to them and did not belong to a specific religious order such as the Benedictines or Franciscans. They also dictated the ways in which the sacraments and other rituals were applied or carried out by clergy or other church personnel. In addition, they were the chief financial officers for their dioceses, collecting tithes and other incomes and distributing the funds among charities and institutions. They depended for their personal finances on income from manorial lands, which made them among the largest landholders in any realm. Finally, they were the chief spiritual teachers in their dioceses. As such they interpreted church doctrine, Scripture, and the events of the day—including plague. But to interpret the plague was not to solve the problems it caused.

The earliest religious impulse when pestilence struck was to hold special civic Masses and processions, thought to be useful in quelling the divine rage and sparking repentance in the people. The Eucharist, relics, paintings, or statues provided the focal points and the spiritual touchstone between heaven and earth. With the development of contagion theory emerged official civic opposition to large gatherings; the fate of a procession was often a sign of the relative power of the religious and secular authorities. Bishops could also grant certain dispensations from formalities made inconvenient by the plague. For example, the bishop of Bath and Wells in a carefully worded statement famously allowed those in his diocese to confess their sins "to any lay person, even to a woman if a man is not available."[1] Other bishops shortened the sacrament of extreme unction, or last anointing, that prepared a seriously ill person for death. Many bishops, including the pope, granted special "indulgences" during plague time. People who carried out certain prescribed charitable or ritual actions or said certain specific prayers with the proper religious intention would be released from some set number of days they would otherwise spend in purgatory suffering for unconfessed sins. The soil of a Christian burial ground was always blessed by a clergyman, usually the bishop, and new graveyards, whether freestanding or attached to a church, hospital, or other institution, required his permission and blessing. In an extreme case the pope himself blessed the Rhône River so that bodies might be properly disposed in it.

PROBLEMS OF THE MEDIEVAL CLERGY

In the Catholic West there were two types of priests who worked in the world outside the monastery. The traditional diocesan priest was ordained by and worked for the local bishop. He was usually attached to a parish and "had the cure of souls," which meant that he was responsible for administering the sacraments to the Christian people. He might be very well educated and even a younger son from the upper classes, or he might be a son of the soil with minimal education or literacy. "Beneficed" clergy had a set position, as in a parish, and could expect an income (benefice) that was set or reflected the wealth of the parish. The bishop and his administrators appointed most of these, unless the parish or other post belonged to the local landlord, for various historical "feudal" reasons, and was thus in his "gift." The advantage of this situation for the landlord was that he could appoint virtually any man he wanted to, including family members. The new pastor was rewarded with the income and could be trusted to lead his flock as the landlord saw fit. In all too many cases the actual appointee was given the position for the income alone, while another less-qualified cleric would actually have the cure of souls (be a curate) and only a fraction of the income. The appointee thus held the benefice but as an absentee with a sinecure—literally "without the cure (of souls)." In this way landlords and bishops could use church funds to support a young man as a university student, private scholar, writer, or bureaucrat without spending their own money. It also meant that congregations were often ill served. Eventually recognized as abusive even by the Catholic Church, the practice was curbed during the Reformation.

In part because of problems like undereducated or absentee clergy, a second type of clergy, known as the mendicants ("beggars") or friars ("brothers"), developed during the thirteenth century. Francis of Assisi and Dominic Guzman, founders of the Franciscans and Dominicans respectively, sought to fill a gap by establishing new orders of clergy that blended a kind of apostolic detachment from the worldly life with a mission to preach and revitalize Catholic spirituality in Europe's burgeoning cities. Usually well educated and trained to preach, unlike the

Væ qui dicitis malum bonum,& bonum malũ,
ponentes tenebras lucem,& lucem tenebras,
ponentes amarum dulce,& dulce in amarum.
ISAIÆ XV

Mal pour uous qui ainſi oſez
Le mal pour le bien nous blaſmer,
Et le bien pour mal expoſez,
Mettant auec le doulx l'amer.

Death prompts the preacher in his pulpit. From
Hans Holbein's *Danse Macabre,* Lyon, 1538. Dover.

typical diocesan priests, the friars lived in loose communities following
rules for life established by their founders. They took vows of poverty,
chastity, and obedience to their superiors and relied solely on gifts from
the people whose spiritual lives they served. They built large churches
in which they preached and said Mass for all who chose to come, but
they had no parishes or set congregations. In many ways they were in
competition with both the diocesan clergy and each other.

Death Stalks the Clergy, 1347–1350 In both normal and plague times, diocesan and mendicant
clergy alike were expected to visit the sick and aid those in
need. The friars and their female branches, the Dominican
nuns and Franciscan Poor Clares, often served or maintained
hospitals and other institutions for the sick or travelers. People of all classes favored friars as confessors and spiritual guides and often
called upon them specifically when death seemed imminent. Technically,

last rites were reserved to the parish priests, but no friar would ignore the call of a soul in need, whether it belonged to a faithful patron and supporter or a homeless vagabond. In plague time this dedication to service placed the clergy directly in the line of fire, repeatedly exposing them to the plague germs, whether from the household fleas or the sputum of the victim. As with notaries and doctors, who also served at victims' bedsides, one would expect high death rates among the dutiful clergy. The monk Gilles li Muisis of Tournai wrote in 1348, "[C]ertainly there were many deaths among the parish priests and chaplains who heard confessions and administered the sacraments, and also among the parish clerks and those who visited the sick with them." Some tried to limit their exposure by reducing the time spent providing the last rites, or hearing confessions from outside the sickroom window or even through a candle flame believed to purify the victim's breath. In some dioceses, such as that of Barcelona in 1651, victims received their communion wafers from a distance, on the end of long silver rod. In 1605 an Anglican theology oral exam queried, "whether at the onset of pestilence pastors should visit the sick."[2] For Catholics it was a given; for non-Catholic clergy it was an open-ended question for debate.

The most comprehensive blow against the Catholic clergy was, of course, the initial outbreak of plague in 1347–1352. Subsequent outbreaks, being both less severe and more localized, were far less drastic in their effects and have been far less diligently studied by scholars. Information on deaths among the mendicant orders clearly shows that casualties were quite high. However, the preplague populations of the local communities are unknown, so to say that among Italian Dominicans 49 died in Siena, 39 in Lucca, and 57 in Pisa is to provide limited information. The huge convent of Santa Maria Novella in Florence could house about 150 Dominicans, and of them 68, or about half, died in 1348. Was this percentage typical? The English friar Henry Knighton reported that at Montpellier in southern France only seven of 140 survived, and at Maguellone only seven of 160. Among the Franciscan Cordelliers at Carcassonne and Marseille, not one survived. All of these communities were rather small and locally based, with administrators who were among the best educated men in Europe, so the figures would seem to be trustworthy. They clearly support anecdotal reports from the likes of the Sicilian Franciscan Michele da Piazza, whose chronicle notes that "the Franciscans and Dominicans, and others who were willing to visit the sick to hear their confession and impose penance, died in such large numbers that their priories [residences] were all but deserted." Shortly after 1350, Pope Clement VI rebuked the diocesan leaders who complained about the new wealth from gifts and bequests that enriched the mendicants:

Why do you complain that the mendicant orders, during the plague, received so much that was offered by the faithful? This money was properly gained. While so many of the parish priests took flight and abandoned their parishioners, the

P· D· IO· BAPTISTA CARACCIOLVS C·R·
Neapolitana Grassante Lue
In Ægrotorum Ministerio absumptus,
Millibus superpositis, effractisque cadaueribus
Angelorum manu extractus;
Vt in Diui Pauli Cœmeterio, quod summe optauerat, conderetur

A seventeenth-century plague-time broadside sheet that would have been hung in memory of the priest who died helping plague victims, in this case Father Giovanni Battista Caraccioli. An angel removes him from the horrible mass grave that has been made of a hillside cave. Naples, undated. National Library of Medicine.

mendicants cared for and buried them. Thus, if they use the gifts that they received in fine construction, and such that it is of a magnificence that honors the universal Church, and in any case, it is better spent in this way than lost in forbidden pleasures and debaucheries.[3]

The numbers and percentages of active diocesan priests who died differ across Europe, but in general they range between 35 and 70 percent with an overall rate of perhaps 50 percent—roughly in line with estimates for deaths among the general population. For English dioceses one finds figures such as 48.8 percent for Winchester and Exeter, 47.6 percent for Bath and Wells, 43.2 percent for Hereford, 39.0 percent for York in the north, and 40.0 percent for Barcelona in Catalonia. These figures are derived from books called bishops' registers, in which scribes recorded (among many other things) appointments to new positions for which the bishop is responsible. For the fourteenth century, England provides by far the best collection of registers, though there are important gaps. These records do not usually list priests who died or priests who were buried, but rather vacancies in positions that were entitled to an income and that needed to be filled. But of one hundred vacancies in plague time, what percentage was due to the priest's flight from his congregation? Or his death from causes other than plague? Or his being moved to another position? If the priest in large, wealthy parish A died, then a vacancy opened. When Priest X was moved to parish A from small and poor parish B, a second vacancy opened: one death, two vacancies. And what of the priest with the sinecure: if his vicar died was the vacancy counted? In addition, some priests received incomes from several parishes, a questionable practice known as pluralism. if a priest with three benefices died, was his a single vacancy or three? As with other medieval sources, bishops' registers provide some fascinating information, but one must use them carefully and understand their limitations.

Noting the problems with using bishops' registers, William Dohar, in his recent study of the Diocese of Hereford, England, relates that of just over 300 benefices, 160 lost their curates and created vacancies in 1349. He appropriately adjusts downward this raw figure of about 54 percent to a "conservative" figure of "thirty-eight to forty percent," or about 120 deaths due to plague. **Filling Vacancies in England** Even with this adjustment, the terrible deviation from the norm is evident: from 1345 to 1348, 28 vacancies opened, an average of only 7 per year. In his early study of the register of John Gynwell, Bishop of Lincoln, Hamilton Thompson found that vacancies averaged about 106 per year before the plague and reached 1,025 in the plague year alone. Because the scribe kept especially good records we know that 824 of these vacancies were due to death, though we do not know how the holder died. The scribe at Coventry was good enough to note the cases in his part of the diocese in which the holder died: Between March 1347 and September 1350—three and a half years—there were a total of 235 death-related vacancies. During the single year between March 1349 and February 1350, 91 percent (214) of the holders who died succumbed to the "epidemic." Among benefices in the gift of the king of England, which averaged about 100 vacancies per year, there were 159 vacancies in 1348 and 899 in 1349. In Norwich the figure rose from an average of 77 to 800, and in Exeter from 35 to 371. In Barcelona, whose episcopal records are also very good, the vacancies rose from 1 in April 1348 to 9 in May, 25 in June, and 104 in July. In Somerset, the bishop had a total of 413 benefices, of which 201 went vacant during plague time. Since several candidates died, it took 249 appointments to fill these openings.

In the very best of times these numbers would have taxed the resources of the typical medieval bishop and his administrators. But bishops themselves lost many of their staff and sometimes their own lives. As previously noted, Canterbury, England's most important diocese, had three archbishops die in a little more than a year. In Avignon the pope survived, but lost about a third of his curial bureaucracy. Scribe William Dene of the relatively small English diocese of Rochester reported that his bishop "lost four priests, five squires, ten household servants, seven young clerks and six pages, leaving no one in any office who should have served him."[4] In Marseille the bishop and all of his canons—priests who were stationed at the cathedral church to aid the bishop—died in 1347 or 1348. In 1349, 54 of the clergy attached to St. Stephen's Cathedral in Vienna died. Six of 36 Irish bishops succumbed. Since the pope had to install any new bishop, and with all of Europe gripped by the pestilence, replacing bishops was rather more difficult than replacing clergy.

Even when bishops remained alive and active, clerical vacancies could stay open for months. Once the patron or diocese officials learned of the vacancy, the diocese's archdeacon confirmed it and suggested candidates. Once the patron and the bishop agreed on a choice, then the ordination took place if needed, the priest was installed, and the installation was formally recorded in the episcopal register. Canon Law allowed for a maximum of six months before a vacancy had to be filled, but issues such as communication, patrons' preferences, and the availability of ordained priests could slow the process down. Bishops were known to flee the cities in which they normally resided for country estates, and they could be difficult to track down. To be ordained a priest a layman had to go through several distinct stages required by Canon Law. Some in the later stages (sub-deacon or deacon) could be fast-tracked to ordination in as little as six months, but during serious epidemics even these candidates were soon in short supply. In Coventry the average time it took to fill a benefice was about 40 days. Of course this meant 40 days without spiritual guidance, and, most importantly as plague raged all around, without the sacraments.

Problems with Postplague Priests

For many parish priests their post was little more than a job, and, being human, when the plague struck they did what so many others did: they fled. The friar Jean de Venette wrote of the French parish clergy, "[T]he cowardly priests took themselves off, leaving the performance of spiritual offices to the regular[5] clergy, who tended to be more courageous." Abandonment or flight by both pre-Reformation Catholic and Protestant clergy is a theme that recurs in plague sources. Some merely sought their own safety, but the worst offenders were those who fled out of greed. William Dene, who was well placed in Rochester cathedral, decried that some

priests, making light of the sacrifice of a contrite spirit, took themselves to where they might receive a stipend greater than the value of their benefices. As a result, many benefices remained unserved by parish priests, whom neither prelates nor ordinaries were powerful enough to bridle. Thus, spiritual dangers sprouted daily among the clergy and the laity.

In the wake of the plague opportunities and higher salaries beckoned the clergy as they did the laboring classes, prompting bishops to issue salary caps as well as the stern rebukes that accompanied them. In introducing his laws limiting clerical salaries and fees to preplague levels, Archbishop Simon Islip wrote ruefully of his clergy, who were "not ashamed that their insatiable avarice is despicably and perniciously taken as an example by other workers among the laity [and] now take no heed to the cure of souls." He continued:

But priests now refuse to take on the cure of souls, or to support the burdens of their cures in mutual charity, but rather leave them completely abandoned and apply themselves instead to the celebration of commemorative Masses and other offices; and for these, too, they are not content with the payment of adequate wages but demand excessive salaries.

During the later Middle Ages the wealthy laity began to demand, and the church provided, Masses that were celebrated not with a congregation but by the priest alone and on behalf of the spiritual needs of individuals or families. Often these Masses were celebrated in commemoration of the deceased, the belief being that they helped lessen his or her time in purgatory. Men and women left provisions for the Masses in wills, sometimes creating a whole ensemble of chapel and permanent priests. Since the priest sang or chanted the Mass, it was known as a "chantry." Such positions certainly paid better than those in some lowly parish and imposed only minimal obligations on the priest. With the uncertainties of plague the demand for these "private" priests grew and drew many away from pastoral duties. In his prologue to *Piers Plowman* William Langland skewers those

> That have cure under Christ and, in token, tonsure,
> A sign that they should shrive [confess] their parishioners,
> Preach to them and pray for them, and feed the poor–
> They lie in London, in Lent and else.

Langland wrote in the 1370s, more than two decades after the initial out-break, but the problems and his disgust were still fresh.

> Parsons and parish priests complained to the bishop
> That their parishes were poor since the time of plague
> So as to have a license and a leave at London to live
> And sing there for simony, for silver is sweet.[6]

The poet considers chantries to be a form of simony, an abusive selling of a church office or service. It is likely that Langland's characters did not want to rid themselves of the parish income, but rather add to it with the chantry service, thereby adding the abuses of pluralism (multiple positions) and absenteeism.

Even when absenteeism, pluralism, or abandonment was not the issue, excessive clerical salaries or benefits remained a problem. As Simon Islip noted, the clergy's demand for high salaries set a bad example for laypeople, which undermined the entire social order. The English friar Henry Knighton claimed that with

such a great shortage of priests everywhere . . . A man could scarcely get a chaplain for less than £10 or ten marks to minister to any church, and whereas before the pestilence there had been a glut of priests, and a man could get a chaplain for four or five marks, or for two marks with food and lodging, in this time there was scarcely anyone who would accept a vicarage[7] at £20 or twenty marks.

Priests may have had a right to a certain presumptuousness refused to the lower, working classes, but as long as the church leaders did not sanction the change in custom, the change was bad. Writing about the same time as Langland (1378), Archbishop of Canterbury Simon of Sudbury characterized his clergy as being

so tainted with the vice of cupidity that they are not content with reasonable stipends, but demand and receive excessive wages. These greedy and fastidious priests vomit from the excess of their salaries, they run wild and wallow, and some of them, after sating the gluttony of their bellies, break forth into a pit of evils.

Nonetheless, he raised their allowed stipend from five to seven marks. Very often in the medieval world it was not *what* was done, it was *who* did it that mattered. It was Sudbury, by the way, whom the angry mob captured and executed during the Peasants' Revolt of 1381.

By Archbishop Simon's time an entirely new generation of clergy had been recruited, prepared, and put in place, but clearly the effects of that disaster were still reverberating. Part of the problem was the character of the new class of postplague priests. Friar Henry continued his contemporary analysis by recording that

within a short time a great crowd of men whose wives had died in the pestilence rushed into priestly orders. Many of them were illiterate [in Latin], no better than laymen—for even if they could read, they did not understand what they read.[8]

Even worse, perhaps, were the new candidates who were younger than 24, the traditional canonical age for ordination. In January 1349, the Archbishop of Dublin received permission to ordain 20 underage men and 30 who were born illegitimately. The diocese received fees and paid Rome a fee for each such dispensation. During the plague of 1363, Dublin's archbishop received a blanket dispensation for illegitimate sons since the need was so great.

In York diocese as well the underaged and illegitimate joined the clerical ranks. From 1344 to 1346 the archbishop ordained an average of 132 men, but from 1349 to 1351 this average rose to 402, with 724 ordinations in 1350 alone. By contrast, Hereford diocese, where these groups were forbidden from the priesthood, ordained 156 in 1346 but only 86 in 1350 and half of that in 1351, with numbers running in the thirties and forties throughout the 1350s.

The mendicant clergy, who had suffered no less than the diocesan, had similar problems replenishing their ranks. Unlike the local bishop, however, the Dominican or Franciscan leadership did not have an immediate need for curates; nor were friars tempted away by chantry stipends. The Chapter General of the Dominicans, an order that especially valued a recruit's intellect, met in the midst of the 1348 outbreak. They agreed on the need for attracting young and apt candidates to all of their convents, and decided that the less-successful communities would help support financially the greater numbers in the larger ones. They also forbade the resale of dead brothers' university textbooks that would be useful in educating new Dominicans. In addition, they saw the value in establishing local grammar and music schools through which they might recruit suitable candidates. Twenty-eight years and three major plagues later, the Chapter General admitted that the order was reduced to admitting children from 10 to 14 years of age, most of whom had little intellectual aptitude or spiritual fortitude. Among these boys few could read or write going in and far too few learned while in the order. As in most niches of society, the ones with the skills and who taught had been killed off, and the craft suffered. A Franciscan chronicler reflected on this effect:

In this year 1348, there rages so great an epidemic in the entire world that fully one-third of the order was living on its feet. This is why the Franciscan family, which had shone so splendidly in the Church of God, began to decline and to grow dark, because of the deaths of so many holy and learned fathers and brothers.

In the later 1470s the Dominican biographer Giovanni Caroli reflected similarly on the spiritual and intellectual losses of his order:

As the chief men died and novices replaced them, the religious orders themselves fell to ruin. How painful it is, whenever men have been trained for many years and with great effort that they pass away in scarcely one hour. All that diligence, which men previously applied in preparing and supporting outstanding careers, is rendered vain and useless.[9]

Ironically, because of their dedication and institutionalized poverty the mendicants benefited greatly from the redistribution of wealth that resulted from the exorbitant plague deaths. Though Pope Clement had praised the mendicants' self-sacrifice and given his blessing to their new wealth, the Benedictine monk John of Reading, writing in the 1360s, decried its effects:

The mammon of iniquity wounded . . . the mendicants fatally. The superfluous wealth poured their way, through confessions and bequests, in such quantities that they scarcely condescended to accept oblations.[10] Forgetful of their profession and rule, which imposed total poverty and mendicancy, they lusted after things of the world and of the flesh, not of heaven.[11]

Anticlericalism   John's remarks reflect a newly energized trend in European society known as anticlericalism. Many in society, even clerics themselves, grew increasingly critical of the clergy at all levels. Poets and theologians lashed out against the removal of the papacy from Rome to Avignon (1309–1378) and the high life that was lived at the papal court. Monks had long suffered a reputation for sloth and gluttony, and parish priests were condemned for fornication, greed, ignorance, and general corruption. Anticlerical literature dates back to the 1100s, but anticlerical expressions and actions gained in frequency and vehemence after 1350. The strongest criticisms came from frustrated bishops like Simon of Sudbury and outraged members of the clergy like John. The more dangerous insults were those of outsiders like Petrarch and Boccaccio, Chaucer and Langland, the Lollards and the Hussites. The cowardly or immoral actions of some priests during the early plague outbreaks fueled popular attacks on the clergy, as did the oftentimes harsh actions of church and secular authorities following plague outbreaks. Sometimes the attacks were carried out with more than just words. Physical assaults on priests and bishops, especially during plague outbreaks, grew increasingly common in the later fourteenth century.

In the sixteenth century Protestantism would redefine its Christian church leadership away from the voluntary caste system of the Catholic priesthood. While one cannot meaningfully attribute the Reformation directly to the Black Death, one can see in its effects the roots of the changes that reshaped the religious landscape of late medieval Europe. Open dissatisfaction with and distrust of the clergy led to greater spiritual self-reliance among many believers. Generations of recurring plague chipped away at the cherished notion that the clergy was necessary for mankind to maintain good relations with God. The economic dislocations that enriched many townspeople and peasants also enriched the church and its leaders, which drew fire from the envious as well as the saintly.

THE BLACK DEATH AND THE MONASTERIES

The Monastic Life   Unlike diocesan and mendicant priests, whose lives were devoted to the cure of souls, monks and nuns lived in seclusion in monasteries and dedicated their lives to the "prayer and work" dictated by the father of Roman Catholic communal monasticism, St. Benedict. Founded in the sixth century, Benedictine monasticism was the dominant Western form, though there were Catholic variations and the Orthodox world had its own traditions.

Some men and women chose to live as hermits, or anchorites, either off in the literal wilderness or completely isolated in a cell in a church. Benedictine monks and nuns followed strict schedules of daily Mass and group prayer and meals. They took vows of poverty, chastity, and obedience to the rule and the abbot or abbess (women had their own monasteries). The ideal monastery was a self-contained community on whose land all the monks worked to grow the necessary food and in whose workshops they toiled to produce everything else they needed. In fact, however, some monasteries became centers of production for export, making especially high-quality beer or wine, jewelry and religious craftworks, or copies of brilliantly illustrated manuscripts. Many also provided schools that prepared young boys for careers in the clergy or for the university, or young girls for lives in the monastery or broader society as wives and mothers.

In these ways, and many others, medieval monasteries served the world from which their members were drawn. Over time, however, the demands of the workshop and monastic choir pulled them away from the soil. Over many centuries pious Christians gave or bequeathed an enormous amount of land to monasteries in return for the monks' prayers, and under the manorial system the land was furnished with laboring peasants. Monasteries thus became great landlords whose acreage rivaled that held by the highest nobles. Their wealth ensured security and a standard of living that was well above that of most Europeans. As long as will-makers and others continued to support the monasteries and young men continued to seek out their prayerful communities they would thrive. In 1348 the monastic system was still deeply entrenched in the European landscape, though the newer mendicant orders as well as the growth of cities with their own schools and craftspeople and money economy had begun to erode it.

Monastic communities differed from all other medieval communities in several ways. There were **Monastic Medicine** neither families nor social (class) distinctions; the entire population was adult, or nearly so; aside from servants and peasants, the entire community was literate and had access to what were often the best libraries in the region; and all except the abbot were supposed to sleep in a common dormitory. The Benedictine Rule dictated an ascetic vegetarian monastic diet but provided for rather well-balanced nutrition. It also insisted that clothing be appropriate to the climate. Because they were meant to stand forever, monasteries tended to be very well constructed of stone and solid wood. They were certainly drafty but were far more substantial than the wattle-and-daub thatched structures in which most well-off peasants resided or even the half-timbered houses increasingly found in European towns.

Because of the close living arrangements, maintenance of a healthy population was a chief concern. Benedict himself had written, "Before all things and above all things let care be taken of the sick," and he made provisions for sick monks, allowing them special foods, including meat, and reduced work loads. In the famous ninth-century Plan of St. Gall, a ground plan for an ideal monastery, accommodations and services for the sick are located together in one corner of the compound. Here one finds a chief physician's quarters, a medicinal garden, a storeroom for medical supplies, a room for the critically ill, a room for regular bloodletting of the monks, and a special chapel, cloister, kitchen, and bath for the sick. By the High Middle Ages larger monasteries had infirmaries to isolate the sick and care for the elderly, and a specially appointed Master of the Infirmary, who had assistants known as *infirmarii*. At Christchurch, Canterbury, the master made his daily rounds, feeding the ill, sprinkling holy water on them, and praying with or over them. His infirmary was a hall 237 feet long with beds placed perpendicular to the wall and separated by portable screens or curtains. By the later fifteenth century the space was divided into smaller, permanent wards of six beds each. These monastic facilities were the models for later urban hospitals, which in turn were often served by religious orders in Catholic countries. By the fourteenth century many of these institutions were centuries old and held collections of medical texts and herbals, which described the medicinal properties of plants.

Death in the Cloister

Though often geographically isolated or walled off from neighboring urban build-up, Europe's monasteries received a constant stream of visitors. From imperial, royal, or papal delegations to poor pilgrims; from merchants with carts piled high or the cash to purchase the monastery's goods to ragged peasants with in-kind rent; from local nobles and benefactors to brothers or sisters from other monasteries, the gates swung open for all, sick and well together. However the pestilence entered the cloister, once inside it spread like fire through tinder. Because of the monks' literacy and tendency to keep written records, they left numerous accounts of the effects of plague on their communities.

No one has surveyed all the existing literature on monastic death tolls, but published numbers and anecdotal evidence from the later 1340s make for grim reading. Gherardo, the younger brother of the famed poet Francesco Petrarch, was a Carthusian monk at the Chartreuse (monastery) of Montrieux in southern France. Carthusians lived in communities of hermits, each of whom had his own cell and avoided unnecessary human contact. Even so, Gherardo tended his 35 brothers as each fell ill and died, until only Gherardo was left standing—the only survivor. Typically the order lost about 100 men each year in France, but this number rose to 465 in 1348. All of the 28 Camaldolese[12] monks of Florence's Santa Maria degli Angeli fell ill, and only 7 survived. In England Meaux Abbey lost 33 of 43 brothers and all their lay servants. The Benedictines of Westminster Abbey near London lost their abbot and suffered a death rate of half their brothers, while 20 of 23 Cistercians died at Newenham. Ely Cathedral lost 26 of 54 canons, priests who lived together like monks.

In the larger houses, at least, the level of medical care and personal attention had to be as good as that received almost anywhere. Monastic herbalists may have been able to dull the pain more readily than other apothecaries (pharmacists) were willing to do, and none had to worry about money being an object in medical treatment. The monastic life was founded on an ascetic ideal that valued suffering as spiritually beneficial, a message that validated the horrific experience the community was sharing. Given the Christian view of the necessity of self-sacrifice for salvation and the ultimate mortality of the physical human body, health care outside of the home was really more important to the caregiver than to the patient. The exercise of Christian charity could save the soul in a way no human medicine could ever save a body.

The sufferings of the various monastic houses in the later 1300s undermined the institution itself, leaving it weaker than it had been. Like many peasant villages, some monasteries simply closed their doors, the survivors moving to less-devastated residences. The lands of an abandoned house would be consolidated with those of the stronger one or otherwise redistributed. Monasteries, like other landlords, suffered from reduced rents, a shattered workforce, and deserted villages; unlike the others, monks could afford to lose income since their mission in the world required little in the way of cash outlays. Northern Italian monasteries complained of the high cost of hiring workers, the depredations of war, shortages of wine and grain, violence unleashed by feuding local nobles, and "burdens, imposts, taxes, subsidies, [and] exactions"[13] that were growing almost every day. Many released their suddenly greedy servants and even removed certain expensive foods from their tables. Some of this loss was made up for with a rise in cash and in-kind gifts from dead benefactors' bequests, including chantries. With reduced numbers, individual monks in northern Europe benefited even more, which helped recruitment; local studies of monasteries tend to show that the losses in numbers rebounded rather quickly. Studies of wills, however, demonstrate that in the longer run, popular support for monasteries declined as people gave more to the mendicants. With a society-wide impulse to procreate, the numbers of young women entering monasteries dropped off considerably, as did the value of gifts and bequests to female houses and orders.

Plague's Impact on Monasticism

Russian Orthodox monasteries provide an interesting contrast to those of the Catholic West. Following a pattern set by Sergius of Radonezh, new monasteries budded off of a motherhouse when a single hermit-monk moved away and settled, drawing new brothers to his camp. Under the local system of landholding these small, new communities were able to grow by taking over land that had been cleared and worked by plague-decimated peasant communities. The monks' role in the market for agricultural goods expanded rapidly in the wake of massive peasant deaths, and their various religious immunities from local fees and taxes gave them a decided advantage. Inside city walls new communities also grew in influence and power thanks to gifts, bequests, and simple usurpation of abandoned church land and structures. Where the West had developed a complex network of numerous religious orders—monastic and mendicant, alongside the parish and diocese—the situation in Orthodox Russia was far simpler and the pious benefactor's options far fewer.

The impacts of the plague on the church were complex. Like medicine, religion failed to control the pestilence or its effects. Those charged with praying for the good of humanity clearly failed to placate an angry God, while those responsible for tending to people's spiritual needs often imitated the Gospel's "bad shepherd" and fled in terror. Many religious leaders did, however, stay at their posts and direct their charges: bishops labored to replace dying clergy; monks stayed by their dying brethren; priests risked their lives providing last rites to parishioners and strangers alike. The church was enriched financially, but that very wealth spawned corruption, prompting the criticisms that sparked the Reformation.

NOTES

1. Rosemary Horrox, ed., *The Black Death* (New York: Manchester University Press, 1994), p. 272.

2. Horrox, *Black Death*, p. 54; Charles F. Mullett, *The Bubonic Plague and England* (Lexington: University of Kentucky Press, 1956), pp. 113–14.

3. Horrox, *Black Death*, p. 36; Jacqueline Brossollet, "Quelques aspects religieux de la grande peste du XIVe siècle," *Revue d'histoire et de philosophie religieuses* 64 (1984), p. 60.

4. Horrox, *Black Death*, p. 71.

5. Priests who were members of an order and followed a specific rule for living or *regula*; includes the mendicants.

6. Horrox, *Black Death*, pp. 55, 72–73, 307; J. B. Trapp, *Medieval English Literature* (New York: Oxford University Press, 1973), p. 354.

7. A position as a substitute parish priest, usually very low paying.

8. Horrox, *Black Death*, pp. 78–79; Christopher Harper-Bill, "The English Church and English Religion after the Black Death," in *The Black Death in England*, ed. W. M. Ormrod and P. G. Lindley (Stamford, UK: Paul Watkins, 1996), p. 91.

9. Brossollet, "Quelques aspects," p. 56; David Herlihy and Christine Klapisch-Zuber, *Tuscans and Their Families* (New Haven: Yale University Press, 1985), p. 85.

10. Free-will offerings.

11. Horrox, *Black Death*, p. 75.

12. The Camaldolese and Cistercian orders were reformed branches of the Benedictine Order.

13. Samuel Cohn, *Death and Property in Siena, 1205–1800* (Baltimore: Johns Hopkins University Press, 1988), p. 33.

6

AT THE PEST HOUSE

However strongly people wanted to believe that plague originated in God's wrath, celestial conjunctions, or corrupted air, they decided quickly to act as though it spread directly from person to person and from "infected" goods. In his *Decameron* Boccaccio famously relates how a pig rooting among a plague victim's clothing rapidly took ill and died. Touch (the origin of the word *contagion*), breath, body odor, even the "rays" that were supposed to emanate from people's eyes were thought to pass along the disease. When people fled they were fleeing not only bad air, but the company of the sick from whom they might "catch" plague. Boccaccio and many other writers in 1348 and 1349 remark on the abandonment of children by parents, brothers by brothers, and so forth—clearly a moral failing, but also a prudent act of self-preservation if indeed one could catch the disease. Civic authorities tended to be slow to develop the implications of this theory into official action, but once they did, they acted with a brutality that often seemed inhumane. The first step was to isolate in their own homes the sick, then those possibly infected. Officials eventually augmented "shutting in" with the creation of special quarters for the victims, often little more than huts located outside the town walls. With time, authorities took over larger quarters, such as hospitals and monasteries, to serve as plague hospitals. Finally, larger cities constructed special "pest houses" in which to tend the sick and isolate the potentially infected. By the mid-seventeenth century officials all over Europe were desperately utilizing all of these practices.

SHUT-INS

**Voluntary
Isolation**
          On July 14, 1665, as plague swirled all about, a London gro-
cer locked himself, his wife, his son, three daughters, and an
apprentice in their house. He had stored up ample supplies of
food, water, and medicine, and relied upon a servant, Abraham, who remained stationed outside his employer's window, for contact
with the broader world. When Abraham brought needed supplies or the
latest "Bills of Mortality" the grocer opened a second-story window, fired
off gunpowder to cleanse the incoming air, and pulled the goods up in a
basket. The servant fumigated arriving mail with burnt sulfur or gunpowder and sprinkled vinegar on it before sending it up in the basket, and
the grocer smoked it again as he opened it. Eventually Abraham died of
the plague, and an old woman recommended to the family one Thomas
Molins, who had already contracted and survived the plague. When the
family began to suffer from scurvy, Molins brought them lemons and limes.
They had a scare when one of the family caught a cold, but all survived.
When Molins died, a watchman whose family had all succumbed took his
place until the family relocated to the suburbs in December, a move the
grocer based upon death trends indicated in the official Bills of Mortality.

One might compare this type of self-isolation with that of Dr. Burnet,
physician and neighbor of Samuel Pepys of London. On June 11, 1665,
Pepys walked past the doctor's residence and

saw poor Dr. Burnet's door shut. But he hath, I hear, gained great goodwill among
his neighbors; for he discovered himself first [that his servant, William, had the
plague], and caused himself to be shut up of his own accord—which was very
handsome.

Burnet was later accused falsely of killing William and died on August 25
of plague. Pepys found this turn of events quite "strange, his man dying so
long ago and his house this month open again. Now himself dead—poor
unfortunate man." In fact Burnet died after performing an autopsy on a
plague victim.[1]

A third example, without doubt the most famous, is that of the entire English village of Eyam, in Derbyshire. Though far from London, the folks of
Eyam caught the pestilence, it is said, from a load of cloth that arrived from
the plague-infested capital in August 1665. The tailor who received it was
first to die, and many followed. Convinced by the pastor, 28-year-old William
Mompesson, that their best course of action was for all to remain and none to
flee, everyone stayed put and suffered the plague's wrath. The people of Eyam
and their neighbors laid out a cordon sanitaire, a boundary no one would cross
with designated points where needed supplies would be left. Eyam lived off of
the charity of surrounding villages, which in turn were spared by its sacrifice.
With their own hands mothers buried their children and sons their parents.

The epidemic lasted 14 months and took the lives of some 260 villagers, leaving fewer than a hundred survivors in the immediate area.

It is one thing to choose to isolate oneself, one's family, or one's community; it is another to have this isolation imposed **Coercion** by force of arms. Milan began the practice of forced isolation **in Europe** when a few plague cases first appeared in 1348. Headed by a lord, Bernabò Visconti, rather than an elected council, the Milanese government could act swiftly and ruthlessly. They sealed off the first few victims and their families in their houses until all had died or the survivors had proved their good health. Agnolo di Tura reported deaths in only three families, and so Milan was spared the horrors suffered by so many other Italian cities. But Milan was not to repeat its success during subsequent plagues, nor did other Italian cities follow suit until the later fifteenth century.

Whether discouraged by the theory of corrupted air, the lack of organizational resources, or the assault on human dignity that shutting in entailed, few later medieval cities practiced this method. For the most part the governments that pioneered the policy—Visconti Milan, grand ducal Florence, and Elizabethan England—were well-organized and authoritarian governments. In many ways this behavior echoed a new and ruthless tone in political theory and practice. In one of his many letters from the early sixteenth century the Dutch humanist Desiderius Erasmus described and addressed the moral issue of forced isolation: "In Italy buildings are locked up at first sign of pestilence; those who attend the sufferer are quarantined. Some call this inhumanity, though actually it is the highest humanity, for because of this precaution the plague is checked with few fatalities."[2] The practice would remain hotly controversial for two centuries.

WHY 40 DAYS FOR QUARANTINE?

For Hippocrates, the fortieth day of an illness is "crisis" day: if one survived that long, he was cured.

In Judeo-Christian tradition, 40 days is the period of ritual purification.

The so-called alchemist's month had 40 days.

In 1557 Dutch plague victims were harshly treated. Family members could choose whether to remain in the house with the victim, but once in they stayed. Authorities wrapped the entire house with a padlocked chain and a fence and marked it with a bundle of straw over the door. From that point, Leiden straw merchants were forbidden from using actual bundles as advertisement; they were now to display painted pictures of straw. In The Hague plague houses were marked with "PP" for "plague present," and in Roermond authorities affixed tin plates with "Jesus" on them to front doors of plague houses. All windows and doors had to remain shut (a common provision), though the top half of Dutch doors could remain open for short periods each day. Anyone who visited a victim's house had to carry a white wand in public for two weeks thereafter. For six weeks after the last sick person died or recovered, those who remained could leave to buy things or attend church, but in Amsterdam only at St. Anthony's Chapel. They, too, had to carry the white wand and could not go near wells or other water supplies.

Development in England   The practice of shutting in plague victims in London began in 1518 under the administration of Cardinal Wolsey. It was applied sporadically until Queen Elizabeth's government, which was established during a plague year, began taking stronger and coordinated measures to limit the effects of pestilence. In 1568 the houses of plague victims were shut up for 20 days with all family members, sick or well, inside. To their doors were nailed paper signs praying, "Lord have mercy on us." An "honest and discrete person" paid by the parish provisioned them each day and called the gravediggers as needed. The city paid for food if necessary, and officers burned all the victim's clothes and bedding. In 1578 the statutory plague orders were revisited and the quarantine period extended to six weeks. The trend was toward greater coercion: in 1604 Parliament declared that watchmen could use "violence" to keep shut-ins restricted; people out in public with evident plague sores could be considered felons and hung; and a healthy person who had been shut in and was found outside illicitly could be whipped as a vagrant. Provincial English towns had their problems with the policy, especially providing for the poor shut-ins who could not earn a living. Seeking aid from the county in 1593 Leicester's mayor complained to the Earl of Huntingdon that funds to support the shut-in poor were hard to come by; plague expenses had risen to over £500. The town was now supplying each house with "meat, drink, fire, candle, water, soap, [and a] keeper." But there was no guarantee of support, even in the nation's capital. In 1593 the London Puritan William Reynolds wrote in a scathing letter to Queen Elizabeth's Lord Burghley,

a woman of mine own knowledge, being sick and great with child, ready to be delivered, travailed in great anguish, and both she and her child died, having no help of man nor woman. O you dogs, O you devils, you villainous villains, that lock up the sick in outrageous manner, not regarding them to visit them as their necessity requires.[3]

About the same time the equally rhetorical physician Simon Forman, who had been a plague doctor earlier, found himself shut in with an apparently sick servant and he was none too happy for it. He wailed in a later plague tract:

O how much is the malice of cursed caterpillars of a commonwealth. They might have considered that I bought not the plague with money, neither did I go abroad to seek it. But it was the visitation of the most highest [God] . . . In the last plague I fled not from them, they were glad then of both my presence and counsel. I did not then shut up my compassion from any, nor my doors as they have done to me.[4]

In 1604, 20 percent of Salisbury's population found itself shut in (411 houses with 1,300 people), while the small village of Stone in Staffordshire was supporting 115 shut-in families. The well-off tried to avoid being shut in by concealing plague deaths, a trick even arrogant authorities played. A servant at the home of John Taylor, an alderman of Gloucester, died of plague in 1604 and the family secretly buried him. A second servant also contracted the disease and underwent treatment by a female medical practitioner. At a dinner party the suffering servant even waited upon several of Gloucester's civic leaders. After he and several others died, the deception was uncovered, Taylor fined £100, and the Taylor house shut up. Taylor's son broke out, however, and threatened to shoot anyone who tried to close up the house again. Constables captured him and locked him in the town's stocks.

The practice continued during the Great Plague of 1665 and the controversy still raged. Some complained of sacrificing the sick to save the well, some claimed that this action angered God and prolonged the epidemic, and others pointed to the fact that the policy actually backfired. In his tract entitled *Shutting up Infected Houses,* an anonymous author noted that "infection may have killed its thousands, but shutting up hath killed its ten thousands." Twenty years earlier John Fealty, chaplain to King Charles I, wrote *Tears against the Plague* as a devotional for a "gentlewoman of his acquaintance." Reprinted during the Great Plague, it retained its terrible currency:

Pestilence consumes and hunger cries; thus the visited die they know not of what; for sickness calls, and hunger calls, and want calls, and sorrow calls; all of them join in their hideous concord, in their horrid discord, and call for our ruin and yell for our destruction.[5]

The stench inside shut-up houses must have been profound, as normal human and animal odors blended with the smoke of materials burnt for fumigation: niter, tar, tobacco, resin, sulfur, gunpowder, and aromatic woods in wealthier homes, old shoes and leather scraps in poorer ones. Little wonder that people fought the authorities, people like young Taylor or the three men from Hamburg, Germany, a city that also practiced shutting in, who broke out and fled into the countryside. They were found dead of the disease in a barn by officials who promptly burned the structure to the ground. Half a century after the Great Plague of 1665 Englishman Daniel Defoe wrote his stunning "history" and cautionary tale *Journal of the Plague Year* at a time when Marseille, France, was suffering an especially horrific plague episode. His protagonist, H. F., admits the problem of balancing personal liberty with public necessity, but rails against the practice on three grounds: people escape, so it does not work; shutting the well in with the sick is both inhumane and "medically outrageous"; and those who have the disease but no signs still roam about freely. Voluntary isolation was fine, thought H. F., but coercion futile. Nonetheless, fear was a powerful impetus: At Bubnell near plague-wracked Eyam an ill man was supposed by his neighbors to have the plague, so they posted a guard outside his door to pelt him with rocks should he try to walk outside. A doctor's examination revealed he merely had a cold.

HOSPITALS

Medieval Hospitals and Leprosaria   In antiquity Romans had borrowed from the Greeks healing shrines *(asklepieia)* where the sick waited and prayed to the gods for healing. In their *valetudinaria* ill or injured slaves and soldiers found relief. It took the Christian concept of charity, however, to inspire hospices and hospitals where all injured and sick found refuge and care. These facilities took root in the fourth century and paralleled the development of monasteries—isolated residences of men or women (monks and nuns) who dedicated themselves to prayer and community life. The Greek-speaking St. Basil is thought to have created in Caesarea the first hospice for lepers *(leprosarium)*, who suffered from a hideous disease long considered a punishment from God. Leprosaria sprang up in the Eastern Empire to remove lepers from society, moving west with returning Crusaders—especially the Knights Hospitaller—in the twelfth century. By the later thirteenth century there may have been as many as 19,000 of these charitable institutions scattered across Europe. In larger Muslim cities *bimaristans* had been tending the sick since the tenth century, and Jewish communities in German cities established their own hospitals as early as 1210. In France, church councils in 506 and 511 declared that each diocese should create and support at least one hospital, following the example of the *Maison-Dieu* (House of God) in Arles, founded in 503.

England's earliest hospital was St. Peter's, York, which was established with the support of King Athelstan, and by the 1270s there were several hundred in Britain. As with hospitals elsewhere, those in Britain were usually associated with monasteries, convents, or priories and staffed by monks or nuns, though lay nobles, wealthy merchants, urban guilds, and even city governments generally established them. Hospitals supported themselves with the gifts of money, land, or buildings provided by living donors or through wills. They tended or simply housed the unwell, the poor, the cleric, the orphan, the aged, and the pilgrim as each institution saw fit. Larger cities had several hospitals that often specialized in one or more of these clienteles; for example, some that handled mainly orphans also set up grammar schools. The sick received rudimentary treatment from nurses and surgeons, though rarely physicians. The point was not to cure the person so much as to provide relief during natural recovery or prior to death. The famous Heilig Geist Spital (Holy Ghost Hospital) in Nuremberg, Germany, was established in 1339 by a rich merchant and run by three female administrators responsible for, respectively, general care of the sick, food preparation, and provision of alms to the poor and their inspection for diseases. The medieval Maison-Dieu in Paris had a staff of 47 nuns. Medieval cities tended to be well served by hospitals, but these often served multiple purposes and among these the least important was curing illness.

By the mid-sixteenth century several trends had changed the face of hospitalization in Europe. Lepers and leprosaria had all but disappeared. Many smaller foundations had also closed their doors as donations dropped off or larger **Early Modern Hospitals** institutions filled their roles. In Protestant areas Catholic monasteries shut down and hospitals either closed or became wards of the city or state. The Black Death had forced hospitals into a corner: either they had to expand significantly and make special arrangements for plague victims, or they had to exclude plague patients. One way to make more room was to limit their functions as way-stations and hospices, allowing them to concentrate on the sick, especially the poor.

Florence had 35 hospitals by the 1520s. Its largest, with 260 beds (most serving two patients at a time), was Santa Maria Nuova, which was founded by a rich merchant in 1288. Target of much generous giving, it was the size of a large church and similarly cross-shaped, with an altar at the crossing so all patients could witness the daily Mass. Englishman Thomas Linacre studied in Florence and brought the plans and statutes for the institution back to London. Following this model King Henry VII began a new hospital, St. John of the Savoy, in 1505, and Henry VIII finished it a dozen years later. As in a modern homeless shelter the poor were admitted to fill empty beds on a nightly basis; only the sick could stay longer. The guests, all males, were formally welcomed at the main door, led to the chapel to pray for the founder, then to their beds and to women who bathed them and cleaned their clothes. Twelve women worked here, none under 50 years of age. By the Reformation era London had 34 hospitals and almshouses (for the poor). As part of his reformation, however, Henry closed many of these religious houses, including the Savoy in 1553, but created or reestablished five as royal hospitals between 1547 and 1553.

In France the Wars of Religion and conflicts with the Habsburgs drove off many of the orders that ran the hospitals, leaving the buildings to serve as warehouses, schools, and even brothels. Fewer women entered nursing orders, and secular authorities often assumed control of the hospitals that remained, funding them from the taxes designated for the poor. The church and government maintained many hospitals

Interior of the Hôtel Dieu in Paris in the sixteenth century. The king looks on as the patients in the middle ground receive attention, food, or communion; corpses are sewn into their shrouds in the foreground; and the altar stands empty in the center background. National Library of Medicine.

in sixteenth- and seventeenth-century Paris, offering asylum, hospitality, assistance, alms, medical care, and a place to await death. By the mid-1600s, 10 percent of Parisians died in the Hôtel-Dieu and almost 28 percent in hospitals generally. One did not choose to go to these places, and primarily the poor populated their wards. Surgeons rather than physicians tended the sick in most hospitals, but under royal patronage physicians began to serve in the seventeenth century. Louis XIV was an especially caring patron.

Elsewhere in Catholic Europe the Council of Trent and Catholic Reformation movement spurred piety and the provision of hospitals for "God's poor," and female nursing orders thrived. Meanwhile, Protestant city governments, challenged by the closures of monastic hospitals and the banning of religious orders, fully secularized health care and poor relief. Yet even at their best, hospitals were wretched places. In seventeenth-century England critics complained of ignorant and useless nurses, lack of privacy, the scarcity and filthiness of linens, absent doctors, and a lack of isolation of contagious patients. Today we would add horribly unsanitary conditions and a lack of antiseptics, though neither was much of a concern at the time.

In 1442 the local indigent hospital at Bourg-en-Bresse, France, accidentally admitted a patient with the plague. **Hospitals** As others took sick the local authorities locked everyone **and Plague** in. Within a few weeks, all had died. At a similar rural **Victims** hospital for poor men near St. Flour in the Haut-Auvergne of France, plague likewise struck the population. When the administrators sought to lock everyone in, the residents rebelled, seeking to be separated from the infected. They won, and the sick were taken to live in a tumble-down farmhouse near the local mill. Soon the local villagers caught the plague and all ended up wandering the fields together. Around 1400 Paris's Hôtel-Dieu had a normal occupancy of 100 to 400; in plague time the actual occupancy rose to between 1,000 and 1,500, with inexperienced lay staff replacing the religious caretakers who had died. The hospitals of medieval and early modern Europe were in no way prepared to deal either with those dying of plague or the scale on which they died. Nonetheless, in lieu of shutting in or when dealing with homeless plague victims, hospitals were the first places that the sick were warehoused. The Carmelite friar Jean de Venette wrote of the situation in 1348:

The mortality was so great that, for a considerable period, more than 500 bodies a day were being taken in carts from the Hôtel-Dieu in Paris for burial in the cemetery of the Holy Innocents. The saintly sisters of the Hôtel-Dieu, not fearing death, worked sweetly and with great humility, setting aside considerations of earthly dignity. A great number of the sisters were called to a new life by death . . .

Townspeople in Dijon, Burgundy, rioted in 1553 and 1629 to force the authorities to allow plague victims to enter the local Hôtel-Dieu, from which they had been banned for their supposed contagiousness. In Florence through much of the fifteenth century Santa Maria Nuova served as a plague hospital; after 1479 Santa Maria della Scala filled this role, and in the early sixteenth century San Bastiano outside the city walls and the convent of San Salvi housed plague victims. For a Roman Catholic the advantage of dying in a hospital was ready access to the sacrament of extreme unction, or last rites, which had to be performed by a priest. An official of Santa Maria Nuova wrote around 1500 that after the sacrament, "we place before [the dying victim] an image of Christ on the Cross, and a nurse watches over him, never leaving him, and reading him the Creed, the Lord's Passion, and other holy texts."[6] Yet no matter how dignified the care they provided in normal times, when plague struck hospitals were simply overwhelmed.

The Roman plague hospital of Santo Spirito with its palisade and guards. In the foreground an animal catcher drags a dead dog to be thrown into the Tiber River. National Library of Medicine.

HUTS AND CABINS

With or without hospitals and shutting in, most large towns and cities during plague time had a surplus of victims that had to be either driven away or housed cheaply and at a distance from the town. In the late 1300s Milan's Giangaleazzo Visconti ordered that the sick who had houses would be shut in with their families while the many homeless would be housed outside of the city in a "healthy" area. For these people the state built *mansiones* that were 6 meters (19 feet) broad with painted walls and furnishings, located a "stone's throw" from each other so inhabitants did not have to hear each others' groans. These unfortunates would be served by a state-supplied doctor, barber, and apothecary.

When plague struck Edinburgh in 1529 the city's magistrates decided to house victims in huts built on the "sick moor," denying them access to the city. During the epidemic of 1565–1566 both the infected and those suspected of infection were marched to huts on the "foul moor." Family members could visit them, but only in the company of an official and only after 11:00 A.M. The death penalty was decreed for those who entered the grounds earlier. Afterward, visitors were quarantined for several days in huts built on the "clean moor" before being allowed to return home. "Bailies of the Moor" dressed in gray robes with white crosses oversaw the pitiful village. The city of York constructed a virtual village of huts in nearby Layerthorpe for the sick in 1538, but squatters moved in afterward. By the next epidemic in 1550 it had grown into a real suburb and the authorities had to run the inhabitants out to allow the victims to reuse the quarters. In the 1590s Carlisle leased land near the water for plague lodges or "shields." These small huts had timber frames and bundles of brushwood for walls, doors but no windows, straw-covered dirt floors, and roofs made of turf. Each was served by a nurse who made two shillings plus per week at a time when grave-diggers were making ten. In Huby, Yorkshire, the commons came to be called Cabinlands from the pesthuts constructed there during each epi-demic. Oxford, home of the university and brilliant men, built cabins that could be dismantled, stored in the Guildhall, and rebuilt quickly when needed. That these cabins were often the simplest of shelters is clear from the Nottingham Council's order of 1646: "that the tops of trees be kept to make huts for people infected or suspected to be infected with the plague." Leicester housed its victims in shacks built in a garden plot the city bought for ten guineas. Life in these shantytowns could have been nothing better than horrible, even when the sick were tended regularly. Those who retained their strength often assaulted the guards and ran off, or otherwise ignored or defied authority, despite heavy pen-alties. In the plague village near Manchester in 1605 one male victim became notorious for his behavior and was chained in his cabin. Even so he broke free several times. The magistrates in Manchester complained that people like this needed to be treated like slaves and kept in chains lest they revolt together and burn Manchester to the ground.

In Shakespeare's time London built and administered scattered huts derisively called "cages," each of which could hold a single victim. As the new king, Charles I, approached London's government for his coronation in 1625 the royal Privy Council feared that he might contract the plague; they ordered that "small Tents and Cabins" be built outside of town in open spaces. The infected were to stay one month, but whether they lived or died their possessions and the cabin would be burnt to ashes. The coun-cil tried this tactic again in 1630, but to little effect; nonetheless, in 1636 London authorities authorized justices of the peace to build timber huts as necessary, grouping them in small communities with stinking burial pits close at hand. Men received 7 shillings per week to carry corpses from the huts to the pits, while the gravediggers made 11 shillings per week. As the plague gained strength again in spring 1637, the magistrates decreed that all members of any infected house were to be removed to the pest cabins in an attempt to stanch the pestilence before it washed over the city again. At one point during the Great Plague of 1665 London authori-ties ordered all the sick removed to pest houses, sheds, and huts so that

Broadside memorializing Theatine Catholic priest Giulio a Ponte, who died while serving plague victims in the streets. Note the crucifixes clutched in their hands, and the simple shelter in which one sick priest is housed. Genoa, seventeenth century. National Library of Medicine.

the family members might stay and have a chance at survival. The Earl of Craven rented four acres—an area later known as Pest House Close—near St. Martin's in the Fields on which he had 36 huts built for victims. Even with these measures, over 100,000 Londoners died by year's end.

On the continent similar dreadful villages sprang up, often outside overcrowded plague hospitals. Beginning in the 1520s the Florentines had to augment their hospitals with a shantytown of plague huts. In 1576 the landscape of San Erasmo Island in the Venetian lagoon sported 1,200 such huts. When the plague summer of 1630 turned toward a potentially deadly winter, the Senate had shipbuilders construct a shantytown; in December they ordered construction of several thousand beds for sufferers. Miquel Parets, a tanner of Barcelona, relates how he and his family escaped the city during the plague of 1653 and traveled to stay with relatives. Before being allowed to enter their village they had to be quarantined in a simple lean-to for several weeks. As late as 1771, near Starodub, Ukraine, a quarantine station consisted of "straw huts and dugouts . . . in a remote forest."[7] Shacks, shelters, sheds, cabins, huts, lean-tos, *mansiones,* and tents all served to house the unfortunate. Perhaps grimmest of all were those created in 1628 by the Hôpital Saint-Laurent of Lyon on the right bank of the Saône River. With the pest house holding up to 4,000 at a time, alongside timber shanties temporary shelters were built of stiff corpses piled one upon another.

THE PEST HOUSE

Hospitals were not designed to isolate individuals or to deal with contagious diseases;[8] leprosaria served this function.   **Origins** For reasons not entirely understood the incidence of leprosy in Europe declined radically with the onset of the Second Pandemic. From the beginning some of the leprosaria scattered about the countryside took in plague victims. Dublin's Leopardstown was once Leperstown, and, before the euphemistic name change, served the city's plague victims as well. But it quickly became clear everywhere that these leprosaria were too small to handle the vast numbers affected at one time. Nonetheless, the idea of an isolated, specialized treatment facility like the leprosarium for plague victims caught on. These buildings would be known as pest houses, lazar houses, or *lazaretti* (Italian, singular *lazaretto;* variously spelled in different languages), named, as were many leprosaria, for Lazarus, the poor man with sores in the Gospel parable whom the rich man ignored at the peril of his soul (e.g., Luke 16:19–31).

In much of Europe a lazaret was simply a large facility such as a monastery or hospital that was seized by authorities for use in plague time. For its first pest house Barcelona purchased the Dominican convent of *Angels vells* (Old Angels) outside of St. Daniel Gate in 1562 and forced the community out. In the case of the Florentine-controlled town of Prato, Italy, the Tuscan Health Magistracy denied the town's request for a pest house as plague approached in the summer of 1630, wishing not to appear alarmist. By October local authorities had turned the hospital of San Silvestro into a plague facility, with beds, fuel, food, and medicine provided by the town's other large hospital, the Misericordia. The city paid salaries for about 25 medical personnel, gravediggers, messengers, cooks, and others. But San Silvestro was inside the town walls, and escaped inmates who wandered about threatened Prato's healthy citizens. The authorities decided to move the victims and targeted two large monasteries outside of town. Neither community wanted the burden, and both argued against having to receive it. In the end, both religious communities relocated; one monastery served temporarily as the lazaretto and the other as a convalescent home for those who survived.

In many cities, especially ports, governments did build permanent quarters for plague victims or quarantine stations for incoming people and merchandise, often using them or leasing them out for other purposes when the plague was absent. These measures were, however, both expensive and depressing, as they served as an admission that pestilence was likely to return. In contemporary documents the terms pest house and lazaretto also referred to the shantytowns of tents and huts that were either freestanding or surrounded the actual pest house building, as at Pest House Close. At Leicester the "pest house" was tossed together in a garden bought for 10 guineas, while Dublin's was put up in the garden of shoemaker William Stuoks, who occupied a house in what had been the Augustinian convent of All Hallows, later the site of Trinity College. Additionally, "pest houses" may have served only as leprosaria or for later, nonplague epidemics such as smallpox. Indeed, the many "Pest House Lanes" in England are not all directly connected to the Black Death at all. All of this makes historical reconstruction of "pest houses" in Europe rather complicated.

Examples of Pest Houses One of the earliest known isolation facilities developed in the later 1300s near Venetian-governed Ragusa (Dubrovnik) on the Island of Mljet in an old convent transformed for the purpose. A second, specifically built as a lazaretto, was added in 1429 on the Isle of Supetar. Venice herself opened a temporary isolation hospital in 1403, and the Senate built a permanent facility in 1424. In plague time this facility was inadequate to handle both cases in the city and the quarantining of (generally quite healthy) ships' crews and travelers. The Senate added a second lazaretto, the *lazaretto nuovo*, in 1468. In the 1440s Milan used the Villa at Cusago as a hospital for the poor and ill, converting it to a plague hospital in 1451. But the notary Lazzaro Cairati, who worked for the Ospedale Maggiore, dreamed of a great pest house on the Venetian model. He proposed to the duke a facility of 200 small rooms that opened onto an enormous square courtyard, as in Venice, a space that would house a plague village of huts during epidemics. He recommended locating it in Crescenzago, a small town about five miles from Milan and connected to the city by a canal down which the sick could be transported. Uncharacteristically for a Milanese duke, Giangaleazzo Maria Sforza heeded the complaints of the locals and shelved the plan. During the plague-ridden 1480s his successor revived it, locating the pest house much closer to the city. The cornerstone was laid in 1488 and it took two decades to complete; even then, it was not fully operational until 1524. San Gregorio Lazaretto at Porta Orientale had 288 rooms that measured 15 feet to a side, and an

Nineteenth-century woodcut of the courtyard of the Milanese pest house. Note the chapel in the middle. National Library of Medicine.

open altar for Mass dominated the middle of the courtyard that measured 413 × 405 yards. In Naples in 1587 the Brothers Hospitaller of St. John of God built the lazaretto connected with Santa Maria della Pace as a single great hall, 30 feet wide and 180 feet long, with a frescoed ceiling 36 feet above the floor.

NOVELIST ALESSANDRO MANZONI DESCRIBES THE CHAPEL IN MILAN'S LAZARETTO

The octagonal chapel which arises, raised on a few steps in the middle of the lazaretto, was open in its original construction on all sides with no other support than pillars and columns—a building, as it were, in filigree. In each façade there was an arch between two columns, while inside, round what might be called the church proper, ran an arcade composed only of eight arches, corresponding to those on the façades, with a cupola on top; so that the altar erected in the center could be seen from the window of every room in the enclosure, and from almost any point in the camp.

From Alessandro Manzoni, *The Betrothed* (New York: Dutton, 1951), p. 557.

The earliest known formal pest houses in France appeared in the later 1400s. Bourg-en-Bresse, whose indigent hospital had suffered thirty years earlier, built a permanent isolation facility in 1472, the *maison de pesti-fiérés*. The town may have been spurred to do so by neighboring Brou, to whose designated plague house they had been taking their sick since 1472. In 1477 the lazarette was filled and Bourg again sent many of its sick to Brou, though this time offering to provide them with food. Parisian authorities expressed the need for a lazarette as early as 1496 but did not begin one in earnest until 1580, when they enacted numerous other anti-plague measures. Modeled on the Milanese lazaretto, the structure was never completed and the foundation was eventually demolished. Henry IV spearheaded the effort to build a new lazarette, however, and his Hôpi-tal St. Louis was constructed between 1607 and 1612.

Agnes van Leeuwenbergh of Utrecht bequeathed her fortune to the city to be used for the poor. City officials decided to use it to build a *pesthuis* near the city's eastern wall. Still standing, its 5,400-square-foot open floor is covered by two gabled roofs that run down the length of the structure, meeting in an arcade that splits the hall in two, one side for women and the other for men. When not used for plague victims it served as a guest-house for the needy and travelers. In contrast, pest houses in the English countryside were often little more than large houses, as those that survive at Findon, Suffolk, and Odiham, Hampshire, which locals built in 1622. Croyden's stood in the Commons, at a distance from the town, and was a two-story structure of brick and tiles. Today, *pesthuizen* and *Pesthäuser* in Dutch and German cities may only be noticeable from plaques or sculp-tures on the façades, or from the small doors embedded in the street-front portals, through which trays of food and medicines were passed to the inmates.

Personnel and Administration   Throughout the Second Pandemic those who worked directly with plague victims ran a very high risk of con-tracting the disease, and thus a very high risk of dying. Those who had passing contact, like doctors, notaries, or clergy, covered their noses and mouths with vinegar-soaked cloths or used other filters, or maintained their distance by serving communion at the end of a long rod or examining the patient's urine while standing out-side a window. Those who worked in pest houses, whether religious or lay, convicted criminals or selfless volunteers, were threatened by death at every turn. Thomas Lodge suggested they carry pomanders, apples, oranges, or lemons near their noses as prophylactics, while Cardinal Geronimo Gastaldi, the head of Rome's Plague Magistracy in 1656, rec-ommended the dried-toad powder touted by Dr. Van Helmont. By the seventeenth century pest-house workers, like gravediggers and corpse-carriers, often wore waxed or oil-cloth gowns to thwart the contagion, however it spread. The staff lived together—Milan's huge lazaretto had 8 of its 288 rooms set aside for staff—and were never to interact with the healthy outside the facility. The Florentine lazaretto at the Benedictine monastery of San Miniato above the city in 1630 had a staff of 2 physicians, 9 surgeons, 5 friars, and 134 lay personnel to serve nearly 800 patients at a time. It was typical in Italy for friars to serve as administrators and as confessors in lazaretti.

It was also typical to have few, if any, physicians on staff. When the Florentine Health Board required the College of Physicians to provide the two doctors, the College replied that such was "tantamount to a death sentence" and would gladly examine and certify anyone from another part of Tuscany that the Board recommended. During the same plague, the physician's guild in Bologna complained that this service was "certain death" after eight of their colleagues had succumbed. A quarter century later Cardinal Gastaldi reflected that coercion was the only way to staff lazaretti since "high fees and special prizes were not enough to induce doctors to go and tend people in the pest houses."[9] In Geneva the candidate Jean Pernet offered himself as a candidate for pest-house physician, but he first "was examined to discover if he was wise enough to console the poor plague victims and to provide them with treatment." Pernet served with a barber-surgeon and a minister and received a house and an annual salary of 240 florins. He died after two weeks. Three years later a much less skilled barber-surgeon from Dutch Zeeland was hired at an annual salary of 360 florins and a free house, a sign of the soaring demand for medical staff.

Aside from the doleful sights, the omnipresent threat of death, and the profound stench, the medical staff, like the inmates, suffered from fleas. Father Antero Maria wrote of Genoa's lazaretto in 1657,

I have to change my clothes frequently if I do not want to be devoured by fleas, armies of which nest in my gown . . . If I want to rest for an hour in bed I have to use a sheet, otherwise the lice would feast on my flesh; they vie with the fleas—the latter suck, the former bite . . . All of the bodily torments which are of necessity suffered in the lazaretti cannot compare even to the fleas.

At least the good father had a change of clothes:

As pest house surgeon in Tuscany Diacinto [Gramigna] had served for almost eight months lancing buboes, cauterizing wounds, practicing bloodletting, catching the plague, recovering from the plague—and he always wore the same suit of clothes.

As a *recognitione* by the authorities, when the plague had subsided Diacinto was awarded 15 ducats, specifically for a new suit. Wise administrators rewarded personnel who did their duty and did it well, like Matron Margaret Blague of St. Bartholomew's Hospital in London. When both of the institution's physicians fled to the countryside in 1665, she remained at her post and received recognition "for her attendance and constant great pains about the poor in making them broths, candles, and other like comfortable things for their accommodation in these late contagious times, wherein she had adventured herself to the great peril of her life."[10]

The records, however, tell us far more about the sinners than the saints. In 1630 Father Dragoni, the main plague official in tiny Monte Lupo, Tuscany, had to evict and lock up the lazaretto's apothecary "because he played cards and had dealings with everyone indiscriminately, and I discovered he introduced women from Monte Lupo into the pest house to eat and drink and at night to sleep with him." The tanner Miquel Parets of Barcelona wrote of how orderlies in the pest house there preyed on attractive female plague victims for sex: "only bad women had good food." He continued, "It was truly said that there was great lewdness in the pest house regarding women; that it was like a little brothel." At Haverfordwest, Wales, one female patient complained of being treated "worse than a whore." At San Miniato the assistant Federigo Tergolzzi was caught stealing mattresses, blankets, and pillows to resell. Other workers were jailed and punished for stealing the belongings that inmates brought with them lest thieves rob their empty houses—a reasonable fear, as court cases and Archbishop Federico Borromeo of Milan testify. Locks, bars, and chains proved to be mere challenges, not deterrents. Miquel Parets tells us that Barcelona's authorities solved the unskilled-personnel problem by sending convicted thieves to work in the pest house—if they were not working there already. The tanner complained of the terrible general conditions of the pest house: "It is known for certain that more people died in the [pest house] of bad organization and poor food than of the plague itself." In England nurses were accused of killing off their charges by smothering or poisoning them, and doctors and surgeons by malpractice or malice. Incompetence and a lack of the spirit necessary to deal with the horrors crippled many medical professionals, as Dr. Leandro Ciminelli reported in 1630 to the Florentine chancellor. Ciminelli described working conditions at San Bonifazio Hospital in Naples:

Crowds of plague-stricken people are coming here, and it is impossible to stem the tide of pestilence with inexpert people who are not used to witnessing death, and it will grow all the more as the doctors' own fear grows . . . Now we have to [ensure] that all hospital doctors know how to deal with this disease and to assist patients . . .[11]

Finally, in 1530 a number of Geneva's pest-house attendants were accused of deliberately spreading plague by smearing a plague ointment on healthy people's doors. One confessed under torture; two were tortured with hot pincers and then beheaded; two women had their hands cut off in front of their "victims'" houses before being executed; the priest Father Dufour was first defrocked and then executed by the civil authorities.

Although Archbishop Borromeo claimed that most people who entered Milan's great lazaretto did so in order to die with the plenary indulgence[12] granted by the pope to all who died there, one can hardly imagine people willingly **Life in the Pest House** condemning themselves to its horrors. In every large town and city huge carts collected the sick and dying—and often the well who lived with them—each day. The practice of mixing the sick to be treated and the well to be quarantined was not uncommon in Continental Europe, but rare in Britain. In 1644–1646 the city of Bristol experimented with this practice, but it proved too expensive and was greatly and vociferously resented by the public. From Brescia, Italy, and Marseille come reports that in the terrible plague of 1630 carts picked up 10 or 12 people at a time, only one of whom was showing plague symptoms; in time all died. At Milan 50 to 60 arrived at a time, among whom only one was sick and taken to the infirmary; the remainder were quarantined elsewhere and survived. Borromeo paints pathetic pictures of the sick headed for the lazaretto:

Often were seen sons carrying parents on their shoulders on their way to recover in the courtyard of the Lazaretto with great weeping by he who carried them and they fell under the weight . . . Parents carried away their children to the Lazaretto and with their own hands place them on the wagons, not permitting the *becchini* to touch them."[13]

In London in 1603 patients were expected to bring money for their maintenance with them, even though most were quite poor, and families were also expected to pay for their servants. At Barcelona in 1651 the carts carried the mattresses and bedding of the sick while the gravediggers carried

A street scene in plague-time Rome during the seventeenth century. Corpses are loaded onto the tumbrel at right, sick people are taken to the pest house in the carriage at center, and armed guards look on from the left. National Library of Medicine.

the sick themselves. Here the pest house was so crowded, Parets says, "that a sick person who did not bring along a mattress and bedclothes had to lie on the [bare] ground." At Barcelona and Leiden, Holland—and no doubt elsewhere—the sick were transported only at night, which had to mean terrible jostling and much stumbling about as workers toiled by flickering torch or pale moonlight.

Viennese plague victims in 1712 were transported to the Pesthaus in special sedan chairs carried by porters. An official took data (name, age, occupation, etc.) on the arrivals and recorded their sedan chair numbers. A surgeon examined and questioned the patients and priests offered last rites to those who were Catholic. Patients were then placed in the appropriate ward (male or female) with their medical histories attached to the foot of each bed. Each ward had two attendants on duty at all times, and a fire burned to purify the air. The sick, arranged by severity of symptoms, received visits twice a day by a physician and a surgeon who wore amulets of mercury and arsenic around their necks to absorb the "poison" in the breath of the patients. The poor received free treatment; the wealthier were tended to in private rooms at cost. Officials burned all of the victim's belongings, and the victim's family was quarantined in their home, with food regularly left for them at a distance from their front door. This comparatively civilized manner of treatment dates from the end of the pandemic, though, and would have proved impractical under most serious epidemic conditions.

Testimonies to the plight of plague patients are legion and horrifying. In Bologna during the 1630 plague Cardinal Spada reported that

here you see people lament, others cry, others strip themselves to the skin, others die, others become black and deformed, others lose their minds. Here you are overwhelmed by intolerable smells. Here you cannot walk but among corpses. Here you feel naught but the constant horror of death. This is the painful replica of hell since there is no order and horror prevails.

In the wake of the same epidemic the notary and reformer Rocco Benedetti reported to the Venetian Health Office:

[T]he Lazaretto Vecchio[14] seemed like Hell itself. From every side there came foul odors, indeed a stench that none could endure; groans and sighs were heard without ceasing; and at all hours clouds of smoke from the burning of corpses were seen to rise far into the air. . . . Nobody did anything but lift the dead from the beds and throw them into the pits. It often happened that those who were close to death or senseless, without speech or movement, were lifted up by the corpse-bearers (*pizzicamorti*) as though they had expired, and thrown onto the heap of bodies. Should one of them be seen to move hand or foot, or signal for help, it was truly good fortune if some corpse-bearer, moved to pity, took the trouble to go and rescue him. . . . Sometimes at the height of the plague 7,000 to 8,000 sick persons languished in the Lazaretto Vecchio.

Francesco Borromeo echoed the regime of chaos in that pest house:

A woman, pushed to madness by the sickness, for five days ran around naked in a headlong course and chewed through and broke the ropes with which she had to be tied down, and with equal violence tore up the clothes thrown on her for the sake of modesty.[15]

Pistoia's Dr. Arrighi sent in a requisition to the Florence Health Board in 1630 for leather straps "to tie down patients who go out of their minds." In another (almost comic) case, Borromeo relates how a plague sufferer came to believe he was the pope and became agitated when none of the friars would kiss his foot. He went on a hunger strike for five days, stopping only when the prior had some of them kiss his foot as a joke. The man calmed down, ate, and recovered.

When G. B. Arconato, president of Milan's Board of Health, visited the pest house in 1629, "he went into a dead faint for the stinking smells that came from all those bodies and those little rooms." In San Miniato near Florence plague victims slept five to a bed for lack of facilities. Dr. Arrighi reported the same conditions, adding that in Pistoia "nothing we need is here: there are no bandages for bloodletting, nor cloth for dressing tumors, and there are no attendants!" There and elsewhere pest-house staff went door to door seeking donations of bedding, clothes, and other necessities. In one campaign the director received 1 old feather mattress, 3 old feather pillows, 3 wooden bed-frames, 4 blankets, and 22 sheets. Some resourceful and pragmatic administrators gathered up the bedding and clothes that were set to be burned by officials: even if the stuff was "infected," so were their patients.[16]

Mothers who were pregnant or nursing infants provided some of the sorriest sights. All records of the Second Pandemic that mention pregnant women relate terrible mortality rates during plague times. In the pest house the situation was exacerbated. Pisan officials reported that of about a thousand pregnant women who entered their facility none survived, and of the many children who were born, only three lived. Borromeo recounts how a newborn cuddled in the arms of his dead mother survived by suckling for several days. In Barcelona, Parets tells us, the children

were labeled with a ribbon or tag around their arms or legs with the names of their parents on it, so that the parents would know if they ever got out, but hardly any of the babies sent there managed to survive because so many were sent there.

At Pistoia, Milan, and no doubt elsewhere, surviving infants were provided goat's milk, sometimes directly from the source. Borromeo noted that one nanny goat became so fond of her human charge that she would let no other suckle. Barcelona's pest houses hired wet nurses, often employed by upper-class families in normal times—each with five or six infants to care for. Parets claimed the nurses "are normally like cows, and are evil and uncaring women who would rather the children die than live . . . not changing or cleaning them." Many of these babies, he wrote, died of neglect rather than disease. Those who survived and were orphaned were often left to wander the streets untended.[17]

MANZONI ON THE "CAMP" IN THE MIDST OF MILAN'S LAZARETTO IN 1630

The reader must picture to himself the precincts of the lazaretto filled with sixteen thousand plague-stricken people; the whole area cluttered with cabins and sheds, with carts and human beings; those two unfinished ranges of arcades to right and left filled, crowded, with a confused mass of sick and dead, sprawling on mattresses or heaps of straw; all over this immense sty a perpetual movement like waves on the sea; here and there a coming and going, a stopping, a running, a bending and rising of convalescents, of madmen, of attendants.

From Alessandro Manzoni, *The Betrothed* (New York: Dutton, 1951), p. 544.

The "Italian model" that developed in the seventeenth century included provisions for convalescing plague victims, recognizing in part their need for comfort and in part the threat they still posed to society. In the case of Prato, recovering victims arrived at the convent of Sta. Anna in groups of up to 60 and stayed together for 22 days. Upon leaving Sta. Anna they all were to be washed thoroughly, their clothing burned and replaced with a new set. They were also to receive alms of 10 soldi (which were often not available). With or without the alms, these men, women, and children were the survivors, who, as nineteenth-century Italian novelist Alessandro Manzoni so eloquently put it in his great novel *The Betrothed*, "seemed to each other like people risen from the dead."[18] In 1656 at the gate to Rome's lazaretto on Tiburtina Island, once the site of a famed pagan healing shrine, officials posted lists of the dead to provide loved ones with some closure.

THE VENETIAN SENATE CREATES A PLAGUE-RECUPERATION HOSPITAL, 1468

The [pest house] called Nazareth, as everybody knows, has been and is of extraordinary assistance in preserving this city from the plague; but it cannot be wholly effective because those who leave Nazareth after being cured return immediately to Venice and infect and corrupt those persons with whom they associate. Measures must be taken to set matters right.

Be it therefore determined that our Salt Office shall by the authority of this council cause a hospital [lit. a *place*] to be built on the Vigna Murata ["Walled Vineyard" on the Island of Sant'Erasmo], as they see fit, and those who have left Nazareth must go to this hospital and remain there for forty days before they return to Venice. The expenses incurred in building this hospital shall be met from the proceeds of renting out the shops and quays which are government property. And, since the Vigna Murata belongs to the monks of San Giorgio, be it resolved that the [Salt] Officials shall pay these monks an annual rent of fifty ducats. The Officials shall be fully entitled to incur any expense, both in building the aforesaid place and in other matters, as they are with Nazareth.

By 1541 the "new" facility of 1468 was being called the Lazaretto Nuovo, and Venice had a Health Office, which issued the following decree:

To avoid all possible dangers, it must be noted that, when someone has recovered in the Lazarretto Vecchio [Nazareth] (his abscess [bubo] having been lanced and healed), he shall be sent to the Lazaretto Nuovo, taking no goods with him. There he shall stay for thirty days—that is, fifteen in the part of the Lazaretto called *prà* and fifteen in the part called *sanità* [health]— and then he shall be sent home, there to be under a ban for ten days. But, if someone has an abscess which has not been lanced but has resolved itself, he shall stay in the Lazaretto Nuovo for forty days—that is, twenty in the *prà* and twenty in the *sanità*. Then he shall be sent home, where he shall stay under a ban for ten days.

From David Chambers and Brian Pullen, eds., *Venice: A Documentary History, 1450–1630* (New York: Blackwell, 1992), pp. 115, 116.

The numbers of people crammed into pest houses during plague times are staggering. The largest are reported from Milan's vast lazaretto: up to 10,000 at a time in 1629 and 15,000 at the plague's peak in 1630. At its peak Florence's San Miniato's 175 beds held 900 patients, Padua's lazaretto over 2,000, and Verona's some 4,000. Hamburg's general hospital served as the *Pesthof* in the later seventeenth century and handled between 850 and 1,000 victims at a time, while Seville's well-run lazeret was stuffed with 2,600 patients when a group of monks established another facility.

Death in the Pest House

Even with such overcrowded and often horrible conditions the survival rate of pest-house inmates was quite high. Records show that 5,886 victims entered the lazaretti of San Miniato and San Francesco near Florence between September 1 and December 20, 1630. Of these, 2,886 died, for a survival (or at least discharge) rate of just about 50 percent. Historian Carlo Cipolla found very similar rates, between 50 and 60 percent—in other Italian towns of the period such as Pistoia, Prato, Empoli, Trent, and Carmagnola. These figures correspond to modern mortality rates of about 50 percent for untreated bubonic plague cases and compare very well with the situation in Ukraine in the 1770s, when pest-house mortality rates reached 76 to 80 percent.

For Daniel Defoe, looking back a lifetime to the horrors of London's Great Plague and the awful phenomenon of the pest houses, their very necessity was merely a part of God's punishment of vile humanity. He believed

Outside of the palisade of one of the Roman pest houses a crowd gathers to read the names of the latest plague victims to die within. Note that three gates separate the interior of the pest house from the general public. National Library of Medicine.

it was a great mistake that such a great city as this had but one[19] pest house: for had there been, instead of but one pest house . . . where at most they could receive 200 or 300 people . . . been several pest houses, everyone able to contain a thousand people without lying two in a bed, or two beds in a room; and had every master of a family as soon as any servant (especially) had been taken sick in his house, been obliged to send them to the next pest house . . . not so many, by several thousands, had died.[20]

Defoe, opponent of coerced shutting in and fan of pest houses, was quite correct in his characterization of the limitations of London's facilities. During the Great Plague of 1665, which took the lives of over 100,000 Londoners, the bills of mortality list a mere 312 plague deaths in all of the pest houses in the city and Westminster, or about one-third of 1 percent of all plague deaths in the city. This pales beside the figures for Worcester (25 percent) and Norwich (10 percent). In Prato, Italy, about 27 percent of the town's plague victims died in the lazaretto in 1630.

Often the central burial ground for a smaller town or rural area was directly associated with the pest-house grounds. Scattered reports describe the sick arriving in carts with the dead. This centralizing of function made both carting and grave digging much more efficient, and here the practice of mass burial in long trenches continued. And so the grunting of the corpse-bearers and the creak of the tumbrels' heavy wheels joined the low din of sighs punctuated with screams of pain and death's agony that wafted across the shantytowns and lazaretto courtyards day and night, season following deadly season of the Second Pandemic.

Barges filled with seventeenth-century Roman plague dead move along the Tiber River, passing the lazaretto of San Bartolommeo. National Library of Medicine.

Defoe's support aside, many people across Europe spoke out about the terrible policies and conditions of pest houses. Though the sick themselves were often too weak to resist, both convalescents and forcibly detained **Resistance and Resentment** family members often escaped or caused problems for the staff. At Norwich in 1631 a special prison was set up for these rowdies, and in 1666 a whipping post and stocks appeared at the pest house itself. Dr. Arrighi's leather straps no doubt kept down the rebellious as well as the insane. People complained of the mixing of well with sick, the breaking up of families, the prison-like conditions, the poor quality or lack of food, and the fact that the wealthy could avoid the pest house. Administrators and health boards bore the brunt of resentment, but civic leaders usually made the decisions that resulted in forced quarantining. When the mayor of Salisbury, England, tried to enforce the law he was challenged "whether I came of a woman or a beast that I do so bloody an act upon poor people in this condition."[21] In eighteenth-century Temesvár, Hungary, the locals resented their pest house so much that they burned down the houses surrounding it with the aim of destroying it. The closing and cleansing of the local pest house marked the official end of a time of terrible trials for the entire community, however small or large. It provided a moment for communal and personal hope and prayer and resolution to do and be better, lest God unleash his awful wrath yet again.

The growth of coercive power in the hands of the early modern state can easily be seen in the policies and practices dealing with plague victims. Forced shutting in and mandatory detention in pest houses of all types constituted an erosion of traditional rights that even medieval kings and clerics had respected. Christian charity may still have influenced the hearts of many who worked in the hell-holes that were the society's plague facilities, but the pragmatically defined necessity of stemming the tide of plague once it had settled in became paramount. Moreover, one should never forget the 50 percent of those who entered and suffered the experience and then found their way back into "normal society." Isolation, however inhumane, was the path to eradicating epidemic plague and creating a Western society that keenly protects human dignity and the rights that attend it.

NOTES

1. Robert Latham and Williams Matthews, eds., *The Diary of Samuel Pepys*, vol. VI (Berkeley: University of California Press, 2000), June 11 and August 25, 1665.

2. W. R. Albury and G. M. Weisz, "Erasmus of Rotterdam (1466–1536): Renaissance Advocate of the Public Role of Medicine," *Journal of Medical Biography* 11 (2003), p. 132.

3. William Kelly, "Visitations of the Plague at Leicester," in *Transactions of the Royal Historical Society* 6 (1877), pp. 403–4; Katherine Duncan-Jones, *Shakespeare's Life and World* (London: Folio, 2004), pp. 92–93.

4. Barbara Howard Traister, *The Notorious Astrological Physician of London: Works and Days of Simon Forman* (Chicago: University of Chicago Press, 2001), p. 13.

5. Paul Slack, "Responses to Plague in Early Modern England," in *Famine, Disease and the Social Order in Early Modern Society*, ed. Walter R. Schofield (New York: Cambridge University Press, 1989), p. 182; John Fealty and Scott Rutherford, *Tears Against the Plague* (Cambridge, MA: Rhwymbooks, 2000), p. 9.

6. Rosemary Horrox, ed., *The Black Death* (New York: Manchester University Press, 1994), pp. 55–56; Katherine Park and John Henderson, "The 'First Hospital among Christians': The Ospedale di Santa Maria Nuova in Early Sixteenth-Century Florence," *Medical History* 35 (1991), p. 183.

7. N. K. Borodi, "The History of the Plague Epidemic in the Ukraine in 1770–74," *Soviet Studies in History* 25 (1987), p. 41.

8. Though not understood at the time, bubonic plague is not contagious, though pneumonic plague is.

9. Carlo Cipolla, *Public Health and the Medical Profession in the Renaissance* (New York: Cambridge University Press, 1976), p. 78.

10. Carlo Cipolla, *Fighting the Plague in Seventeenth-Century Italy* (Madison: University of Wisconsin Press, 1981), p. 12 n. 12; Carlo Cipolla, *Cristofano and the Plague* (London: Collins, 1973), p. 118; Liza Picard, *Restoration London* (New York: Avon Books, 1997), p. 93.

11. Carlo Cipolla, *Faith, Reason and the Plague in Seventeenth-Century Tuscany* (New York: Norton, 1979), pp. 20–21, 82; Miquel Parets, *A Journal of the Plague Year: The Diary of the Barcelona Tanner Miquel Parets, 1651*, trans. James S. Amelang (New York: Oxford University Press, 1991), pp. 57–58, 67.

12. The church's guarantee that one would be absolved of all spiritual penalty for otherwise unforgiven sins. One also had to leave all belongings to the church.

13. Federico Borromeo, *La peste di Milano* (Milan: Rusconi, 1987), pp. 80, 81, 85; Parets, *Journal*, p. 55.

14. The "Old Lazaretto" was the primary pest house of the city of Venice.

15. Cipolla, *Cristofano*, p. 27; David Chambers and Brian Pullen, eds., *Venice: A Documentary History, 1450–1630* (New York: Blackwell, 1992), pp. 118–19; Borromeo, *Peste*, p. 67.

16. Cipolla, *Cristofano*, pp. 27, 88–89, and *Fighting*, pp. 61, 62.

17. Parets, *Journal*, p. 61.

18. Alessandro Manzoni, *The Betrothed*, trans. Archibald Colquhoun (New York: Dutton, 1951), p. 584.

19. There were in fact several, including two in Westminster.

20. Daniel Defoe, *A Journal of the Plague Year* (New York: Norton, 1992), pp. 63–64.

21. A. D. Dyer, "The Influence of Bubonic Plague in England, 1500–1667," *Medical History* 22 (1978), p. 319.

7

At City Hall

GOVERNING EUROPE'S CITIES

Long before the Second Pandemic European towns and cities had developed governing bodies and rules for administration that suited their size and relations to the larger duchy, kingdom, or empire in which they were located. Most governments used some form of classical Roman model that included one or several law-making councils, usually consisting of well-off citizens, and one or more major executives (mayors or consuls) responsible for overseeing the administration of law and justice. Both were assisted by record-keepers and scribes known as notaries, a profession developed in ancient Rome and revived with Roman law in the twelfth century. The notary had neither the university education nor status of a lawyer, but was well trained in the "notarial arts." These skills included Latin and its use in creating formal private documents such as wills and contracts as well as public documents such as charters, laws, diplomatic letters, and minutes of council meetings and criminal proceedings. Notaries, who often also served as local historians or chroniclers, penned most of the existing records of activities of medieval Europe's city governments.

Like members of most other skilled trades, crafts, and professions, notaries were organized into occupation-specific guilds. With their roots in ancient Rome, these officially chartered and oath-bound organizations regulated every aspect of a member's work life: employment as helper in a master's shop, training as an apprentice, development as a journeyman, and practice as an independent master. Guilds established acceptable wages, prices, training periods, and qualifications for entry. They also regulated the quality of products and restricted competition, both among members and from outsiders. To be a merchant, baker, banker, carpenter, lawyer, apothecary (pharmacist), physician, goldsmith, or even a judge meant being an active member of a self-regulating guild. In turn, city governments were often run by and for the guilds, with seats allocated to each of the more important ones. With a total population in the 1340s of around 35,000 people London had some 1,200 different guilds and fraternities (brotherhoods), while much-larger Florence (around 100,000) had only 73.

The elected members of city councils might directly represent the economic interests of the "bourgeois" (*burgher*, burgess, *borghese*) class, but in many parts of Europe nobles and landowners also had a place at the table; in some areas the local bishop or his representative did as well. The right to make even local laws had to be granted by the ultimate authority in a kingdom, generally the monarch or his council. As cities like London, Paris, Vienna, and papal Avignon and later Rome developed into national capitals royal councils directly affected local affairs and laws. In relatively independent Italy powerful men and their families such as the Visconti of Milan and the Medici of Florence seized power and ran territorial states that included numerous towns and cities. As in the developing nation-states of northern Europe, governors or other officials represented the central authority and in plague time helped shape the local civic reaction.

During an epidemic, death and flight reduced the effectiveness of most municipal governments, but scholars have concluded that in general civic life and at least the basic rudiments of administration went on. Initially, the Black Death overwhelmed later medieval city governments, but over time they adjusted to the plague's recurrence. Through legislation and the development of health boards they established patterns of response that directly addressed the plague's worst effects. They hired doctors and gravediggers, guards and corpse-inspectors, nurses and pest-house administrators. They sanitized, quarantined, shut in, regulated, prosecuted, isolated, fumigated, and incinerated. They created mortality records, built hospitals, instigated religious rituals, and encouraged the repopulation of their cities as the pestilence subsided. And when the specter appeared again after a few years' respite, so did the cycle of civic response.

EFFECTS OF PLAGUE ON GOVERNANCE

Death and Flight   The deaths of council members and administrators resound like a drumbeat through the official records of the early years of the Second Pandemic. In 1348 four-fifths of Barcelona's city councilors died, as did nearly all of the Council of One Hundred. In Orvieto, Italy, the council of The Seven lost 6 of its members, and all 12 of The Twelve died—4 in one month—along with half the population. London lost 8 of its 24 aldermen, and the city government of Pistoia, Italy, simply stopped meeting between June 30 and October 18, 1348, due to the massive death toll. Since there was little division of labor in these early governments, notaries bore a large share of the administrative functions and often provided important continuity among administrations. Notaries also routinely visited the sick and dying to help them prepare their last wills and testaments. When these clients were victims of plague, the notary's task became very risky indeed, and many died in the line of duty. Survivors could certainly inflate their fees, but this monetary reward hardly compensated for the risks. After losing two dozen notaries, the Guild of Judges and Notaries in Orvieto declared that only officially inscribed members of the guild should be allowed to practice as notaries; apparently others were doing so without such authorization.

Qui obturat aurem fuam ad clamorem
pauperis,& ipfe clamabit,& non exau=
dietur.

PROVER.   XXI

Les riches confeillez toufiours,
Et aux pauures clouez l'oreille.
Vous crierez aux derniers iours,
Mais Dieu uous fera la pareille.

E ij

Death confronts a wealthy magistrate, who is followed by a hapless supplicant. From Hans Holbein's *Danse Macabre*, Lyon, 1538. Dover.

By the end of the plague only seven licensed notaries had survived. In Siena, Italy, only one notary's surviving business record book (cartulary) spans the deadly summer of 1348. For the first time in over a century, the government decided to allow clergy to practice as notaries public due to the shortage. Perpignan in southern France lost at least 68 of its 117 legal professionals, a fatality rate of 58 percent, which was probably greater than that of the population as a whole.

If notaries were not among the wealthier of a city's citizens—and they generally were not—those elected to a city's councils often were. These men naturally sought to preserve themselves and their families in the face of imminent death and usually had the means to do so. From the first outbreak to the last, civic leaders fled their plague-infected cities as often as anyone else, which helped cripple city governments as much as deaths did, since either way they lacked the quorums necessary to conduct business. The people who remained behind resented the flight of those for whom the demand was even more acute in plague time: doctors, clergy, and civic leaders. Time and again short-handed governments levied fines against those who sought to shirk their duties. During the plague of 1665 the deputy mayor of Southampton, John Steptoe, was fined £20 for fleeing and "failing to give aid." At the same time four of the town's churchwardens, three collectors for the poor, the town steward, chief bailiff, water-bailiff, three market officials, and three law court officials were each fined £3 to £10 for desertion of their posts. The fourteenth-century Florentine chancellor Coluccio Salutati railed against such people as traitors. Perhaps the cult of local patriotism embodied in the "civic humanism" that Cicero inspired and Salutati championed developed as a means of stiffening the backs of wayward leaders in the face of plague.

Effectiveness Both death and flight sapped the strength of local governments. Where they disintegrated, no new laws were passed and the administration of existing laws fell by the wayside. In the absence of effective government offices went unfilled, taxes uncollected, records unkept, personnel unhired, salaries unpaid, criminals unpunished, wills unproved, and key decisions unmade. Without notaries and last wills, orphans were often left without their inheritances or had them plundered by "false friends," unscrupulous and parasitic adult kin or family friends. Fraudulent or inexperienced "notaries" created flawed and ineffective legal documents, and men of ill will took advantage of chaos to steal public funds and other resources. In the wake of the plague both guild and municipal councils often had to lower qualifications such as age and experience to fill positions and replenish guild rolls.

Modern scholars seem to agree that despite the disruptive effects of plague on civic governance, the overall picture is far from disastrous. Studies from across Europe echo the conclusion of historian Christopher Dyer, who wrote that for England "the main impression is of a civilized and organized society doing its best to make decent arrangements in desperately difficult circumstances."[1] Governments were not overthrown and were only rarely challenged seriously. Surviving records indicate that bills were paid and personnel were hired and criminals were punished. The French city of Toulouse licensed 97 new notaries between September and December 1348, and another 108 in 1349 to carry on with legal business. The official records of Marseille fail even to mention the plague—which reached its height there in the summer of 1348—until May 1349. Notarial business seems to have continued, though an unusually high number of new licenses were issued. Historian Daniel Smail comments that the "availability of notaries and their willingness to handle transactions in the midst of death played a crucial role in minimizing the worst effects of the mortality." Indeed, the legal court of Marseille continued its business, though a notary recorded that it changed locations due to "the terrible stench of the dead from the cemetery of Notre Dame de Accoules."[2] Studies from France, Spain, and Italy demonstrate that even where civic affairs suffered during the epidemic recovery was swift and fairly complete. In his work on the Hanseatic League Philippe Dollinger notes that, despite a few new names on the lists of city councilors, the same old patrician families continued to rule German cities before and after the Black Death. Continuity and stability rather than upheaval and change seem to have followed in the immediate wake of the plague. Indeed, during the following three centuries civic governments across Europe, often borrowing ideas from one another, made slow but huge strides in confronting plague and its effects.

GENERAL CIVIC RESPONSES TO PLAGUE

By the sixteenth and seventeenth centuries the last thing a municipal government wanted to do was to declare officially the presence of plague. After two centuries of experience, civic magistrates well understood the impacts that **Declaring an Epidemic** such a declaration had, however warranted it might be. First, it immediately put all outsiders on notice that people and goods from the affected city and its region were potentially tainted. Orders for its products immediately dried up, guards at territorial borders or city gates turned away its citizens, and foreign ports quarantined ships with the city's goods. Second, it struck fear in its own citizens at home and abroad. Shops closed, the well-off fled, and people stopped reporting the sick in their families for fear of being shut in with them or carted off to a pest house. Third, it meant the imposition of special laws—usually quite intrusive—both time-honored and novel. This legislation was crafted at first to keep the plague contained and later to deal with its spread and the dead it produced. Fourth, a declaration of plague necessitated the hiring of special personnel to handle the crisis, from civic physicians to help the sick to gravediggers to bury the dead. Fifth, by the later sixteenth century such a pronouncement required the purchase of new graveyards and the construction and staffing of special facilities for victims and often for their families. Overall it meant lowered civic revenues from gate taxes and other commerce and increased expenditures on the sick, the dying, the dead, and those left without jobs or other means of support. It is no surprise to learn that time and again governments hesitated to declare a state of epidemic even in the face of clear evidence. In 1630 Archbishop Federico Borromeo of Milan blamed the local government for letting the plague enter through gates kept open "by their preoccupation with the gate taxes and customs duties."[3] Over time the means for ascertaining and telling the world that plague was "visiting" a particular city became more formal and sophisticated as states recognized the importance of very quickly and accurately identifying potential sources of pestilence.

LOCAL COMMERCE DURING PLAGUE-TIME BARCELONA, 1651

When plague struck Barcelona officials dug deep ditches around the city's perimeter. Tanner Miqual Parets tells us:

> In the middle of the ditch three long planks were placed going from one side to the other, with a pole in the middle attached to a strong metal axle, which held up the middle plank and allowed it to turn around like a toy wheel. When the farmer brought his goods, chickens or eggs or fruit or anything else, he put them on the end of the plank and spun it around to the other side. If the buyer liked it, they agreed on a price, and then the person from the city put the money on the plank and spun it again. And the farmer put the coins in a pot of vinegar he brought with him [to disinfect the coins].

From Miquel Parets, *A Journal of the Plague Year* (New York: Oxford University Press, 1995), p. 51

Record Keeping   Before the sixteenth century demographic records of any kind were rare and usually very flawed. In Catholic Europe public registering of those who had died served little purpose unless the deceased person's will required masses, prayers, or other special remembrances. Since every Christian European theoretically belonged to a parish community, regular record keeping first appeared at this level. As in many administrative innovations, Italian city-states were the first to require registry of burials: Arezzo in 1373, Siena in 1379, and Florence in 1385. The city's Grain Office maintained Florence's death registry, due initially to the need to estimate demand for grain: the more deaths, the lower the demand. Cause of death was only added in 1424. Milan began its record in 1452 with the date, name, age, address, cause of death, and duration of illness of the deceased. Mantua followed only in 1496 and Venice in 1504. In 1520 the city council of Barcelona was troubled by rumors of plague and ordered all parishes to record the dead and causes of death to quash these rumors. (In fact, 1,519 people died of plague that year.) Henry VIII required all English parishes to keep detailed records of deaths and burials from 1537, and two years later the French crown made a similar demand. Despite great strides in developing business records, the Dutch did not keep death registries until the seventeenth century, and Catholic German parishes until after the Council of Trent (1543–1562).

Of course, good records required care in the making, and often the necessary meticulousness was lacking. For example, England relied on old women who were otherwise unemployed and supported by parish funds to determine cause of death, and these "searchers" regularly came in for criticism. Their age, ignorance, "sloth," and propensity to be bribed made many wary of their conclusions. A dire report from Yarmouth, written in 1664 as plague wracked nearby Amsterdam, ended, "if the reports of the searchers . . . are true, but they are drunken persons and very poor and may make false returns because of the large allowance (wage) they have for this work."[4] One of the biggest problems was with the searchers' conclusions on causes of death. "Causes" listed in surviving records included not only true causes like plague or accident, but also symptoms like fever, ailments like rickets, and characteristics like "lunacy." Other "causes of death" included "disappointed in love," "suddenly," "blasted," "planet-struck," and "old age." Venice in the early 1630s created what were probably the most reliable death records of the era. In plague time every sick person was required to see a doctor, and every deceased person—including Jews and other non-Catholics, foreigners, and infants, all of whom were often left out of such records—appeared in the *Necrologi*. Notaries recorded each entry in a set format: name, age, surname, occupation, cause of death, number of days sick before death, and place of residence.

London's bills of mortality are the most famous of these records, in part because they were regularly published. From the 1530s the clerk of each Anglican parish was responsible for hiring the searchers, who were at first paid two pence per body examined, and collecting their reports each week. By the 1560s royal officials standardized the forms and process for reporting the results. Each Tuesday the clerks collected the reports and placed them in a locked box at the top of the stairs at the Guildhall. On Wednesday civic officials tallied the totals and set the results in type for printing. The week's results first went to the civic and royal authorities and then to the general public, sold for a penny or two. Every parish appeared with the total number of deaths and number of plague deaths listed in columns beside. The City's total dead and plague toll for the week appeared at the bottom; the authorities added sex ratios in 1629. By the early seventeenth century the crown licensed private printers to produce the listings, which were often accompanied by graphics, prayers, recipes for antidotes, and eventually advertisements for pills or potions. In 1618 a year's subscription cost four shillings or three pence for a single copy. Businessmen and city officials became very reliant on these sources of

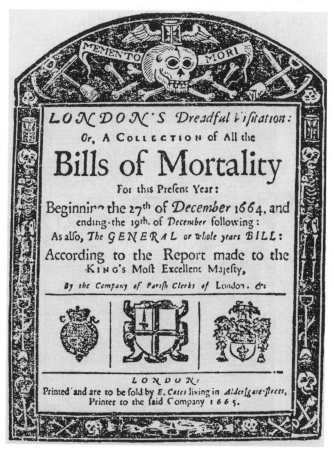

A printed tombstone for an entire city: the cover of *London's Dreadful Visitation*, a compilation of the bills of mortality for the year of the Great Plague in London, 1665. Dover.

information. Even slight changes could cause disproportionate concern: In the wake of the Great Plague of 1665, Samuel Pepys of London wrote in his diary for February 23, 1666, "We are much troubled that [deaths from] sickness in general should be [up] by 3, and yet of the particular disease of the plague, there should be 10 encrease [sic]."[5] Merchants refused to entertain customers or suppliers from parishes or towns whose numbers had increased, and they would not visit towns with troubling statistics. Individuals decided whether to stay or flee London and officials whether to close theaters and open pest houses based upon a handful of deaths in a city of 50,000. The last recorded plague death appeared in 1679, but the column "plague" remained for another three decades. Such was the power of pestilence.

Though London's parish clerks had many responsibili-
ties, and searchers eventually became full-time personnel, **Personnel**
with plague came the need for an ever-expanding corps of
civic employees. On July 25, 1603, the Great Court of Ipswich, England,
commanded four bailiffs to

find out of the Town, four of the fittest men to attend upon the infected houses
and people for the burial of the dead, and for the delivery of the meat and drink
to them that are sick, and two women for the lying of them forth in death [prepar-
ing the bodies for burial], and for viewing them, and attending to them in their
sickness.[6]

Even for a small town this was a skeleton crew. Ipswich had gates that
needed guarding and a pest house that required medical personnel, cooks,
laundresses, a chaplain, and a steady supply of food and medicine. The
houses of the "visited" victims needed to be fumigated or scrubbed out
with disinfectants by cleansers, who, along with the rest, ran the risk of
contracting the disease. In Austria friars of various Catholic orders performed this dangerous business, with the added benefit that they were
unlikely to steal from the victims. Florence's plague workers—fumigators,
cleansers, nurses, gravediggers, guards—were despised and nicknamed
nibi (scavenger kites). In the early 1630s they were charged with and tried
for crimes ranging from theft to violent intimidation and rape. In Carlisle,
England, corpse-inspectors and house-cleansers received wages of 10 shillings per week, a rather large sum designed to discourage criminality. In
1583 London added "viewers" to look after the searchers and keep them
honest. Watchers and warders armed with pole-weapons appeared in the
1590s to guard "visited" and shut-up houses during daylight lest anyone break in or out; in May 1609 this job became a 24-hour commitment.
These men received the keys to the houses, the responsibility to feed the
inhabitants, and the brunt of popular and official complaint. In 1630 King
Charles' Privy Council formally upbraided the lord mayor of London for
the poor choice of searchers and the careless vigilance and supervision of
the watchers. Yet even good performance drew popular ire, as one Londoner noted in 1665: "Death is now become so familiar and the people so
insensible of danger that they look upon such as provide for the public
safety as tyrants and oppressors."[7]

From late antiquity medical care outside of the home had
been the responsibility of the church, especially monasteries. In **Civic**
the early thirteenth century, closely following the development **Physicians**
of medical schools, Italian urban governments began hiring
communal physicians to meet the medical needs of the poor. The earliest was employed by the Po Valley town of Reggio in 1211, though better known was Ugo Borgognoni of Lucca, hired by Bologna three years
later. By century's end civic physicians were fairly common in Italy: Milan
had three in 1288, and by the 1290s Venice was paying £2,000 per year

Roman authorities fumigate books and papers from a victim's house, while a corpse is loaded onto a tumbrel in the background. National Library of Medicine.

in salaries. By 1324 there were 13 physicians and 18 surgeons working for Venice. Many of these men served in its colonies or tended the galley fleet; they also tended the poor and tortured prisoners (ensuring that they would not die while suffering). The first arrived in Venetian Ragusa in 1301 and served a two-year term, with a house and office provided. He was to treat everyone, but never charge any Ragusan for his services. In Florence Master Jacopo de Urbe served the needy from 1318 until 1348, when he was succeeded by his two sons. He received the modest sum of five florins per month and also had the duty of surgically removing the hands, feet, or limbs of convicted criminals. Germany, Burgundy, and northeastern France had the earliest communal doctors outside Italy, dating from the end of the thirteenth and first half of the fourteenth century (Bruges in the thirteenth; Wismar, 1281; Munich, 1312; and Lille, Ypres, and Dunkirk later). Thanks at least in part to the recurring plague most French towns and cities had civic physicians on staff by the fifteenth century. In fact, municipalities employed 15 percent of the physicians we know from this period by name.

In plague time communal doctors and surgeons were especially important, since many private practitioners fled, and few of these would treat the needy in any case. Often, cities would hire additional—or replacement—physicians to handle the awful burden. Pope Clement VI hired several doctors to tend the plague-ridden Avignonese in 1348, as did a number of French city councils. In Venice only 1 of 18 public physicians remained on the books in 1349, but only 5 were listed as having succumbed to plague: Did the other 12 simply flee? On October 24, 1348, Orvieto hired Matteo fu Angelo at four times the 50-florin annual salary it had been paying. In 1479 Pavia, Italy, hired Giovanni Ventura for 30 florins per month, with full citizenship and a free house. The pope and many city governments gave public surgeons and physicians free reign to perform autopsies on plague victims as part of the search for a cure, an otherwise closely guarded privilege. As time went on, both communal physicians and plague doctors (*physici epidemie* in Italy; *pestmeesters* in Holland; *Pest-medici* in Germany) became quite common—and quite valuable—in European cities. In 1650 Barcelona sent two of their physicians to help plague-struck Tortosa. Guerillas captured them en route and held them for a ransom that Barcelona readily paid. Observers in both England and Italy comment that

The well-dressed seventeenth-century French plague-doctor's suit, complete with the required wand. From Thomas Bartholin's *Historiarum anatomicarum*, 1650s. National Library of Medicine.

plague physicians tended to be inexperienced, second-rate, and too few in number. William Boghurst complained in 1665 that in London

But two or three of the youngest are appointed in plague time to look to thirty or forty thousand sick people, when four or five hundred are too few; and at another time, when there dies but two or three hundred a week, you should have five or six hundred [doctors] hanging after them if they be well lined with white metal [silver]. Tis the rich whose persons are guarded by angels.[8]

The plague physicians' principal tasks were to tend the sick and dying and certify plague deaths for the sake of public records. In France and Holland pest-doctors were sometimes neither trained surgeons nor physicians but non-professional "empirics"—in one Dutch case a fruit-seller. To help protect themselves many seventeenth-century practitioners adopted the distinctive suits of long waxed-cloth coats and hats with a bird-like mask. The "beak" was filled with aromatic stuff meant to filter the "corrupted air"; one recipe for this included laudanum, amber, rose petals, storax, myrrh, balm-mint leaves, cloves, and camphor.

ENCOURAGEMENT FOR CIVIC PHYSICIANS: BREMEN, 1582

And these being hired [by the health magistrates] for an appropriate stipend, and bound by oath to the commonwealth, so that they take no occasion to flee for fear of the sickness greatly increasing (such is human weakness), each one of them must have the duties of his office made clear: namely, that manfully shaking off the fear of death they diligently employ themselves to prove their faithfulness and service both to God and man—considering that God is the beholder and judge of the things they do, howsoever these things may be hidden from the common people unskilled in the art [of medicine]. If they do anything through error or deceit, it shall not go unpunished; but if they shall behave themselves in their office diligently and faithfully then they shall receive a far greater reward after this life than they can receive from people in this world. [. . .]
The health magistrates must recommend privately to the physician that he often consider how great the hope of all people he takes upon himself, wherefore all the citizens will hold him in admiration, and reverence him as if he were some god sent down from Heaven.

An adaptation of John Stockwood's 1583 translation of town physician Johan Ewich's *Of the Duty of a Faithful and Wise Magistrate* (1582), in Peter Elmer and Ole P. Grell, eds., *Health, Disease, and Society in Europe, 1500–1800: A Source Book* (New York: Manchester University Press, 2004), pp. 98–99.

Health Boards   Though physicians both private and communal provided a great deal of advice to individuals, medical advice did not become part of civic planning and decision making until much later. When plague hit the Italian city-states in

1348 the famed physician Gentile da Foligno provided a *consilium,* or letter of professional medical advice, to the "Venerable College of Masters" of Perugia. To stave off the epidemic he recommended prayers for God's mercy, moderation in food and drink, purgations and bloodletting, certain medicines, and disinfection of places suspected of having the disease present. He also suggested that a panel of "substantial citizens" join with a group of physicians to "make arrangements for preserving the health of the people of the city." Most Italian cities responded to emergencies by appointing temporary, ad hoc commissions of citizens, and so many did in 1348. Florence appointed an eight-man *balía* and Siena a three-man committee. In 1347 Venice's Grand Council sent three "knowledgeable men" *(savi)* to Istria, Venetian territory across the Adriatic Sea, to study the new epidemic disease; on March 30, 1348, they charged a new panel of three *savi* with "the conservation of the health and the elimination of the corruption of the environment."[9] Since the *savi* accepted miasma theory, their laws emphasized deep and distant burial of the dead and cleaning of filth in the streets. The Senate's new laws of July 10 reflected a subtle but important understanding of the plague: officials were to control incoming people and goods and stop anything or anyone suspected of having the infection.

Their understanding of the plague being vague, civic authorities tended to apply both miasma theory, which recommended sanitation measures, and contagion theory, which prompted the isolation of the sick to protect the well. Yet, for over a century no permanent health boards existed in Italy, nor for over a century longer did any medical professionals serve on the ad hoc boards that did. In January 1486 the Venetians created a permanent Commission of Public Health with twelve-month terms of office, providing a model for city councils as far away as Holland. With extensions of the concept of "public health," by 1540 its authority covered parish poor relief, the suppression of begging, and the control of prostitution. The Florentine permanent magistracy known as the Otto di Guardia, a kind of political police, was given in 1448 the responsibility to "preserve public health, keep off the plague, and avoid an epidemic." They provided bread for the poor, established the hospital of Santa Maria Nuova, one of Europe's biggest, and hired 4 physicians and 4 surgeons as well as 40 women and 12 men to oversee the plague victims. These extraordinary powers, however, were only granted for three months. Only after the outbreak of plague in 1527 did the rather new Grand Ducal government of Florence institute a permanent five-member health magistracy with the means of coercion to enforce its laws throughout Florentine territory. None of its members, however, was a medical professional. During the well-documented plague of 1630–1631 the Health Magistrates appointed five "Commissioners-General" to oversee the five administrative districts of the Grand Duchy of Tuscany. Each traveled his territory with a notary, an officer, and guards, and had "supreme authority" over all aspects of life in his district. Preceded by a trumpeter, the commissioner was to visit every village and town to announce the plague laws of the magistrates. He was then to set up a residence and inspect the region regularly, establishing pest houses, shutting in victims and their families, and forcing physicians to serve as he saw fit. In an age often associated with the rise of science, the magistrates added that should the commissioner see a need to change the ordinances he was to enforce, "then you shall advise us of this in your letters, specifying the reason that inclines you to revocation or change so that . . . we may with your opinion ever apply ourselves to reaching better decisions." In the city of Florence itself agents of the magistrates were not only to oversee victims, but "to visit the homes of the poor and have them thoroughly cleaned and repainted in order to get rid of anything that would produce foul odors, because filth is the mother of corruption of the air and the latter is the mother of the plague."[10]

The pattern evident in other European countries is similar: first ad hoc citizen committees with limited oversight, then permanent boards with increasing power over citizens. But these authorities were not all-powerful. Clergy resented and flaunted restrictions on church services, innkeepers ignored bans on guests, merchants smuggled goods in contravention of quarantines, and everyone badmouthed the guards they set at gates and on houses. At St. Lô, France, in the seventeenth century the town's chief medical officer was imprisoned as a witch when he proved suspiciously successful in damping an episode of plague.

LEGISLATIVE RESPONSES TO PLAGUE

The plague-related official actions of city councils, health boards, and magistracies fall into five major categories. Though all were related to either preventing the plague (prophylaxis) or dealing with its effects and bringing it to an end, the actions of city councils often had mixed motives. Most early laws were enacted piecemeal rather than as part of a comprehensive program. By 1437 Ragusa had one of the earliest full ordinances, with 35 chapters. Within a few decades most larger Italian cities had similar sets of regulations, as did many French cities by the early sixteenth century. Paris codified its measures in 1531 and London by 1583; northeastern European cities followed during the later sixteenth century.

Sanitation Legislation The oldest type of public-health legislation by medieval cities entailed the paving and maintenance of clean streets and alleys and removal of sources of foul odors, such as rotting animal and vegetable matter and human waste. Stench had long been associated in Galenic medical theory with "corruption" of the air, and corruption with disease and its spread. The university town of Cambridge, England, had a constant stream of anti-filth statutes from the time it was chartered, in 1267, and Florence from a few years later. Florentines regulated the sale of meat, fish, and fruits and required that the sewers be cleaned twice each year. The 1319 Florentine law prohibiting the slaughter of animals in certain parts of town explained that to continue allowing it "provoked illness among their inhabitants through their pestiferous exhalations." Essentially, stink made people ill and the city had the right to intervene.

In plague time these efforts were redoubled. In March 1348 Florentine sanitation legislation was peppered with phrases like "putrefaction and corruption of things and bodies" and "corruption and infection of the air," and directions "to remove and carry away from the City of Florence and its suburbs any putrid thing or things and infected persons and similar things, from which could [proceed] corruption of the air and infection."[11] The government of Rouen, France, enacted laws restricting the sale and disposal of fish in 1394, banning certain animals in town a decade later, and three years later prohibiting the flinging of human waste into the streets. In 1606 Hull, England, required that fish livers be kept and cured at least a half-mile from town, and about the same time Périgueux, France, banned the dumping of chamber pots into the streets each day after the Angelus bell (about noon). Presumably the streets were swept of filth each day after that.

In London, subject to both civil and royal authorities, the plague prompted a series of antilittering laws in 1353, 1354, 1356, 1357, 1362, 1366, and 1370. In 1354 the king demanded that all butchers locate their slaughterhouses along the Thames for refuse disposal. When one shop lost its place and had to move inland, the government demanded that its offal be barged out to the middle of the river at ebb tide so it would be readily flushed out to sea. Yet London's earliest comprehensive set of laws on public sanitation, the Statute of the Streets—again prompted by the plague—dates only to the early seventeenth century. Among many other things these laws required that "every householder must cause before his door to be paved and swept; the filth of houses to be carried daily away." The raker of each of London's 26 wards, who had this responsibility, drove a great two-wheeled cart and blew a horn before each door to announce his arrival. Privies were not to be dumped in gardens, and dunghills were to be removed out of the city. Officials known as beadles levied and collected fines or jailed lawbreakers and oversaw the constables who patrolled the streets.[12]

Another type of "sanitary" legislation had its foundation in the Christian belief that sin angered God, who expressed his divine wrath through plague. In what historian Ann Car-michael has aptly labeled a "secularization of older moral laws," city governments legislated against sexual immorality—especially sodomy and prostitution—official corruption, and eventually the supposedly vice-ridden poor.[13] Florence kicked out all prostitutes in 1348 and later passed laws against street-walking prostitutes (1403; brothels were permitted), immoral activity in religious convents (1421), official

Moral Legislation

malfeasance (1429), and sodomy (1432). Venice very tightly regulated prostitutes beginning in 1486, as did other Italian cities such as Perugia, Siena, and Mantua in the later fifteenth century. Even before the advent of terrible venereal diseases in Europe at the end of the century the Venetians noted that openly available sex drew into town unsavory foreigners and encouraged intimate relations that could help spread disease.

FLORENCE'S GOVERNMENT DEBATES POOR RELIEF IN PLAGUE TIME, 1430

Messer Lorenzo Ridolfi . . . said that it is to be feared that the pestilence will become worse. The poor are in a very bad condition, since they earn nothing, and in future they will earn less. . . .

Antonio Alessandri said that on account of the plague which is imminent, it is necessary to provide for the preservation of our regime, keeping in mind the measures which were taken at similar times in the past. First, we should acknowledge our obligation to God, taking into account the poverty of many citizens, that is, by distributing alms to the needy and indigent persons, appointing for this task men who are devoted to God and who lead good lives, and not those who are active in the affairs of the state. But since not all are quiet, and in order to instill fear into some, foot soldiers should be hired who are neither citizens nor residents of the *contado*,[14] and who will serve the needs of the Commune and not private citizens. . . .

Messer Rinaldo Gianfigliazzi said that the poor should be subsidized with public funds since they are dying of hunger. God will be pleased, and their evil thoughts [of crime or rebellion] will disappear. God should be placated with processions and prayers. . . .

Buonaccorso di Neri Pitti said that the poor should be assisted so they can feed themselves. Those of our indigent citizens who are capable of doing evil should be hired as soldiers and sent to those places where troops are stationed, and their salaries should be increased.

From Gene Brucker, *The Society of Renaissance Florence* (New York: Harper, 1971), pp. 230–31

Following Christian teachings, early medieval people tended to see the poor as deserving of support and care, and worthy advocates whose prayers to God held special power. As European society changed and cities grew, however, poverty came to be associated with vice and sin, which provoked God's anger and resulted in plague. Lacking economic and social resources the urban poor—a population often swelled in plague time as desperate country folk came looking for aid—came to be seen as a social and economic burden on the broader community and a threat to its moral health. In 1348 the town of Uzerche simply expelled all of its sick, as did Basel in 1370 and Reggio in 1375, leaving the poor victims of plague to die in ditches and fields. Over time, observers concluded that plague carriers tended to be poor—itinerants, vagabonds, beggars, day laborers—and that plague tended to start in the poorest sections of town.

Plague legislation often targeted the poor, whether residents or travelers. On October 22, 1630, in the midst of plague, Venetian authorities ordered the forcible removal of the poor from the neighborhood of San Rocco. They were shipped to the beggars' hospital of San Lazzaro on a distant island in the lagoon. When plague first struck a poor quarter of London in the seventeenth century, authorities barricaded the roads and boarded windows to wall the inhabitants inside, hoping to contain the disease by shutting in the entire neighborhood. They always failed. Sadly, these societies decided to combat the poor rather than poverty.

The prevention of plague, or prophylaxis, meant not only eliminating corrupt air, but avoiding people and things that **Prophylaxis** had become corrupted. As Frenchman Oderic Raynold put it, "the villages that want to avoid the plague keep all strangers out." But it also meant keeping the villagers from visiting and returning from areas with "corrupt air," and carefully screening all goods from suspect places. In 1348 Pistoia landed on a simple answer: "Any cloth brought into the city must be burned in the main square of the city."[15] By the seventeenth century prophylactic measures included isolating those places that had the plague, lest it spread elsewhere. In a famous case of self-sacrifice, the villagers of Eyam, England, voluntarily remained in their homes and suffered tremendous losses to prevent further spread of the pestilence. Digne, France, on the other hand, found itself virtually besieged by its neighbors, who seriously considered firebombing the entire town to stop the plague. Instituting a cordon sanitaire—without the firebombs—became a regular means of insulating a neighborhood or small town from a clear source of epidemic.

In 1348 Florence and Venice closed their gates to any people or goods from Genoa, Pisa, and other plague-ridden cities, but to no avail. On the other hand, Milan's virtual self-isolation seems to have prevented a major outbreak there. Port cities all around Europe banned ships from suspect areas, though this move led to secret landings and the smuggling of contraband. As Italian city-states began to cooperate in halting plague, they exchanged information on plague reports and developed health passes or "bills of health" that certified a traveler as coming from a plague-free area and being healthy at the time of its issuance. To prevent forgeries, these documents were soon being produced on city presses and constitute some of Europe's earliest printed official forms. In May 1630, after plague had been reported in Bologna, Florence required health passes from all travelers from the north and posted troops along the northern frontier at positions three miles apart. From June 13, local residents were to help watch for any surreptitious border-crossers, ring bells if they spotted any, and follow them until troops arrived.

Eventually both goods and people suspected of carrying plague found their way into special quarantines. Named for the generally imposed isolation of 40 (*quaranta*) days, such places included ships anchored off the coast, coastal islands, secluded monasteries, or special quarters outside a city's gates. The idea was to isolate apparently healthy people and ensure that no sickness developed, and to cleanse "infected" goods by washing or fumigating them or exposing them to "good" clean air and sunlight. People rinsed coins from suspect areas in vinegar or running water and purified correspondence by passing letters through fire or smoke or placing them in special ovens. As brutal or silly as some of these measures may seem, many modern scholars believed they may have played a vital role in removing the threat of plague from western Europe.

Dealing with Disaster   Once the plague struck a town the sick needed to be tended and isolated, the healthy protected, and the dead buried. On January 17, 1374, after milder actions failed, Milan's lord Bernabo Visconti simply ordered plague victims in his town of Reggio expelled into the countryside to live or die as God desired. Cities developed two approaches to isolating the sick: shutting them up in their own houses, often with all who lived there, and providing special pest houses in which victims received some succor and might recover or die (see Chapter Six). Often a city employed both approaches, with the pest house, horrible as it was, serving the poorer people, while the wealthier stayed locked inside their houses. Like other measures, isolation of the sick assumed that people themselves spread the disease (contagion), a theory that prompted governments to limit the congregation of people whether sick or well. To this end authorities closed theaters, discouraged large religious gatherings, and canceled markets and fairs when plague threatened. They prohibited meetings of guilds and other civic groups, feasts, neighborhood games, musical performances, and militia drills.

Civic authorities even regulated funeral processions, especially those to the graveyard or church. In Tournai, Belgium, still known for its annual "Great Procession," funerals were typical and could be quite grand, and bells tolled day and night for the dead. City magistrates reined this pageantry in, regulating the number of mourners, restricting bells to Sunday at Mass-time, banning the wearing of black mourning clothes, and requiring a simplification of funerary rituals that treated rich and poor equally. Restrictions on bells were meant at least in part to have a salutary psychological effect: The constant tolling and reminder of death depressed people, which supposedly made them more susceptible to the plague. Samuel Pepys noted that "it was a sad noise to hear our Bell to toll and ring so often, either for deaths or burials," and certain Aragonese towns specified that the ban was "to avoid frightening people." Venice forbade any public display of plague bodies, and Pistoia commanded that "dead bodies are not to be taken out of the houses where they died unless they are put in a wooden box bound together with string so that the odors do not escape." Like other cities, Pistoia required that corpses be buried at least two and a half meters beneath the surface.[16]

Once victims had been carried to the pest house or the grave, their houses and goods had to be cleansed to eradicate any "seeds" of plague. When clothing, bedding, and furniture were simply incinerated, the victims or their heirs might receive compensation: In 1630–1631 the government of Prato, in Tuscany, paid 50 percent of the claimed value. In some cases, as at Troyes in 1495, entire houses—presumably of the poor—were torched; in 1499 the practice was banned. Most often houses were fumigated with some combination of burning aromatic woods and minerals such as sulfur, then scrubbed down with vinegar or another disinfectant. In 1636 the authorities of Bourg-en-Bresse, France, paid children to live in fumigated houses to ensure that there was no danger of contagion after treatment. Magistrates might also mandate repainting, which was thought to trap any "seeds" beneath the paint. The illustrious London bureaucrat and diarist Samuel Pepys declared himself quite content not to have visited the second floor of a friend's house, the usual place for entertaining guests, since his host had yet to repaint it after his servant had died of plague. Following his visit he drank heavily.

The chaos of plague time presented ample opportunities for criminal behavior, and plague legislation presented new laws to **Crime** break. These often turned ordinary activities like walking in the street or even opening a window into crimes. Common criminals were punished even more severely for stealing plague-tainted goods or breaking into shut-up houses or sexually violating plague victims. Victims

Roman officials dump the belongings of a victim to be incinerated in the fire below. The cross-staffs held by several men were signs of their plague-time authority. National Library of Medicine.

and their families broke laws by failing to report illnesses and deaths; by disposing of a victim's clothes and other belongings in an improper manner; by leaving shut-in houses or entertaining guests when shut in; by refusing to relocate to a pest house when ordered; or by interfering with the directions or activities of the plague authorities. These authorities broke the law by abusing their access to homes and helpless people; by selling goods they should have burned; by stealing funds, food, or medicines meant for plague victims; by taking bribes for special treatment; or simply by doing their jobs poorly (corpse-tending, guarding, fumigating, digging graves, administering funds, tending the sick, etc.). Other citizens had to be wary of dealing in tainted goods or money, illegally assembling with others, visiting shut-up houses, insulting plague officials, attending illicit funerals, hosting visitors from banned places, traveling abroad, and disposing of waste improperly. People readily ignored, resisted, and even defied plague laws, as many contemporaries remark. In 1603 one Londoner wrote that "the poorer sort, yea women with young children, will flock [illegally] to burials and (which is worse) stand (on purpose) over open graves where sundry are buried together, that (forsooth) all the world may see that they fear not the plague." Some victims were downright malicious, as Thomas Middleton reported to Samuel Pepys: "people are so wicked in Portsmouth that it is reported that they take their foul plasters [bandages] from their sores and in the night throw them into the windows of fresh houses."[17]

MURDER MOST FOUL IN PLAGUE-TIME FLORENCE, 1400

The court of justice in Florence tries siblings Francesco and Tomasia for their plot against Tomasia's wealthy stepdaughter:

> Francesco brought a notary and certain witnesses to Lena's house while she was lying ill [of the plague] in bed. And after being persuaded by Francesco and by Tomasia, Lena was interrogated by the notary and she consented to have Francesco as her husband. [They were quickly married.] Then two days after the wedding Francesco had a conversation with certain persons from whom he sought counsel about arranging that Lena would not recover from her illness but instead would die. And since the pestilence was then (and still is) raging, he would never be suspected by anyone. Having received advice on this matter, Francesco went personally to the shop of Leonardo di Betto, a druggist in the Mercato Vecchio, and bought from him eight portions of arsenic and took it home. With Tomasia he placed that arsenic in a small loaf of bread and gave it to Lena to eat, for the purpose of poisoning and killing her. Lena ate that mixture and on the second day she died.
>
> The pair confessed to the crime and was sentenced to death. Francesco was executed but pregnant Tomasia's sentence was first postponed and later cancelled.

From Gene Brucker, *The Society of Renaissance Florence* (New York: Harper, 1971), pp. 141–42.

With the criminal courts often suspended during plague time, suspects sometimes spent many sweltering months in jails or prisons awaiting trial. When plague caught hold **Punishment** in one of these places few survived. In cities with health magistracies, special tribunals rather than normal courts often tried criminal cases related to plague laws: Florence generated 332 such criminal proceedings during the plague years 1630 to 1632. Many of those tried were charged with multiple offenses, and almost all were from the working or poorer classes of society. In Lausanne, Switzerland, during the plague year of 1536 the drunken Jacques Bovard visited the house of the local gravedigger and continued his drinking. He was caught and fined 25 florins for both drunkenness and being with a man who was supposed to remain isolated from healthy people. For crimes such as failing to report plague, selling victims' goods, or removing them while not carrying the required white wand, the city council in Dutch Leiden in 1515 determined an appropriate punishment to be a fine of 2,000 bricks for the town wall or the severing of the convict's right hand and banishment. About the same time the Scots handed out penalties ranging from confiscation of property or branding to eternal banishment or hanging. By the later sixteenth century one of the first acts of a city council faced with plague was to erect a gallows in a central and very public place. Geneva and surrounding Alpine cities seemed to suffer from a peculiar crime in the later sixteenth and early seventeenth centuries—that of purposefully smearing on doorposts and other common places a goo that was thought to spread the plague. Trial transcripts report that the grease was made by boiling down the flesh of dead plague victims. Numerous people, usually plague workers who supposedly wanted to retain their jobs by prolonging the epidemic, were convicted of this atrocity, the punishment for which was "to be burnt in a raging fire until reduced to ashes."[18]

Those who broke various laws imposed during plague time in seventeenth-century Rome were punished severely. National Library of Medicine.

The place of punishment, Milan, 1630. Those accused of plague-related crimes are tortured and executed in the background, as two notorious "plague-spreaders" are brought to justice in the foreground. A popular graphic from the 1630s. National Library of Medicine.

AFTER THE PLAGUE

In the wake of plague civic governments had three major tasks: sort out private matters of orphans, wills, and property distribution; address the economic disaster caused by disrupted markets, shattered tax bases, and huge public debt; and, especially in the early years, repopulate their half-empty cities.

Wills, Orphans, and Property The initial onset of plague in the late 1340s caught many Europeans unprepared, without having made clear arrangements for the disposition of their property and children after their deaths. Those who had done so generally left spouses or other family members or friends as executors, but these individuals often died in quick succession before a new document could be drawn up. Death also seized the heirs stipulated in wills, negating the effects of even the clearest instructions. Wills from plague times often have several versions written over a short period or long codicils—statements of changes—appended to them. As notaries died off the opportunity to make these changes disappeared, leaving people's estates in legal limbo. Children orphaned by plague generally became wards of friends or relatives specified in their parents' wills, but often these guardians died as well. Yet other kin or friends might step up, especially if the children had inherited a substantial amount of money or property. Unscrupulous custodians, known in Italy as "false friends," were known for squandering or simply stealing their wards' inheritance, behavior considered criminal when detected. Many poorer children were simply left wards of the state or church. To help remedy this problem in 1410 the wealthy Tuscan merchant Francesco Datini, himself orphaned in 1348, left large parts of his fortune to establish orphanages in Florence and his hometown of Prato. In the absence of such institutions civil and church courts had to make many decisions regarding inheritance and wardship, and do so quite rapidly before real damage was done.

IN HIS WILL FRANCESCO DATINI ESTABLISHES THE OSPEDALE DEGLI INNOCENTI IN FLORENCE, 1410

Also, in order to increase the alms and devotions of the citizens and rural folk and of others who have compassion toward the boys and girls that are called 'throwaways'; and so that these children might be well fed, changed, and looked after, and so that the effects of the giving of the alms might be unrestrained; and lest they fear that the alms might be appropriated and sent outside the city: he willed and ordered that a new place be built, where and how the below-written superintendent in the said city of Florence will desire, of which institution let the first superintendent be the superintendent of the Hospital of Santa Maria Nuova of Florence, whoever he will be at the time. The superintendent shall provide for and cause to be fed those children who will be left or abandoned there, with good diligence and prudence. There are to be given to the said superintendent of Santa Maria Nuova, from the wealth of the said testator, one thousand gold florins; and from this the superintendent is to begin to build the new facility, and not do otherwise.

Translated by author from the document in Cesare Guasti, ed., *Lettere di un notaro ad un mercante del trecento*, Vol. II (Florence: Le Monnier, 1880).

The death of half a town's or city's population, typical in the earliest plague epidemic, caused enormous economic problems for the survivors. Highly skilled professional and craftspeople disappeared, leaving few masters and many untrained students behind. Debts and taxes went unpaid, the demand for many goods and services dropped off, and crops went untended or unharvested. Those who survived could often demand very high wages, a free-market intrusion on guild economics. Tax rolls had to be rewritten to reflect the dead and those who had permanently fled. They also had to reflect the many and varied changes in property ownership due to death and inheritance. As cities became more active fighting the effects of plague their expenses shot up while their revenues from

Economic Effects and Actions

taxes on commerce dwindled. Personnel, facilities, poor relief, medicines, even wands, carts, and shovels cost money that cities could ill afford. In the 1630s Venetian Padua spent the enormous sum of 57,000 ducats on maintenance of the local pest house, and another 12,000 on poor relief. During London's so-called Dread Visitation in 1665 the single parish of St. Margaret's Westminster paid 350 women for nursing service at least once at a rate of about four shillings per week. At the same time the parish paid the apothecary Loveday Fenner £570 for his services and medicines, and physician Nathaniel Hodges £100 for his services. Nurse Littlejohn rated a measly three pounds eight shillings. In 1603 the City of London paid a total of £153 for plague expenses; 20 years later the total was £1,571. London and Oxford began taxing inhabitants to support plague measures in 1518. York was the first provincial English city to do so, requiring 10 pence from each alderman and one penny from every "honest" man who had never held an office. Beginning in 1603 England's Parliament levied taxes on the county in which the affected town was located, or in the case of London, the surrounding counties. Each parish was assessed a certain amount, and parish authorities distributed the levy among all landowners. Constables who collected the sums were also to keep a close watch for signs of plague. They were also specifically authorized to seize and sell the goods of any who refused to pay.

LONDON'S PLAGUE EXPENSES: 1625

Poor relief for shut-in victims	£171
Medical personnel	290
Pest house	315
Relief for poor in hospitals	333
Relief for poor in Bridewell Prison	400
For marshal and men	111
Printing costs	51

Repopulating   The only certain way to revive urban life after a sweep of the plague was to encourage repopulation. Every major city experienced growth by a natural migration from the countryside, and the population ballooned further after plagues because of the higher wages, low rents, poor relief, and generally better living conditions available within the walls. Many towns with fewer economic opportunities never recovered their lost populations or lost even more to the burgeoning cities. Postplague cities needed skilled and ambitious people and not merely laborers, and many offered incentives to immigrants from towns as well as the countryside. For example, in 1350 Orvieto, Italy, promised the full rights of citizenship to all who settled in the city or its hinterland, without any taxes or military service due for 10 years. Other cities' guilds encouraged settlers by shortening apprentice periods or lowering the ages at which masters might begin practicing professions, crafts, or trades. Professionals in very high demand, such as physicians, apothecaries, and notaries, could command extremely high wages and perks such as free rent or waived guild fees.

EXCERPT FROM A POEM ON POSTPLAGUE NATALISM IN THE ITALIAN CITY OF AQUILEIA, RECORDED BY BUCCIO DA RANALLO (D. 1363)

When the plague was over, men revived:
Those who did not have wives took them now,
And women who were widowed got remarried;
Young, old and spinsters all went this way.
Not only these women, but many nuns and sisters
Threw away their habits and became wives,
Many friars ruined themselves to do such things;
And men of ninety took spinsters.
So great was the rush to remarry,
That the numbers by the day could not be counted;
Nor did many wait for Sunday to hold weddings,
They did not care for things, no matter how dear they were.
People were fewer but greed was greater:
From now on women who had dowries,
Were sought after and requested by men . . .
Worse than this, some were abducted.

Excerpts from Trevor Dean, ed., *The Towns of Italy in the Later Middle Ages* (New York: Manchester University Press, 2000), p. 194.

The other way to repopulate a city was to encourage natural growth through increasing the birth rate. Cities generally experienced high marriage and birth rates following plague as widows and widowers, and young men with new wealth, quickly constituted new families. After the outbreak of 1361 Englishman John of Reading complained of

Widows, [who] forgetting the love they had borne toward their first husbands, rushed into the arms of foreigners or, in many cases, of kinsmen, and shamelessly gave birth to bastards conceived in adultery. It was even claimed that in many places brothers took their sisters to wife.[19]

In Vic, Catalonia, the average annual number of marriages from 1338 to 1347 was about 23; in 1349 the total shot up to 73. In Givry, Burgundy, a city of about 2,100 people where 615 died of plague in 1348, the picture was similar: the average of 17.5 rose to 86 in 1349. In 1351 local governments in Castile unsuccessfully petitioned the king to waive the requirement that widows wait six months before remarrying. Other cities introduced policies that are collectively known as "natalism": public means to encourage marriage and births. Florence, for example, established a dowry fund in which fathers invested money for their daughters' dowries. Should the girl die or enter a convent, the family lost the investment. Across Europe both donations and new entrants to women's convents and monasteries fell off in the second half of the fourteenth century as people felt the acute need to be fruitful and multiply.

Europe's city governments faced horrors and enormous challenges as wave after wave of pestilence washed over them. They suffered criticism from their constituents, the church, and royal governments for doing too little, too much, and the wrong things. Yet once in a while one runs across a rare statement of appreciation. In 1652 surgeon José Estiche, of Saragossa, Spain, recognized and praised

the great zeal, care, piety and generosity of those who, in such a stormy year, and thanks to the special providence of heaven, governed this commonwealth. These men, in a rare example of paternal care, preferring the public good to their own comforts, resolved in their council not to spare any effort, no matter how great, nor any expense, no matter how large, in their struggle against the invasion of so fierce an enemy.[20]

NOTES

1. Christopher Dyer, *Making a Living in the Middle Ages* (New Haven: Yale University Press, 2002), pp. 272–73.

2. Richard L. De Lavigne, "La peste noire et la commune de Toulouse," *Annales du Midi* 83 (1971), pp. 413–41; Daniel L. Smail, "Accommodating Plague in Medieval Marseille," *Continuity and Change* 11 (1996), pp. 14–17, 20.

3. Federico Borromeo, *La peste di Milano* (Milan: Rusconi, 1987), p. 50.

4. A.G.E. Jones, "The Great Plague in Yarmouth," *Notes and Queries* 202 (1957), p. 108.

5. Robert Latham and William Matthews, eds., *The Diary of Samuel Pepys*, vol. VII (Berkeley: University of California Press, 2000), p. 52.

6. A.G.E. Jones, "Plagues in Suffolk in the Seventeenth Century," *Notes and Queries* 198 (1953), p. 384.

7. Paul Slack, "Metropolitan Government in Crisis: The Response to Plague," in *London: 1500–1700*, ed. A. L. Beier and Roger Finlay (New York: Longman, 1986), p. 73.

8. William Boghurst, *Loimographia: An Account of the Great Plague of London in the Year 1665* (New York: AMS Press, 1976), p. 60.

9. On Gentile see Jon Arrizabalaga, "Facing the Black Death: Perceptions and Reactions of University Medical Practitioners," in *Practical Medicine from Salerno to the Black Death*, ed. Luis Garcia-Ballester et al. (New York: Cambridge University Press, 1994), p. 271; on Venice see Luigi Parentin, "Cenni sulla peste in Istria e sulla difesa sanitaria," *Archeografo triestino* 4th ser. 34 (1974), p. 11.

10. Carlo Cipolla, *Public Health and the Medical Profession in the Renaissance* (New York: Cambridge University Press, 1976), p. 13; Carlo Cipolla, *Faith, Reason, and the*

Plague in Seventeenth-Century Tuscany (New York: W. W. Norton & Co., 1981), p. 98; Carlo Cipolla, *Fighting the Plague in Seventeenth-Century Italy* (Madison: University of Wisconsin Press, 1981), p. 15.

11. Ann G. Carmichael, *Plague and the Poor in Renaissance Florence* (New York: Cambridge University Press, 1986), p. 96; John Henderson, "The Black Death in Florence: Medical and Communal Responses," in *Death in Towns*, ed. Steven Bassett (New York: Leicester University Press, 1992), p. 143.

12. Robert Gottfried, "Plague, Public Health, and Medicine in Late Medieval England." in *Maladies et société (XIIe-XVIIIe siècles)*, ed. Neithard Bulst and Robert Delort (Paris: Editions du C.N.R.S., 1989), p. 351; E. Sabine, "City Cleaning in Mediaeval London," *Speculum* 12 (1937), pp. 19–24, 40.

13. Carmichael, *Plague*, pp. 107, 123.

14. The rural area around Florence.

15. Quoted in Monique Lucenet, *Les grandes pestes en France* (Paris: Aubier, 1985), p. 49; Henderson, "Black Death," p. 143.

16. Latham and Matthews, *Diary*, Vol. VII, July 30, 1665; J. Gautier-Dalché, "La peste noire dans les états de la couronne d'Aragon," *Bulletin hispanique* 64 (1962), p. 71; Henderson, "Black Death," p. 145.

17. Slack, "Metropolitan," p. 75; J. Taylor, "Plague in the Towns of Hampshire: The Epidemic of 1665–1666," *Southern History* 6 (1984), p. 117.

18. William G. Naphy, *Plagues, Poisons, and Potions* (New York: Manchester University Press, 2002), p. 129.

19. Rosemary Horrox, ed., *The Black Death* (New York: Manchester University Press, 1994), p. 87.

20. Miquel Parets, *A Journal of the Plague Year: The Diary of the Barcelona Tanner Miquel Parets, 1651*, trans. James S. Amelang (New York: Oxford University Press, 1995), p. 101.

8

ON THE STREETS AND ROADS OF EUROPE

In normal times roads and byways, streets, alleys, bridges, and plazas connected the people of rural and urban Europe. They made movement, trade, and communication between regions not only possible, but increasingly safe, fast, and reliable. Late medieval and early modern people continued to improve and extend the roads and bridges that ancient Romans had laid out more than a thousand years before. Within cities, streets and alleyways allowed the circulation of people and goods among houses, shops, churches, and the increasingly specialized buildings that were reshaping the European city. Citizens lived much of their lives in the streets and plazas that defined neighborhoods and regulated many of the relationships of those who lived there. Pageantry regularly filled these open spaces: sacred and secular; religious, royal, and civic; promoting guilds, families, and fraternities; honoring saints, sacrificing criminals, and celebrating the betrothed. The walls of the buildings that lined the streets and plazas echoed with the regular drumbeat of horses' hooves, the clatter of carts and intoning of church bells, and the general din of conversation and negotiation, argument and lecture, joke and insult. Through streets and roads ran the lifeblood of European society.

In plague times, however, this network played other, more ominous roles. Travel may have been necessary but it could also be terrifying. Along the roads crept Death, whether embodied in the imagination as miasmic clouds, wraith-like old women or young girls, carts loaded with plague-infected goods, or poisoners set on killing the innocent. Through the great stone gateways of cities and towns entered the region's sick and dying who sought alms and medical aid inside; passing them, fleeing in the other direction, sped the wealthier city-dwellers, seeking the uncorrupted countryside or unstricken towns. Through city streets wound anemic funeral corteges and fear-induced religious processions whose members sought divine forgiveness. The sick and those who served their needs walked the streets with colored sticks that warned away any healthy person who ventured into the often deserted and desolate urban landscape. Along the roads traveled pilgrims and flagellants, soldiers and deserters, thieves and cutthroats, refugees, quacks, and administrators. What the urban denizen, villager, and traveler alike confronted were the horrors of the great mortality. Along city streets rumbled tumbrels piled high with the sick destined for the pest house and the dead to be swallowed by mass graves. Bodies, some with life still faintly within, were dumped unceremoniously in alleyways and ditches and courtyards by parents and children, brothers and sisters, masters and hosts. Many who lay dead along highways and byways had simply dropped, exhausted, while desperately seeking help or wandering aimlessly in the dementia that accompanied the plague. In later years, thanks to city regulations, streets were filled with supposedly "infected" mattresses, furniture, linens, and clothing that awaited fumigation or incineration. Bonfires appeared in many early modern streets as magistrates sought to purify the plague-saturated air. The stench of human filth and rotting flesh wafted along narrow streets, broad boulevards, and back alleys, along with the dreary, echoing clangs of tolling church bells and the gravediggers' cry, in every European language and dialect: "Bring out your dead!"

CITY STREETS

Sanitation   The streets of ancient Roman cities were paved with stones and sculpted in a way to encourage drainage. After the disappearance of classical civilization, these well-dressed stones often found their way to other building projects or were buried beneath the debris of generations of medieval people. For centuries these once-great cities had streets of dirt. The economic and demographic boom of the later twelfth and thirteenth centuries reinvigorated Europe's ancient cities and led to the creation of new ones. By 1300 major cities like Paris and Florence were well paved in stone once again, though only major streets in smaller towns had this amenity. Paving kept the dust down in summer and the mud clear in winter, and also provided a sounder and safer base for carts, wagons, and, later, carriages. In addition to rainwater, paved streets also drained away other types of urban filth, including human and animal waste and the blood of butchered animals. Where pavement did not exist, this foul matter was usually simply ground into the hard-packed dirt or well-churned mud.

All large cities and many smaller ones had begun trying to limit the accumulation of filth in the thirteenth century, but most efforts had limited results. The medical theories surrounding the Black Death amplified the message that "stench causes death," and Europeans began to take clean streets more seriously. Royal and civic governments alike demanded that sources of "corrupt air" such as piles of manure and open cesspits or drains be tended to or removed. People in odiferous trades such as butchery, tanning, and fish-mongering were often ordered to relocate to riversides or the outskirts of towns, or dispose of their wastes more efficiently. That laws mandating such sanitation measures were passed time and again is not a sign that they were effective, but that they were ignored. By the sixteenth century cities like London developed specific means for clearing street filth. Each London ward appointed two "scavengers," unpaid householders who swore an oath to oversee the "rakers" who kept the streets cleared. The salaried rakers proceeded every Monday, Wednesday, and Friday through each street of the ward, blowing a horn before each house and calling for the family's waste and garbage. Later, this work became a daily task that had to be completed before 6:00 P.M.

In plague time, of course, such amenities disappeared as civic governments shifted their priorities, and collecting corpses became more vital than retrieving rubbish. The problems were exacerbated when cities began "shutting in" whole families suspected of plague, quarantining them for six or seven weeks at a time. Those trapped had no choice but to toss household garbage and waste out their windows and into the street. Since cities had rid streets of swine in normal times, and purposely killed off dogs and other scavengers during plague, the sanitation problems only grew worse.

ARCHBISHOP FEDERIGO BORROMEO OF MILAN ON THE CORPSE-BEARERS, 1630

The *becchini*, taking and placing them on their wagons, were not able to cover or veil nor lay them out properly because of their great number, but they were transported with their legs and arms dangling down. Even heads hung over in the cases of bodies that were a little taller than normal. And yet the *becchini*, something that would seem impossible to say, were used to dealing quite familiarly with the dead and the cadavers that they would sit upon them, and while sitting there, continue drinking. They carried away cadavers from houses as was their custom, over their shoulders like a knapsack or sack, and threw them onto the wagons. It often happened that while some corpse was being removed from a bed, an arm that the *becchino* perchance grasped, its articulation being then so putrefied and loose, broke off from the shoulder, and then hugging the horrible weight they committed it to the wagon, as if they were carrying any other merchandise. Sometimes one could see thirty wagons in an uninterrupted row as heavily laden with cadavers as their yoked horses could pull.... How rapidly the bodies deprived of life became corrupted and once corrupted how disgustingly they stank.

From Federigo Borromeo, *La peste di Milano* (Milan: Rusconi, 1987), p. 73.

Plague dead are picked up off the street by corpse-bearers who smoke pipes to fumigate the air they breathe. From a contemporary English engraving. National Library of Medicine.

Death Stalks the Streets   In "God's Terrible Voice in the City" (1667) Thomas Vincent paints a desolate picture of London in the grip of plague:

[T]here is a dismal solitude in London streets. . . . Now shops are shut in, people rare and very few that walk about, in so much that grass begins to spring up in some places, especially within the Walls; no rattling coaches, no prancing horses, no calling in customers, no offering wares, no London cries sounding in the ears; if any voice be heard it is the groans of dying persons breathing forth their last; and the funeral knells of them that are ready to be carried to their graves.[1]

The cries of those who were there to carry the dead were also all too audible. According to the Milanese carpenter Giambattista Casale, in the summer of 1576 "one heard nothing else in Milan save the cry 'The gravediggers are coming with their cart,' which carried the sick and the dead to the pest house." The Barcelona City Council Minutes for June 5, 1651, read in part:

These gravediggers stop their carts at a street corner in the city and cry out for everyone to bring the dead from their houses . . . and it often happened that the gravediggers would carry dead babies or other children gravely ill with plague on their backs.

The Barcelona tanner and diarist Miquel Parets described how corpses "are often thrown from the windows to the street and then carried off in the carts by the gravediggers, who go about playing their guitars, tambourines and other instruments in order to forget such great afflictions." Indeed, keeping one's spirits up was considered an excellent prophylaxis against plague, however inappropriate it may have seemed. Elsewhere Parets more fully described the grim work of the cadaver-carriers:

They had to use carts to carry the dead, and the gravediggers themselves carried the sick [to the pest house] on cots. Each cart was accompanied by a deputy of the plague warden whose job it was to keep people out of the streets when the carts passed by. . . . To see them move through the streets filled with the dead, some fully dressed and others naked, some wrapped in sheets and others with only their shifts on, was a terrifying sight.[2]

The carts were usually two-wheeled tumbrels, which could be easily tipped backward for dumping the grisly cargo directly into the grave. Reflecting on the egalitarian nature of the plague, an author in Vienna around 1680 wrote,

Whole carriages were seen full of nobles and ignobles, poor and rich, young and old, of both sexes, driven through all the streets and out of the city gates. If a corpse fell from a carriage the corpse bearer threw it back like a piece of wood, frightening those who, waiting in the streets, observed the spectacle.[3]

In the later seventeenth century coaches and even sedan chairs conveyed the stricken to the pest houses of Europe. Over time cities prescribed means of protecting the public from infected vehicles: Vienna licensed special curtained chairs with numbers printed on them for identification, while London required that any coach that had carried a plague victim be aired out for five to six days. Owners who wanted to protect their coach horses sometimes stuffed the animals' nostrils with fragrant herbs meant to filter corrupted air; one in London in 1603 hung rue all over his coach "to keep the leather and nails from infection."[4]

Despite the practice of "shutting in" and the existence of pest houses in many European cities by the later sixteenth century, one was still likely to meet with the infected and those suspected of infection. Many had been abandoned by their friends and relatives; others had arrived from the surrounding countryside in search of medical aid or alms from the wealthier citizens. In sixteenth- and seventeenth-century London those with plague and those who served them were required while in the streets to carry wands, short sticks about a yard long. These were distinctively colored (both used white before 1583; plague-workers carried red ones thereafter). In 1582–1583 the small London parish of St. Michael Cornhill purchased 50 red ones just for the corpse inspectors. Other cities in England and on the Continent established similar requirements. Often these wands were carried by homeless infected beggars who sought charitable alms from passersby, and sometimes otherwise healthy beggars used the wands as a ruse. "As I entered the city gate, I met a man and a woman bearing the white plague wands in their hands and asking for alms; but some believe that this was merely an artifice on their part to gain money,"[5] the Venetian ambassador to Paris noted in 1580. At the same time, in London, people claimed that beggars with these wands aggressively threatened "to infect" those who refused to hand over their money.

Many chroniclers record cases of delirious plague victims running amok in the streets. Fear of such folks continued to grow: By 1636 those walking about with clear plague sores in London could be killed summarily as felons, while any vagabonds found roaming about were subject to a whipping and a bond for "good behavior." Amsterdam was less strict, requiring the infected and their family members to carry openly a four-and-a-half-foot white wand and merely avoid other pedestrians and narrow alleys if at all possible. Other Dutch cities restricted those who were recuperating and wished to walk for exercise to paths in the suburbs or along the town walls or ramparts. Among the most pitiful of the abandoned were the children. The shopkeeper Andrés de la Vega of Seville lamented in 1649 of having

to see many small children in the streets whose parents had died, and lacking help they went about looking for some food, and if anyone gave them something it was by throwing it to them like dogs. They could be found near the city gates, where they died either from hunger or disease.

Milan's very dutiful archbishop Federigo Borromeo also witnessed the dire effects of being orphaned in plague time:

And I saw one day going through the crossroad of the city a group of young children, among them a girl of seven or eight years who, lurching this way and that by the violence of the sickness, was kept on her feet by a younger brother. They made their way thus to the pest house together, and to death.[6]

Sum quidem & ego mortalis
homo.

S A P.   V I I

Ie porte le fainct facrement
Cuidant le mourant fecourir,
Qui mortel fuis pareillement.
Et comme luy me fault mourir.

E iij

Ringing the bell and carrying the lantern, Death
leads the priest and his acolytes who bring
the last sacrament to the dying. From Hans
Holbein's *Danse Macabre*, Lyon, 1538. Dover.

For over three hundred years chroniclers of plague time wrote with
horror of the dying and dead in the streets. In Catholic countries where
priests did their duty, the dying were at least provided with the last
rites of confession, communion, and anointing that constituted the
sacrament of extreme unction. Many prints and paintings in sixteenth-
and seventeenth-century Europe celebrated these acts of heroic self-
lessness, helping rehabilitate the priesthood recently undermined by
the Reformation. Other Good Samaritans may have helped the poor
wretches, but of them little account remains. English Navy administrator and tireless diarist Samuel Pepys reminds us of how quickly and
severely the plague could overcome a victim. On a coach ride in mid-June

of the plague year 1665, Pepys and his driver rattled along until "at last [the coach] stood still, and [the driver] came down [from his seat] hardly able to stand; and told me that he was suddenly stroke very sick and almost blind, he could not see." True to form, Pepys had "a sad heart for the poor man," but was more troubled for his own health, "lest he should have been stroke with the plague."[7]

In cities that practiced shutting in, families wanted to avoid being caught with a plague victim, whether dead or alive. Servants, guests, and apprentices often resided with urban families; when any of these fell ill, they could find themselves hidden away from the authorities in attics or outbuildings. If they died, their corpses were likely to be disposed of surreptitiously, usually at night. The bodies might be placed carefully on pallets or the gravedigger's cart, or unceremoniously dumped in some

Eighteenth-century etching of plague dead in the streets of a classical or neo-classical city. National Library of Medicine.

open area where they would be found easily and buried the next day. When gravediggers were few or overworked, rotting bodies might be found scattered along every street, with bloating, decay, and the effects of scavengers adding to the awful appearance and smells of the plague-ridden corpse. Like other sources of stench, this putrescence was considered a continuing source of "corruption" and plague to be avoided by any passerby and whose immediate removal was greatly to be desired.

During epidemics few people were in the streets needlessly, but one was likely to meet civic officials, **Signs of Plague** physicians, clergy, notaries, and criminals. Some adopted distinctive clothing to ward off the infection. Doctors in many places wore a waxed or oilcloth robe to which the plague could not cling; French doctors added a bird-like head-covering and "beak" that was stuffed with aromatic herbs and served as an air filter. Some claim that the round, pleated ruff that surrounded the necks of several generations of upper-class western Europeans was originally designed as a type of air filter to avoid airborne contagion. Federigo Borromeo warned his priests during plague time to cut their robes very short (to avoid stirring up contagious dust) and to wear over them garments of slick black linen. Upon returning from any errand they were to change shoes and clothes immediately, advice he disseminated throughout his flock. Doctors, surgeons, nurses, apothecaries, and others who served the infected were also required to carry colored wands when abroad to warn the healthy to stay away. Sometimes a small group of men would be found gathered outside of a plague victim's lower window. These men, who feared to go inside, might include a doctor, who examined sweat and urine passed to him; a priest, who heard confession and passed the Eucharist through the window on a long silver spoon; an apothecary, who took down the doctor's orders for medication; and a notary, ready to record the victim's will, with the others as witnesses.

Civic officials and those meeting the needs of shut-ins also roamed the streets. Inspectors were required to confirm causes of death; others made sure the shut-ins remained inside or locked new ones in; some brought shut-ins food, medicines, and other necessities to be handed in through ground-floor windows or higher with buckets on ropes. In London in 1665 male "warders" earned five shillings per week overseeing these activities. Constables or citizen watches patrolled the streets, both to deter and interrupt criminal activity. The social disruptions of plague time led to crimes of opportunity and of desperation as people took advantage of the administrative chaos that often left easy targets. Gravediggers who collected bodies were notorious for stealing anything and everything on which they could lay their hands. Professional thieves and even neighbors ransacked houses left empty by flight or death. In Paret's Barcelona the trouble-makers were often soldiers barracked in the city. Here apprentices were supposed to patrol the night streets to keep order, which they did in armed groups of 18 to 20 for their own protection. "One couldn't leave one's house at night,"

Parets wrote, "thanks to the muggings and thefts and murders and such shamelessness that many nights the watch itself was shot at."[8] Other thugs dressed as soldiers and bullied anyone they met. By the later fifteenth century, city governments regularly erected gallows in prominent places when plague broke out as a reminder of the long arm and short rope of the law.

In the early stages of a plague episode local authorities typically trimmed back public funeral rites, including processions to the church or graveyard. During the initial outbreak of plague in 1348, the papal musician Louis Heyligen wrote of funeral processions in Avignon:

So it happens every day that a rich man is carried to his grave by these ruffians [the gravediggers: "boorish yokels from the mountains of Provence"], with just a few lights [candles] and no mourners apart from them, for while the corpse is going along the street everyone else hides away indoors.[9]

Large, well-attended funerals were a mark of status and dignity and in normal times displayed the honors accorded both deceased and his or her family. In the mid-seventeenth century a London funeral of a prominent person—what Pepys referred to as "The Show"—had in addition to family and friends one paid mourner for every year of the person's life. These processions were sources of income for the poor, since wills often left money to be distributed among them at the funeral. Some cities forbade nighttime burials, since it was so easy to slip in uninspected corpses; others forbade daytime burials to prevent all sorts of unauthorized gathering and pageantry. There was no point in either if no one could see the fancy procession. Punishment for participation in prohibited funerary rituals could be harsh, as when 11 London trumpeters were jailed at Newgate Prison for accompanying the night burial at Shoreditch of their fellow musician, Samuel Underhill. As early as September 1348 the officials of Tournai, Belgium, regulated funerals. The Benedictine abbot Gilles li Muissis recorded their decision: " . . . that nobody at all should wear black, or toll bells for the dead, that palls should not be placed over the bier, and that crowds should be invited, as usual, to attend the funeral, but only two to pray for the dead and to attend the vigils and Mass."

In Catholic countries other processions, which were called to beg God for forgiveness and a lifting of the plague, were more difficult to control. Oftentimes the civil authorities demanded these public displays, though they believed that plague spread easily in such gatherings. In any case it was hard to deny to a city of believers such a spiritual remedy. Louis Heyligen described the earliest of these gatherings:

It is said that these were attended by 2,000 people from all the region round about: men and women alike, many barefoot, others wearing hairshirts or smeared with ashes [traditional signs of penitence]. As they proceeded with lamentations and tears, and with loose hair, they beat themselves with cruel whips until the blood ran.[10]

Pope Clement VI, who ruled the city, not only participated in these demonstrations, but ordered them, as his predecessor Pope Gregory the Great had done in Rome during an epidemic in the early seventh century. With the later condemnation of the flagellant movement, the more excessive elements of self-mutilation generally disappeared, but processions continued throughout the era, often centered on a patron saint's relics, a "miraculous" painting or statue, or the Eucharist itself, displayed in a huge, gold monstrance for all to see. There was an air of normalcy in these great displays, as processions regularly punctuated the church's year: on patron saints' feast days, in commemoration of Jesus' Passion on Good Friday before Easter, and, after 1320, on the Feast of Corpus Christi (The Body of Christ).

From the sixteenth century most European cities suffering pestilence sported three other clear signs of plague in their streets: signs on houses, piles of "infected" cloth goods, and bonfires. Marking the houses of plague victims was a long established practice. In Vienna in 1562 a white cross appeared on the front doors; in Hoorn, The Netherlands, a bundle of straw hung over the door as the indicator; and in Tuscany a simple cross or X sufficed. Historian Frank Wilson nicely summarized the history of such signs in London legislation. In 1518 plague houses were marked with either a red cross and the words "Lord have mercy upon us" upon the front door or a 10-foot-tall pole with a bundle of straw hanging from it posted outside the front door. In 1521 authorities adopted the T-cross associated with St. Anthony painted on blue or white paper and affixed to the front door. These appeared again in 1563 and 1568, and parish clerks had the task of ensuring they were where they belonged each morning. In 1578 the city officials chose a simple sign: a "large sheet of paper printed with a great red circle of the circuit of a foot and a breadth of two inches and the words Lord have mercy upon us, printed in the midst." This image lasted until July 1593, when red crosses were nailed to the front doors. In 1603 authorities decided on a paper sheet with the inscription and a cross painted in red oil paint, fourteen inches in each direction. The sheets were cheap, but the oil paint hard to efface: a perfect pair. Witty commentators of the early seventeenth century had their characters remark on the signs; one dull country lad visiting London was made to wonder at the great devotion of the people, what with so many crosses and prayerful sentiments. More soberly, poet Abraham Holland wrote of the signs' omnipresence in 1625: "So many houses you shall meet/As if the city were one Red Cross Street."[11]

During plague time the streets of early modern cities that were generally kept free of rubbish were suddenly transformed into trash heaps. Piles of clothing, bedding, mattresses, and other furnishings belonging to plague victims were hurled into the streets. As Archbishop Borromeo of Milan put it, "The streets of the city were seen to be full of junk, of tables and all kinds of clothing and obstacles to the point that there didn't remain any empty place."[12] According to Parets, people living with the victims threw out their tainted belongings under the cover of darkness. In other cases these items were discarded by those charged by the city with cleaning out plague houses. In some cities these goods would be "disinfected" by fumigation and/or careful washing, in others burned in great public fires. Tuscan authorities incinerated such stuff in bonfires held near the city gallows: a reminder of the punishment for stealing such—literally—tainted goods. Some officials, however, halted the practice of burning infected goods when they came to believe that doing so simply released the plague back into the air, prolonging the civic agony. Other types of bonfires, however, were thought to help purify corrupted air. In 1352 the people of Novgorod, Russia, set bonfires near the places they thought plague had entered the town. In July 1563 London authorities required bonfires be lit every Monday, Wednesday, and Friday evening at 7:00 P.M. The frequency was changed to twice a week between 8:00 and 9:00 P.M. in 1603, and in July 1625 fires were replaced with great outdoor charcoal braziers on which coarse myrrh, frankincense, or stone pitch were burned. Londoners tried bonfires again in 1665, but after only three days rain put them out, and the plague continued unabated.

ROADS AND TRAVEL

The Highway of Death   Despite the early, widely accepted, and persistent theory that pestilence was caused by corrupted air, Europeans consistently accepted that plague was something that arrived from somewhere else and via some carrier. The very earliest explanation for the initial outburst in southern Europe set the tone: Genoese seamen from Caffa brought the plague from the Black Sea. The Genoese notary Gabriele de' Mussis wrote

When the sailors reached these places and mixed with the people there, it was as if they had brought evil spirits with them: every city, every settlement, every place was poisoned by the contagious pestilence, and their inhabitants, both men and women, died suddenly.

In the popular imagination, any tainted person was a threat to life itself. De' Mussis noted that "one infected man could carry the poison to others, and infect people and places with the disease by look alone." Typically, the register of the town hall in Coggeshall, England, reported in 1578: "This Lore Smith [wife of Joseph Smith] was the instrument the Lord used to bring the infection of the plague into the town."[13] In port cities like Genoa, Marseille, and Hamburg, and on islands like Sicily, Iceland, Ireland, and Britain, chroniclers—and very likely the populace as a whole—pinpointed the arrival of plague to the arrival of a single ship whose crew or cargo planted the seeds of disaster. Towns and cities that lay along rivers also blamed boatmen and cargoes, but often the geographic progress of the disease indicated otherwise. Both observers at the time and modern-day scholars have concluded that plague seemed to follow the road systems of Europe. To contemporaries, in plague time every traveler was potentially a harbinger of death: the merchant carried it in his wares, the refugee in his clothing, the stranger in her touch, and the vagabond in his very stare. Paranoia, and some torture-induced testimony, led people at specific places and times to believe that individuals—Jews, Gypsies, Turks, witches, Muslims, Catholics, Protestants, thieves (anyone of ill will would do)—traveled the roads with poisons meant for doorposts and water supplies and holy water basins.

POPE CLEMENT VI ON PERSECUTING JEWS FOR WELL-POISONING, 1348

Recently, however, it has been brought to our attention by public fame—or more accurately, infamy—that numerous Christians are blaming the plague with which God, provoked by their sins, has afflicted the Christian people, on poisonings carried out by the Jews at the instigation of the devil, and that out of their own hot-headedness they have impiously slain many Jews, making no exception for age or sex; and that Jews have been falsely accused of such outrageous behavior so that they can be legitimately put on trial before appropriate judges—which has done nothing to cool the rage of the Christians but has rather inflamed them even more. While such behavior goes unopposed it looks as though their behavior is approved.

Were the Jews, by any chance, to be guilty or cognizant of such enormities a sufficient punishment could scarcely be conceived; yet we should be forced to accept the force of the argument that it cannot be true that the Jews, by such a heinous crime, are the cause or occasion of the plague, because throughout many parts of the world the same plague, by the hidden judgment of God, has afflicted and afflicts the Jews themselves and many other races who have never lived alongside them.

We order you by apostolic writing that each of you [bishops] upon whom this charge has been laid, should straightly command those subject to you, both clerical and lay, when they are assembled in worship at Mass, not to dare (on their own authority or out of hot-headedness) to capture, strike, wound, or kill any Jews or expel them from their service on these grounds. . . .

From his *Sicut Judeis*, in Shlomo Simonsohn, *The Apostolic See and the Jews, Vol. I: Documents, 492–1404* (Toronto: Pontifical Institute of Mediaeval Studies, 1991).

Whether plague arrived by design or accident, it traveled down roadways that could be blocked and through gateways that could be barred. Healthy travelers were first issued "bills of health" by Italian city officials in the fifteenth century, allowing unhindered passage through the city's own territory and that of neighboring states. Though often-bellicose rivals, these cities had to trust each other when it came to plague security, and they did so with a sense of "mutual assured destruction." Guard posts appeared along main arterials and mountain passes whenever plague was in the neighborhood. Suspicious goods and people underwent quarantine or fumigation to lessen any threat they posed. As time passed, increasingly powerful governments used their military forces to regulate the flow of people and goods in plague time, often surrounding infected areas with a strict blockade or cordon sanitaire intended to keep plague localized. Trade and travel were severely restricted, and terrible hardships often attended this practice, but the greater good appeared to have triumphed as the spread of plague came under control and eventually died away altogether. The specific action that is most often credited with eliminating western European plague is the great cordon sanitaire erected by the Austrians along their border with the Turks in the eighteenth century. By carefully regulating the flow of people and goods, they seem to have blocked the reinvigorating flows of pestilence.

War and Plague   In the Bible's Apocalypse, a sword-brandishing horseman on a blood-red mount unleashes war on earth. In the popular imagination the armies that slogged down Europe's roads brought plague, which in turn brought famine, the two combining to bring death to the innocent in their villages, towns, and cities. In many cases plague blunted the horseman's sword by murdering soldiers and sailors before they could murder each other. During fourteenth-century plagues the warring Venetian and Genoese fleets were regularly undermanned, and many ships on both sides lacked crews. Both the Dutch and English fleets that battled one another in the wake of their respective plagues in 1664 and 1665 suffered the strains of depleted manpower. On land, plagues often brought sudden ends to sieges and invasions. When plague struck the English army along the northern border with Scotland in the fall of 1349, the Scots were jubilant, praising God for his favor. After they attacked and contracted the disease themselves, they sang a different tune. At about the same moment, the great Muslim historian Ibn Khaldun records, plague broke out in a southern Spanish Muslim city besieged by King Alfonso XI of Castile. Many Muslims took this as a sign of divine displeasure and began seeking baptism—until the Christian army began to disintegrate due to the same disease.

War mobilized a greater number of people than any other human activity, keeping them together, moving them around through diseased areas, and spreading the disease. Scholars including Jean-Noël Biraben and Edward Eckert have demonstrated that plague moved precisely with armies that had contracted it.[14] From the Hundred Years War to the great Russo-Turkish conflicts of the later eighteenth century, when an army on the move contracted the plague the effects were felt all along its path. Diseases of all types spread like wildfire in army camps and densely packed garrisons. The Milanese Dr. Tadino described the German soldiers that approached Mantua in 1629: "most of these Germans are infected with plague because of their wantonness and dirtiness." From their camps came "unbearable odors due to the rotting straw on which they sleep and die. . . . [They] roam without health passes and they stay wherever they will."[15] Soldiers foraged and pillaged and bullied their way through enemy territory, sometimes contracting the disease, at other times spreading it. Civilians living in such places suffered miserably, and refugees—among them the plague-ridden—fled to nearby towns or wandered the countryside. Soldiers raped women, stole or burned food supplies, and occupied and then destroyed entire villages. They dragooned young men into the army to replace the fallen. Deserters were nearly as bad, and in addition hungry, angry, and utterly unsupervised. Soldiers were brutal, crafty, resourceful, unscrupulous, and unafraid of civilians. None of these men paid attention to the niceties of "bills of health," quarantines, or cordons sanitaires, nor did they recognize other plague-fighting efforts of towns or states. They marched roughshod and unaware through infected territories, seizing grain stores and cloth goods and stirring up the rodents with their deadly fleas. The English delegation to the Convention of Regensburg reported on a village in the Danube basin that had been pillaged by passing armies 18 times in two years. Even those fortunate enough to return home from war could bring the pestilence with them, as did the 1,500 defeated English defenders of Havre who sparked London's epidemic of 1563. During the Thirty Years War alone hundreds of thousands were displaced; somewhere between 6 million and 14 million people died, only a small fraction of whom found death in battle.

"Flee quickly and far and stay away a long time" was standard advice during plague time. Though it may have moved along highways and onboard ships, **Plague and Flight** plague was generally associated with a specific place, and flight from that place was deemed the surest prophylaxis. But flight was a complex phenomenon that had economic, social, moral, and even medical aspects. Giovanni Boccaccio, in his *Decameron*, the earliest literary treatment of flight in plague time, wrestles with some of the issues. He condemned those who "callously maintained that there was no better or more efficacious remedy against a plague than to run away from it." Such people spared "no thought for anyone but themselves," abandoning "their city, their homes, their relatives, their estates, and their belongings," and the suffering victims left behind.[16] Foolishly they thought they could escape God's wrath, which all agreed lay behind the epidemic, by taking to the roads. Rather than pleasing God, such people angered him further with their impudence. Nonetheless, Boccaccio's protagonists, having rationalized their situation, agree with clean consciences to flee the city for an estate in the hills, where they while away 10 days telling stories.

The ambiguity with which Boccaccio treated flight must have reflected the feelings of many throughout the era. A generation later the Florentine chancellor Coluccio Salutati, who lost his own son to plague, vilified those who fled the *patria:* flight was evil and treasonous and in any case all too useless for many. Florence, Venice, and other cities forbade flight and punished those who took to the road. In French Cahors, whose tax base had shriveled after 1350, the town's consuls generated much-needed revenue by fining those who had fled. After numerous waves of pestilence had washed over Europe, flight carried less of a stigma. The Barcelona tanner Miquel Parets opined that "it is just as right to flee in order not to witness the travails and misfortunes and privations that are suffered wherever plague is found." About the same time Englishman William Boghurst, along with many clerics, argued that those who fled should help relieve the suffering left behind by sending aid. He also believed that the "more the fuel the greater the fire,"[17] the fewer people in town, the quicker the plague would

A late-fifteenth-century German family on the road. Woodcut from the 1498 edition of Sebastian Brandt's *Ship of Fools,* Lyon. National Library of Medicine.

subside. Around 1520 the famous Italian physician Girolamo Fracastoro counseled flight, noting that medical treatment for plague should be only for those required to stay.

Over the three centuries of the Second Pandemic, those who remained behind were generally of the lower classes, often servants left to guard houses and shops. Those without much money or property abroad or family in unaffected areas had little chance of escape. Bishop John Hooper of Norwich noted in the 1550s that "there be certain persons that cannot flee although they would: as the poorer sort of people that have no friends nor place to flee unto, more than the poor house they dwell in."[18] The wealthy, on the other hand, could avoid the plague. Many sent their women and children into the country, to the houses of friends and relatives. In early stages of plague the roads were crowded with carts loaded with refugees and their goods, prime targets for highwaymen. In seventeenth-century England many families found that inns and whole villages that had welcomed them in better times shunned them as potential plague-carriers. Left with no alternatives, travelers camped out along the roads until they reached their destinations. In 1625, poet and clergyman John Donne wrote to Sir Thomas Roe:

The citizens fled away, as out of a house on fire, and stuffed their pockets with their best ware, and threw themselves into the highways, and were not received, so much as into barns, and perished so, some of them with more money about them than would have bought the village where they died.

Poorer refugees from Barcelona in 1651 camped out on Montjuich or the Plain of Valldonzella, "making huts out of dirt and sticks or of timber and branches," Parets related.[19] Having used up what food they brought, however, quite a few had to return to the plague-besieged city for more, and many of these ended up diseased and dead. Those who traveled elsewhere were happy to build small quarantine huts near friends or kin, who would warily supply their needs from a short distance.

But terror also isolated the refugees themselves, as each group feared the other carried the plague. The Beggar character in William Bullein's *Dialogue* recalled, "I met with wagons, carts, and horses fully loaded with young children, for fear of the black pestilence, with their boxes of medicines and sweet perfumes. O God, how fast did they run by hundreds, and were afraid of each other for smiting."[20] Other dangers lurked as well. In 1534, while the English fought with the Irish rebel "Silken" Thomas Fitzgerald, plague struck Dublin, forcing hundreds of noble and wealthy children into the countryside for safety. Fitzgerald and his men grabbed up many of these for ransom, but were thwarted by a force of angry parents.

Though pilgrims had been a common sight along Europe's highways for centuries, the Black Death created special spiritual needs and special types of pilgrims. Abbot Gilles of Tournai chronicled the spike in   **Pilgrims and Flagellants** devotion in 1348 for the plague-saint Sebastian, some of whose relics lay in French monasteries:

While the mortality was at its height an enormous number of people (including those of noble birth, knights, matrons, ecclesiastics, canons and members of religious orders, as well as ordinary men and women) flocked to the monastery of St. Peter at Hennegau.

And a bit further along he recorded that "while the pestilence raged in France pilgrims of both sexes and every social class also poured from all parts of France into the monastery of St. Médard at Soissons, where the body of that martyr St. Sebastian was said to lie."[21] In both cases the frenzy was short-lived. Nonetheless, during each plague episode many Catholic Europeans took to the road singly or in large processions to visit local shrines where prayers for God's mercy flowed heavenward. Even the imperial physician, the Belgian Dr. Paul de Sorbait, led a pilgrimage to the shrine at Mariazell, about fifty miles from Vienna. The pilgrims brought the disease with them, spreading it in their wake. A distinctive variety of pilgrimage was the so-called Bianchi movement of 1399. Plague was approaching Italy yet again, and spontaneous three-day processions of penitent townsfolk led by clergy wound their way to neighboring towns, sparking yet more processions in a vast wave of popular piety. Though people's motives were no doubt mixed, the movement may be seen as a positive response to the horrors that they saw descending upon them yet again. Sadly, their prayers went unanswered and the region was struck the following summer.

The flagellant movement that was spawned during the first year of the Second Pandemic was less a popular manifestation of piety than a traveling penitential pageant. Originating in eastern or central Europe—some say in Hungary—small troupes of male penitents took to the roads for 33 days of walking and praying in silence, whipping themselves and each other in imitation of Christ's Passion. By thus imitating Christ, they hoped to bring down divine mercy and thus avoid the plague in the areas through which they marched. Most of their activity was centered in Germany, and an anonymous monk at Neuburg described how they

went devoutly in procession from church to church, walking two by two, totally naked except for a white cloth covering them from their loins to their ankles, singing beautiful hymns in honor of [Christ's] Passion in their mother tongue and beating themselves so hard with knotted whips that drops of blood spattered the roadway.

Another German, the Dominican friar Heinrich von Herford, whose account is the most detailed source on the movement, explained "they were called flagellants because of the whips [*flagella*] which they used in public penance." He described these nasty tools in detail:

Each whip consisted of a stick with three knotted thongs hanging from the end. Two pieces of needle-sharp metal were run through the center of the knots from both sides, forming a cross, the ends of which extended beyond the knots for the length of a grain of wheat or less. Using these whips they whipped and beat their bare skin until their bodies were bruised and swollen and blood rained down, spattering the walls nearby. I have seen, when they whipped themselves, how sometimes those bits of metal penetrated the flesh so deeply that it took more than two attempts to pull them out.[22]

Crowds gathered to watch as the flagellants sang and prayed and beat themselves and one another; some observers even collected their blood as a sort of relic. After a day or two, they moved along to the next town and another performance. Hugo of Reutlingen wrote that a broad range of people participated in the movement: "priest and count, soldier and arms-bearer joined with them, as well as the master of the school, monks, burghers, peasants, and scholars."[23] Their apparent fervor and piety obviously inspired many, but they also brought serious charges of fanaticism and even heresy. The suspicious Henry called them "fools" and despised their lack of clerical leadership. Both Emperor Charles and the powerful theology faculty of the University of Paris called upon Pope Clement to condemn them. In September 1349 the Flemish Benedictine monk Jean de Fayt, who had witnessed the flagellants in action, spoke directly with the pope and convinced him to act. Clement condemned them on October 20, 1349: calling them cruel and impious, he linked them directly to massacres of Jews in German towns and forbade good Christians to participate with or support them. Since the spring, clerical and civic authorities in cities like Lübeck, Erfurt, and Strasbourg had barred flagellants for being disruptive, but now imperial and civic forces actively suppressed the flagellants, often violently. This independent movement went "underground" in Thuringia in early 1350, but thousands joined local, authorized brotherhoods of flagellants directly controlled by the local clergy.

The traveler in plague time confronted a world transformed. The people of the day write of the roadblocks, closed gates, and shuttered inns; the refugees, scoundrels, vagabonds, pilgrims, army deserters, rural processions, **Plague Along the Way** and most of all about the dead. In an age beset by the ravages of war and famine, plague brought a special kind of horror. While none can adequately summarize it, two witnesses may help us feel it. Miquel Parets, the tanner of Barcelona, recalled how in 1651

many poor people fell sick while walking the roads and kept walking as well as they could, and when they could not walk any more they lay down in a ditch gasping for breath until they died. Even when people passed by, they fled, for no one would dare get near enough to say anything to them or give them anything.

Bishop Borromeo of Milan was especially graphic:

Many, while they proceeded on their own legs toward the Pesthouse or the shelters prepared outside the city, fell, having hastened death, and joined the cadavers already spread along the ground; and it was almost impossible to take a step or even set one's foot down without touching the limbs of the dead. And these bodies, whether because of the mud and slime caused by the continual rain, or their nudity, or the corruption of the ulcers, upset people's hearts and filled them with terror.[24]

NOTES

1. Watson Nicholson, *Historical Sources of De Foe's Journal of the Plague Years* (Boston: The Stratford Co., 1919), p. 29.

2. Miquel Parets, *A Journal of the Plague Year: The Diary of the Barcelona Tanner Miquel Parets, 1651,* trans. James S. Amelang (New York: Oxford University Press, 1995), pp. 90, 106, 55.

3. Boris and Helga Velimirovic, "Plague in Vienna," *Review of Infectious Diseases* 2 (1989), p. 820.

4. Frank P. Wilson, *Plague in Shakespeare's London* (New York: Oxford University Press, 1962), p. 98

5. Susan Scott and Christopher Duncan, *The Return of the Black Death* (New York: Halsted Press, 2004), p. 81.

6. Parets, *Journal,* 100; Federico Borromeo, *La peste di Milano* (Milan: Rusconi, 1987), pp. 79–80.

7. Robert Latham and William Matthews, eds., *The Diary of Samuel Pepys,* Vol. VI (Berkeley: University of California Press, 2000), p. 131.

8. Parets, *Journal,* 40.

9. Rosemary Horrox, ed., *The Black Death* (New York: Manchester University Press, 1994), p. 44.

10. Ibid., pp. 53, 44.

11. Wilson, *Plague,* pp. 61–64; Scott and Duncan, *Return,* p. 92.

12. Borromeo, *Peste,* p. 74.

13. Horrox, *Black Death,* p. 19; Charles F. Mullett, *The Bubonic Plague and England* (Lexington: University of Kentucky Press, 1956), p. 68.

14. Jean-Noël Biraben, *Les hommes et la peste en France et dans les pays européens et méditeranéens,* 2 vols. (Paris: Mouton, 1975, 1976), pp. 140–45; Edward A. Eckert, *The Structure of Plagues and Pestilences in Early Modern Europe: Central Europe, 1560–1640* (New York: S. Karger Publishing, 1996); see p. 147 for a concise summary of movements during the later Thirty Years War.

15. Carlo Cipolla, *Cristofano and the Plague* (New York: Collins, 1973), p. 15.

16. Horrox, *Black Death,* pp. 29–30.

17. Parets, *Journal,* p. 59; William Boghurst, *Loimographia: An Account of the Great Plague of London in the Year 1665* (New York: AMS Press, 1976), pp. 58–61.

18. Roy Porter, *The Great Plague* (Stroud, Gloucs., England: Sutton, 1999), p. 5.

19. Wilson, *Plague,* p. 157; Parets, *Journal,* p. 64.

20. William Bullein, *A dialogue against the fever pestilence,* (Millwood, NY: Kraus Reprint, 1987), p. 8.

21. Horrox, *Black Death,* p. 54.

22. Ibid., pp. 60, 150.

23. Richard Kieckhefer, "Radical Tendencies in the Flagellant Movement of the Mid-Fourteenth Century," *Journal of Medieval and Renaissance Studies* 4 (1974), p. 160.

24. Parets, *Journal,* p. 65; Borromeo, *Peste,* p. 77.

9

AT THE BOOKSELLER'S AND THE THEATER

In Verona, Italy, a 13-year-old girl entrusted a vital secret to a clergyman who was to deliver it to her young lover in a distant city. The friar had every intention of carrying out his mission, but on the way found himself shut in by the authorities with a family suspected of plague. Left clueless, the young man returned to Verona to find his beloved laid out as for burial. Grief-stricken, he rashly took his own life rather than live on without her. Upon awaking from her feigned sleep of death and seeing her dead suitor, the distraught girl took her own life. And so the plague claimed two more lives, at least indirectly. Or so went Shakespeare's story of the "star-crossed lovers," Romeo and Juliet.

During the sixteenth and seventeenth centuries in major cities and provincial towns across Europe the plague provided a somber and shifting backdrop to the newly emerging art of the theater. In a single generation, playgoers watched as drama emerged from its medieval liturgical and religious cocoon into the richly textured Renaissance product that blended classical secular subjects and forms with a new naturalism. The plague found its way into the plots and settings of numerous plays, and references to astrology, medicine, and pox pepper many more. In Protestant England, moralists blamed the theater's players for spreading God-provoking licentiousness among the lower-class audiences and the audiences for spreading the plague. When the authorities shut down the theaters for public-health reasons, playwrights were often forced to produce alternative forms of art: Shakespeare created his immortal sonnets between 1592 and 1596, and in the early 1600s poet and dramatist Thomas Dekker turned his hand to writing popular moral pamphlets about the plague and London society.

During the first outbreak of the plague, physicians penned professional medical works on the disease in Latin, some of which found their way into the vernacular and even verse. With few changes in medical theories or advice, until the early eighteenth century medical men continued to produce tracts "explaining" the plague and recommending individual or civic actions to avoid or counteract it. Increasingly these writings were in the vernacular and for a popular audience. Between Giovanni Boccaccio's *Decameron*, written during the first years of the Second Pandemic (c. 1351), and Daniel Defoe's *Journal of Plague Year*, published in Europe's last great plague year (1722), literary authors wrote countless popular books, poems, dialogues, plays, pamphlets, almanacs, broadsides, and other literary materials concerning the plague. Though plague literature for the masses appeared only with the introduction of Gutenberg's printing press in the 1450s, popular works such as Chaucer's *Canterbury Tales* and *Piers Plowman* by William Langland displayed the social effects of the Black Death and circulated widely in manuscript. By the 1550s, during each plague cycle the literate public was devouring a diet of inexpensive medical manuals, prayer sheets, bills of mortality, astrological tracts, moral lessons, cure-all recipes, and luridly illustrated reports on plague at home and abroad. Apothecaries, surgeons, quacks, physicians, poets, preachers, priests, and playwrights filled people's heads with advice good and bad, consolation, fear of damnation, food for thought, and fear of foods thought harmful in times of plague. Street vendors, booksellers, druggists, innkeepers, doctors, coffeehouse owners, and even tobacconists (the weed was thought to be a prophylactic against the airborne plague) peddled the day's popular plague literature, which helped to shape the common people's understanding of the phenomenon and their many reactions to it.

MEDICAL LITERATURE AND THE PLAGUE

Medieval Plague *Consilia* from 1348 to 1350

The oldest form of plague literature dating from the Second Pandemic was the professional medical treatise known as the *consilium*. These "counsels" had long been written in Latin by practicing and well-known physicians for specific patients who suffered from any sort of illness. Usually the author lived at a distance and would have been informed by letter—often written by another physician or surgeon—of the patient's condition and symptoms. Trusting the accuracy of the information, the author of the *consilium* would make a diagnosis and provide a regimen of diet and medicines he thought appropriate to the case. When the plague suddenly confronted well-off Europeans in 1348 and 1349 they sought the advice of their own physicians, who in turn invoked the expertise of the best doctors they knew. From Llerida in Spain to the capital of the Empire in Prague, Europe's best medical minds wrestled on paper with the great pestilence.

Gentile da Foligno, who died in June 1348, was one of the first to address the new disease. Perhaps the most famous physician of his day, he addressed *consilia* to the civic governments of the Italian cities of Genoa, Naples, and his own Perugia. He followed the basic outline of the traditional medical *consilium:* the nature and cause of the disease, its signs both in nature and on the human body (symptoms), means of avoiding or preventing the illness (prophylaxis), and the means of treating it (therapy). His ideas and advice were strictly Galenic and mainstream for his day, and thus ineffectual. In Naples, the university medical professor Giovanni della Penna responded in his own *consilium* by criticizing specific elements of Gentile's work, from how the corrupted air affected the human body to which fruits were best to eat. Since he worked within the same incorrect framework, however, Giovanni's advice was no better than Gentile's. Both of these works were written in Latin and circulated in manuscript among Italian doctors and literate laypeople, and Gentile's was first printed in 1472.

In Prague, Emperor Charles IV requested a *consilium* from his imperial physician Master Gallus, who also wrote one entitled "Preventives and Measures against the Disease" for the margrave of Moravia. As his model and chief source Master Gallus used the most famous and often copied *consilium,* that of the medical faculty of the University of Paris. Their jointly composed "Compendium on the Epidemic" was ordered by the French king in October 1348 as a means of helping him understand the disease and apply the measures to prevent it in his kingdom. Unfortunately, none of the Paris scholar/doctors had had any experience of plague victims, so their expertise was based solely upon general medical principles of epidemic disease and what they had heard from other doctors. The modern historian of French literature Alfred Coville characterized the resulting piece as a "mélange of prejudices, fantastical interpretations, and ingenious and useful observations, presented with discretion and piety."[1] Within a year it was circulating in a vernacular version. Even though it was the first major work to come from the recently founded medical faculty at the university, copies quickly found their way into Switzerland, Spain, Poland, Italy, and, of course, the Empire, thanks to the school's prestige. Several fourteenth-century copies can still be consulted in European libraries. Seventy-five years after it first appeared, the French poet Olivier de la Haye transformed the dry Latin work into French verse (with its own glossary), and the original was still being copied in the seventeenth century.

Other *consilia* from the years 1348–1350 were composed by groups like the five physicians of Strasbourg, whose humbly titled *Treasure of Wisdom and Art* offered to the leaders and people of Strasbourg professional advice based upon the doctors' experience of the disease. Most *consilia,* however,

were written by individuals, such as Tommaso del Garbo, the Italian doctor
whom the poet Petrarch claimed capable of raising the dead, even if they
had been buried for years and turned green. In Aragon, the civic-minded
Master Jacme d'Agramont presented the "lords and Council of the City
of Llerida" with his "Letter" of advice on the plague, written in Catalan
and dated April 24, 1348. He clearly stated that he wrote this work "for
the benefit of the people, not the instruction of the physician," and elsewhere "it has been written for the common and public utility." At about
the same time in Montpellier the Spaniard Alfonso of Cordoba composed
a very optimistic "Letter and Regimen on the Pestilence." He boldly stated
that humans could affect the natural causes of the plague, and that natural
philosophy—the academic study of nature as it was before the Scientific
Revolution—gave men the knowledge necessary to control nature. He did,
however, note that medical wisdom and art could be used for good or evil,
and, sadly, blamed epidemics that lasted more than a year on well water
poisoned by Jews and Muslims.

Later Medieval Plague Tracts and Manuals

A total of 18 *consilia* are known to have been written
around 1350, but at least another 200—perhaps over
900[2]—similar tracts, most of them in the European vernaculars, appeared over the next century and a half.
These works reflected their origins in the *consilia* tradition, but were broader in scope and generally composed for the public
rather than specific patrons. Some carried stringent moral messages along
with the medical advice. The anonymous Portuguese author of "Preventive Regimen against the Pestilence" dutifully blames the disease on corrupted air, counseling the removal of corpses, dead animals, cesspools,
sewers, and dunghills. But his first level of advice is for the reader to "put
his evil practices to one side, and to embrace the good ones; that is, a man
must first confess his sins humbly, because holy penitence and confession
are a great remedy as they are more valuable and efficacious than all medicines."[3] Writing around 1485, the Norman physician Thomas Forestier
blamed original sin as one of the causes of plague, and the mid-fifteenth-
century "Canutus" plague tract attributes it at least in part to "lust for
women."

Like the *consilia*, the later medical tracts relied heavily on the standard
medical authorities of the day, including Aristotle, Galen, Hippocrates,
the classical Muslim physicians Avicenna, Ali-Abbas, and Razes, and the
plague-era Spanish Muslims Al-Khatib and Ibn Khatimah. Their inclusion
was clearly meant to reassure the reader that the author knew his medicine and was indeed an expert. Many tracts also emphasized the practical experience of their authors: the author of the "Canutus" plague tract
offers the slogan "trial by experience emerges as the final assurance of
effectiveness," and following one recommendation the French "Damouzy
Consilium" of 1360 or 1361 reassures its reader that "no one who uses this
[remedy] dies from plague." Clearly, some of these tracts were meant to

draw new clients to their authors, and more than one assures the reader that the remedies outlined had saved even the author's life. One of these authors was the physician of Belluna, Italy, Dionysius Secundus Colle, who recommended in his "About the Pestilence of 1348–1350 and Pestilential Peri-pneumonia, and Malignant Likewise" a disgusting concoction of human and animal offal.

Despite the inability of traditional Galenic medicine to affect the disease or cure its victims, it remained the basis of standard medical theory and practice until the eighteenth century. Renaissance-era medical texts profited from their authors' access to better editions of Hippocrates and Galen, but the flawed foundation remained flawed. Medical writers continued to pen works in Latin for their fellow professionals, but the development of the printing press in the 1450s and the general increase in vernacular literacy across Europe created a new and very broad market for medical advice in the languages of everyday speech. The inability of local doctors to affect the epidemics, the high cost of professional health care, and its general unavailability to all but the wealthiest prompted many early modern Europeans to seek out professional medical advice in relatively cheap manuals, tracts, and books.

Galenic Medical Texts of the Sixteenth Century

Of course, plague was only one disease among many afflicting Europe's population in the 1500s and 1600s, among which were various forms of "the pox," dysentery, whooping cough, numerous diseases of the stomach and bowels, a wide variety of fevers, in Tudor England the mysterious "sweating sickness," and the new (or increasingly reported) maladies typhus, influenza, and venereal disease. Books on general matters of health and medicine included "*practicae,*" which were encyclopedic reference works on medicine; "regimens," which concentrated on Galenic notions of health maintenance through proper diet, drink, and exercise; "*experimenta,*" in which "proven" remedies for a whole host of ailments could be found; "herbals," often of classical or medieval origin, in which the medicinal properties of hundreds of plants were listed; and general and very practical medical handbooks known in England as "leechbooks," from the popular term for a physician or surgeon. Some of these were translations from earlier Latin works, others translations from other vernacular languages, and still others were composed in the vernacular for a contemporary audience. Often the translators were people other than physicians, such as lawyers, clergy, apothecaries, scholars, or teachers.

Sir Thomas Elyot's *The Castle of Health* of 1534 is a well-known example of a popular English medical manual. Elyot's work is a very strict treatment of Galen's writings, which he was able to read thanks to their earlier translation from Greek to Latin by the English physician and humanist Thomas Linacre. Elyot lays out the theory of humors, the factors that affect their balance, and the ways to treat the imbalances

Popular Medical and Plague Texts in Tudor England

known as diseases. In 1528 Thomas Paynell, an Augustinian clergyman at Merton Abbey, Surrey, freely translated into English the *Regimen sanitatis salerni* (The Regimen of Health of Salerno), a late fourteenth-century regimen in Latin verse by the physician of Salerno, Italy, Giovanni da Milano.[4] Salerno had long been a center of medical education in Europe, and Paynell counted on its reputation to help sell his own version. Though it was a fully medieval example of Galenic medicine, Paynell's regimen enjoyed great success, going through nine editions between 1528 and 1634.

At least 23 books specifically on the plague were published in English—often with multiple editions—during the Tudor era (1485–1603), and many more general works contained detailed sections on the plague. The earliest medical prose work in English on plague was the translation of the Swedish "Canutus" tract. In 1485 it appeared in print as *A Little Book the Which Treated and Rehearsed Many Good Things Necessary for the . . . Pestilence*. It was reprinted in 1488, 1490, 1510, 1520, and 1536; additionally it appeared in translation in France around 1498 and Antwerp in 1520. Thomas Paynell also translated the "Canutus" text in the 1520s, entitling his work *A Much Profitable Treatise against the Pestilence*.

The persistence of the plague clearly drove the popularity of medical literature, as is evident from the title of the English Dominican Thomas Moulton's *The Mirror or Glass of Health: Needful for Every Person to Look in That Will Keep Their Body from the Sickness of the Pestilence: And Showeth the Remedies for Many Diverse Infirmities and Diseases that Hurt the Body of Man*. Considered the most popular medical book in sixteenth-century England, this example of a leechbook went through 21 printed editions from the 1530s to 1580. Moulton probably wrote the book in the 1490s, and it is essentially a retread of a plague tract by John of Burgundy from about 1350. Its popularity from the 1530s stems at least in part from Thomas's harsh and condemning moral tone, which he applies even to the plague's victims, whose immorality he is certain has angered God and brought down the divine punishment. Further, and fittingly for the England of Henry VIII, Thomas ultimately blames the "head men and the governors of the [Roman Catholic] Church," the corrupt popes and cardinals. That his work was composed for the people at large is clear from the inscription with which Moulton opens his work: "that every man both learned and lewd may the better understand it and do thereafter, and to be his own physician in time of need against the venom and the malice of the pestilence."[5]

Popular Medical Texts Elsewhere in Sixteenth-Century Europe

Equally moralistic was the earliest plague tract in the Scots dialect, Gilbert Skeyne's *A Brief Description of the Pest Wherein the Causes, Signs, and Some Special Preservation and Cure Thereof Are Contained*, published in 1569. Skeyne was a professor of medicine at King's College, Aberdeen, and royal physician to Scotland's King James VI, yet much of his preventive advice revolved around personal and social morality, including the necessity of unselfishness, humility, and repentance for sin. Of course, many Galenic medical books appeared elsewhere in Europe, such as the *Regimen of Life* by the Dutchman Jehan Goeurot, which saw 10 printed editions between 1549 and 1596. Even longer lasting was the *Sure and Certain Methods of Attaining a Long and Healthful Life* by the Italian physician Luigi Cornaro, which went through 12 editions between 1558 and 1724. In the Tuscan countryside, where professional medical help was scanty, medical recipe books were extremely popular. Giulia Calvi, a modern scholar of plague in Italy, has referred to the printers' output as a "vast body of pamphlet literature" on plague and other medical conditions.[6]

In Denmark, the University of Copenhagen's first Professor of Medicine, Christen Morsing, published in 1546 a short plague tract that he dedicated to the school's chancellor. Early printed German plague tracts include the 1473 *Little Book of Rules* by Ulm's city physician Heinrich Steinhöwel. He offers the usual Galenic advice about exercise and diet, but gives special attention to animals and meat products. For example, animals should be left out to pasture rather than kept in stuffy, badly ventilated stalls with their noxious odors, Steinhöwel wrote, and people should avoid consuming all organ meats except chicken livers, sheep or goat brains, and rooster testicles—and these should be eaten with plenty of ginger and pepper.

Between 1510 and 1600 printers in France produced 48 original plague tracts in the vernacular for the general public—a quarter of all the century's medical books in French. Physicians penned nearly half of these works on pestilence; clerics wrote three, surgeons three, an apothecary one, and one was by a magistrate. The audience for these works differed somewhat from that for which English authors wrote. Many, indeed, targeted the general public, as shown in the introduction to Nicolas Nancel's 1581 tract in which he explains his use of French instead of Latin: "The reason is that I wanted to accommodate to the capacity and intelligence of the vulgar."[7] Some wrote their tracts in French specifically for surgeons and apothecaries, who were the physicians' social inferiors and normally did not understand Latin. A number of plague works are aimed at civic leaders and contain lots of advice for public action against the plague, much of which involves keeping the plague out of the city by harsh police measures. Some authors wrote in the vernacular in order to educate common people away from the advice and potions of charlatans and quacks, an increasingly large and troublesome group that preyed on the unwary during plague times. Laurent Joubert pioneered this genre with his 1579 book *Popular Errors*, which was reprinted well into the 1700s. Joubert challenged four particular types of "popular errors": those stemming from the occult and its practitioners, from magic or conjuring, from household manuals written by misleading or ignorant authors, and the so-called "empirical lore" being sold by surgeons, doctors, and apothecaries. While these French works generally avoided the heavy moralizing of their English contemporaries, most open with warnings against God's anger and punishment and calls for reform of life. In the latter half of the century this message may reflect the influence of the Calvinist Huguenots, who were often well-off—and book-buying—bourgeois.

Popular Medical Works and Plague Tracts of the Seventeenth Century   The trend of popularizing medical literature continued into and even expanded during the seventeenth century. At mid-century the English physician and political radical Nicholas Culpepper wrote, "All the nation are already physicians: if you ail anything, everyone you meet, whether man or woman, will prescribe you a medicine for it."[8] Unlike the vast majority of medical men of his day, Culpepper truly wanted to see this effect. He strove to make professional knowledge available to common people and even produced an unauthorized translation of the *Pharmacopoeia*[9] of London's College of Physicians. His goal as a social reformer was to free people from the grasp of the clergy, lawyers, and physicians who kept them under their power by keeping them ignorant. Others, of course, simply sought profit, and the same combination of perceived need and the high cost and unavailability of professional service continued to drive sales of plague books. The author "A. M." noted that he composed his *Treatise Concerning the Plague and the Pox* of 1652 for those in both "a necessitous time and in places remote, both from able physicians and surgeons."[10] The advice in most plague literature was still Galenic, and the prophylaxes and cures were still largely dietary in nature. Unlike apothecaries, who sold herbs and ready-made medicines, the authors of most seventeenth-century plague books emphasized recipes for homemade remedies in their publications. Books like Robert Pemel's *PTOCHOPHARMAKON or Help for the Poor* (1650) or *The Poor Man's Physician and Surgeon, Containing Above Three Hundred Rare and Choice Recipes . . . Published for the Public Good* by Launcelot Coelson, a "student of Physick and Astrology" in 1656, empowered commoners in town and countryside alike.[11]

In France, the Counter-Reformation led to an intensified emphasis on the laity aiding their poor neighbors, including the sick poor. As in the case of the earlier feudal notion of noblesse oblige, upper-class women were expected to practice charity by tending to the medical needs of the needy, especially in the physician-poor countryside. Books like *Medicine of the Poor* (c. 1620) by "Praevotius," *Physician of the Poor* (c. 1650) by Lazar Meysonnier, and *Operator of the Poor* by the "Surgeon Vaussard" were goads to charitable activity as well as how-to manuals on basic medical procedures and remedies. Over 200 plague tracts in French—from 4 to 400 pages in length—appeared in the seventeenth and eighteenth centuries. Nearly half were published in Paris, though the percentage originating in the provinces increased as time passed. From Troyes, for example, came the especially cheap "Blue Library" editions of the seventeenth century.

As in England, the trend was toward instilling both greater self-reliance and better morals. As to the first, a good example is found in the text of Jean Cottin's 1635 manual, which he wrote "so that each of you can profit from my book: for in the judgment of Galen, every prudent man serves as physician for himself." In this he echoes the sentiments of Culpepper and of Guillaume L'Erisse, who wrote in his 1628 tract *Excellent and Quite Familiar Method for Curing the Pest and Preserving Oneself from It*, "All can be physicians themselves, helping each other without the ministry of a physician." Regarding the moral tone found in French plague literature, historians Laurence Brockliss and Colin Jones recently wrote that each work is "less a medical prescription than a pedagogic, proselytizing text, a parable about the Christian community's repentance."[12] Good health was both a medical and spiritual matter.

An example of a plague tract composed by a student of the era's chief alternative medicine, Paracelsianism, is *Guardian [against] Pestilence*, written in 1612 by the Jesuit priest Hippolytus Guarinonius of Ingolstadt, in the Austrian Tyrol. Paracelsus was a Protestant German physician and radical medical thinker active in the mid-sixteenth century who wrote a plague tract of his own. His approach to medicine differed substantially from that of the Galenists. In general, Paracelsus saw human health as a matter of the balance not of humors but of certain inorganic chemicals such as salt and sulfur in the body. His therapies and remedies were therefore more chemical and mineral-based than dietary in nature, often blending alchemical processes with notions of occult spirit powers residing in such things as stones, roots, and seeds. In his own writings Paracelsus saw his radical challenge to traditional Galenism as being parallel with Martin Luther's contemporary challenge to traditional Roman Catholic beliefs and practices. His popularity among Protestants sprang as much from his Lutheran sensibilities and published railings against Catholicism as from his new-fangled chemical medicine. The Counter-Reformation–era Jesuit Guarinonius discarded Paracelsus' anti-Catholic elements but accepted the therapeutic and disinfectant qualities of minerals, especially salt. His *Guardian* is a blend of Galenic and Paracelsian theories and remedies. Its readers learn that the "miasmic cloud" associated with plague contains poisonous "seeds" that are breathed in and against which the best remedies are fire and salt. He recommended boiling "infected" clothing and linen in salt water rather than burning them, a real boon to poorer folk with few belongings. Extra salt was to be baked in bread; in victims' houses woodwork, furniture, and floors were to be washed down with salt water; and church floors were to be strewn with salt during services in plague time. He further recommended firing muskets with sulfurous gunpowder in victims' rooms "until the walls grew warm." He wrote his work in German and designed it "for persons of every station"; the result is a kind of people's catechism on the plague whose author is blunt, preachy, and shockingly colloquial.[13]

MEDIEVAL POPULAR LITERATURE AND THE PLAGUE

Like sculpted and painted medieval visions of hell meant to scare medieval Christians straight, literary works containing the threat or horrors of plague time carried with them a grim moral message of human sinfulness, divine anger, and the necessity of repentance and change of life. Just as medieval artists conveyed the point that sin led to hell, early modern plague writers almost invariably intoned that sinners and sinful societies brought down upon themselves divine wrath and the Black Death, truly a hell on earth. Writers used every literary form and technique at their disposal to link their moralizing with the extraordinary experiences of plague time. Their poetry, drama, fiction, medical advice, short stories, chronicles, reports, sermons, histories, even arguably the first modern English novel by turns informed, terrified, sobered, warned, shamed, and drew empathy from their readers, for whom the plague was no far-off apocalypse but an all-too-real experience.

The Medieval Tradition: Boccaccio
In an article published in the *Journal of the American Medical Association* in 1997, S. S. Yom wrote that living through plague time meant "the ultimate confrontation with suffering and horror."[14] According to Yom, the author who chooses to write about the plague does so from one or a combination of motives: sheer horror, the need to bear witness to the events, or the desire to affirm the human will to survive. It may be that since he is writing in the context of the modern scourge of AIDS he purposely omitted one of the clearest and most consistent motives of writers during the Second Pandemic: to use the disease and the events surrounding its epidemic as a parable for human immorality and divine punishment. In the Introduction of his popular collection of often raunchy short stories known as the *Decameron* (c. 1350), Giovanni Boccaccio recounts in vivid and sickening detail the disease, its victims, and Florentine society's reaction to both. As an early member of the humanist movement he is aware that he is chronicling—or bearing witness to—the event for posterity, since all of his readers had experienced in some form what he described. Yet by placing the horrors of the plague right beside the young, fictional survivors, their escape, and their temporarily idyllic life in the country villa, Boccaccio affirms for his readers the beauty and joys of life and of survival. He was not writing of or for the dead but for the living, many of whom no doubt suffered the kind of vague guilt that often dogs those who live on when so many loved ones die tragically.

The Medieval English Tradition
After successive waves of plague in the 1360s and 1370s, Europeans came to realize that God's scourging was not a one-time matter, but a recurring punishment for sinful human behavior. When observers noted that the Black Death had caused many social dislocations, including

making many rich and poor people better off economically, raising laborers' wages, and dissolving traditional feudal ties between peasants and their "betters," they began to link God's wrath to specific social "sins." In England the natural disasters of plague and a 1382 earthquake were linked to the social upheaval of the Peasants' Revolt of 1381. For the anonymous author of the popular "Dives and Pauper: A Warning to Be Ware," the cause of both types of events was clearly the greed of the wealthy, whose exploitation of the working poor angered God. On the other hand, in the same decade the anticlerical William Langland in his *Piers Plowman* casts his critical net more widely. Indeed, he chided, greater individual wealth in postplague England had led doctors, clergy, and some landholders to become slothful, corrupted, and greedy. But equally problematic were the slothful and gluttonous beggars whose sinful behaviors were enabled by the alms of the God-fearing wealthy, and the high wages they paid for minimal effort. While the lower classes could cheer the warnings to the elite, they also had to endure the critique of their own. The answers that Langland presented to his audience included changes in societal attitudes that made both the wealthy and the laborers more responsible: the lower classes more humble, reliant, and hard-working, the upper more honest and helpful. For those seeking to avoid another round of plague he also recommended a diet that followed the Galenic patterns of the day.[15] This blending of theological, social, and practical elements would become a hallmark of English plague literature.

Readers' desire for the religious element waned in the next century, as evident in the English monk and poet John Lydgate's "A Diet and Doctrine for Pestilence." In many ways this work is a Middle English versified form of a physician's plague tract, but it also carries an important message about the need for stability and harmony in the social order. In the midst of his discussion of the humors, upon whose proper balance good bodily health depends, the poet intones:

> All infirmity comes from too much or too little—
> Lack of self control in balancing these extremes
> Drives one away from the mean, to excess or scarcity:
> Set your sights on moderation.[16]

Like Langdon, Lydgate stressed that maintaining harmony in the social order and one's own relationships is important to social and individual health. Lydgate's original patron may have been Duke Humphrey of Gloucester, a member of the royal family, but his message circulated widely, and 55 manuscript copies have survived. Its popularity probably stemmed from its practicality as well as the fact that there was virtually nothing else of its kind written in English until the translation of the Canutus tract in the 1480s.

FROM JOHN LYDGATE'S "A DIET FOR PLAGUE," EARLY FIFTEENTH CENTURY

Befitting a work by a Catholic monk, Lydgate's poem is not entirely free from moral advice:

[Stanza 16]

> Dress cleanly, and according to your status;
> Don't exceed your limits; keep your promises faithfully,
> Avoiding discord especially with three groups of people:
> First, be wary of contests against your betters;
> Don't seek quarrels with your fellows;
> And it is shameful to fight with those subject to you.
> Therefore, I counsel, seek all your life
> To live in peace and acquire a good reputation.

[Stanza 17]

> While fire in the morning and in the evening before bed is useful
> Against black mists and pestilential air,
> Even better is being on time for Mass,
> Doing God reverence upon first rising in the morning,
> Diligently visiting the poor,
> Having pity and compassion on all who are needy—
> Then God will send you grace and influence,
> To increase you and your possessions.

Excerpts from "A Diet for Plague" by John Lydgate, published in Joseph P. Byrne, *The Black Death* (Westport, CT: Greenwood Press, 2004), pp. 165–66.

Plague's Impact on Religious and Moral Literature
The medieval plague also spurred the writing and publishing of a number of other types of literature. Just as the failure of the medical profession helped spawn self-help books, the failure of the clergy to appease God sufficiently to stop the plagues led to an increase in individual piety and spiritual activity. Some, especially the wealthy, used "books of hours," which were collections of prayers to be said during the course of a day. Modeled on the monastic hours of worship prescribed by St. Benedict in the sixth century, these books included prayers specifically written for the lay man or woman. Many of these prayers begged God for mercy and avoidance of or release from illnesses such as epilepsy and, of course, the plague, but also for safety while giving birth or undergoing a bloodletting, and ultimately for a "good," holy death. The monastic concept of a good death was also translated for the general public from the fourteenth century, and books known as *Ars moriendi*—Art of Dying [Well]—also became quite popular.[17] They advocated the patterns of life that would direct one toward a death leading to heavenly rewards and prescribed the rituals and prayers that would protect the dying from the

As family members look on, the demons of Avarice (greed) torment the dying man, whose wealth is signified by his large house, well-stocked cellar, and fine horse. Woodcut from a French *Ars moriendi of* 1465. Dover.

snares of Satan and ensure a perfect passing. Both books of hours and *Ars moriendi* were often rather expensive, illustrated, and likely to be passed down within families.

Less hardy and more ephemeral were cheap illustrated pamphlets that linked short moral verses with striking pictures. One popular theme was the Meeting of the Three Living with the Three Dead, according to which three young, startled, well-off aristocrats are reminded by three decaying corpses that one day death would be their fate, too. In the thematically similar *Danse Macabre*, Death, in the form of a skeleton, dances dismayed men and women from their daily pursuits off to the netherworld.[18] Like

Death confronts the queen and the duchess. From the *Danse Macabre des Femmes,* printed by Guyot Marchant, Paris, 1486. Dover.

the manifold characters in Geoffrey Chaucer's *Canterbury Tales,* the dancers reflect a full range of human types, from popes to peasants, a feature that gives these a populist appeal. A later fifteenth-century Parisian version by Martial d'Auvergne is peopled exclusively with women, specifically Parisian women. They constitute a rather independent lot that includes shopkeepers, a queen, noblewomen, nuns, a prostitute, and even a female theologian. Unlike the more general *Danses* that feature the full range of the Seven Deadly Sins, D'Auvergne's focuses on stereotupical female covetousness and greed, and the dancers all display some symbols of their materialism.

DEATH AND THE SALESWOMAN

Death:
Come closer, Saleswoman,
Without waiting any longer.
You don't pause, night and day,
Earning to be respected.
Respect that doesn't last long;
It is gone in one minute.
Nothing is certain in this world.
Who laughs in the morning cries at night.
Saleswoman:
Yesterday I had earned two ecus
Through clever overcharging,
But I don't know who took them from me.
Money gained dishonestly
Doesn't ever do any good.
Alas, I'm dying, that's another matter.
Let me have a priest quickly,
Better late than never.

From Ann Tukey Harrison's, *The Danse Macabre of Women* (Kent, Ohio: Kent State University Press, 1994), p. 100. With permission of The Kent State University Press.

THE EARLY MODERN POPULAR PRESS

The best-known edition of the *Danse Macabre* was printed in 1546 and illustrated with the woodcuts of the German master Hans Holbein. Like other typically medieval allegories, however, the theme rather rapidly disappeared **Almanacs and Ballads** in the tumultuous sixteenth century. The popular press, however, kept very busy supplying new types of inexpensive material for general audiences. Printed under license in London, Oxford, or Cambridge on cheap paper and meant to be carried rolled up in one's pocket, almanacs cost no more than a few pence and were readily available. The standard almanac that the public came to expect by 1600 contained a calendar of political events and holidays along with the predictable movements of the planets and stars and expected conjunctions. Legal and medical terms were sometimes listed, along with simple "zodiac man" charts that presented the best times for bleedings and other medical procedures. From their origins in the mid-fifteenth century they also provided predictions of, among other things, weather events and epidemics. In 1545 Mathias Brothyel used his list of expected plagues as a basis for urging social harmony and peace, lest "stiff-necked or unobedient persons" be visited with the divine fury of pestilence. The pseudo-science of astrology was on full display in these booklets, and sharp publishers made the connection between the stars and plague that had long been supposed by natural philosophy and medical science. They also blended in folk medicine, moralizing, tips on plague-time hygiene and diet, and pharmaceutical quackery, providing advertising space to the vendors of pills, potions, and secret recipes. Since almanacs were sold in the same places as these remedies—tobacconists, apothecaries' shops, coffee shops, inns—the natural connection between the two helped sales. Literally millions of these circulated in seventeenth-century England; in its best years Vincent Wing's *Almanac* sold 50,000 copies annually. And the bestsellers returned to the shelves year after year. Those composed by William Lilly, the most popular astrologer of the day, sold well from 1644 to 1681. Of course, rumors of plague drove sales up, as people sought information that would help them decide whether to flee the cities or stay put. Unfortunately for them, only one of the almanacs published in late 1664 or early 1665 predicted the horrendous epidemic of 1665, London's Great Plague. But God's Will was God's Will and not necessarily predictable from celestial conjunctions, according to astrologer John Gadbury, who had failed to make the prediction. Almanacs were also prime forums for brief moralizing about social ills, individual sins, and consequent divine wrath. Gadbury welcomed the plague as "a broom in the hands of the Almighty with which He sweepeth the most nasty and uncomely corners of the universe, that the more noble parts of it may remain secure and safe."[19]

ADAM VON LEBENWALD WARNS AGAINST ALARMIST PUBLICATIONS, 1695

Credence should not be given to every tramp, false prophet, and news reporter who of every black cloud construct a bier, of every shooting star a flying dragon or comet, from the reflection of starlight foretell I know not what judgment and affliction, and in every fiery celestial phenomenon see an opening of the heavens, and who then in uneven rhymes chant these miracles to the populace, even causing lying sheets to be printed by which they inspire the simple with great fear and tribulation, but themselves reap a rich harvest of money.

From his *Town and Country Book of House Medicine,* in Johannes Nohl, *The Black Death* (New York: Ballantine Books, 1961), p. 49.

Single-page broadsheets and printed ballads also carried messages of the need for repentance and social reform. Some broadsheets offered comic images drawn from the *Danse Macabre* tradition, making light of the figure of Death and the gravity of the plague. Others were more serious, making the usual connection between sin and plague. William Birch targeted whoring, gambling, and drunkenness in his ballad "A warning to England, let London begin: To repent their iniquity, and fly from their sin" of 1565. A popular ballad from the plague year of 1593 bore the title "A heavenly proclamation sent from God, declaring his great Love towards London, and his mercy to all them that repent." Such works were the printed side of a largely oral culture that was entertained and informed, and perhaps even inspired, by song in the country's taverns and inns.

The plague of 1603 inspired a flood of literary works that revolved around the triad of man, God, and pestilence. The coincidence of the epidemic with the end of Queen Elizabeth's long reign (she had ruled since 1558) and the acces-

The Moral Dimension in Early Seventeenth-Century English Plague Literature

sion of the Scots ruler England's King James I Stuart made for an especially unsettled time. A preacher with the oddly apropos name James Godskall published two sermons during the plague season. One homily was entitled "Ark of Noah, for the Londoners that Remain in the City to Enter in, with Their Families, to Be Preserved from the Deluge of the Plague"; and in "The King's Medicine" he lays out a regimen of Galenic diet and exercise combined with Christian virtue and uprightness. Among other clerics, Roger Fenton penned *A Perfume against the Noisome Pestilence*, which he based on a verse in the biblical book of Numbers, and Nicholas Bownd wrote *Medicines for the Plague* based on the text of Psalm 20. In "London's Mourning Garment" poet William Muggins advised the capital's leaders:

Reform these things, you heads of London City.
Punish lewd Vice, let virtue spring and grow:
Then God's just wrath, now hot will turn to pity;
And for His children, you again do know:
Your former health, on you He will bestow,
The Plague and Pestilence, wherewith He visits still,
To end or send, are in His Holy Will.[20]

The humanistically educated physician Thomas Lodge admitted that he was baffled by the plague and attacked those, including other doctors and astrologers, who claimed to have found the causes in nature. His *Treatise on the Plague* of 1603 is a compendium of biblical and classical moral and medical sentiments on sickness and plague from the Old Testament, Neo-Platonists, Avicenna, Hippocrates, and even Homer. Ultimately the matter was simple: God unleashes the plague. To help assuage the angry deity, printers produced small, cheap, single-sheet posters known as broadsides that featured prayers and were meant to be affixed to a prominent wall in a house. From 1603 came "A Prayer very comfortable and necessary to be used of all Christians every morning and evening amongst their families," and four years later, "In the time of God's visitation by sickness or mortality especially, may be used by governors of families." A 1636 example by Michael Sparke prints a plague remedy that begins with walnuts, treacle, and endive water and continues, "[f]irst, fast and pray, and then take a quart of Repentance of Niniveh,[21] and put in two handfuls of Faith in the blood of Christ, with as much Hope and Charity as you can get, and put it into the vessel of a clean conscience." In the corner of the poster he advertises his book, *Crumbs of Comfort*, from which he drew the "recipe." In Catholic countries similar broadsheets featured prayers to Mary and plague saints like Sebastian and Roche and were illustrated with their images. In England after the plague year of 1625 they sported skulls and corpses.

The most prolific and best known of London's moralizing pamphleteers was the poet and playwright Thomas Dekker. He used satire rather than straightforward preaching and began this phase of his career when the playhouses were closed down because of the plague in 1603. Author or co-author of some 60 plays, he knew well the public's taste and translated his acerbic social commentary into colorful and compelling narratives. He was foreshadowed by the satirist Thomas Nashe, whose *Pierce Penilesse* (1592), *Unfortunate Traveler* (1593, on the plague in Rome), biting *Christes Tears over Jerusalem* (1594), and *In Time of Plague* (1600) assailed the failures of Christian virtue and charity and incompetent government that he believed angered God and brought the plague. But Calvinistic Dekker outdid his Anglican rival in drawing vivid verbal pictures and marshalling steamroller rhetoric. In his *Seven Deadly Sins of London* of 1606 he excoriated its citizens for committing his colorful version of the vices: Fraud (false bankruptcies), Lying, Candle-Light (secret transgressions like boozing and gambling performed under the cloak of night), Sloth, Apishness (vain stylishness), Shaving (swindling), and Cruelty. As plague looms just outside the city, each vice in turn parades through the city he relabels "Babylon." *The Wonderful Year* (1603) opens with the death of Queen Elizabeth and rise of King James and quickly turns to the plague, which leaves London

a vast charnel house; hung (to make it more hideous) with lamps dimly and slowly burning in hollow and glimmering corners[.] Where all the pavement should, instead of green rushes, be strewed with blasted rosemary, withered hyacinths, fatal cypress, and yew, thickly mingled with dead men's bones. The bare ribs of a father that begat him [the work's protagonist], lying there; here the chapless hollow skull of a mother that bore him. Round about him a thousand corpses; some standing bolt upright in their knotted winding sheets; others half moldered in rotten coffins that should suddenly yawn wide open, filling his nostrils with noisome stench, and his eyes with the sight of nothing but crawling worms. And to keep such a poor wretch waking, he should hear no noise but of toads croaking, screech-owls howling, mandrakes shrieking.

"Were not this an infernal prison?" he asks rhetorically. Dekker thundered against the mistreatment of the poor and the practice of shutting in the poverty-stricken and powerless victims of the pestilence; against the fraudulence and cowardice of physicians; against "the worm-eaten generation" of Anglican clergy.[22] Dekker continued his barrage with plague-themed works like *News from Gravesend Sent to Nobody* (1604), *A Rod for Runaways* (1625), *London Look Back,* and *The Black Rod and the White Rod* (both 1630). In *Work for Armorers* (1609) the ineffectual rulers of the city dither and society crumbles. He compares the strife between poor and rich in plague time to the contest between yelping dogs and the powerful bear in a bear-baiting arena: in the end, he notes, the dogs are usually all trampled.

Dekker was followed by a platoon of plague-time authors like the Puritan soldier and poet George Wither, in whose 600-page *Britain's Remembrancer* (1628) he painted the horrors, praised the honest folks, and reviled the spiritually weak of the 1625 outbreak. In "The Fearful Summer," John Taylor, an Oxford-educated ferryman known as the "Water-poet," assaulted those quacks and apothecaries who took advantage of the sick and fearful and called out gravediggers and sextons who fleeced victims' relatives. A reader of Dekker's works, he also described the plight of Londoners who sought refuge in the countryside in 1625, lamenting that they were often left to die in open fields without the least shelter. He railed against those who refused succor as "murderers of your Christian brothers and sisters." Far less strident was *Tears against the Plague* written in 1646 by John Fealty, an exiled high-church Anglican chaplain of King Charles I. A female friend complained that there was no devotional plague material that had a woman's voice, so he penned *Tears* in the voice of a dispossessed woman fleeing from the pestilence. Its meditations on Old Testament plagues and prophetic admonitions and prayers for deliverance from the plague made it so popular that it appeared again two decades later amid of the flood of tears that accompanied the 1665 Great Plague.

PLAGUE AND THE ENGLISH THEATER

European drama evolved in the fifteenth and sixteenth centuries from three distinct traditions. The first was the liturgical use of drama in Roman Catholic services to bring to life the stories from biblical and church history; this trend resulted in the religious mystery or miracle and morality plays performed by community or traveling players on church steps or pageant wagons. The second was popular miming, jesting, and buffoonery offered by visiting professionals or local talents. Highly comedic in nature, performances were satiric and naturalistic, irreverent and highly entertaining with no redeeming social value beyond letting people "blow off steam" in hearty laughter. The third tradition was that of Greco-Roman drama of the classical era that was revived in the late fifteenth century and generally presented to social elites. By the late sixteenth century these three streams had flowed together to produce golden ages of drama in Spain and England, and playwrights used the pestilence their audiences knew so well as foreground, background, and by allusion. For various reasons the plague also interfered with public performances, prompting authorities to cancel entire seasons and alter the course of theater history.

Late Medieval Drama and the Plague

The dramatic horror and steady recurrence of the pestilence meant that no one ever had to produce a play specifically about plague and the sufferings it caused.[23] It rather lurked in the background as a looming presence, threatening all with sudden death and the wicked with the pains of hell. A morality play like the anonymous English *Everyman* should be viewed in this context: Death arrives suddenly and unpredictably, and nothing but moral virtue will stand with Everyman in the last stage of his earthly pilgrimage. The vanities of wealth and beauty and knowledge are of no use when the time of the final reckoning arrives. Sermons and popular tracts echoed these sentiments, but their embodiment in living actors added an immediacy that transcended even the spoken word. Miracle or cycle plays that reenacted biblical scenes could also take on contemporary relevance, as in the York Corpus Christi play entitled "Moses and Pharaoh." The Hebrew people of God have grown greatly in number and desire to flee Egypt. Their Egyptian masters react by increasing their burdens and oppression rather than releasing them, and Pharaoh plots to kill Jewish infants at birth. Moses calls down God's plagues of boils, darkness, and a river of blood on the unrepentant Egyptians as punishment, reaching his climax with the deaths of each firstborn in what the anonymous dramatist calls the "grete pestilence."[24] In this populist drama God's people become England's lower classes, whose growth in number and power threaten the social order. The prideful elites who seek to thwart God's will and oppress his people will instead find themselves despoiled as divine retribution sweeps them away. And so the play embodies the contemporary themes of lower-class power and aspirations and God's wrath in the pestilential massacre of children in later fourteenth-century and fifteenth-century plagues, which seemed to fall most heavily on the young.

Plague and the Playgoer

The religious York Cycle dramas drew huge crowds into the city, and by the middle of the sixteenth century civic authorities began to regulate performances to reduce the risk of plague entering York. In 1551 they severely scaled back the program and in 1550 and 1552 cancelled performances altogether. London's church-inspired drama received an even deadlier blow when the new monarch, Queen Elizabeth I, banned religious theater altogether in the 1570s. She and the Anglican Church hierarchy agreed that morality and mystery plays carried too much Catholic baggage to suit Protestant English sensibilities. The very Protestant Bishop Edmund Grindal had unsuccessfully sought to ban all public dramatic performances in London, whether religious or secular. The players were blasphemers and men of ill repute, he charged; young people avoided their duties at work or school to join audiences which themselves could be seedbeds for resistance to the state. Though Grindal failed, from 1563 church, civic, or royal authorities could close down performances of any kind, and they kept a keen eye on the emerging secular dramas being performed in guildhalls and the court-yards of inns. Plays with themes that were considered lewd or that dealt with social or political issues of the day could be every bit as dangerous to the Elizabethan government as "Catholic" theater.

Fear of plague as well as issues of public morality helped keep theaters out of the City of London and restricted to outlying areas. When a perma-nent "common playhouse" was proposed for the Blackfriars neighborhood in 1596, the locals filed a complaint with the Privy Council, warning of "the great pestering and filling up of the same precinct, if it should please God to send any visitation of sickness as heretofore hath been, for that the same precinct is already grown very populous."[25] Performances in London were banned in 1569 and 1572 for no particularly compelling reason, but church-men and politicians agreed that the plague presented a compelling reason to bar the doors. In nearby Westminster, seat of the royal court, plays were prohibited or shut down in 1577, 1578, 1580–1582, and 1583. In 1584 London's civic government wrote to the royal Privy Council, "To play in plague-time is to increase the plague by infection: to play out of plague-time is to draw the plague by offendings of God upon the occasion of such plays."[26] Recognizing that even a few reported plague deaths indicated that a much larger number were infected and presumably walking about, they established the rule that as long as the reported number of plague dead remained smaller than 50 in London for "two or three" weeks, the plays could go on. This had, in fact, been suggested in the first place by the acting troupe known as the Servants of Queen Elizabeth. The city fathers had countered with a benchmark of 50 *total* deaths, but this was an unacceptably low threshold and so plague deaths it was. After his brush with pestilence in 1603, King James lowered this thresh-old to 30 plague deaths. But the government and church leadership were not alone in their disdain for drama: as a popular preacher announced very logi-cally from St. Paul's Cross in London, "The cause of plague is sin, if you look to it well; and the cause of sin are [sic] plays: therefore, the cause of plague are plays."[27] Indeed, theaters became focal points of sin and lawlessness: the poorer and presumably less law abiding were drawn to them from their lairs, as were the drunken and violent and thieving and idling. The threat of plague contagion was really only the icing on the moralists' cake.

The only play of the Elizabethan or Stuart eras that overtly relies upon the use of a plague-struck city for its setting is Ben Jonson's comedy *The Alchemist* of 1610. His plot unfolds in a London largely denuded of the proper-tied class because of the plague:

Pestilence and the Playwrights

> The sickness hot, a master quit, for fear,
> His house in town, and left one servant there.[28]

Jeremy, protector of the wealthy Lovewit's house, like many London servants in plague time, becomes a "temporary aristocrat." He uses the otherwise empty house as a front for an intrigue with two other rogues—one of whom,

Subtle, is by turns alchemist, cunning man, and doctor—to fleece the greedy and gullible. A knight (Sir Epicure Mammon), an apothecary, and a group of religious Separatists fall prey to the charlatans' promises, paying dearly for expected wealth, love, and the "philosopher's stone," which the alchemist guarantees will transmute any metal object into gold. The confederates babble convincingly to Mammon in the obscure language of alchemy. To stall him further the alchemist reassures:

> Son, be not hasty, I exalt our medicine,
> By hanging him [the "stone"] in *balneo vaporoso;*[29]
> And giving him solution; then congeal him;
> And then dissolve him; and then again congeal him;
> For look, how oft I iterate the work,
> So many times I add unto his virtue.

The stone's power is not only metallurgical but medicinal as well. Mammon describes the alchemist as "An excellent Paracelsian," who "will not hear a word of Galen or his tedious recipes." As Mammon tells a skeptical friend, the stone

> is the secret
> Of nature naturized 'gainst all infections,
> Cures all diseases coming of all causes . . .
> I'll undertake, withal, to fright the plague
> Out o'the kingdom, in three months.

Convinced they will have ample notice of the householder's return,

> O, fear not him. While there dies one a week
> O' the plague, he's safe from thinking toward London.

the conmen reach the climax of their plot. Then, suddenly, Lovewit arrives. Stalling his master at the door while the others clear out, the servant claims the house had been shut up for a month since a serving girl was thought to have contracted the plague and the place needed fumigating:

> [I was p]urposing then, sir,
> T'have burnt rose-vinegar, treacle, and tar,
> And ha' made it sweet, that you should ne'er ha' known it,
> Because I knew the news would but afflict you, sir.

His chicanery exposed nonetheless, Jeremy puts a good face on his shenanigans, is forgiven, and lets his accomplices slip away empty-handed. Though the knight is compensated, the other marks are driven off and social stability returns.[30] Jonson had lost his seven-year-old son Benjamin, Jr., to the pestilence in 1603, and then in 1605 his dear friend John Roe, who in some ways had replaced Benjamin in his affections.

While never making light of the city's suffering, nor even mentioning it, Jonson does use comedy to display the moral diseases that accompany the epidemic, and perhaps London society in general.

"PLAGUE" IN SHAKESPEARE'S DRAMAS

Timon of Athens (set at the time of the fifth-century plague in Athens; apparently never performed; the word "plague" appears over a dozen times)
Timon curses his world:
> "O blessed breeding sun, draw from the earth
> Rotten humanity; below thy sister's orb
> Infect the air!" (IV 3: 1–3)

Timon spurs Alcibiades to slaughter without mercy:
> "Be as a planetary plague, when Jove
> Will o'er some high viced city hang his sick poison
> In the thick air. Let not thy sword skip one." (IV 3: 107–09)

Cursing, Timon calls down a plague on the Athens that rejected him:
> "Plagues incident to men
> You potent and infectious fevers heap
> On Athens, ripe for stroke!
> . . . Breath infect breath,
> That their society, as their friendship, may
> Be merely poison." (IV 1: 21–23; 30–32)

Troilus and Cressida (I 3: 95)
> The planets "in evil mixture to disorder wander"

King Lear (III 4: 69)
> "the plagues that in the pendulous air Hang fated o'er men's faults"

A report on Scotland during the pestilence, written during the plague year 1603:

MacBeth (IV 3: 166)
> "It cannot
> be called our mother, but our grave; where nothing
> But he who knows nothing, is once seen to smile;
> Where sighs and groans, and shrieks that vent the air
> Are made, not mark'd: where violent sorrow seems
> A modern ecstasy: the dead man's knell
> Is there scarce ask'd for who,[31] and good men's lives
> Expire before the flowers in their caps,
> Dying, or ere they sicken."

The plague interferes with Juliet's plans as the Friar reports:

Romeo and Juliet (V 2: 5–12)
> "Going to find a barefoot brother out,
> One of our order, to associate me
> Here in this city visiting the sick
> And finding him, the searchers of the town,
> Suspecting that we both were in a house

Where th'infectious pestilence did reign,
Seal'd up the doors, and would not let us forth,
So that my speed to Mantua [to inform Romeo] was stay'd."
As Mercutio dies in the street fight he curses the Montagues and the Capulets,
"A plague o' both your houses!" (III 1: 87)
The "plague" of love:

Twelfth Night (I 5: 273–74)
Olivia is surprised by love's onset:
"How now!
Even so quickly may one catch the plague?"

Loves Labor's Lost (V, 2: 420–24)
"Write 'Lord Have Mercy on Us' on those three;
They are infected, in their heart it lies;
They have the plague, and caught it of your eyes:
These lords are visited; you are not free,
For the Lord's tokens on you do I see."[32]

In his *Work for Armorers* of 1609, Thomas Dekker described the theaters closed down because of the plague:

Playhouses stand (like taverns that have cast out their masters) the doors locked up, the flags (like their bushes) taken down; or rather like houses lately infected, from whence the affrighted dwellers are fled. . . . The players themselves never did work till now, their comedies all turned to tragedies, their tragedies to nocturnals. . . . Their muses are more sullen than old monkeys."[33]

Even so, some playwrights simply exchanged muses. During the disruptions Shakespeare fled to Stratford and turned his pen to writing poetry for his patron, including his famous sonnets, and in the early 1600s Dekker and Thomas Middleton began their careers as moralistic pamphleteers. For all three these very lucrative pursuits enjoyed a broad public following. In contrast, dramatist John Fletcher found his flight from plague-filled London delayed in 1625 as he waited for a tailor to finish his new suit; he died of the disease before it was ready.

When London theaters closed, acting companies took to the inns and barns of rural England or the somewhat nicer accommodations of larger towns. During the outbreak of 1603 Shakespeare's King's Players toured Bath, Coventry, and Shrewsbury. Rather uncharitably, Dekker mocked the provincials who happily flocked to watch plays that had had their runs in London and were thus "so stale and therefore so stinking." The King's Players also performed for the royal court, which spent much of 1603 at Wilton and Hampton Court. In April 1609 the king provided £40 "for their private practice in time of infection" so the troupe could be well prepared to perform before the court.[34] Theater-owners suffered most when the "flags were taken down" to signal a closing. In October 1608 William Pollard and Rice Gwynn were jailed in Newgate Prison "for that they yesterday last suffered a stage play to be publicly acted in the White-friars during the time of the present infection contrary to His Majesty's late proclamation."[35]

Though too horrible to be portrayed on a stage, the plague's carnage often appeared on the printed page in the cruelest of language. But the cruelty was not gratuitous. Like the plague itself even the most graphic literature had a deeper, moral meaning that remained downright medieval. Humanity had not only to be informed, but "scared straight" lest it be destroyed.

NOTES

1. See his "Écrits contemporaines sur la peste de 1348 a 1350," in *Histoire litteraire de la France,* vol. 37 (Paris: Imprimerie Nationale, 1938), pp. 325–90.

2. Between 1910 and 1925 the German scholar Karl Sudhoff published or specifically referred to a total of 288 *consilia* dating between 1348 and 1500 in his periodical *Sudhoffs Archiv.* More recently historian Samuel Cohn has provided the higher number, noting that Sudhoff had missed many Italian consilia (*The Black Death Transformed: Disease and Culture in Early Renaissance Europe* [New York: Oxford University Press, 2002], p. 66.

3. A. H. de Oliveira Marques, *Daily Life in Portugal in the Late Middle Ages,* trans. S. S. Wyatt (Madison: University of Wisconsin Press, 1971), p. 140.

4. This was an extremely popular source that blended Arabic and Galenic medicine. Authors all over Europe used or translated it. Between 1474 and 1846 some 300—often very cheap—editions appeared in France alone.

5. G. R. Keiser, "Two Medieval Plague Treatises and Their Afterlife in Early Modern England," *Journal of the History of Medicine and Allied Sciences* 58 (2003), pp. 298–99.

6. Giulia Calvi, *Histories of a Plague Year: The Social and the Imaginary in Baroque Florence* (Berkeley: University of California Press, 1989), p. 26.

7. Colin Jones, "Plague and its Metaphors in Early Modern France," *Representations* 53 (1996), p. 107.

8. Andrew Wear, "The Popularisation of Medicine in Early Modern England," in *The Popularisation of Medicine, 1650–1850,* ed. Roy Porter (New York: Routledge, 1992), p. 32. See also Benjamin Woolley, *Heal Thyself: Nicholas Culpepper and the Seventeenth-Century Struggle to Bring Medicine to the People* (New York: Harper Collins, 2004).

9. The official catalogue of the supposed medicinal effects of herbs, drugs, and other pharmaceuticals.

10. Doreen E. Nagy, *Popular Medicine in Seventeenth-Century England* (Bowling Green, Ohio: Bowling Green State University Press, 1988), p. 7.

11. Wear, "Popularisation," p. 29.

12. Jones, "Plague," p. 107; Laurence Brockliss and Colin Jones, *The Medical World of Early Modern France* (New York: Oxford University Press, 1997), p. 67.

13. Ailene Sybil Goodman, "Explorations of a Baroque Motif: The Plague in Selected Seventeenth-century English and German Literature" (Ph.D. dissertation, University of Maryland, 1981), p. 128.

14. S. S. Yom, "Plague and AIDS in literature," *Journal of the American Medical Association* 277 (1997), pp. 437–38.

15. In general see Bryon Lee Grigsby, *Pestilence in Medieval and Early Modern English Literature* (New York: Routledge, 2004); on Langland see in particular pp. 103–15.

16. Excerpts from "A Diet for Plague" by John Lydgate, translated by Margaret Monteverde, appears in Joseph Byrne, *The Black Death* (Westport, CT: Greenwood Press, 2004), pp. 162–66.

17. These are discussed in detail in Chapter Three.

18. See Chapter Four for a fuller discussion of both of these themes.

19. B. Capp, *Astrology and the Popular Press: English Almanacs, 1500–1800* (London: Faber and Faber, 1979), p. 112.

20. Charles F. Mullett, *The Bubonic Plague and England* (Lexington: University of Kentucky Press, 1956), p. 130.

21. The sinful city to which the reluctant Old Testament prophet Jonah was sent; it repented and was saved from God's anger.

22. George Richard Hibbard, *Three Elizabethan Pamphlets* (London: Harrap, 1951), pp. 179, 185.

23. Historian Rudolf Starn's comments are apropos: "As a social drama the plague was the supreme theater of the Old Regime, in which the binding ties and the divisive conflicts, the assumptions, rituals, and symbols of the afflicted community were acted out"; in foreword to Calvi, *Histories*, p. xi.

24. Grigsby, *Pestilence*, p. 122.

25. Andrew Gurr, *Playgoing in Shakespeare's London* (New York: Cambridge University Press, 1996), p. 219.

26. F. P. Wilson, *Plague in Shakespeare's London* (New York: Oxford University Press, 1999), p. 51; see also Mullett, pp. 99–100; J. C. Robertson, "Reckoning with London: Interpreting the Bills of Mortality before John Graunt," *Urban History* 23 (1996), p. 337.

27. Liza Picard, *Elizabeth's London: Everyday Life in Elizabethan London* (New York: St. Martin's, 2004), pp. 276–77.

28. All quotations from *Ben Jonson: The Alchemist and Other Plays*, ed. Gordon Campbell (New York: Oxford University Press, 1995).

29. *balneo vaporoso:* a vapor bath; *virtue:* ability to transmute base metal into gold.

30. C. L. Ross, "The Plague of the Alchemist," *Renaissance Quarterly* 41 (1988), pp. 439–58.

31. A line echoed three decades later by poet John Donne: "Ask not for whom the bell tolls, it tolls for thee."

32. These are lines filled with plague language: "Lord . . ." was written on the doors of plague victim's houses; the belief was that the plague "poison" directly affected the heart; they also believed one could pass the plague through a glance; "visited" was a term for having the plague; and the "Lord's tokens" were the buboes and other signs on the body of the disease.

33. Quoted in John Leeds Barroll, *Politics, Plague, and Shakespeare's Theater: The Stuart Years* (Ithaca: Cornell University Press, 1991), p. 176.

34. F. P. Wilson, "Illustrations of Social Life. 4. The Plague," *Shakespeare Survey* 15 (1962), pp. 125, 126.

35. Barroll, *Politics*, p. 190.

10

IN THE VILLAGE AND
ON THE MANOR

The plague spread ferociously in Europe's densely populated urban
centers. Recent studies of early modern documents show fairly clearly
how the disease first appeared in one small area and disseminated along
streets and alleyways. One of the problems for modern epidemiologists
is how bubonic plague, assuming that was "the plague," spread into the
countryside, and why it seems to have skipped some locales altogether
while devastating others. Another interesting phenomenon is that over
time plague seems to have become much more an urban disease than a
rural one. Though plague certainly appeared in Europe's small towns
and villages after 1400, its incidence became much less widespread and
its effects rather less deadly. Local or regional practices of isolating villages that had even a few plague victims appear to have had some effect
in reducing plague dissemination, but if migrating rats and their infected
fleas were the ultimate culprits, then no level of interference with human
trade or travel should have stopped them. The fact that these interdictions
seemed to have worked has led some researchers to identify "plague" as
something other than rat-borne bubonic plague: perhaps plague borne by
human fleas, or pneumonic plague spread directly by victims to others,
or some pathogen other than *Yersinia pestis* that was passed along directly
among people (see this volume's introduction).

In any case, the plague's greatest impact on rural life came during the
second half of the fourteenth century. The combination of rural depopulation by disease and rural laborers' search for higher wages and more
opportunities in underpopulated cities and towns caused a huge drain

on the countryside's labor supplies. Those who remained in rural areas improved economically, as landlords had to offer higher wages and make other advantageous arrangements with them. In England and elsewhere the state stepped in to regulate these new economic conditions that favored workers and, from its point of view, undermined the social fabric. In turn, members of the lower classes organized and opposed these new regulations that, from their point of view, interfered with their traditional rights and customs. With the expansion of peasant options and the contraction of landlord power came the disintegration, especially in England, of what is often referred to as feudalism. As later medieval urban and rural populations became balanced and the new economic arrangements took hold in the fifteenth century, Europe entered a new era in its history, the early modern period. Though plague returned repeatedly, its effects on the countryside diminished for not only what appear to be natural reasons, but also because European society adjusted to its depredations.

THE PLAGUE IN THE COUNTRYSIDE

Sources of Information
One of the characteristics that distinguish the modern from the medieval world is the modern person's attitude toward numbers and quantification. In the medieval West people often used numbers symbolically rather than realistically, a trait borrowed from Platonism and the Bible. Of course, folks knew and easily understood the specific number of furlongs a peasant family plowed or children they had or days of road-repair service they owed, but in matters beyond daily experience there was little use for exactitude. Manorial and monastic administrators who collected dues and taxes had a better sense of quantity and record keeping, and the growing class of merchants in larger cities invented accounting and replaced Roman with Arabic numerals in bookkeeping and computation. Even so, when faced with having to provide the number of men engaged in a battle, or the population of a city, or the number of plague deaths in a region, the European chronicler of the fourteenth or fifteenth century was ill-equipped. He generally settled for numbers that, rather than accurately reflecting reality, registered an emotional response in the reader. By the end of the Second Pandemic in the early eighteenth century, quantification had become far more sophisticated and accurate record keeping a mark of a modern government. Yet despite 150 years' experience with the bills of mortality, commentators during and after London's Great Plague of 1665 utterly distrusted the official final count: student of the plague and novelist Daniel Defoe thought the figure should be 50 percent higher, and a physician at the time reckoned it three times larger than the official count of 68,596 dead.

Those estimating rural losses face even greater problems. Northern Italy was one of the few regions where city-states took anything like full censuses of the countryside. These surveys began only in the fifteenth century, were limited to a few city-states, undercounted women and children, and occurred only sporadically. Estimating rural plague deaths in most of Europe is thus a very inexact science. This process entails estimating the population of an area (country, village, parish, or manor) sometime before 1348 or 1349 (or any other epidemic period), and again sometime after the pestilence struck. Tax records often exist and may seem to be a sound source of information. The problem is that only households—often referred to as "hearths"—rather than individuals were taxed, and we know only the number of households before and after the event rather than their size. Modern assumptions about the number of people in an average household can have a huge effect on estimations of loss.

As an example, assume that 40 percent of a village's 100 households (hearths) disappear between 1345 and 1355. If one estimates 4 persons per

Death leads off the peasant's child. From Hans Holbein's *Danse Macabre*, Lyon, 1538. Dover.

household, then the loss was 4 × 40 or 160 people; if the average is 6, then the total is 240 people, a 50 percent increase. And the "what ifs" continue: What if only one half (or any fraction) of each household actually died, with the rest relocating to live in towns or with kin or friends? What if all in the 40 percent died and a considerable number of the remaining households also suffered losses but remained intact? What if hearths disappeared for reasons other than plague? Clearly, our "40 percent" is only a convenient number that may approach some useful level of accuracy if enough samples are used. In France, another problem is that sometime around the 1380s the government switched from counting "real hearths" to "fiscal hearths." The basis for these new units remains unclear, but the effect is to nullify a lot of otherwise comparable data. In St.-Flour, Auvergne, we know that there were 744 "real" hearths in 1380 and 433 in 1390, an apparent drop of 42 percent during a plague-struck decade. In 1382, however, tax documents record only 65 "hearths"; clearly these are "fiscal hearths" and bear little relation to the actual population.

In England, researchers commonly use manorial court rolls that list tenants of the manor and their annual dues or rents. Heriots were a form of death tax paid by serf families to lords upon the death of the head of the peasant household. Generally a son or brother of the deceased assumed the role of tenant and paid an additional tax for the privilege. Both this action and the heriot would have been recorded by the landlord. He did not, however, record any other deaths in the tenant families, so unless the head of the family died, no loss of life appears in these records. Of course, some families hid the deaths of their heads to avoid the heriot and assumption tax, making modern interpretation of these records even more difficult.

Although some peasants made wills, will-making was usually an activity of the wealthier classes. These documents were recorded as public records and they survive in huge numbers, generally in the form of abstracts of the original. Some scholars have interpreted the sheer increases in the numbers of wills produced in a region or city as a sign of epidemic; others have looked at the numbers that were legally "proved" in court after the death of the will-maker (testator). These "inquisitions post-mortem" determined the authenticity of the will and protected the heirs from having assets stolen or hidden. Yet again only the head of the family—the testator—appears in lists of wills, and the documents themselves usually refer only to living friends and relatives. These records can give only an impressionistic view of overall patterns of death since they are not representative of the whole population. Nor do we usually have a clear idea what percentage of the total number of wills made in a particular place and time still exists. Though wills are wonderful sources of information on family structure (how many children a testator had living, for example), material wealth, and patterns of landholding, they can leave only impressions about death patterns or rates.

PARISHES IN AMOUNDERNESS, LANCASTER, ENGLAND: POPULATION LOSSES IN 1349 AND THE PERCENT WHO MADE WILLS

Parish	Deaths	Number of Will-makers	% Who Made Wills	Declared Intestate[1]
Preston	3,000	300	10	200
Kirkham	3,000	600	20	100
Poulton	800	200	25	40
Lancaster	3,000	400	13.3	80
Garstang	2,000	400	20	140
Cockerham	1,000	300	33.3	60
Ribchester	100	70	70	40
Lytham	150	80	53.3	80
St. Michael	80	50	62.5	40
Bispham	60	40	66.6	20

The document that contains these figures was created by the archdeacon of Richmond, who stood to benefit from the administration of the wealth of those who died intestate. Although used as evidence in a legal case, the heavily rounded figures are clearly an approximation by the cleric rather than the actual numbers. This illustrates the difficulty in trusting medieval statistics.

Source: A. G. Little, "The Black Death in Lancaster," *English Historical Review* 5 (1890), pp. 524–30.

Church records—including burials—become more reliable from the early sixteenth century, especially in England and Germany. Prior to 1500 there are only three known European parish record series that are reasonably complete: for Givry in Burgundy, St. Nizier in Lyon, France, and St. Maurice in Valais, Switzerland. While both the complete and incomplete records count all bodies that pass through for burial, they do not include those that did not do so for various reasons: some families buried members, especially young children, on their own land; nonmembers of the parish or denomination were buried elsewhere; or clergy may have wanted to keep burials "off the books" to hide their income from diocesan auditors. To conclude, none of the records utilized below may be considered more than an impression that confers a sense of the disaster on the reader. Yet in itself this information is valuable in understanding the economic, social, and political effects of the Black Death on rural society across Europe.

English historian Christopher Dyer, in one of most recent attempts to characterize the information we have on the plague, concludes

The Initial Outbreak: 1347–1352

it would be reasonable to estimate the death rate in 1348–1349 at about half of the English population. Its effects were universal, and no village, town, nor region for which records exist escaped. If the total population stood at about 5,000,000 or 6,000,000, then there were 2,500,000 or 3,000,000 casualties.[2]

According to inquisitions postmortem, among 505 English tenants-in-chief that held land directly from the king, 138, or about 27 percent, died in 1348 or 1349. This figure of 27 percent is the death rate most often provided for English nobility, and its small size probably reflects the mobility, relative isolation, and better living conditions (diet, general health, and housing) of the wealthy in the countryside.

ENGLISH VILLAGE/PARISH HOUSEHOLDS LOSSES, 1348–1349

Dry Drayton	47%
Cottenham	57%
Oakington	70%
Halesowen	40%
Coltishall	60%
Waltham	65%
Bishop of Winchester's Estates (avg)	66%
Glastonbury: range = 33–69% (avg)	55%
Bishop of Worcester: r = 17–80% (avg)	42%

Sources: S. L. Waugh, *England in the Reign of Edward III* (Cambridge: Cambridge University Press, 1991), p. 88; Yves Renouard, "Conséquences et intérêt démographiques de la peste noire de 1348," in his *Etudes d'histoire médiévale* (Paris: SEVPEN, 1968), p. 160; Richard Lomas, "The Black Death in County Durham," *Journal of Medieval History* 15 (1989): 130–31.

The manorial court records of Hunstanton, Suffolk, provide a glimpse into village life during the plague year 1349. On March 20 they report the recent death of a woman; on April 22 they were to hear 5 disputes, but of the 16 male witnesses or parties, 11 had died; on May 22 there were 3 debtor suits on the docket, but 1 of the debtors and 1 creditor had just died. Because of the plague, hearings were suspended until September, when the roll records that the local priest had died. On October 16 local officials reported that 78 people had died over the previous two months. Over an eight-month period, 172 tenants died, with 74 leaving no male heir. Records at Christ Church, Canterbury, show that on their estates only one in three families remained as tenants between 1346 and 1352. The other two-thirds disappeared, making way for new tenants who kept vacancy rates low. In a study of the Hundred of Farnham, which consisted of 12 villages controlled by the bishop of Winchester, Etienne Robo demonstrated that of 562 tenants, 185 (33 percent) died between September 1348 and September 1349. He estimated that three dependants died for every tenant, making a total of 740 deaths. Why three deaths? He needed a number, admitting that it "should probably be higher."[3] The bishop received only £101 in fines ranging from £8 to £20 each from new tenants, implying a poor replacement rate, and 189 head of cattle as heriots.

In his recent study of 28 Durham County townships, Robert Lomas found that 16 (57 percent) lost more than half of their tenants; overall, 362 out of 718 tenants died (50 percent). Even contiguous townships could lose very different percentages of their tenants: Monton lost 21 percent while contiguous Jarrow lost 78 percent; Over Heworth lost 36 percent while next door Nether Heworth lost 72 percent of its tenants.[4]

REDUCTIONS OF SOUTHERN FRENCH HEARTHS

Region	Pre-1348	1350s	% drop
Aix-en-Provence	1,486	810	45
Apt	926	444	52
Forcalquier	600	281	53
Moustiers	619	204	67
Riez	680	213	69
8 parishes near Montmelian	303	142	47
10 locales in Provence	8,511	3,839	55
30 villages in Provence	7,860	4,069	48

Sources: Emmanuel Ladurie, "A Concept: The Unification of the Globe by Disease," in *The Mind and Method of the Historian*, trans. Siân and Ben Reynolds (Chicago: University of Chicago, 1981), p. 44; Henri Dubois, "La dépression: XIVe et XVe siècles," *Histoire de la population française, vol. 1: Des origines à la Renaissance*, ed. Jacques Dupaquier, et al. (Paris: Presses Universitaires de France, 1988), p. 44.

The very complete parish vicar's account book for Givry, Burgundy, records 615 burials between July 28 and November 19, 1349, out of a population of an estimated 2,100 (29 percent). The excellent St. Nizier, Lyon, parish register shows between 900 and 1,000 deaths by plague (teasing these out from other deaths is the problem) out of a total of 3,000 to 4,000 parishioners, about 25 to 30 percent. St. Maurice's records indicate between 30 and 40 percent losses. Even these excellent records, however, have three problems: they cannot tell us the total population of the parish; they do not count infants and children; and they do not separate plague deaths from other deaths. Modern studies of hearths in France (see table) and Spain also show dramatic drops in population over the decade from about 1345 to about 1355. According to tax records from Navarre only 15 of 215 locales escaped the pestilence, and the region suffered an overall mortality rate of 45 to 50 percent. On the Plain of Vic in Catalonia a preplague census counted 643 hearths *(fuegos)* and postplague only 204 remained, for a loss of 68 percent. May one conclude that 68 percent of the population therefore died of plague? No, for the picture is far more complex.

One final consideration concerns the specific people who died in a community. If infants and children died in great numbers, the growth of their generation would be stunted, leaving a dearth of births 20 or 30 years later. If fertile women died disproportionately, then there would be fewer children born immediately to repopulate the area. When men or women with special skills died, their skills often disappeared with them, leaving certain tasks unfilled at least in the short run. Rural priests, notaries, and medical practitioners were especially difficult to replace since survivors were quickly drawn to the cities where the pay was much better.

The Continuing Crisis   A single blow of this magnitude to the population of Europe would have been bad enough, but just as people were getting back to their normal lives, the same disease struck again about a decade later. It was the first in a three-century series of epidemics that depressed Europe's population and economy for a century and a half. For example, in Hainault in the Netherlands, rural population dropped by about a third between 1349 and 1400 and dropped by another third by 1479. In the northern Italian Valdelsa region, the population fell continuously from 1350—after the initial plague—by about 40 percent. In eastern Normandy between 1358 and 1374 the number of hearths dropped off by 20 percent. The same pattern is evident in England, with recovery stalled until the 1480s. The hammer blows of plague occurred about once a decade, and even when they did not massacre the rural population, the urban losses almost always invited rural migration. This pattern continued to drain a significant segment of the rural population, perhaps many of the best and brightest, or at least the more ambitious. When these migrants were women, their home communities lost an important source of regeneration; when they were skilled men, their skills left with them. Between plague deaths and this drainage, landlords were left with a shrunken labor pool, while the laboring class embraced new opportunities.

REDUCTIONS IN HEARTHS IN PROVENCE, 1339–1475

Gresvaudan	Champsaur	Faucigny	Viennois-la-Tour
83 communities	24 communities	33 communities	82 communities
1339: 8,873	1339: 2,577	1339: 4,440	1339: 7,312
1394: 3,083	1394: 870	1412: 2,173	1394: 3,251
1475: 3,553	1475: 729	1470: 1,875	1475: 3,871

Source: Henri Dubois, "La dépression: XIVe et XVe siècles," *Histoire de la population française, vol. 1: Des origines à la Renaissance,* ed. Jacques Dupaquier, et al. (Paris: Presses Universitaires de France, 1988), p. 331.

NEW OPPORTUNITIES

Redistribution of Wealth   All those who remained alive became rich, because the wealth of many remained to them.

Anonymous author from Lucca, Italy, 1348

By the fourteenth century European villagers were far from being an undifferentiated mass. Serfs who owed special duties to their landlords and who could not permanently leave the manor lived side-by-side with free peasants who could relocate as they pleased, according to agreements or leases they drew up with their landlords. Some villagers had had ancestors on the spot for centuries; other residents had just moved to the neighborhood. Some had developed special, useful skills—carpentry, animal husbandry, smithing, midwifery, roof thatching, masonry, butchery—that, along with special equipment, they passed down generation to generation within the family. Over time, some families accumulated great relative wealth, possessing enough land to require hired help at harvest time. Others held no land, merely a cottage to live in, and made do by hiring themselves out as day laborers. Some lived in well-constructed houses built of planed wood, logs, or stone, others in wattle-and-daub huts. Money had begun to circulate in the countryside so that villagers could purchase goods sold at markets and in nearby towns. Traveling salesmen also provided goods, and sometimes services, that were otherwise hard to come by. Iron, pewter, glazed pottery, and brass replaced implements and wares made of cheaper wood or clay. Records show that average households owned more furniture, farm implements, and farm animals after the plague than before.

Both common sense and surviving economic records indicate that the typical survivor of the first outbreak of plague emerged richer in material and monetary wealth. Unlike war, plague had little effect on family wealth, and that which had belonged to the victims now passed down immediately to heirs or was there for the taking. Many survivors married heirs and amalgamated their fortunes, or simply married into new wealth. Men with new wealth could now afford to marry earlier, and many did, starting families and repopulating the countryside in the short run. The amount of cultivable land also remained the same in the short run, and many took advantage by leasing suddenly tenantless holdings, a move of which landlords heartily approved. Some families appropriated better housing by stripping the useable parts of abandoned dwellings or taking possession of better houses in the village. Many improved their outbuildings, such as barns or pens, while some could now afford to hire carpenters to improve their houses.

With the huge population losses across Europe came a general fall in demand for goods of all types. Consequently, prices tended to fall in the short run, making goods much more affordable to survivors. Cheaper cloth meant more and oftentimes better clothing. Since animals—rats aside—did not die of plague, far fewer people now controlled the same supply of draft animals (horses and oxen) and those that were commercially viable (cows, pigs, sheep, and goats). Cheaper foods meant better diets, in terms of variety, calories, and food value (proteins especially). Wheat replaced inferior grains in bread; fresh meat of all sorts augmented salt pork; the consumption of ale rose. In his modern study of the diets of English harvest workers in Sedgewick, Norfolk, historian Christopher Dyer demonstrates that in 1256 the male laborer consumed nearly 13,000 calories per day, of which 74 percent was from barley bread. Boiled grain or pottage, meat, fish, and dairy made up the rest. In 1424 he found that the total number of calories plummeted to about 5,000, of which only 40 percent was bread (wheat) and almost a quarter was meat. In both cases they ate fish and cheese on days of church-mandated fast or abstinence from meat (Fridays, Saturdays, vigils before feast days, maybe Wednesdays). They ate their morning meal *(prandium)* in the fields, with bowls, plates, cups, and spoons brought out by the landlord's servants. The day's later meal was served in the manor house. Harvest workers put in long days, often sprinting to finish before rains came, and were always in great demand because of the short window during which crops had to be brought in. As a result, landlords treated them very well, providing far nicer fare than for any other group. Dyer points out that this change in diet evolved over the years, but that much of this took place following 1348. Certainly the stereotype of the fat, lazy peasant, derided by the poet William Langland and others, is a postplague character.[5]

THE PREPLAGUE FOURTEENTH-CENTURY ENGLISH DIET

ARISTOCRATS

Beef, pork, mutton (salted and fresh); poultry, game, fish (salmon, eels, pike, bream, or salted cod or ling); sauces made of prunes, figs, dates, raisins with sugar, cinnamon, mace, ginger; barley-malt ale, wines; wheat-bread; dairy, fruit, vegetables; often three or four courses at a meal.

PEASANTS

Milk, ale, bread (rye, millet, acorn, chestnut), vegetables, salt pork.

From Simone MacDougall, "Health, Diet, Medicine and the Plague," in *An Illustrated History of Late Medieval England*, ed. Chris Given-Wilson (Manchester: Manchester University Press, 1996), p. 86.

The Rise of the English Yeoman Class

The plague put tremendous strains on what remained of the medieval manorial system, with its great noble and ecclesiastical landlords and peasant laborers. The rapid growth in population across Europe in the thirteenth century was damped in the early fourteenth, especially by famine, but land was still relatively scarce and labor relatively abundant and cheap. The feudal system held enough sway to ensure that most of the cultivated land remained in the hands of the "lords" of the knightly or higher class while the peasants commanded little more than their own labor. Long before 1348, this system began to change with the rise of the money economy. Cash-strapped landlords began selling off their property to other aristocrats, urban merchants, and even some peasants with enough cash. For various reasons this process developed most rapidly in

England, creating a class of rural landholders (owners and leaseholders) that stood below the knightly or gentry class and above the small farmers and peasants. Whereas the landowning gentry evolved from the traditional military knightly class, the yeomen rose up from the laboring class, accumulating land and wealth but lacking the blood and social background of the "gentleman." Income also played a role: in the early fifteenth century a yeoman's annual income from his land was about £5 to £10; among the gentry the gentleman's ran from £5 to £20, the esquire's from £20 to £40, and the knight's from £40 to £200.

Clearly the Black Death created opportunities by concentrating wealth in the hands of survivors and opening access to land. Though a distinct minority in the later Middle Ages, the yeomen farmers developed into a force for change in England. They were willing to experiment with the uses of their land, following changing economic conditions and unfettered by either class traditions or existing tenant arrangements. They invested in village life in ways that contributed to the general prosperity, building mills or bake-houses that traditionally had been the responsibility of noble landlords. They housed their families in comfortable, well-constructed residences and took pains to maintain their properties for the greatest profit. By Elizabethan times the yeomen were the backbone of English society; lacking the pretenses and distractions of the gentry, they were far more stable and economically secure than those beneath them.

The smaller farmers, later called husbandmen, were also able to consolidate their holdings and increase their incomes in the wake of the plague. At Coltishall, Norfolk, preplague plots were typically half an acre in size. By 1400 this area had tripled, and by the 1470s the typical size was nearly seven acres. At Stoneleigh Abbey in the Midlands the customary allotment of land to a tenant was 25 acres. In 1280 only 5 percent held more than 45 acres; by 1392 57 percent did. While yeomen were peculiar to England, the upper classes of peasants in other countries benefited in similar ways: in his study of the rural economy across Europe, French scholar Georges Duby concludes that after 1350 "well-to-do peasants were in fact more favored by economic conditions than any other group in rural society."[6]

Stadtluft Macht Frei[7]

The growth of cities during the High Middle Ages had always beckoned rural folk with economic opportunities and freedom from serfdom. Bustling city life needed the skilled and the unskilled alike, and population growth fed the need as cities expanded in number and size. Some of this demand for rural immigration dried up in the early fourteenth century, but urban plague deaths on the scale of 50 percent created a huge and immediate need. City guilds and governments made it much easier for rural folk to relocate, often shortening the time necessary to prepare for a trade or craft, exempting newcomers from taxation, or providing immediate citizenship.

The enrollment of new citizens in German Hansa towns in 1351 reflects this trend. Hamburg's annual average was 59 new citizens, but in 1351 it was 108; Lübeck normally welcomed 175 each year, but increased the number to 422; Lüneburg's average of 29 rose to 95. Wealthier city-dwellers replaced or acquired domestic servants, building projects needed laborers, and the guild masters who survived had to find new apprentices. These opportunities were tailor-made for landless but imaginative and ambitious peasants. With village social order disoriented by the pestilence, women found it far easier to flee to cities that welcomed them; some studies suggest that more women than men migrated to certain cities.

Although scholars argue over the extent of this migration from countryside to city, it must have had an effect on already depopulated villages. Some scholars contend that this trend combined with repeated attacks of plague to keep population growth depressed until the sixteenth century. For those who remained in rural areas, however, the departure of thousands of country folk opened even more opportunities in the forms of land to till and higher wages for services.

THE LANDLORD'S SQUEEZE

Among the rural landlords of the upper and lower nobility the economic benefits of the first outbreak of plague were limited. It is true that under primogeniture[8] young heirs profited by the deaths of their fathers or older brothers, and even without primogeniture the deaths of siblings and a father concentrated the family's wealth in fewer, younger hands. When wealth was in a form that could be easily spent, the demand for luxury goods like fancy clothing, jewelry, art, and exotic spices jumped and helped fuel the cultural movement known as the Renaissance. When the inheritance was in the form of agricultural land worked by tenants, however, it was a mixed blessing. Labor shortages and falling commodity prices forced landlords to make adjustments that included paying higher wages, abandoning marginally productive land, and converting cropland to pasture.

The Effect of the Black Death on Markets   Apart from crops like flax, from which linen was made, and plants like woad or saffron that were used to dye it, the soil of rural Europe produced foodstuffs that had fairly limited markets. While some commodities like olive oil, wine, or citrus fruits might find customers hundreds of miles away, most cash crops were consumed locally. As cities grew they demanded an ever-increasing supply of food, and those who supplied it found ready markets. With the onset of plague, however, demand plummeted and with it the prices of many of these goods. The 189 head of cattle collected as death taxes by the bishop of Winchester at Farnham in 1348 were worth only a third of their earlier market value. Some crops were merely used differently: The barley no longer used in bread was malted and brewed into beer. The oats that had been used in brewing were now fed to horses. Wheat that had been boiled for pottage was baked into bread. In the longer run, however, the depressed markets made large-scale landowning a losing proposition as the value of the land itself fell with the prices of the crops it produced. Only with the marked growth of population in the later fifteenth century would this situation change.

With the growth of population and the expansion of agricultural (arable) land, people began farming soils **Retreat from** that were not particularly fertile or easy to work. These **the Margin** "marginal" areas were the last to be farmed and, after the plague, the first to be abandoned as land and labor were reshuffled. But not only marginal land was "placed in the Lord's hands." Modern studies have shown that all grades of cropland reverted to the wild. It is

Death goads a plowman's horses. From Hans Holbein's *Danse Macabre*, Lyon, 1538. Dover.

sometimes difficult to tell from late medieval records whether cultivated land was actually abandoned or was absorbed by another landowner and added to his holdings. In Norway, for example, the number of farms fell from around 55,000 in the 1340s to an estimated 25,000 in 1520, but do these figures mean that the amount of arable land also diminished by 54 percent? It is clear that in many places the cultivated acreage did shrink. Scholars have estimated that half of the farmland in southern Jutland (Denmark) reverted to wild terrain.

In England and elsewhere there was no clear pattern of land abandonment, due in large part to the mobility of the rural population. At Battle Abbey's Marley Manor, cultivated acreage fell from 404 to 141 acres during the 1350s, while the extensive estates of the bishops of Winchester and Westminster suffered a reduction of only five acres between 1350 and 1380. In many parts of France, Germany, Austria, and England the relegation of cultivated land to pasture began long before the Black Death, which may explain why some areas experienced less of an immediate impact. One effect of this change was to increase the area of land that was wooded, and another was to make a farmer's work more efficient: good soil takes much less work to produce a yield comparable to that of poor soil. Fewer acres produced more food, which meant that landlords and peasants alike benefited when the price of food was reasonably high.

Occasionally not only tilled acreage but entire villages disappeared from the map. Some of them were utterly depopulated by the first outbreak of plague in 1348–1349, but these instances seem to have been few when compared with the many that were deserted over the following century. The hamlet of Quob in Hampshire was indeed depopulated by the plague, as noted in a manorial record from 1350: "all and each of the tithing (tenants) died in the present pestilence."[9] After three years, however, the buildings were once again let out and the fields put under the plow. Tilgarsley, Oxfordshire, was also utterly depopulated, but it was never again settled. The modern researcher can identify these deserted villages in England by comparing poll tax rolls and checking manorial records for the value of grain grown, acres cultivated, acres put into pasture, tenancy patterns, and rent payments. Poll tax records, for example, show that most of the villages eventually deserted were still paying the tax in the late 1370s. The recurrence of plague and the steady loss of people to thriving villages and towns gradually weakened most of these communities. Gloucestershire, Worcester, and Warwickshire counties lost a total of 240 villages, and across England perhaps 20 percent, or around 1,300 villages, disappeared between 1348 and 1500. Other parts of Europe suffered similarly: eastern and southwestern Germany suffered 20 to 30 percent *Wüstungen* (lost villages) between 1350 and 1500; by 1445 about one-fifth of all Icelandic farms were still deserted; after a terrible plague in 1372 only 11 of 72 villages remained in the countryside of Pola in Istria; and Castile suffered a loss of almost 20 percent (82 of 420) of its villages during the plague's first outbreak alone.

The European landlord made much of his income in the form of rents and manorial dues paid by those who lived in his villages and worked his land. While manorial dues—such as heriots—were generally set as a matter of custom, rents typically depended on the expected crop yield and its value. **Labor and Income Problems** Plague and flight removed rent-paying tenants, and low grain prices in the market meant low rent yields. The combination was devastating. Some French and English rents continued to plunge long after the Second Pandemic began, with the decline lasting well into the fifteenth century. Of course plague was not the only factor in these fluctuations: the Hundred Years War continued over much of this period; crop failures tended to raise prices by reducing supply, but they also tended to kill people; the value or purchasing power of currency changes over time. But none of these factors made the landlord's life any easier. As in any enterprise someone—usually the landlord—had to invest capital into production and upkeep. A profit was necessary to maintain production from year to year, and this margin was often very thin indeed.

NOMINAL[10] DECLINE IN RENTS IN FRENCH LIVRES OR ENGLISH PENCE

St. Germain-des-Pres average per year	Beaufour, Normandy	Forncett, England average per acre (in pence)
1360–1400: 84	1397: 142	1376–1378: 10.75
1422–1461: 56	1428: 112	1401–1410: 9.00
1461–1483: 32	1437: 52	1421–1430: 7.75
	1444: 10	1431–1440: 8.00
		1441: 7.75

Source: Georges Duby, *Rural Economy and Country Life in the Medieval West,* trans. Cynthia Postan (Columbia: University of South Carolina Press, 1968), pp. 329–30.

The brothers of the French Cistercian monastery near Ouges in Burgundy did much of their own work on their demesne[11] land but had to hire help as they needed it. From their demesne the brothers ended the year 1379 with 131 *setiers*[12] of grain; 27 of these were needed for seed and another 80 to feed the workers, leaving 24 to be sold for an income of 173 *livres*. During the growing and harvesting season of 1380 the brothers spent 100 *livres* on wages, 29 on building upkeep, 35 on tools and equipment, and another 4 on farming incidentals, for a total expenditure of 168 *livres*. The profit that remained was a measly 5 *livres*. The brothers leased out all of the manor's land in 1382. In doing so they followed the lead of their fellow Cistercians around Paris and in Brandenburg and Liège, Belgium, who had leased out all of their demesne land by 1370.

In the case above, the Cistercian brothers' biggest prob-
Golden Age   lem was not low rents, but the high wages demanded by the
of Labor   agricultural workers they had to hire. Across Europe huge
(and recurring) death rates meant that wage workers were
far fewer and could now demand much higher wages than before, whatever the value of the product. At the Earl of Norfolk's manor of Forncett
eight or nine wage-earning people made up the *famulus*, or permanent
staff of workers: four plowmen, a carter, a cowherd, a swineherd, a dairy-
maid, and a cook. Of course these would be supplemented with masons,
carpenters, smiths, tailors, and other skilled craftsmen through the year,
and by harvest workers in the late summer or fall. At a time of falling rents
these folks demanded substantially more, and they received it. During the
plague years of 1348 to 1350, vinedressers working for the duke of Burgundy saw their salaries triple. On the bishop of Winchester's land wages
roughly tripled in real terms over the century from 1350 to 1450. There
was real competition in the labor market among landlords and between
countryside and city, where wages even for unskilled laborers were at
all-time highs. In England this inflation in wages prompted royal laws
against paying or receiving high wages, in turn leading employers and
workers to negotiate nonmonetary payments that avoided the penalties
of the law but ensured a loyal workforce. These arrangements often raised
eyebrows and led to prosecutions, whose records attest to the inventive
deals. In 1394 Roger Hert of Sedgebrook, who worked as a plowman on
the monastic lands of Newbo, received 16 shillings cash as his monthly
salary. The court was concerned that he also received a cartload of hay
worth 3 shillings; pasture for a cow worth 18 pence; 15 loaves of bread
(7 of white wheat, 8 with varying grains), and 7 gallons of ale each week.
Other cases list rent-free land, cash or clothing "gifts," room and board,
the use of plow teams, free meals, and even banquets.

But what of enserfed agricultural labor (villeins) that lived in the villages and had carried out additional tasks like carting and plowing for
landlords for centuries? Quite simply, in England manorial villeinage was
on its last legs. It had meant in practice that one paid with one's labor—
working for the lord as well as oneself—and that leaving the village for
greener pastures cost a good deal if the lord allowed it at all. The growing
money economy meant that landlords needed cash at least as much as
labor. The first step was to commute servile dues in kind and labor to cash
payments or rents. The second was to commute the lord's own demesne
land to leased land, or to alienate it altogether by gift or sale. Leasing was
the preferred option since it meant a predictable flow of cash with few
of the obligations of the feudal landlord. The archbishop of Canterbury
began leasing out his estates in the 1380s and had let them all out by 1400.
This was a process that had begun at the end of the thirteenth century, but
with the Black Death it picked up speed until, by the sixteenth century,
little if anything was left of the old system. Of course, after 1348 no one

was willing to become another's villein, and desperate landlords increasingly replaced tenure in villeinage with free tenantry in order to repopulate their lands. This process, often referred to as the "death of feudalism," is one mark of the closing of the Middle Ages.

In much of northern Italy another solution emerged that also helped wipe away the last vestiges of feudalism. Deaths in land-owning families resulted in a great deal of rural real estate entering the urban land markets.

Sharecropping in Italy

Newly wealthy merchants and urban patricians bought up this property and, where possible, consolidated it into fairly large holdings. They could have hired laborers to work the land, but "wage fever" made this option very unpalatable, as expressed in this preamble to a Sienese law written in the wake of the plague:

The workers of the land, and those who customarily worked the lands and orchards, because of their great extortions and salaries that they receive for their daily labors, totally destroyed [economically] the farms of the citizens and inhabitants of the state of Siena and deserted the farms and lands of the aforesaid citizens . . . [etc.].[13]

The citizen-run state laid heavy taxes on the farm workers and brought in "foreigners" (non-Sienese) to supplement their labor. Over the longer run the Sienese and many others acquired tenants who entered into what amounted to sharecropping (*mezzadria*) agreements, whereby the landlord provided the land, some tools, and seed, and the tenant the labor. The tenant grew some crops for himself and the pair shared the profits from the sale of the cash crop according to a predetermined formula. In central Italy the consolidated plots ran from 25 to 75 acres. Around Milan, landlords leased even larger plots of from 125 to over 300 acres to entrepreneurs who paid a set fee and made their own arrangements for labor and expenses. Unlike English landlords, who were usually satisfied with most of their land yielding a single crop, the Italians produced a mixture of cash crops that served as a hedge against price fluctuations: if one commodity dropped in value, another was sure to rise. In addition to grains, they grew grapes, olives, fruits, flax for linen, dyestuffs like saffron and woad, and silkworms in mulberry trees.

One way landlords or employers could avoid the high cost of wages was simply to hire fewer people. Labor-saving devices and animal power that might replace human power were in great demand. Shifting land from

Other Landlord Strategies

labor-intensive agriculture to virtually labor-free pasturage became very popular in England and elsewhere. In Spain and southern Italy the shift to sheep-raising proved very profitable. Some English landlords began to enclose their arable land with fences, let it revert to pasture, and raise a variety of animals once the markets had picked up. At Radbourne in

Warwickshire 1,000 acres were enclosed in the early fifteenth century and given over to sheep and cattle. The value of the income in 1386 as arable land had been £19; by 1449 it was £64. This increase was accentuated by the fact that the owner needed only five or six hands to do all the work. By the early sixteenth century this practice was under attack, famously by Sir Thomas More, who wrote in his *Utopia* of "man-eating sheep" that deprived the growing population of needed agricultural land in the name of profit. At about the same time, however, Sir Edward Belknap defended the past practice before Parliament: "for at that time there was a great scarcity of pasture in that part, and arable land was in such abundance that men could not get tenants to occupy their lands."[14]

The newfound economic power of the peasantry in Europe did not everywhere lead to a brave new world. Where they could, landlords increased the burdens and penalties on their laborers in order to squeeze more out of them. In Catalonia and eastern Europe, where few burgeoning cities provided few viable options, landlords imposed stricter terms and shorter leases, tightening rather than loosening the feudal choke-chain. In Catalonia the price of redeeming oneself from servile status was raised from 64 to 133 *sous,* and the church blocked bound peasants from entering the clerical ranks. In German, Slavic, and Spanish lands the lords gained even greater power to seize, retrieve, or even "mistreat" servile laborers. In eastern Germany and western Poland a "refeudalization" took place under landlords who felt the need to keep their scarce human resources under control.

COERCION AND STATE INTERVENTION

English Labor Laws In England King Edward III reacted almost immediately to the labor shortage and consequent rise in wages by issuing the Ordinance of Laborers of June 18, 1349, in the form of a letter to the sheriff of the county of Kent and the bishop of Winchester. Its preamble clearly stated the government's concerns:

Because a great part of the people, and especially of workmen and servants, late died of the pestilence, many seeing the necessity of masters, and great scarcity of servants, will not serve unless they may receive excessive wages, and some rather willing to beg in idleness, than by labor to get their living; we, considering the grievous incommodities, which of the lack especially of ploughmen and such laborers may hereafter come . . . ordained . . . [etc.].

In the body of the ordinance the king laid out his expectations for all able-bodied people in his kingdom. First he dealt with rural folk:

That every man and woman of our realm of England, of what[-ever] condition he be, free or bond, able in body, and within the age of threescore [less than sixty] years [who is not otherwise settled and working] . . . be required to serve, he shall be bounden to serve him which so shall him require; and take only the wages, livery, meed,[15] or salary, which were accustomed to be given in the places where he ought to serve, the twentieth year of our reign of England (1346), or five or six other common years next before.

In short, everyone who could work was expected to find a willing employer and serve him or her at wages and other compensation no greater than what had been customarily paid before the plague. Those seeking work were first to apply to noblemen and only then to commoner landlords. On their part, employers were told that they had no right to more laborers than they could put productively to work. Those who could work and chose not to would be jailed; anyone who left employment before the terms were up was to be imprisoned, as was the person who chose to hire him or her afterward. Employers who chose to pay higher wages and compensation were to be fined twice the amount offered. Craftspeople like "cordwainers, tailors, smiths, carpenters, masons, tilers, [shipwrights, and] carters" were likewise not to charge or be paid more than was customary before the plague. In towns and cities merchants, craftspeople, servants, and laborers were also to refrain from profiting from the great loss of life. Edward further instructed each bishop and his colleagues to be sure that the clergy preached obedience to the new laws to their parishioners and that the clergy themselves not receive salaries or fees greater than before 1346.

By 1351 it had become clear that market forces rather than royal will were directing the depleted labor pool to seek the highest wages available. Noting this situation, king and Parliament issued the very similar Statute of Laborers.

[T]the said servants having no regard to the said ordinance, but to their ease and singular covetise [greed], do withdraw themselves [refuse] to serve great men and other, unless they have livery and wages to the double or treble of that they were wont to take the said twentieth year, and before, to the great damage of the great men, and impoverishing of all the said commonalty. . . .

The statute was more specific in its terms and more rigorous in its penalties than the ordinance:

In the country where wheat was wont to be given, they shall take for the bushel ten pence, or wheat at the will of the giver, till it be otherwise ordained. And that they be allowed to serve by a whole year, or by other usual terms, and not by the day; and that none pay in the time of sarcling [hoeing] or hay-making but a penny the day; and a mower of meadows for the acre five pence, or by the day five pence; and reapers of corn [grain] in the first week of August two pence, and the second three pence, and so till the end of August, and less in the country where less was wont to be given, without meat or drink, or other courtesy to be demanded, given, or taken; and that such workmen bring openly in their hands to the merchant-towns their instruments, and there shall be hired in a common place and not privy [private or secret].

One of the great freedoms of the newly unfettered laborer had been the right to make work contracts for very short periods, even by the day, which allowed him or her to bargain again soon for even better terms or to leave for a better position. The statute forbids this practice as well as that of secretly hiring seasonal day labor at undisclosed wages.[16]

In many ways this legislation was an unprecedented interference by the royal government in matters of the economy and the traditional right of contract. The working classes had no voice in the matter, and both they and the employer class honored the law in the breach. Christopher Dyer claims that there were "hundreds of thousands" of infractions across the later fourteenth century. In Essex County in 1352 alone there were 7,556 people fined for breaking the law, and 20 percent of these were women. The number fell to one-tenth of that (791) by 1389, probably due more to lax enforcement than a reduction in infringements. The demographic crisis also prompted other royal laws that were designed to—among other things—undermine the monopoly of London's guilds in order to lower prices (February 1351); force English landlords in Ireland to remain on their estates (1350, 1351, 1353, 1359, 1360, 1368, and 1380); limit expenditures by both the upper classes and the newly wealthy members of the lower classes on luxury items (the sumptuary laws of 1363 and following); and keep beggars from wandering about (Statute of Cambridge, 1388). While none of these laws achieved its goals, together they paved the way for ever-greater intrusions by the English crown into its subjects' private lives.

The Rise of the English Gentry
Edward III and his government relied upon, and indeed recruited, the lower nobility—often referred to as the gentry—in their attempts to control the suddenly mobile lower classes. Due in large part to social and political changes brought about by the Black Death, the gentry as a class developed a distinctive outline in the fourteenth century. The knights who lived on manors and administered much of England's agricultural activity were not a uniform group but had evolved into three social levels determined by the extent of and income drawn from their landholdings and their family's social standing. The gentleman was at the lowest level, with resources limited to the local parish or thereabout; the esquire occupied a middling stratum with resources spread about the county; the wealthiest level of knights had the broadest holdings and interests. Upwardly mobile yeomen with large estates could often pass for gentlemen as long as the status was loosely defined. One attempt to define it more strictly was embedded in the Statute of Additions of 1413, which required participants in legal court actions to specify their social standing as knight, esquire, gentleman, and so on.

Because of its long association with the nobility, the royal government trusted the gentry as a class to be a force for conservatism and stability in a rapidly changing world. From this elite, local crown officials were chosen to enforce the laws and, when they were broken, to conduct judicial proceedings. From among the knights came the more prestigious rural officials, including members of Parliament; justices of the peace and judicial officials tended to be esquires, and the lower constables and enforcement personnel were usually gentlemen. As court records demonstrate, these men were quite persistent in seeing that those who caused problems for the landholding class were dealt with harshly if fairly. They pursued and punished overdue debtors, tax evaders, runaway laborers, and aimless vagabonds with the same diligence as they did murderers and thieves.

Several factors quite unrelated to the plague exacerbated the tensions in rural English society following the Black Death. One such factor was the spread of Lollardy, a popular religious move-   **The Lower** ment based on the teachings of the radical priest and theolo-   **Classes** gian John Wyclif. His ideas undermined the foundations of   **Revolt** late medieval Catholicism by discrediting the priesthood and sacraments and insisting that the Bible be made available to all in English. This attack on the church hierarchy and its control of the Christian religion appealed greatly to otherwise disaffected members of the lower classes. Were the church to fall, so would its control of vast tracts of English soil, which some expected to be redistributed downward. Mandatory tithes to the church would also, presumably, come to an end.

Famines, wars, and taxation continued unabated during the era of the Black Death, and each of these fell very heavily on the rural lower classes. Until nearly 1450 England was entangled in the Hundred Years War, and though the fighting took place in France the money and men needed to support it were drawn largely from the English countryside. As serfdom declined and the English peasant class found its material conditions generally improved, the crown decided in 1377 to levy a series of poll taxes, taxes not on land or income but simply on subjects over a certain age. The first was a mere four pence per person, but to a man making a penny a day with three dependents over sixteen, it was half a month's wages. A mixture of anger at these exactions, Lollard radicalism, and frustration based on the government's attempts to minimize the lower classes' social and economic gains erupted into the famous English Peasant's Revolt of 1381. Recent studies have demonstrated that this event was a culmination of a series of protests by both the upper and lower classes, and that the "peasants" of 1381 included many with yeoman and even gentleman status. In many ways, the failure of this revolt helped strengthen the king's hand, demonstrating to the masses that rebellion was useless.

England's lower classes were not the only ones in Europe to feel the postplague tensions and revolt in the hope of relieving them. In the region around Paris a large-scale rebellion of peasants (nicknamed *Jacques*) against nobles and landlords broke out in June 1358. The *Jacquerie* was sparked by the failure of the French nobility to protect the peasantry from the English armies in the midst of the Hundred Years War. The brutality of the violence by both peasants and nobles was well beyond anything seen during the English revolt. The *Jacquerie* was key in convincing the French crown and nobility that the peasantry should receive absolutely no social or economic concessions in the wake of plague or other major disruptions. In Florence, Italy, it was the low-level wool workers known as *ciompi* who rose against the guilds and civic government in 1378. They demanded that Florentine wool-cloth manufacturers raise production levels to ensure higher employment levels and insisted that they be allowed to organize a guild and participate in civic government. Significantly, all three of these movements sought to redress ills that had long been a part of the medieval social system but that had been made worse by the plague. In all three cases they were repressed with some degree of violence, leaving the governing class shaken but not stirred to make conditions better.

The vast majority of people killed by the plague in the later Middle Ages lived in the countryside, and most of these were laborers rather than landowners. On the one hand plague made life somewhat better for the laboring classes by reducing the competition for land and concentrating material and monetary wealth in fewer hands. On the other, it forced the landowning and ruling classes to raise their demands on these same people in order to make up for the reduced labor force. The shifting around of burdens and resources, of opportunities and restrictions, was never smooth, and the adjustments led to social rebellion on a scale never seen in medieval Europe. As plague steadily became a disease of the urban world its effects on the social and economic structures of the countryside lessened, but the forces it unleashed in the fourteenth century were never reversed.

NOTES

1. Given their wealth—more than £5 worth—by law they should have made a will but did not.

2. Christopher Dyer, *Making a Living in the Middle Ages* (New Haven: Yale University Press, 2002), p. 233.

3. Etienne Robo, "The Black Death in the Hundred of Farnham," *English Historical Review* 44 (1929), p. 560.

4. Richard Lomas, "The Black Death in County Durham," *Journal of Medieval History* 15 (1989): 127–40.

5. Christopher Dyer, "Changes in Diet in the Late Middle Ages," in his *Everyday Life in Medieval England* (New York: Hambledon and London, 2000), pp. 83–90.

6. Georges Duby, *Rural Economy and Country Life in the Medieval West*, trans. Cynthia Postan (Columbia: University of South Carolina Press, 1968), pp. 339–40.

7. "City air makes one free"; medieval German proverb.

8. Primogeniture: the practice by which all land is inherited by the oldest or "firstborn" son.

9. B. T. James, "The Black Death in Hampshire," *Hampshire Papers* 18 (December, 1999), p. 6.

10. Not adjusted for inflation or deflation.

11. Land that was farmed to benefit only the landlord.

12. A *setier* was about 3 hectolitres or 78 gallons liquid.

13. William Bowsky, "The Impact of the Black Death upon Sienese Government and Society, " *Speculum* 39 (1964), p. 26.

14. Dyer, "Everyday Life," pp. 36–37.

15. Meed: a merited wage or gift.

16. Ordinance and statute texts found in *Source Problems in English History,* ed. Albert White and Wallace Notestein (New York: Harper and Brothers, 1915).

11

IN THE MEDIEVAL MUSLIM WORLD

In the early seventh century C.E., the Arab merchant Muhammad declared to the world that he had been chosen to be the final prophet of Allah, the one God whom, he proclaimed, Christians and Jews knew and worshipped imperfectly. Those who chose to submit to the will of Allah as recited to Muhammad from heaven itself and recorded in the Quran were the Muslims (from "submission"). Together they formed the religion of Submission, or Islam. Yet Islam has always been more than a religion: it fully prescribes a way of life—outlined in the Shariah or Shariat law—for the individual and the community. True believers who stray from this path imperil their very souls.

Islam spread from Arabia with an astonishing rapidity and within a century dominated the lives of people from the Pyrenees to Central Asia. So that all Muslims, regardless of their ethnicity, could read the Quran, Muslim leaders and teachers implanted the Arabic language throughout the Muslim world or House of Islam. Despite the political divisions that inevitably emerged in the far-flung empire, the religion of the Quran and its Arabic language provided powerful elements of cultural unity across this broad arc. After the Moroccan religious scholar Abu Abdullah ibn Battuta completed the 73,000-mile voyage that took him to virtually every corner of the vast fourteenth-century Muslim world, he remarked that he felt at home everywhere the Quran was read, from southern Spain to the isles of the Indian Ocean.

PLAGUE IN MEDIEVAL ISLAMIC SOCIETY

Muslim Medicine before the Plague

As Islam spread it not only connected countless millions of people by religion, but by commerce as well. Ibn Battuta traversed ancient trade routes along which traveled scholars and pilgrims like himself, as well as consumer goods, ideas, and secular cultural artifacts. From the societies it absorbed the Islamic world adopted and spread whatever it valued. During the ninth century the leaders of Islam, or *caliphs*, developed in their capital city of Baghdad a thriving center for both religious and secular studies known as the House of Wisdom (Bayt al-Hikmah). On the shelves of its library, the *caliphs* collected scientific, mathematical, and philosophical manuscripts from all parts of their empire and the neighboring Byzantine world. Spurred by the recent horrors of the First Pandemic, Baghdad's scholars read and translated into Arabic the highly respected Greek biological and medical books of the classical physicians Hippocrates and Galen and the philosopher Aristotle. For more than three centuries Muslim scientists and physicians pored over and commented on these works, integrating them into their own highly influential medical texts.

Informed by books and their own clinical experiences, Muslim physicians made huge strides in virtually every field, from brain surgery to internal medicine. Since the Islamic world and its trading network provided access to a far wider range of herbs and other medicines than had the Greek world, Muslim pharmacology expanded its scope well beyond what had been available to the Greeks and Romans. Pioneering Muslim physicians and scientists communicated their findings widely in Arabic works that ranged from short tracts to the encyclopedic tenth-century *Kanon (Qanon)* of the Persian Avicenna (Abi Ali al Hosain Ibn Sina). Many of these books became classics in both the Islamic and—once translated into Latin—Christian academic worlds. After the destruction of Baghdad's House of Wisdom by the Mongols in 1258, these Arabic classics dominated Islamic medicine and, by their very success, discouraged further medical advances. Despite a vital intellectual life in Damascus, Cairo, and other major Islamic cities, when plague arrived in the House of Islam in the 1340s Muslim physicians and scientists found themselves incapable of moving beyond the medicine of previous centuries.[1]

Plague in the House of Islam

Epidemic disease was far from unknown in the Islamic world. The First Pandemic of bubonic plague that rocked the entire eastern Mediterranean in the sixth and seventh centuries weakened the Persian and Byzantine (Eastern Roman) empires and facilitated the spread of Islam. The contemporary Arab poet Hassan ibn Thabit captured the devastation of one outbreak:

Its [the plague's] banners descended on Basra [Iraq], and in Rumah
Like whirlwinds it left the smoke of its blazing passage.

It wreaked havoc in Dhu Ba'l until its inhabitants were wiped out,
And destroyed every inhabited compound in al-Khamman.
Thus were the people hurried on from their requisite tasks
By the distracting stinging of *jinn*[2] well known in the land of the Romans.

At least nine major outbreaks of epidemic diseases occurred between 1056 and 1340, though most were limited in geographic extent. That of 1056–1057 was the most widespread and left an impression on Islamic culture similar to that of the Second Pandemic. Nearly four centuries after the fact the Muslim chronicler Ibn Hajar related:

The epidemic occurred in Samarkand and Balkh and killed every day more than 6,000 inhabitants. The people were busied night and day with washing, shrouding, and burying the bodies. Among the people whose hearts were split, blood welled up from their hearts and dropped from their mouths, and they would fall down dead.[3]

ABU ISHAQ AL-RAQIQ DESCRIBES TIIE PLAGUE IN TUNISIA, 1004–1005 C.E.

To all the calamities [famine, economic inflation, rural flight] were added *waba* [disease] and *ta'un* [epidemic disease; plague], which carried off the greater part of the population, both rich and poor. One hardly saw people busy except caring for or visiting the sick, performing the last rites for a dead person, following a funeral procession, or returning from a burial. In Qayrawan the bodies of the destitute were gathered at Bab Salim. Communal graves were dug for them and in each grave a hundred corpses or more were buried. . . . The mosques in Qayrawan were deserted; the public baths and ovens were still. People were even reduced to burning the doors of their houses and the rafters of their roofs [as firewood]. Many city dwellers and rural folk emigrated to Sicily. . . . It is even said that in the country people ate each other.

Quoted in Mohamed Talbi, "Laws and Economy in Ifriqiya (Tunisia) in the Third Islamic Century," in *The Islamic Middle East, 700–1900,* ed. Abraham Udovitch (Princeton: The Darwin Press, 1981), p. 223.

The plague of the 1340s appears to have moved along the very network of trade routes that facilitated the **The Black Death** spread of Islam and provided it with a measure of cultural unity. Like Christian commentators, Muslims report that the plague had its origins in China or southern Central Asia and advanced westward. Writing in the early fifteenth century, the chronicler Muhammad al-Maqrizi relates that

[i]t started in the land of al-Qan [the Khanate] al-Kabir . . . and this was in the year 742[4] [1341/1342 C.E.] and news of this arrived from the land of the Uzbeks . . .

and [the plague] spread throughout al-Qan killing the al-Qan [Khan] and his six children . . . and then it spread throughout the Eastern Countries and the Bilad al-Uzbek, Istanbul, Qaysiriyya, and Rum.[5]

Scholars face a dearth of known sources that would allow them to reconstruct the actual point of origin of the plague or to determine its effects in China and the Mongol-dominated regions of Central Asia. The generally accepted picture assumes that human activity along the very active trade and travel routes between China and the Black Sea region scattered native rodent colonies that harbored plague-carrying fleas. As these fleas infested new rodent colonies that had no immunity, huge die-offs occurred and the fleas began to feed off of people, spreading the disease from the rodent to the human population. Advocates of this model believe that hungry rats or other flea-infested rodents traveled with grain supplies along Central Asian trade routes westward into Islamic territory (and probably eastward into China) and eventually along the Muslims' own well-developed travel network.

First-hand sources of information on the spread of the Black Death in the Muslim world are relatively scarce, and little exists in the way of the diaries, housebooks, and letters that illuminate the European experience. There are official records, such as the chronicles known as *diwans*, though a good deal of this type of material remains to be studied. More personal accounts come from travelers' narratives like that of Ibn Battuta, histories like Al-Maqrizi's, poems, and anecdotes in various kinds of written sources. Two Andalusian physicians, Abi Gafar Ahmed ibn Khatimah and Abu Abdallah Muhammad ibn al-Khatib Lisad-ad Din, who witnessed the first epidemic in the late 1340s, left their plague tracts as primary sources. In his poetic 1348 "Essay on the Report of the Pestilence," historian Abu Hafs Umar ibn al-Wardi declared, "It began in the land of darkness."

IBN AL-WARDI ON THE ADVANCE OF THE PLAGUE, 1348

Oh, what a visitor: it has been current for fifteen years. China was not preserved from it nor could the strongest fortress hinder it. The plague afflicted the Indians in India. It weighed upon the Sind. It seized with its hand and ensnared even the lands of the Uzbeks. How many backs did it break in what is Transoxiana! The plague increased and spread further. It attacked the Persians, extended its steps toward the land of the Khitai, and gnawed away at the Crimea. It pelted Rum with live coals and led the outrage to Cyprus and the islands.

. . . it directed the shooting of its arrows to Damascus. There the plague sat like a king on a throne and swayed with power, killing daily one thousand or more and decimating the population. It destroyed mankind with its pustules. May God the Most High spare Damascus to pursue its own path and extinguish the plague's fires so that they do not come close to her fragrant orchards. Oh God, restore Damascus and protect her from

insult. Its morale has been so lowered that people in the city sell themselves for a grain. . . .

Then, the plague sought Aleppo, but it did not succeed. By God's mercy
the plague was the lightest oppression. I would not say that plants must
grow from their seeds. The pestilence had triumphed and appeared in
Aleppo. They said: it has made on mankind an attack. I called it a pestilence. How amazingly does it pursue the people of each house! One of them
spits blood, and everyone in the household is certain of death. It brings the
entire family to their graves after two or three nights. I asked the Creator
of mankind to dispel the plague when it struck. Whoever tasted his own
blood was sure to die. Oh God, it is acting by Your command. Lift this from
us. It happens where You wish; keep the plague from us. Who will defend
us against this horror other than You the Almighty? God is greater than the
plague which has captured and entered like an army among the peaceful,
even as a madman. Its spearheads are sharpened for every city, and I was
amazed at the hated thing [i.e., the plague] which lies on the sharpened
points. How many places has the plague entered? It swore not to leave
the houses without its inhabitants. It searched them out with a lamp. The
pestilence caused the people of Aleppo the same disturbance. It sent out its
snake and crept along.

From Michael W. Dols, "Ibn al-Wardī's 'Risālah al-naba' 'an al-waba,' A Translation of a
Major Source for the History for the Black Death in the Middle East," in *Near Eastern Numismatics, Iconography, Epigraphy and History,* ed. Dickran Kouymjian (Beirut: American University of Beirut Press, 1974), pp. 443–55.

The Persian chronicler Abu Bakr al-Ahri mentions plague in Azerbaijan
in 1346/1347 and explains that the khan of the Golden Horde, Djanibeg,
took advantage of the disruption in the region to invade the Crimea, which
brought him into contact with the Italian trading post in Kaffa. Ibn Khatimah
traces the plague's spread from Kaffa on the Black Sea to Constantinople
and thence to Cilicia. Al-Maqrizi and other sources date the arrival of plague
in Egypt to the fall of 1347, about the time it appeared in Sicily. He attributes it to the docking in Alexandria of a single merchant and slave ship.
Its 32 merchants and 300 slaves and crew were reduced to 4 merchants and
41 others by the time it made land; within a few days all had succumbed.
Alexandria was ravaged: clerics in the Grand Mosque prayed over 700 coffins at one time. The following spring, pestilence began to flow down the
Nile Valley, striking Cairo in April 1348 and reaching Upper Egypt in early
1349. In and around Cairo the dead were carried to their graves two or
three at a time on planks, ladders, shutters, or doors. Corpses and trash
littered the streets. Many bodies remained where they had died along the
roadside, and others were cast there by overwrought friends or family. Ibn
Ali Hajalah wrote of "these dead who are laid out along the highway like
an ambush for others." To the east, Tabriz suffered the epidemic in the fall
of 1346. The army of Malik Ashraf, which was besieging the city, broke off

its attack and turned on Baghdad, bringing the disease with it. Ibn Battuta noted that plague had hit Gaza in early 1348, probably spread from Egypt: "We went to Gaza and found most of it deserted because of the numbers that had died during the plague. The qadi told me that only a quarter of the eighty notaries were left and that the number of deaths had risen to 1,100 a day."[6] The thriving city of Damascus lay prostrate by June 1348, and in the same month 1,000 people a day were dying in Tunis, Tunisia. In the midst of this carnage the poet Abu l-Qasim ar-Rahawi wrote,

> Constantly I ask God for forgiveness.
> Gone is life and ease.
> In Tunis, both in the morning and in the evening
> —And the morning belongs to God as does the evening—
> There is fear and hunger and death,
> Stirred up by tumult and pestilence.[7]

At that time Abu l-Hasan, the ruler of Fez, Morocco, was fighting for control of Tunisia. After plague struck his military camps, his men scattered to Tlemcen and elsewhere in North Africa, taking the disease with them. Physician Ibn Khatimah's native city of Almería in Muslim Spain suffered its first case in June 1348 as well, and was soon losing 70 people a day. As European observers would later claim about plague in their regions, it originated in a house in the poorest quarter of town. Further north, along the border with the Christian armies of Castile, Muslim troops were ordered to attack their plague-stricken enemies. Though they won several skirmishes, they also contracted the plague and returned with it to their homes and loved ones. Finally, in late 1348 or early 1349 Mecca hosted its first victims as pilgrims on the hajj brought the disease from parts unknown. Ibn Khatimah listed the death tolls for a single day in May of 1348: Tlemcen, 700; Tunis, 1,202; Majorca, 1,252; and Valencia, 1,500.

In Egypt the epidemic of 1429–1430 was second in its destructiveness only to the original outbreak. Maqrizi noted that at its height in two days funeral services were held for 13,800 victims at the gates of Cairo. This number underrepresents the entire toll, since it leaves out those who died in the heavily populated suburbs and those who had no one to organize a service. Ibn Taghri Birdi described the houses and shops left empty by those who died and those who fled. He estimated that 100,000 people died in the outbreak, a death toll that modern scholars accept as reasonable.

Over the following two centuries plague returned to the western part of the Islamic world with roughly the same levels of intensity with which it returned to Europe.[8] To take centrally located France as an example, between 1347 and 1534 plague is recorded somewhere in 176 of 189 years, but only 16 major outbreaks occurred. In relatively isolated Egypt plague was reported in only 55 of the years between 1347 and 1517 (the end of the Mamluk[9] dynasty) but 21 of these outbreaks are considered major epidemics. In Mamluk-ruled Syria/Palestine the picture is similar, with 19 major plague years among 51 years with reports of plague.

During the era of Ottoman domination after 1517 the pattern continued unabated, with sporadic outbreaks occurring well into the nineteenth century. While western Europe may have been able to curb and eventually eliminate the recurrence of plague by controlling its ports and eastern frontiers, the Ottoman Empire remained wide open to sources of plague in western Asia and perhaps the Nile Valley. A recent study states that the annual flooding of the Nile regularly forced out burrowing rodent colonies—some of these plague-infested—bringing them into direct contact with the human population as they searched for food.[10] It may also be that the Muslim attitude to plague, conditioned as it was by the Quran and religious teaching, discouraged the kind of civic and personal measures that European Christians employed in battling the Black Death.

Metaphors for the plague abounded among Muslims. It was a cup of poison, an invading army, a sword or an arrow, fire or a bolt of lightning; poets imagined it as a snake or any of a number of predatory animals. It was swift, stealthy, and deadly. Muslim intellectuals who contemplated the plague were heavily influenced by both their religion and classical, Galenic medicine. Like Christians, they believed that the *ta'un*, or pestilence, was an action of God first and foremost. Religious teachers declared that for the righteous Muslim death by plague was a blessing *(rahma)*: a martyrdom like death in defense of Islam, which ensured the victim a heavenly reward. For the unobservant Muslim or infidel (non-Muslim) death by plague was punishment for sin that condemned one to hell. As with all acts of Allah, the pestilence was just, merciful, and good, and could not be avoided. Since God specifically chose each victim, there could be no random spreading of the disease by contagion, nor could one escape death by flight or medication. Muhammad himself had overturned Arab tradition in denying the possibility of contagion. He also taught that during times of epidemic disease—as his own was—a Muslim was neither to enter nor flee from an area in which the disease was found. An early Muslim commentary on this injunction stated that "God has created every soul: He has ordered its span of life on earth and the time of its death, the inflictions it will suffer and the benefits it will enjoy."[11]

Religious Theories of the Plague

IBN AL-WARDI ON THE DIVINE SOURCE OF PLAGUE, 1348 C.E.

This plague is for the Muslims a martyrdom and a reward, and for the disbelievers a punishment and a rebuke. When the Muslim endures misfortune, then patience is his worship. It has been established by our Prophet, God bless him and give him peace, that the plague-stricken are martyrs. This noble tradition is true and assures martyrdom. And this secret should be pleasing to the true believer. If someone says it causes infection and destruction, say: God creates and recreates. If the liar disputes the matter of infection and tries to find an explanation, I say that the Prophet, on him be peace, said: who infected the first?

From Michael W. Dols, "Ibn al-Wardī's 'Risālah al-naba' 'an al-waba,'" A Translation of a Major Source for the History for the Black Death in the Middle East," in *Near Eastern Numismatics, Iconography, Epigraphy and History*, ed. Dickran Kouymjian (Beirut: American University of Beirut Press, 1974), pp. 454.

Some Muslim clerics, like the Syrian legal scholar Muhammad al-Manbiji, who wrote his *Report on Plague* in 1363–1364, and Ibn Hajar in the 1440s, held that the spirits known as *jinn* directly attacked plague victims by pricking them as with arrows. While a few contended that the *jinn* acted on their own, most accepted that the *jinn* did their deeds according to the will of God, as his instruments. The theologian and physician Ibn Qayyim al-Jawzziya, who died shortly after the first outbreak of plague, attributed the plague to "satanic spirits." These beings continue to do their damage until they are "repelled by some defense stronger than their causes," which included remembrance of God, prayer, giving to the poor, and reciting of the Quran. "These deeds will invoke the angelic spirits who can conquer the evil spirits, make void their evil, and repel their influence," Al-Jawzziya wrote.[12]

THE MEDIEVAL PLAGUE AND ISLAMIC MEDICINE

Medical Practitioners in the 1340s

A variety of medical practitioners worked in any given Islamic city. Physicians trained in the Greco-Arab tradition of medicine commanded the most social prestige and served at the courts of Muslim rulers. For example, the Andalusian Al-Khatib, who had studied medicine in Granada, became an influential counselor and secretary to Granada's rulers Yusuf I and Muhammad. Muslim physicians were also important in administering the great urban hospitals and as educators in both medicine and science. New physicians had to pass strict examinations, and all were expected to carry out charitable visits to prisons and rural areas that lacked permanent health services.

Sheikhs were Muslim holy men who, among other things, practiced both physical and spiritual faith healing, as did certain "wise women" who were especially adept at handling women's health matters. It appears that average Muslims resorted to the *sheikhs* and wise women when the matter was either not terribly serious or when the physicians admitted an inability to treat the problem, as in the case of mental illness or a slowly debilitating disease. These healers often offered the patient prayers, spells, amulets, and unorthodox medicinal concoctions and herbal remedies. As in the medieval and early modern Christian world, Muslim popular healers combined religion, herbs, and ancient folk superstitions in their medicine. Some prescribed writing "sacred words" on bread before eating it, or on paper in ink that was then washed off and drunk by the sick person. Other word-oriented prescriptions involved writing secret letters on doorposts and drinking the water in which a specially engraved ring had been dipped. These last remedies were meant to combat specifically the plague. Al-Jawziyya said that the faith-based medicines practiced by the "village healers" were not only effective, but "that the powers contained in the formulas of taking refuge and in spells and supplications are superior to the power of medicines, even counteracting the force of deadly poisons."[13]

In the ninth century the Muslim *caliph* declared maintenance of the health and physical welfare of the people to be a duty of the Islamic state and established the *hisba*, an office held by the *muhtasib*. The state chose **Public Health and Hospitals** *muhtasibs* from among the religious judges known as *qadis*—learned and wealthy men who interpreted Shariat law and acted as moral watchdogs in the community. *Muhtasibs* were regulators of the weights and measures used by merchants in the great urban marketplaces. They were to protect the customers from any sort of fraud or deception as well as the selling of spoiled or otherwise tainted products by sellers who might come from any corner of the known world. By extension, the *muhtasib* oversaw the confection and selling of drugs and herbs by apothecaries (pharmacists), and by further extension monitored medical practice itself, both internal medicine and surgery, through which such goods were usually prescribed and distributed. By an odder extension the *muhtasib* was also to oversee licensed prostitutes. According to a fourteenth-century treatise on *hisba*, "It is necessary that the *muhtasib* make [them] fearful, try them, and warn them against imprisonment." A terser statement of their duty was "Command to do good; forbid to do evil."[14]

The concern of the Muslim rulers for the welfare of their people led them to build, equip, and staff at least one huge hospital *(bimaristan)* in every major Muslim city. In turn, wealthy and powerful individuals and families provided continual support for these institutions as a form of pious charity. Unlike Christian hospitals, which tended to be multipurpose, Islam's focused on the needs of the ill and education in the healing arts. Some hospitals were their cities' centers of medical scholarship and training. Patients received care and medicines free of charge in generally pleasant surroundings, their senses soothed by fragrant plantings, music, and the splash of fountains. Members of all social classes sought hospital treatment when needed, and, despite the charitable nature of the institutions, no stigma was attached to use of their services. The chief administrators were physicians chosen by the rulers or their ministers, and these men received generous salaries. Since these were formally educated men of medicine, the practice in the hospitals was based on mainstream Greco-Arabic theory.

Islam's physicians recognized the Black Death as *ta'un.*
Medical   In his *Medicine of the Prophet* the theologian and physician
Theories of Al-Jawzziya defined *ta'un* as "a type of *waba* [pestilence]."
the Plague   In early Islamic medical works *waba* is defined variously as
"quickness and commonness of death among men," "a cor-
ruption happening to the substance of the air," and "an unwholesomeness
in the air, in consequence of which disease becomes common among men."
Early in the Second Pandemic, physicians turned to the ninth-century texts
that dealt with the First Pandemic, such as the Egyptian Al-Timini's "The
Extension of Life by Purifying the Air of Corruption and Guarding against
the Evil Effects of Pestilence" (c. 970). Here they found a combination of
Hippocratic/Galenic medicine and elements of clinical experience tempered by Islamic religious teaching. The Spanish physicians Ibn Khatimah
and Al-Khatib, whose writings shape the modern view of mid-fourteenth-
century Islamic medicine, lived on the western frontier of the House of
Islam. In many ways each challenged the scientific and religious ortho-
doxies of the era, usually reflecting the commonsense observations of the
people in the streets and the men who governed them. One may assume,
however, that most physicians, even those who read the Spaniards' works,
operated within the belief system of the day.[15]

Both Al-Khatib and Ibn Khatimah sidestepped widely accepted astrological
medicine in their practice and writings. Ibn Khatimah wrote that medicine
was "an art which through research and experiment has arisen with the
object of maintaining the natural temperament, and of restoring it to him
who has lost it." He admitted that the celestial bodies may have an effect
on human health, but denied that the people of his day understood any
such influence. Likewise, in his "A Very Useful Inquiry into the Horrible
Sickness" Al-Khatib accepted that the stars and planets influenced people
but denied that these effects had anything to do with the practice of medicine. Both physicians explain and describe the plague as a disease spread by
contagion, but Ibn Khatimah steps back from the brink of heresy by avoiding the term and dismissing the possibility of what he has just described.
Al-Khatib, on the other hand, grasps the nettle and directly challenges
Muhammad's teaching: "The existence of contagion stands firm through
experience, research, mental perception, autopsy, and authentic knowledge
of fact, and these are the materials of proof." He went on to note

that most people who have anything to do with the receivers of this sickness die,
and [he] to whom this does not happen remains healthy; and further, that this
sickness appears in a house or quarter because of a garment or vessel so that it
becomes the cause of death of a person who affixes the aforementioned to himself,
and even the entire house shares in the perniciousness.

Al-Khatib lamented the fact that so many victims had died, sacrificed
to the legalistic decisions of religious lawyers and teachers. Admitting

that such men acted in good faith, he nonetheless insisted they were wrong:

But it belongs among evident principles that a demonstration evolved from tradition, if it is opposed to the perception of the mind and the evidence of the eyes, must necessarily be subjected to explanation and interpretation. And this, in the present instance, is exactly the idea of many who defend [the theory of] contagion.

Quite simply, he observed, plague accompanied the plague-ridden, and those who remained isolated from the disease—including certain North African tribes—remained free from it. He also noted that those who lived in areas struck by pestilence seemed to acquire immunity to it. He spoke adamantly about the folly of accepting and imposing the religious taboos:

Already, in fact, have pious people arisen in Africa, who retracted their earlier opinion, and formally proved by document that they withdrew from the earlier fetwa,[16] since they considered their consciences burdened by the view that it is permitted them to surrender themselves to destruction.[17]

Al-Khatib had as much trouble reconciling the standard theory of miasma—the Hippocratic/Galenic idea that the disease is caused by corrupted or putrefied air—with contagion,[18] as did orthodox physicians who tried to reconcile miasma with sharp-shooting *jinn* or the inescapable will of Allah. Miasma theory, blessed by Avicenna in his *Kanon*, held that "[v]apors and fumes rise [from the earth] and spread into the air, and provoke its putrefaction by means of a soft warmth." The "putrefied" air enters the human body and proceeds to corrupt the humors and the heart, which results in a poisoning of the body. In Book IV of his *Canon*, Avicenna wrote,

When the air that has undergone such putrefaction arrives at the heart it rots the complexion of its spirit and then, after surrounding the heart, rots it. An unnatural warmth then spreads all around the body, as a result of which a pestilential fever will appear.[19]

Ibn Khatimah altered this description somewhat, explaining that this pestilence worked in a manner unlike any other disease, which is why contemporary medicine proved so ineffective.

The swelling, or bubo *(dummal* or *khiyara)*, that observers noted on most victims' bodies was caused by the body gathering the poisoned humors and attempting to expel them. Al-Jawzziya cites Muhammad himself as describing the bubo of *ta'un* as "the swelling of a gland like that of the camel," and goes on to define it as

an evil inflammation, fatal in outcome, accompanied by a very fierce and painful burning that exceeds the norm; most of the surrounding area of inflammation becomes black, green, or of a dusky color, and the condition quickly turns to ulceration. Mostly this appears in three places: under the arm in the armpit, behind the ear and on the tip of the nose, and in the soft flesh [of the groin].[20]

Ibn Khatimah explained that the buboes formed either high on the body (neck or armpits) or lower (the groin), depending on the density and consequent heaviness of the corrupted matter. While buboes were a clear sign of the deadly disease, doctors also considered them a lifeline of sorts: if they "ripened," burst, and expelled the putrefied humors with the poison, the patient might well live. Like their Christian counterparts, Muslim doctors recognized that some victims contracted the pestilential fever and died without developing buboes. They rightly considered this variation the most lethal form of the disease, though they had no specific names for septicemic and pneumonic plague. True to their medical heritage, Muslim doctors were careful to note and catalog all of the symptoms related to plague from which victims suffered. Beside the notable buboes Ibn Khatimah lists fever, an erratic pulse, chills and shivering, a blackening of the tongue, cramps, lethargy, and anxiety.

Medical Prophylaxis and Treatment of Plague

As heirs of the Galenic theory of humors, Ibn Khatimah and Al-Khatib believed that a person's physical state—specifically the state of one's humoral balance—predisposed one to avoid the plague, contract the disease and survive it, or die from it. Avicenna had written, "Pestilential fever will spread to any human who is susceptible to it." People whose bodies were naturally "warm" and "moist," such as women, children, the obese, and the highly sensual, were most susceptible to the disease, which was by its nature warm and moist. The simplest means to prevent or treat the plague was to alter the patient's humoral balance to make it cooler and drier. Galen and Arab tradition provided the basic outline: avoid warm and moist foods, activities that excite the body like immoderate exercise, sex, or warm baths, and thoughts or feelings that arouse "hot" passions; consume a diet of cool and dry foods, especially sour, acidic ones; and exercise moderately. Ibn Khatimah also counseled altering the surrounding air, always avoiding corrupted air when possible. He suggested inhaling strong fragrances of many types, rubbing oneself with scents or scented oils, and sprinkling rosewater about the room or burning sandalwood. Dry and warm air was also to be avoided, and people were cautioned against spending time around fires or ovens or remaining exposed to the sun for long periods.

IBN KHATIMAH'S ADVICE FOR AVOIDING THE PLAGUE, 1349 C.E.

1. Keep the air around you pure and sweet, scented with fragrances when possible.
2. Sleep in a room open to the north wind; avoid the south winds.

3. Keep your body quiet and calm, and do not breathe deeply.
4. Keep your mind and spirit calm; relax and read soothing texts, especially the Quran.
5. In your diet avoid eating old meat but eat black bread regularly.
6. Avoid drinking any wine, even if mixed with water as allowed by the shariah.
7. Regularly evacuate your bowels and avoid constipation.

Adapted from Michael Dols, *The Black Death in the Middle East* (Princeton: Princeton University Press, 1977), pp. 101–5.

Muslim religious tenets insisted that people who had the plague should simply surrender to the will of God, dying or recovering as he saw fit. The practice of medicine by its nature interfered with this process, even when all it could do was to comfort the dying or dull their pain. No doubt many Muslims who contracted the disease followed these religious prescriptions and shunned medical aid. Those who sought the physician's help found that he had a limited range of tools. He began with diet and medicines that served to "cool" and "dry" the victim's body, following Galenic humoral principles. Bloodletting was the most frequently used surgical procedure. While some medieval writers advocated letting the "black blood" flow only until it turned red, Ibn Khatimah recommended draining "up to five pounds" of the humor. He tried to reconcile the practice of bloodletting with the Muslim notion of predestination by noting that in his experience, "God has as a result of this enlightenment caused great effects to follow in those whose sparing was ordained." Ibn Khatimah also had buboes surgically removed from sufferers, which, if done properly, could lead to recovery. To draw out the poison, he and other doctors suggested plastering the bubo with various ointments, egg yolk, or a special red clay known as Armenian bol, which is especially rich in iron oxide. They supposed that as it dried it drew the poison out of the swelling. Some drank water with the clay dissolved in it, and according to Al-Maqrizi, "some people devoted themselves to coating their bodies with clay," presumably as a prophylaxis. Al-Jawziyya's patients were probably not heartened to read his conclusion that "physicians have nothing whereby to repel these illnesses and their causes, any more than they have anything to explain them."[21]

IBN AL-WARDI ON THE PLAGUE IN ALEPPO, SYRIA, 1348 C.E.

The buboes which disturb men's healthy lives are smeared with Armenian clay. Each man treated his humors and made life more comfortable. They perfumed their homes with ambergris and camphor, cypress and sandal. They wore ruby rings and put onions, vinegar, and sardines together with the daily meal. They ate less broth and fruit but ate the citron and similar things.

If you see many biers and their carriers and hear in every quarter of Aleppo the announcements of death and cries, you run from them and refuse to stay with them. In Aleppo the profits of the undertakers have greatly increased. Oh God, do not profit them. Those who sweat from carrying the coffins enjoy this plague-time. Oh God, do not let them sweat and enjoy this. They are happy and play. When they are called by a customer, they do not even go immediately.

The Grey [i.e., Aleppo] became blackened in my eyes because of the anxiety and deceit. The sons of the coffins [the undertakers] are themselves about to follow death.

From Michael W. Dols, "Ibn al-Wardī's 'Risālah al-naba' 'an al-waba,' A Translation of a Major Source for the History for the Black Death in the Middle East," in *Near Eastern Numismatics, Iconography, Epigraphy and History,* ed. Dickran Kouymjian (Beirut: American University of Beirut Press, 1974), pp. 452–53.

THE PLAGUE AND ISLAMIC SOCIETY

In Islamic societies the leaders most concerned with religious and administrative affairs were the *ulamas*. They were conservative men who took quranic law very seriously and literally. Apart from the handful of medical tracts by physicians like Ibn Khatimah and Al-Khatib, most of the Islamic plague literature that prescribes particular attitudes and actions was written by *ulamas*. All echoed the Muslim teachings that plague came directly from Allah and brought martyrdom for the righteous and punishment for the infidel, and held that there was no contagion and flight was forbidden. Good Muslims, they taught, accepted God's will, neither praying for protection from the disease nor acting in a way that might seem to allow them to avoid it. Aiding suffering victims was a pious act of charity, but was not to be done with the intention of thwarting God's will.

Preparing for Death In Muslim cities the death tolls were enormous, though exact figures are far from trustworthy. Even so, a figure like 100,000 dead during the Great Extinction of 1429–1430 in Cairo— arguably the largest city west of China—seems far from exaggerated. Victims were both admitted to hospitals and treated by physicians wherever they lay suffering. Despite the comforting sermons of the religious teachers and *ulamas*, Muslim populations seem to have been every bit as anxious about their earthly fates and afterlife as any Christian society. Many desperately sought prophylaxes or cures, fled from their homes, and prayed for deliverance for themselves and loved ones. Abu l-Mahasin ibn Taghri Birdi, the major historian of early fifteenth-century Mamluk Egypt, wrote about those who were resigned to the fate Allah had prepared for them. They repented of their sins, made their wills, prayed in worship and thanksgiving to Allah, and attended funerals out of respect for both the dead and for the will of God. He described the weekly Friday prayer services, whose attendees grew ever smaller in number. Each week the prayer

The final page from a contemporary copy—perhaps
by the author himself—of a sixteenth-century Muslim
plague treatise, *Umdat al-rawin fi bayan ahkam al-tawa
'in*, by the Arab theologian Muhammad ibn Muhammad ibn al-Hattib, who died in 1547. Courtesy of the
National Library of Medicine, Ms. A 80, fol. 40b.

leader compared the number of live congregants with that of the previous
week: a vivid reminder of each person's mortality.

Funeral services were held en masse, with the dead placed in
wooden coffins for the ceremony. The coffins were then lined up **Dealing**
in the mosques, and even the largest, like the Al-Hakim mosque **with the**
in Cairo, were crowded with the dead as well as the living on Fri- **Dead**
day afternoons. On at least one occasion there was an unseemly
scene as families scrambled to retrieve the proper coffins for subsequent
burial. Muslim tradition dictated that designated "washers" prepare the
bodies and the families bury their own dead, though charitable or occupational brotherhoods often performed the duty and professional gravedig-

gers prepared the final resting place. Ibn Taghri Birdi asserts that in the 1420s families indeed cared for their deceased members, even when huge graveyards like that at Qarafa near Cairo were impossibly crowded and the relatives

were unable to bury their dead[. They] passed the night with them at the cemeteries, while the gravediggers spent the whole night digging. They made large trenches, the dead in each one reaching a large number. Dogs ate the extremities of [the unburied corpses], while people searched eagerly all the night for washers, porters [to bear and bury the corpses properly], and shrouds.[22]

In such a situation the corpse was removed from the coffin in which it had lain in the mosque and was buried simply in its cloth shroud. Wealthy or socially powerful people were honored with long funeral corteges that did not cease with the plague or its worsening. At times these processions became entangled in one another as they made their ways through the great cities' dense networks of streets and alleys to the mosque or graveyard.

When the pestilence raged with great fury, the usual customs fell away as the mass of bodies grew unbearably. Coffins disappeared completely, and even shrouds were reused, bodies being placed nude in the great burial trenches and pits. Corpses littered streets and alleys, perhaps laying where death overtook them, perhaps having been dumped. People tossed corpses onto trash heaps, and the Nile became a slow-moving highway for the bloated, floating dead who became entangled in the great reedy marshes, decaying in the midday sun.

Flight and Migration

Despite the religious taboo against flight from an area struck by disease, many Muslims departed the fetid cities for untainted regions. At the same time, a far greater number of rural Muslims fled their villages for the nearest city. Unlike the Christian European country folk who sought out the economic opportunities that opened in the wake of the plague, Muslims began migrating from the countryside as the pestilence raged, searching for anything that could aid their day-to-day survival. Some, of course, did not realize that the cities were suffering as badly as the countryside. Others did not care, and came looking for food and other necessities that had disappeared from their villages. Many sought the services of physicians and other healers who resided in the cities, and the apothecaries who provided drugs, herbs, and other medicines that they or their families needed. Still others sought out the cities for the spiritual comfort of their religious services, shrines, and holy men.

Religious Responses

The most characteristic Muslim responses to the plague were religious, and they took many forms, both personal and communal. Shiite Muslims differ from Sunni Muslims in many ways, but one that surfaced during plague time was Shiite devotion to holy men, living and dead, and to the shrines connected with them, especially if they were associated with healing. Some reported visions in which Muhammad himself presented specific prayers that were supposed to be especially pleasing to Allah. Shiites honored their saints by participating in processions and pilgrimages, though no specific "plague saints" equivalent to Christians' St. Sebastian or St. Roche received special attention. Since they were already a part of Muslim spiritual life, physical objects such as talismans, amulets, and inscriptions as well as spoken incantations became especially popular among the desperate populace. Some of the incantations were cycles or repetitions of prayers that dated back to the First Pandemic; others were found in the Quran. One such formula read, "The Eternal, there is no destruction and cessation of his Kingdom"; reading this 136 times in succession guaranteed protection from the disease. The use of these tools seems to have been most popular among those who believed that the *jinn* were responsible for the plague and could be affected by earthly behavior. Personal prayer to Allah was important to all Muslims, as was the ritual purity that was a part of the prescribed Muslim way of life.

Communities practiced ritual purification and prayer no less than individuals did, but did little else to combat the plague. Spurred by religious leaders, community govern- **Civic Responses** ments laid down strict laws against the use of alcohol and fornication and prostitution. During the 1438 plague Ibn Taghri Birdi wrote with disgust of the Cairo government's edicts against women appearing in the streets—even to attend the funerals of loved ones—under penalty of death. The public uproar was such that the council backed down and allowed servants and old women (who presumably would not fire men's libidos) to carry out necessary errands. When the sultan who supported these measures died soon after the law was adjusted, some critics declared it punishment for the draconian law, others that he suffered for lifting the restrictions. City governments like that of Cairo sponsored special assemblies for prayer and civic processions to shrines and even cemeteries. In spite of Islamic teaching to the contrary, cities like individuals acted as though the plague were a punishment from God, and prayers sought Allah's infinite mercy and the sparing of the townspeople. Other prayers that sought divine mercy on the souls of the departed victims were uttered fervently at the mass funerals and by men stationed around the city for just that purpose.

Al-Wardi, who died of the plague in Aleppo, saw what he felt were positive results of the epidemic in the changed lives of those around him:

Among the benefits of [the plague] is the removal of one's hopes and the improvement of his earthly works. It awakens men from their indifference for the provisioning of their final journey.

One man begs another to take care of his children, and one says good-bye to his neighbors.

A third perfects his works, and another prepares his shroud.
A fifth is reconciled with his enemies, and another treats his friends with
kindness.
One is very generous; another makes friends with those who have
betrayed him.
Another man puts aside his property;[23] one frees his servants.
One man changes his character while another mends his ways.
For this plague has captured all people and is about to send its ultimate
destruction.
There is no protection today from it other than His mercy, praise be to God.[24]

Muslim governments seem to have relied almost exclusively upon spiritual measures and God's mercy when confronting the plague. Many sultans
and other powerful men fled plague-struck cities with their extended families
and servants, while those who stayed did little more than follow the teaching of Galen and Avicenna and burn fires to purify the supposedly putrefied air. None even took the trouble to ban the sale of the clothing of plague
victims in the huge urban markets. Perhaps because they themselves were
both religious and secular figures in society, Muslim leaders did not seek
out medical advice or encourage the study of the plague by secular scholars
or physicians. As a result, Muslim intellectuals did not produce the kind of
speculative literature on the plague that characterized the results of Christian European inquiry. The most comprehensive modern historian of plague
in the Muslim world, Michael Dols, has concluded that the Muslim response
to the plague was remarkably consistent throughout the Second Pandemic
and that there was little in the way of research or theorizing about plague
in the Islamic world until the nineteenth century. This quiescent approach
contrasts vividly with the aggressive experimentation with all manner of
prophylactic and treatment measures by European governments.

**The Plague's
Effects on
Muslim
Society**

The Black Death and subsequent medieval plagues dev-
astated Muslim regions. Travelers report that entire villages
were devoid of human life. The massive depopulation of both
urban and rural areas was quickly followed by economic
depression. Because there was a strong tendency for many
Muslims to abandon the countryside for the cities, harvests
lay unclaimed, often rotting in the fields as urban residents paid increasingly
high prices for even simple fare. In some regions hunger resulted locally
until foodstuffs could be brought in from unaffected areas or released from
great urban storehouses. Of course the plague hindered transportation as
well, slowing the deliveries. Wells and irrigation systems requiring constant
attention fell into disrepair and otherwise fertile fields rapidly reverted to
scrub vegetation natural to the hot and arid climates typical of the Middle
East and North Africa. Tunis in Tunisia, which normally exported wheat,
had to import it from Christian Sicily in the spring of 1350.

The deaths of skilled laborers and craftspeople meant that the prices
of their labor or goods rose rapidly. Despite the lower demand for food

products, the decline in agricultural output ensured that prices would rise and remain high. Commerce among Muslim regions and with the states of Christendom fell off rapidly, and patterns of trade changed as Europeans replaced imports such as fancy cloth with high-quality home-manufactured goods. Increases in per capita disposable wealth in Europe led to an increase in the demand for spices that were shipped through Muslim ports, but this rise in demand simply meant higher prices in local markets. The steady flow of unskilled labor to the cities in times of trouble meant that their wages would remain depressed and their standard of living low.

These trends were especially damaging in Egypt's Nile Valley, which had been ruled by the Mamluk sultans since the thirteenth century. Arable land was divided into quasi-feudal *iqta'at* that centered on one or more agricultural villages. Like a European fief, the **The Case of Mamluk Egypt and Syria: 1348–1517** *iqta* might be held by the sultan, one of his chief military officers, or *amirs,* or by one of many thousands of leading soldiers in the highly professional Mamluk army. These landholders benefited from the land's production, usually overseen by professional managers. The landholders themselves generally lived away from the land in larger cities like Alexandria or the capital, Cairo. Tenure was neither permanent nor hereditary, and even in normal times an *iqta* could change hands frequently over the course of a decade. Therefore, the title-holders had no incentive whatever to improve or invest in their holdings; the villagers were left largely to their own devices.

When plague hit the Nile Valley in 1348, landholders, managers, and villagers died—or fled—in great numbers, leaving little in the way of leadership and relatively few peasants to handle the huge tasks associated with maintaining the Nile irrigation system. Even the sultan fled Cairo for Siryaqus. Amirs sent their troops to harvest the crops, which they did: threshing from horseback and winnowing by hand. Though they offered to split the harvest 50-50 with any peasants who helped, there were few takers. At the end of the season much of the crop remained to rot in the fields. In the Asyut region some 6,000 residents regularly paid the tax, but in 1349 the number had fallen to 116. Around Luxor 24,000 *faddans* of land were normally cropped before the plague; afterward it dropped to 1,000.

Deaths among the soldiers/landholders reached such levels that the sultan granted military rank, privileges, and *iqta'at,* normally reserved for the special Mamluks, to Egyptian commoners. Local breakdown and a failure of the central authority to provide adequate protection virtually invited the highly mobile nomadic Bedouin tribes to move into the lush riverine areas. Content with simple crops for themselves and natural grasses for their horses and flocks, they did little to maintain the infrastructure necessary to commercial agriculture (mainly wheat, barley, and broad beans). In fact, they were known to sabotage the irrigation system to ensure their control over the land. Bedouin leaders captured by Mamluk military expeditions were taken to Cairo, where they were tortured and brutally executed.

Many rural areas recovered over the following decades, and cities like Cairo were quickly repopulated: In his *Muqaddimah* of 1377, Ibn Khaldun claimed, "It is the metropolis of the universe, the garden of the world, the anthill of the human species, the portico of Islam, the throne of royalty, a city embellished . . ." He continued, "At this time, we hear astonishing things about conditions in Cairo and Egypt as regards luxury and wealth in the customs of the inhabitants there." Seven years later an Italian merchant visiting the city remarked, "[T]here is a street which has by itself more people than all of Florence." Even so, the Egyptian economy remained crippled into the sixteenth century, well after the economies and populations of most European countries had made great strides toward preplague levels. A recent study of Mamluk Egypt during the Second Pandemic demonstrates that Egypt's gross domestic product slid to only about 40 percent of its preplague level and stayed there until the regime's end at the hands of the Ottoman Turks in 1517.[25]

Society's surviving leaders appeared to prosper from oppressive taxes and the profits from long-distance trade, and many of these men built lavishly in the cities. In contrast, the working classes suffered and at times complained of what they saw as a decline in social integrity and a rise in corruption. Muhammad ibn Sasra recorded the following bleak poem by an anonymous author in his *Chronicle of Damascus*, which covered the period from 1389 to 1397.

> We have seen that the corrupt gain power and become high;
>   it is fitting that we go mad.
> We have reached the worst of times, so that we envy in them
>   the one among us who has died.
> We have seen what we have never seen, and heard what
>   we had not heard.
> He who died attained deliverance in death, while he who
>   lives is tortured by anxieties.[26]

The decade of the 1390s saw a conjunction of problems in the Mamluk world, including rule by a new group of Mamluks, popular insurrections against Mamluk oppression, pressures from the aggressive Ottoman Empire, the victories of the Mongol khan Tamerlane, and, of course, plague. The recovery of the 1370s and 1380s–especially in Cairo—had ground to a halt, and decay quickly set in. It was during these "bad times" (*fasad al-zama*) that the population of Mamluk Egypt and Syria reached low points from which they scarcely recovered. The stagnant demographic pattern may well reflect later ages of marriage, high death rates among women, or even the prevalence of pneumonic plague with its very high mortality rate. It may also reflect the increased use of both male and female contraception, including early-term abortion. Religious judges, perhaps reluctantly, condoned the practice of birth control, citing *fasad al-zama* as the key factor. Tahtawi opined: "Coitus interruptus is lawful without permission because the times are bad"; his contemporary Ibn Abidin agreed: "Yes, a consideration of how bad the times are indicates that contraception is permitted to both sexes."[27] Islam teaches parents to support their children and other dependents in an appropriate manner, and when economic and social conditions are as threatening as they were, and would continue to be, religious leaders saw fit to relax the general taboo against contraception. This trend, however extensive it may have been, provides a contrast with the contemporary natalism—or pro-procreation stance—of much of Christian Europe.

Maqrizi dates the real destruction of the Egyptian economy from the early 1400s. He writes that villages continued to vanish and the sultan's irrigation system along the Nile had all but disappeared in many places. Against custom, Mamluk landlords forced unpaid peasant labor into repair service, though with mixed results. Textile factories disappeared from Cairo, and roughly half of the city's sugar refineries either closed down or were converted to other uses. A few more than half of the city's bathhouses remained open. As an official market inspector in the 1420s and 1430s Maqrizi was fully aware of the decline in trade and the closing of markets and shops. The city's suburbs were in decay, with occupied houses only scattered about and even mosques left to fall into ruin. A year before the terrible plague of 1429 Ibn Zuhaira wrote that Cairo had been reduced to one-twenty-fourth of its previous size and glory. Only the cemeteries continued to grow. The plague epidemic of 1429–1430 dealt yet another blow to the fragile Mamluk society, killing large numbers of the ruling class and drawing yet more precious labor from the countryside to the cities. Less than a decade later *ta'un* struck again, this time eliciting an apocalyptic response that had Cairo's inhabitants cobbling together their own coffins as they anxiously awaited the prophesied death and resurrection of everyone on a particular Friday.

The Mamluks lost their hegemony after the Ottoman Turks extended their empire down through Syria-Palestine and across Egypt in the early sixteenth century, but the plague remained to harass the House of Islam for centuries to come. With Ottoman support, elements of evolving European medicine and medical education were studied and sometimes adopted by many Muslim physicians. When plague struck Istanbul in the mid-eighteenth century, Sultan Mustafa III ordered a Turkish translation to be made of two recent medical works by the Dutch physician and educational reformer Hermann Boerhaave. Before the twentieth century, however, these imports proved as ineffectual in helping people deal with the plague as Islamic traditions and practice had. As the connective tissue that linked Central Asia with Africa, the Indian subcontinent and the Indian Ocean, the Muslim world of the Ottomans proved to be a biological crossroads that continued to channel and harbor the disease. With its active public programs of quarantine and border and port closure, European countries appear to have successfully blocked new injections of the disease from Ottoman armies or shipping by the early eighteenth century. In the Lands of the Prophet, where few such measures were employed, however, the *ta'un* continued its pattern of sporadic and sometimes devastating destruction.

NOTES

1. Sami Hamarneh, "Medical Education and Practice in Medieval Islam," in *The History of Medical Education,* ed. C. D. O'Malley (Berkeley: University of California Press, 1970), pp. 58–59. Hamarneh does point out that Avicenna was not universally lauded; several notable physicians in Egypt and Andalusia criticized him severely.

2. Spirit entities known to the Arabs.

3. Ibn Thabit in Lawrence I. Conrad, "Epidemic Disease in Central Syria in the Late Sixth Century. Some New Insights from the Verse of Hassan ibn Thabit," *Byzantine and Modern Greek Studies* 18 (1994), p. 18; Ibn Hajar in Michael Dols, *The Black Death in the Middle East* (Princeton: Princeton University Press, 1977), p. 32.

4. A.H., or from the Year of the Hegira (632 C.E.), the Muslim equivalent of A.D. or C.E.

5. Rum (Rome) designated the Christian world from Constantinople (Istanbul) westward. See Stuart J. Borsch, *The Black Death in Egypt and England* (Austin: University of Texas Press, 2005), p. 4.

6. Dols, *Black Death,* p. 238; Abu Abdullah ibn Battuta, *Voyages of Ibn Battuta,* Vol. 4 (#178) (London: Hakluyt Society, 1994), p. 919.

7. Dols, *Black Death,* p. 238; Abu Abdullah ibn Battuta, *Voyages of Ibn Battuta,* Vol. 4 (178) (London : Hakluyt Society, 1994) p. 919.

8. By comparison, the Muslim ruler of Mughal India, Jehangir (r. 1605–1627), was told by his experts that the occurrence of plague in the region from the Punjab to Lahore and Kashmir in 1615 was the first time plague ever hit India. It returned for a three-year stay in 1619 and continued to recur. B. M. Ansari, "An Account of Bubonic Plague in Seventeenth Century India in an Autobiography of a Mughal Emperor," *Journal of Infection* 29 (1994), pp. 351–52.

9. The Mamluks were a slave-soldier nobility who ruled Egypt and Syria from the later thirteenth century; they were conquered by the Ottoman Turks in 1517.

10. Borsch, *Black Death,* p. 25.

11. Lawrence I. Conrad, "Epidemic Disease in Formal and Popular Thought in Early Islamic Society," in *Epidemics and Ideas,* ed. Terence Ranger and Paul Slack (Cambridge: Cambridge University Press, 1992), p. 93.

12. Ibn Qayyim al-Jawziyya, *Medicine of the Prophet,* trans. Penelope Johnstone (Cambridge: Islamic Texts Society, 1998), p. 29.

13. Ghada Karmi, "The Colonization of Traditional Arabic Medicine," in *Patients and Practitioners: Lay Perceptions of Medicine in Pre-Industrial Society,* ed. Roy Porter (New York: Cambridge University Press, 1985), p. 316; Dols, *Black Death,* pp. 131–32; Al-Jawziyya, *Medicine,* p. 29.

14. Martin Levey, "Fourteenth-century Muslim Medicine and the Hisba," *Medical History* 7 (1963), pp. 180–81; Ghada Karmi, "State Control of the Physician in

the Middle Ages: An Islamic Model," in *Town and State Physicians in Europe from the Middle Ages to the Enlightenment* (Wolfenbüttel Forschungen 17: Wolfenbüttel, 1981), p. 63.

15. Al-Jawziyya, *Medicine*, p. 27; Lawrence I. Conrad, "TĀ'ŪN and WABĀ': Conceptions of Plague and Pestilence in Early Islam," *Journal of the Economic and Social History of the Orient* 25 (1982), pp. 271, 274.

16. A fetwa (or fatwa) is a definitive opinion or decision by an established Muslim religious authority. In this case the fetwa confirmed the Muslim taboo against accepting the possibility that the plague was contagious.

17. Anna Montgomery Campbell, *The Black Death and Men of Learning* (New York: Columbia University Press, 1931), pp. 78 n. 44, 56–59; Dominick Palazzotto, "The Black Death and Medicine: A report and analysis of the tractates written between 1348 and 1350" (Ph.D. dissertation, University of Kansas, 1974), p. 241.

18. He seems to have believed that the air that immediately surrounded the diseased person somehow transmitted the poison—accurate in the case of pneumonic plague.

19. Jon Arrizabalaga, "Facing the Black Death: Perceptions and Reactions of University Medical Practitioners," in *Practical Medicine from Salerno to the Black Death*, ed. Luis Garcia-Ballester et al. (New York Cambridge University Press, 1994), p. 251.

20. Al-Jawziyya, *Medicine*, p. 27.

21. Karmi, "Colonization," pp. 319–20; Dols, *Black Death*, p. 103; Campbell, *Black Death*, p. 73; Al-Jawziyya, *Medicine*, p. 28.

22. Abu l-Ma·hasin ibn Taghri Birdi, *An-Nujum az-Zahirah fi muluk Misr wal-Qahirah, History of Egypt 1382–1469 A.D.*, Vol. 18, part 4, ed. and trans. William Popper (Berkeley: University of California Press, 1915–1964), p. 182.

23. A reference to giving property away in the form of a pious endowment or *waqf*.

24. Michael Dols, "Ibn al-Wardi's 'Risalah al-naba' 'an al-waba,' in *Near Eastern Numismatics, Iconography, Epigraphy and History*, ed. Dickran Kouymjian (Beirut: American University of Beirut Press, 1974), pp. 454–55.

25. Gaston Wiet, *Cairo: City of Art and Commerce* (Norman: University of Oklahoma Press, 1964), p. 63; Abd-ar-Rahman ibn Khaldun, *The Muqaddimah* (Princeton: Princeton University Press, 1969), p. 275; Borsch, *Black Death*, p. 83.

26. Muhammad ibn Sasra, *Chronicle of Damascus, 1389–1397*, ed. and trans. William Brinner (Berkeley: University of California Press, 1963), p. 218.

27. B. F. Musallam, "Birth Control and Middle Eastern History: Evidence and Hypothesis," in The *Islamic Middle East, 700–1900*, ed. Abraham udovitch (Princeton: The Darwin Press, 1981), p.448.

12

THE PLAGUE'S LAST STAND IN EUROPE

By the middle of the seventeenth century the plague began to disappear from European soil. Though people did not know it at the time, each country in turn suffered what were to be final agonies from the pestilence. But the subsidence was neither predictable nor swift. The earliest area freed from the disease was rather isolated Scotland in the 1640s, but the last, Russia, continued to suffer until the 1770s. Western Europe's last great epidemic of plague occurred in southern France between 1720 and 1722 and accounted for over 90,000 officially reported deaths. Europe as a whole saw its last major plague outbreak in Russia 50 years later. Centered on Moscow, this epidemic lasted from 1770 to 1772, killing an officially estimated 100,000 Russians in the city and district. Both of these events stand out against a nearly plagueless European century, and each reminded its contemporaries that humanity had yet to defeat the great pestilence. In fact, it would emerge again to ravage East and southern Asia as the nineteenth century was dying, and only then would its secrets be unlocked.

The reason—or reasons—for the disappearance of virulent plague from Europe between about 1650 and 1775 is far from clear. Underdeveloped Scotland was freed in the 1640s, but neighboring England's greatest city suffered its "Great Plague" in 1665. Italy, which remained carved into several states with multiple ports and close proximity to the plague-ridden Turkish world, suffered its last epidemic in Naples a decade earlier. As in many areas of plague study, researchers argue fervently over their pet theories. A key concern for any theorist is the true nature of the disease that disappeared—that must be determined before any explanations for its demise will be universally accepted. The vast majority of scholars who take one position or another on the plague's disappearance assume that the disease was bubonic plague and its attendant forms, septicemic and pneumonic plague. For them, the basic question is whether plague disappeared because of natural factors or human intervention, or some combination of both.

DECADES OF LAST SERIOUS EUROPEAN PLAGUE OUTBREAKS

Scotland	1640s
Italy[1]	1650s
England	1660s
Spain	1680s
Scandinavia	1710s
Central Europe	1710s
France	1720s
Sicily	1740s
Russia	1810s
Ottoman Empire	1840s

Source: M. W. Flinn, "Plague in Europe and the Mediterranean Countries," *Journal of European Economic History* 8 (1979), p. 138.

THE DISAPPEARANCE OF PLAGUE IN EUROPE

Theories for the plague's disappearance are many and not necessarily mutually exclusive. In fact, it would be odd if a single factor accounted for the ending of a four-century-long scourge. Perhaps for this reason most scholars credit a number of factors, often expressing a favorite or most-probable choice. The theories fall into two broad groups: one that credits human activities and intervention and the other that attributes the plague's decline to biological changes in the bacterium, flea, rat, or human host or environmental changes that affected the organisms involved. Scientists and historians accept no single factor, and it seems unlikely that one will surface until there is universal agreement on the nature of the disease itself. In addition, no current theory is without its critics who tend to claim that either the theory does not account fully for the disappearance or there is no evidence to support it.

Natural Factors: Climatic Change The broadest and least satisfying theories point to the so-called little ice age that altered the continent's climate beginning in the sixteenth century. Winters lasted longer than they had, and this "reduced the ability of the plague to reestablish itself after the winter." This may have had the effect of either driving away black rats or interfering with the fleas' life cycles. But where did the black rats go? And if the requisite fleas and their rat hosts were living in buildings with people, they would have been protected by the increasingly well-insulated houses. In fact, when plague hit during the seventeenth century it seems to have concentrated in the coolest of homes, those of the poor.[2]

Explanations that concentrate on the rat and its role in plague epidemiology are of several types. One that has been discredited is that the Norwegian brown rat (*Rattus norvegicus*), which is not a favored host of the X. *cheopis* flea that generally carries the plague, replaced the highly favored black R. *rattus*, greatly reducing the number of essential hosts. The problem is that the brown rat only appeared in great numbers in the middle of the eighteenth century, too late to play a role. Another older theory posited that rats—including plague carriers—simply became more sedentary and did not migrate as much as they had, since urban growth ensured food supplies and nicer homes. More widely accepted modern theories suggest increasing immunity of rats to the plague bacteria, so that they did not die off and thereby touch off the epidemics. During the Third Pandemic rats in Bombay were found to have been immune to plague 90 percent of the time, though there is no evidence for such a condition in Europe's rodents. Historian Andrew Appleby accepted this theory despite admitting that there is "no direct evidence" for it. He went on to question rhetorically why the immunity had not developed earlier or elsewhere, to which he candidly replied, "I have no idea." Indeed, if rats had gained greater immunity, plague would have disappeared gradually, breaking out sporadically, rather than ending abruptly across regions as it did.

Natural Factors: Rats, Fleas, Germs

Critics also maintain that immunity in rats is short-lived, which may explain the pattern of once-a-decade outbreaks, but not the plague's disappearance. A very different view has the plague rats dying off in such great numbers that they could no longer sustain the presence of enough fleas to create a "critical mass" for a plague outbreak. Biologist Stephen Ell dismisses the idea that plague in Europe was ever enzootic—existing in low levels among resident animal populations—and concludes never had to "disappear." This implies that each epidemic was an importation from somewhere else. Soviet antiplague researcher V. N. Fyodorov claims that in central and eastern Europe at least, plague was indeed enzootic, but was carried by squirrels, whose habitats were disrupted by agricultural development that had the effect of "liberating" the region from the rodents and their fleas.[3]

Though few claim that any change in fleas occurred during the Second Pandemic, several surmise that *Yersinia pestis*, the bacterium associated with bubonic plague, underwent some mutation that caused it to change its deadly ways. Since parasites survive better when their hosts survive, some scientists believe that Y. *pestis* became less virulent or deadly over time. The strain present in Europe may have mutated into its close cousins Y. *pseudotuberculosis* or Y. *enterocolitica*. This would probably have affected the rat populations directly, killing far fewer of the animals, so the fleas had less of a need to seek new hosts. Though many find this theory intriguing it lacks any solid foundation in historical evidence.[4]

Natural Factors: People
But if the disease or its carriers did not change, did the human population? The issue of human immunity to *Y. pestis* is complex and unsettled, though it seems that any immunity provided by having contracted the disease is short-lived and is not passed along genetically. It does appear, however, that having had *Y. pseudotuberculosis* confers immunity to other *Yersinia*-type diseases, and that Europe may have had an outbreak that effectively immunized it. Again there is no evidence, and some scientists say that *Y. pseudotuberculosis* did not occur in Europe until the nineteenth century. Some researchers are studying the possibility that genetic mutations in the human body's ability to block the lethal bacteria made an ever-larger portion of the European population immune over time. Critics of these theories point out that had any of these been the key to the plague's extinction, it would have occurred gradually over time and not suddenly, and only after some of the most horrific epidemics of the Second Pandemic.[5]

Human Activity
Although people had long sought the combinations of foods, medicines, and actions that would make them invulnerable to the pestilence, it may be that some simple behaviors unrelated to plague prophylaxis ultimately played a major role. According to some modern historians the key was better nutrition that built up people's immune systems, though Andrew Appleby points out that the wealthy had always had reasonably healthy diets and still succumbed in great numbers. For others it was the building of stone and brick houses with slate or tile roofing rather than the thatch that was so inviting to rats. According to J. F. Shrewsbury, "[T]he national development of this type of dwelling was probably the most important single factor in the eventual disappearance of the house rat from the bulk of England." Nonetheless, cities like Naples and London continued to have enormous slums with substandard housing long after the last appearances of plague in 1656 and 1665 respectively.

People's increasing use of harsh soaps to cleanse their bodies may have had the additional and unintended effect of repelling the deadly fleas. Another aspect of material life that accompanied the early modern period was the greater availability and cheaper price of clothing, so that changing and washing one's wardrobe became more normal. The temperature of cast-off clothing infested with fleas would have quickly dropped, exposing and perhaps killing them, at least in the colder climes. Fleas are also susceptible to being drowned, so washing infested clothing, especially in hot or soapy water, would have killed many of them. Changes in burial practices, including widespread use of sealed coffins and deep burial, may have served to isolate the fleas and appreciably reduce their number. Of course, coffins and deep burial had been used since 1347, and though possibly a minor factor, could hardly account for the plague's disappearance from much of Europe in the mid- and late seventeenth century.[6]

People's efforts to halt the spread of plague did not include the killing off of the flea-bearing rats—since no one had any clue of a connection—but people did begin to use white arsenic as rat poison on a large scale after the mid-seventeenth century. It was a material used in the production of glass in Venice, and huge quantities were created as a byproduct during industrial mining of metal

Human Intervention: Poison and Environmental Clean-Up

ores. Around 1700 a single site near Schneeburg, Austria, was producing 300 to 400 tons per year. It found its way into plague amulets and even medicines and, because it was cheap, tasteless, and highly toxic, rat poisons. Of course, dead rats were the problem (fleas quickly abandoned them for live people) and not necessarily the solution, unless the poison also killed the fleas that ingested poisoned blood or were otherwise exposed to the white powder.[7]

Historian James Riley wrote an entire book about the many efforts by eighteenth-century Europeans to avoid disease by cleaning up their environment: draining large stagnant bodies of water, flushing out filth, increasing ventilation in buildings and cityscapes, even reburying old corpses in deeper graves at great distances from human habitations. They were still operating on the assumption that plague and some other diseases were matters of bad air, or miasma, that was generated in stinky or swampy places. While draining stagnant wetlands was good for destroying the habitat of the mosquitoes carrying malaria ("bad air"), it would have had no effect on plague rats or fleas. Riley concludes "for unknown reasons, the flea's role in transmitting plague was disturbed in the latter decades of the seventeenth century, very probably in some manner unconnected to environmentalist remedies, which had not yet passed from the stage of theory to action."[8]

The human intervention most widely credited with halting the plague in Europe was the establishment of blockades, quarantines, and a buffer zone or *cordon sanitaire* along the border between the Austrian and Ottoman Empires. Avoiding contact with people who had the disease had always been considered the best way to avoid the disease, despite the prevalence of the theory of poisoned

Human Intervention: Blockades and Cordons Sanitaires

air. As time went on, cities, city-states, and nation-states developed ever-stricter rules governing travel and other contact with people and goods from known plague regions. Historian Michael Flinn is convinced that concerted local and national-level activity did the job. First, local measures like shutting people in, isolating the sick in pest houses, burning flea-infested clothing, and posting guards isolated the plague to smaller and smaller locales until it died out naturally. Then the application of strict rules against commerce with plague-infected areas, combined with quarantining and tighter security against smugglers kept the plague from being reintroduced. When plague broke out and began to spread in southern France in 1720 Spain immediately blocked trade with the region and the French government used one-quarter of its royal cavalry and a third of its army's infantry to create a steel ring around the affected region. Both of these efforts seem to have paid off, as the plague spread neither to Spain or the rest of France.

Regarding border patrols, the key for Flinn, as for others, was the development of the *Militärgrenze*, or military border frontier, with the Ottoman Empire. Following the Peace of Passarowitz in 1719, the Austrian border was set deeper in Ottoman territory, creating a wide buffer zone. With special decrees known as *Pestpatente* from the military high command in Vienna (1728, 1737, 1770) the Austrian government enlisted farmers to colonize the new border strip as *Bauernsoldaten*, or farmer-soldiers. Organized into regiments, they actively patrolled the border in five-month shifts, over 100,000 at a time, with more men added when plague was known to be active in Ottoman territory. Their posts were located a gunshot's range apart along a border that ran for over 1,100 miles. Merchandise could cross the border at small and plentiful *Rastelle*, but people with goods crossed

Chains or log booms were effective tools for stopping suspect ships during plague time, as here on the lower Tiber River in the mid-seventeenth century. National Library of Medicine.

only at larger and less-frequent stations known as *Kontumazen*, which were equipped with quarantine facilities and a pest house. Here the travelers and all goods were normally quarantined for 21 days, a period that was doubled when there were rumors of plague, and doubled again (to 84 days) if plague was known to be in the neighborhood. Cotton and wool goods were always aired out first, then menial servants slept on the material to see if they developed plague. Anyone caught trying to evade the border guards was to be shot dead. Even though plague had gradually died out by the 1850s, the *Bauernsoldaten* maintained their posts until 1873. The Austrian model was adopted by the Russian Empire, which also shared a border with the Turks. Only wars and attendant troops' movements seem to have brought the plague into western Russia down to the 1770s.[9]

Austria experienced no large-scale plague outbreaks after Vienna's last epidemic between 1712 and 1714, and many historians credit the tight border security with keeping it out. But critics note that while such measures might keep human or cloth-borne fleas at bay, the border guards hardly kept out migrating rats with their deadly cargoes. The same would hold true for a ship whose plague rats would scurry down mooring lines as soon as it docked, finding new homes and spreading the disease almost immediately. Such measures should also have had no discernible effect on enzootic disease, which would have remained present in European rat colonies with no need for new infusions of the plague bacteria. And what of the many countries released from the grip of recurring plague up to 80 years before the first Austrian border patrols?

The strictly manned Austrian *Militärgrenze* may well have blocked the flow of flea carriers, but it alone cannot explain the disappearance of the plague from western Europe. Some combination of the factors discussed above, perhaps with others yet to be identified, may one day satisfy most students of the Second Pandemic. In the meantime, however, it remains an open question.

WESTERN EUROPE'S LAST GREAT EPIDEMIC: MARSEILLE, 1720–1722

When Captain Chataud's ship sailed from the port of Saida in the Lebanon on January 31, 1720, bound for Marseille, France, its cargo, crew, and passengers were certified free of plague by local authorities. By the time the ship docked in Livorno (Leghorn), Italy, four crewmen and one passenger had died of what an Italian doctor declared to be the pestilence. The vessel continued to its final destination, but instead of quarantining the entire enterprise, the French port officials let the ship dock at a distance from the main port facilities and took its personnel to the local pest house for a two- to three-week quarantine. Other ships also docked in similar fashion, and soon the official in charge of Chataud's merchantman was dead of the plague. On July 8 Chataud's ship and all of its cargo were taken to the quarantine station at the island of Jarre and incinerated. Dr. Jean Baptiste Bertrand reported that the disease spread quickly from the pest house, though by means he did not understand. He believed that the first families to be attacked were tailors and cloth merchants who lived along the Rue de l'Escale in a working-class neighborhood. From mid-June the disease spread through the quarter, he claimed, but little was reported for fear of harsh official actions.[10]

Despite Denials the Plague Spreads On July 18, Dr. Sicard of the Misericorde hospital reported cases of plague to the Marseille health magistrates. The surgeon Bouzon contradicted him, however, claiming they were cases of worm-fever, though he had not examined the patients, "only talked with them at a distance." In his memoir of the epidemic Bertrand lashed out at those in the government and press, and even physicians, who refused to admit that the disease that had been spreading rapidly for nearly a month was in fact the plague. To be on the safe side the civic government sealed off the disease-ravaged neighborhood and sent the friends and family of the victims to the infirmary for quarantining. Finally, at the end of July, city officials formally requested that the College of Physicians send experts to inspect the dead and dying and their friends and family in the hospitals to make an accurate assessment. The College assigned the dangerous task to its newest and only unmarried member, one Dr. Michel, who "accepted the office with the warmest philanthropy." Frustrated, the city council appointed four physicians (including Bertrand) and four apothecaries to inspect the current victims and, in pairs, to serve as civic medical experts to each of the quarters of the city. After two days all eight reported that the plague was raging, but the authorities continued to insist in public posters and publications that the plague was merely "malignant fever" "caused by poverty and unwholesome foods." The practitioners were enjoined to keep silent after being upbraided for "seeking gain" by declaring the epidemic one of plague.[11]

One of the eight, Dr. Peysonnel, related his horror to his son, who began to "talk everywhere and without reserve of the plague being in the city."[12] The young man also wrote to neighboring towns of Marseille's plight, and soon the Parlement of Provence laid out a thin cordon around the city. But both the cordon and the writing campaign occurred too late: the town of Apt reported plague on August 1 and Toulon on August 20. Between August 1 and October 1, 25 southern Provençal communities reported the pestilence. After three more months another two dozen were stricken, including Tarascon and Aix. It appeared in Orange and Avignon as late as August of the following year. Though rural areas also suffered during the fall of 1720, only urban areas reported plague deaths in 1721.

Too Little, Too Late In early August 1720 the Marseille authorities took what Bertrand thought a deadly step and left the victims sealed in their own homes. He argued for a plague hospital and hospices for those recovering. The Hôtel de la Charité could be used to house 600 to 800 poorer residents, he reasoned, but the current inmates would not allow themselves to be evacuated. Five religious monasteries and convents in the city could also be cleared of inhabitants to accommodate over 2,000 more, he estimated. One would serve the wealthy, another clergy and bureaucrats, and the other three people at various stages of the disease or recovery. But the advice went unheeded. By August 10 Bertrand found the city gripped by the pestilence:

No longer were the shops opened; all public works were suspended; commerce ceased; the churches, the exchange, and all public places were shut up; divine service was suspended, and the courts of justice stopped; neighbors, and even relations, ceased to visit each other.[13]

Soon the corpses were accumulating faster than the assigned corpse-bearers could carry them away. Normal graveyards rapidly filled to overflowing, and bodies were left littering the streets as the corpse-bearers died off. Though the bishop and many priests remained in Marseille, the scale of the disaster overwhelmed them, and many of the clergy died. The Catholic Bertrand lamented,

Where [the plague] reigns divine worship is suspended, the temples are shut up, and the public exercise of the holy offices of religion are unavoidably prohibited— while the impossibility of rendering sepulchral honors to the dead increases the horror of their dying moments.[14]

The bishop opened women's monasteries so that the nuns could join their families and help serve the sick and dying. By the first of September over 1,200 orphaned infants were being cared for by nurses appointed to the task. They were fed goat's milk and soup, but still died at the rate of 30 to 40 per day. Once all of the corpse-bearers and gravediggers had died the government pressed into service convicts who normally rowed in the coast-guarding galleys. These rough and sometimes ruthless characters enjoyed the fresh air and exercise, but died in great numbers. Eventually, of 696 who served the city's needs 486 succumbed. The convicts found that the designated burial areas were too far from the port area to be useful, and that corpses tossed out to sea soon floated back in. So they began storing the plague dead in the huge, drum-like towers that served the city's defense.

Since no physicians were allowed to serve on the health board, the College of Physicians provided the board with a copy of *Ranchin's Treatise on the Plague*, which, Bertrand claimed, "contains all the regulations of **Governmental Action** police power proper to be observed in a time of contagion." The civic government expelled vagabonds and beggars, prohibited the trade or even unauthorized moving of victims' clothing, and placed a security guard at city hall. Meanwhile, the provincial government improved the cordon around the city and an increasingly large region. Piedmont, Spain, and Switzerland also closed their borders as tightly as they could. The food supply dwindled and, despite a fine harvest mere miles away, rationing was imposed on the poor. Three food markets were eventually established at a modest distance from the city itself, and buyers and sellers made their exchanges very carefully. The city paid for officers to oversee the process and to ensure that any contact was kept to a strict minimum. Still, "the city soon suffered almost as much from scarcity as from the contagion itself," Bertrand reported. By September 9, all of the city's bakers had fled marseille and all the meat cutters died of the disease, as had all but three of the slaughterhouse workers. Oddly, Bertrand reported that butchers were "immune."[15]

The French royal and provincial governments were terrified that the plague would infiltrate the cordon sanitaire that it had established and ravage the entire country. To treat the victims, the French government sent in physicians and surgeons, who were paid handsomely. Unlike local physicians, these men ministered to the sick free of charge. The local doctors resented these interlopers and actually rioted in Aix. Over the course of the epidemic 17 physicians arrived in Marseille and 3 eventually died, while nearly a third of the 97 surgeons who were sent died, presumably of plague. Across the rest of the plague-struck province 18 physicians and 45 surgeons carried out their mission, with only 6 deaths among them. Six of the 12 local physicians in Marseille died, as did 32 of 35 surgeons. The central government also supplied meat and grain, pharmaceutical supplies (and four apothecaries), fumigants like sulfur and perfumes, quicklime for cleaner burials, and waxed cloth for the coats of physicians and corpse-carriers. When the plague ended, it also provided grants and loans to the needful organizations and a tax remission of 4,500,000 *livres* over a 15-year period.

Lourmarin and England In the end, the city of 90,000 had lost about half of its population, as did cities like Aix, Toulon, and Arles. All told, perhaps a fifth of the population of Provence died.

The village of Lourmarin went unscathed, however, and historians credit a vigorous civic government. They heard of the plague in Marseille on August 12 and immediately formed the Bureau of Health that met every Tuesday, Thursday, and Saturday at noon for 18 months. The body had extensive powers and authority and wielded these to good effect. In January 1721 they had 1,000 bills of health printed in Avignon. These read: "NAME thanks to God has no suspicion of the plague nor any other contagious disease."[16] Traveling without one meant 40 days in prison and a fine of 25 *livres.* They repaired their gates and sealed up any spaces through which an outsider might enter the city. Each night the gates were locked from 5:00 P.M. to 6:00 A.M. and were at all times closely guarded. Members of the village militia visited every family every day to see if all were well. The sick were left in their home and provided with firewood, oil, wheat, and wine; and then the house had all windows and doors plastered over to seal them inside. Anyone who broke in paid a hundred-*livre* fine and spent 40 days in prison. Newcomers to town were quarantined in special quarters for 40 days, and that included the mayor's daughter and her five children.

In England, the royal government sprang into action at the first whispers about the French plague. All ships from the Mediterranean, the Bay of Biscay, or Bordeaux were to be quarantined, and other rules last applied during the Baltic plague of 1711–1712 were reinstated and updated in new laws passed in February 1721. Quarantine stations appeared in the Thames estuary, and all cloth and hair products, feathers, and raw wool were quarantined for 40 days. Unlike the French, the English valued the advice of their physicians, and in the fall of 1721 a group of London's finest advised the Privy Council on better ways to prepare for the plague and to deal with it if it should occur in London. They examined the steps that had been taken in 1625 and 1665 during the last great English outbreaks and wrote new treatises that sound very much like those that came before.[17]

Some were quite positive, but others, especially clerics who retained their moralistic outlook on the plague, were less than sanguine. For example, William Hendley wrote in his *Loimologia sacra* (1721):

We may keep our shipping to strict quarantine, we may form lines [cordons], and cut off all communication with the infected, we may barricade up our cities and our towns, and shut ourselves up in our houses, [but] Death will come into our windows, and enter into our palaces, and cut off our children from without, and young men from the streets.[18]

Of course, prayer and repentance were the only security. It was also in the early days of this outbreak that Daniel Defoe penned his famed *Journal of the Plague Year*, in which he paints one graphic scene after another from the Great Plague of 1665. Though he was only a child in that dreadful year, he later researched the writings of eyewitnesses of all kinds. The result was a powerful and eloquent warning against sloth and half-measures regarding national security, as well as a plea against certain policies such as shutting the sick in. Though sometimes treated as history, it is in fact one of the first great novels in the English language.

RUSSIA'S LAST GREAT PLAGUE: MOSCOW, 1770–1772

The vast expanses of Ukraine and Russia, and their relatively underdeveloped infrastructure of roads, ports, and large cities, did not preserve Europe's eastern edge from regular visitations of the plague. Though the cities of Pskov and Novgorod were the last places in Europe to experience the pestilence during the first outbreak, the Russian chronicles again and again record the horrors of a pestilential season. In the eighteenth century

Ukraine suffered 13 episodes of plague, spaced between 8 and 15 years apart. Soviet researchers claim that in each case the disease was imported from Turkish areas to the west and southwest, and the recorded pattern of dissemination seems to support this conclusion. Historian John Alexander notes that Russian expansion in the eighteenth century brought pioneers into previously undisturbed areas near the Black Sea where colonies of rodents maintained the plague in an enzootic state. Whichever the case, the imperial government established the first medical quarantine station at Vasilkov (Vasylkiv) near Kiev in 1740, and a quarantine service to coordinate efforts to control the movement of suspect people and goods. "Patients with fevers and spots or buboes, or carbuncles . . . shall be immediately brought to the preliminary prepared yards [at Vasilkov] where they shall be nursed by the physician's pupils, treated and fed," read the regulations. Native Russian and Ukrainian physicians, virtually all trained in western or central Europe, understood the pestilence to be a matter of both miasma and contagion.[19]

The great Russian plague of 1770–1772 began in Turkish-controlled Moldavia-Wallachia. Russia had been at war with the Ottoman Empire and its Polish allies since 1768, and armies of both sides marched and countermarched along this frontier area, probably carrying the disease with them. To the west, 18 Transylvanian villages reported 1,624 cases with 1,204 deaths, and many more were reported in southern Poland to the northeast. Kiev was the first imperial city to report plague deaths, beginning in early September 1770. The region's governor reacted by shutting victims up in their houses and burning their goods. Close friends and family members of victims were housed in facilities on Trukhanov Island in the Dnieper River. Rural districts in which plague was found were isolated from all contacts with "clean" areas. Eventually the monastery at Kirillovskii was transformed into a pest house. By year's end a total of 4,000 had died.

Yet even with this outbreak the press and officials in Moscow, a city with perhaps 100,000 souls, refused to acknowledge an epidemic of plague inside Russian territory. After all, Moscow had not suffered a pestilential epidemic in three decades. Denial of plague meant a continuation of business as usual with European merchants and governments, and imperial bureaucrats were loathe to upset this. When the disease reached Moscow the official denials continued, and even foreigners living there were duped. The British ambassador to Russia, Lord Cathcart, wrote his friend Lord Suffolk on August 26:

As to the plague at Moscow your lordship may depend upon it, it has never existed: tho' many principal inhabitants have deserted the town and the government have from complicated reasons of policy, established a quarantine.[20]

In fact the Russians had established a loose cordon between Kiev and Moscow, and one around Moscow itself, but kept the public uniformed. Official deception to the contrary, the English press understood the situation as early as November of the previous year, when the first rumored cases of plague appeared on the Volga. A writer at *London Magazine* took the opportunity to sound the tocsin:

The very stench of it will send thousands to their graves, change mansion-houses into pest houses, and gather congregations in churchyards instead of churches. Every disease turns into the plague; the very breath infects. . . . Art and medicine are entirely useless . . . the people died not only with but without the infection, by fear and surprise.

The author concludes in a familiar vein: "Let repentance and amendment of life, o ye people, be your charms to avert the poisoned arrows of death."[21]

The elite of Moscow, including many government officials, fled the city beginning early in the spring of 1771, often leaving house serfs behind to guard the property. Bodies began to accumulate, filling graveyards. Soon hundreds were dying each day. People who lived in "infected" houses surreptitiously moved their goods to others' homes to avoid their being incinerated by the authorities. Family members of plague victims buried them secretly or tossed their bodies into the street to throw suspicion off their houses. Rumors spread that even the sick were being buried alive by the fearful. Others boldly plundered the homes of those prostrate with the disease, a means by which it may have been spread further. Supervised by the police, condemned convicts dressed all in black with cloth hoods slit at the mouth and eyes carried the sick to quarantines and the dead to mass graves. Food supplies dwindled and prices for what was available skyrocketed. Markets and bathhouses were closed. With the wealthy gone the poor had few to supply them with alms. Moscow was dying.

By late August 1771 the frustration and fear of Moscow's lower classes had reached a flash point. High prices, government closings of needed facilities, a lack of what people conceived of as proper quarantine facilities, a perceived lack of medical care[22]—or medical care by foreigners—and an overwhelming sense of helplessness simmered the people into a mob mentality. On August 29 rumors that physicians were killing patients and healthy hospital staff with arsenic at Lefortovo Settlement raced around the city. A crowd gathered outside the hospital and blocked the doctors from entering while demanding an explanation. The unrest continued on September 1 as another crowd drove away "with blows" soldiers who had been sent to burn victims' belongings. Two weeks later the tinder was rekindled as another rumor spread: the icon of the Virgin Mary of Bogoliubskaia at the Varvarskie Gate could heal those with the disease! Two men began collecting money to fit a silver covering *(oklad)* over the therapeutic image, but the archbishop's police seized them and the cash they had accumulated. On September 15, to prevent the plague-conducive throngs that had begun to gather, the patriarch (archbishop) of Moscow decided to move the icon. The rumors had it that the cleric was going to destroy the icon, and when the men arrived to remove it the crowd beat them back. The official report blamed the "schismatics, factory workers, clerks, merchants, and household serfs,"[23] who then proceeded to pillage and vandalize the patriarch's residence at the Kremlin and the Chudov monastery. Archbishop Amvrosii was beaten senseless, and the prison-like quarantine quarters were broken into and the inmates released.

The following day, when the now-drunken mob returned, the cavalry waded in, sabers slashing. As the terrified mass surged away it was torn into by musket fire and cannon's grapeshot. More wanton destruction followed, but the majority had been cowed or killed. Seventy-eight died and 279 were arrested. Leaders who were not killed were, however, able to voice the people's demands, to some of which the government responded. The demands included burial in churchyards, destruction of the dreaded quarantine facilities, an opening of the public bath houses and markets, and pardons for all arrested rioters. What Moscow received was a Commission for the Prevention and Treatment of the Pestilential Infectious Distemper made up of medical practitioners, administrators, merchants, and clergymen. This body decided to provide better quarantine facilities, to stop the practice of incinerating victims' belongings, and to open bath houses. They also agreed to destroy 3,000 dilapidated residences and to disinfect 6,000 houses.

Official statistics claim that Moscow lost 56,672 to the plague, though the actual figure is probably higher. Across the whole district perhaps 200,000 died. This would make the 1770–1772 plague deadlier than that in London of a century before. Several reasons present themselves: Moscow had a very low percentage of upper-class citizens who could escape the district and a very high percentage—perhaps half of the population—of servants who had no refuge. The government's refusal to admit to the plague's presence probably left many to participate in risky behaviors and omit certain precautions that may have aided their survival. The severity of government policies led many to hide plague victims and otherwise ignore those that were put into place.

EPILOGUE

The West learned a great deal about the Moscow plague through the *Traité de la peste* of Charles de Mertens, a French physician who served in Moscow during the epidemic. His account was originally published in 1778 in Latin as part of a text on plague fever, but appeared separately in Paris in 1784, four years before his death. Fifteen years later Richard Pierson translated the work into English and published it in London. When in 1804 yellow fever appeared in Philadelphia, Anne Plumtre translated and published for her non-French-reading friends the memoir of Jean Baptiste Bertrand, chronicler of the Marseille plague. Ms. Plumtre believed "it may prove essentially useful to them."[24] In 1720 Daniel Defoe scoured what sources he could to reconstruct the sights and sounds of the Great Plague in London 55 years before.

To quote Boccaccio's opening to his *Decameron*, "It is a human thing" to reflect on past disasters as we contemplate our unstable present and uncertain future. Perhaps it is no coincidence that Renaissance humanism and its high standards for recording and reflecting on human history appeared directly in the shadow of the Black Death. As the relentless scythe of pestilence mowed down people by the scores of thousands, by the millions, Europe entered its modern period. Its people proved resilient before the threat of plague and stoical in its presence. They abandoned neither religion nor a hoary medical science that remained powerless before the increasingly visible bacteria. They did, however, change their daily lives, create new institutions, formulate new policies, and implement new practices that directly challenged the pestilential regime. Perhaps at some point someone will be able to say without fear of contradiction that some, or even one, of these measures eliminated the plague as a threat to the Western world.

In the meantime biologists continue to unravel the secrets of the disease and investigate alternatives to the current paradigm of bubonic plague. Historians regularly uncover new sources in archives and libraries that shed light on the epidemics' courses and effects on human communities, and reflect on the longer-term implications for the continent's history. Archaeologists seek new information and insights in grave pits and buildings from the period. And writers digest and share these findings with a world that is increasingly fascinated yet again with the plagues of the past, for they may prove a template for the future.

More than ever in the past 90 years policymakers and average people in the Western world are concerned with the natural and man-made threats posed by viruses and bacteria. This is reflected in the supply and demand for new studies of the Black Death. A quick review of appropriate books with titles (*Black Death, plague*) listed on Amazon.com shows that more books in English that deal substantially with the plague were published or reissued in the first half of the 2000s (83) than over the prior 30 years (67); and most of the latter (37) were written in the 1990s. Some of this interest may be with the gruesome aspects of plague time, many of which were examined in this book, but there is also a sense that a new plague time may appear very soon. If history teaches people anything, it is that humanity has always prevailed over tremendous threats from nature and from its own dark impulses. De Mertens and Bertrand recorded their own observations to decry the errors that people in power made, but also with the assurance that most people survived. Humanity prevailed. And they wrote in profound hope for the future, which is why Pierson and Plumtre translated and disseminated their works. Like

Defoe, these people, too, looked hopefully toward the future, though not without some sense of dread. In the end, it was a dread very much like that we sense today, a dread tempered by hope founded in history and science, and trumped by the conviction that humanity will prevail.

NOTES

1. Excepting Sicily.

2. Susan Scott and Christopher Duncan, *Biology of Plagues: Evidence from Historical Populations* (New York: Cambridge University Press, 2001), p. 245, though they dismiss this factor; also their *The Return of the Black Death: The World's Greatest Serial Killer* (New York: Halsted Press, 2004), p. 246; Stephen Porter, *The Great Plague* (Stroud, Gloucs.: Sutton, 1999), p. 172; Ann Carmichael, "Bubonic Plague: The Black Death," in *Plague, Pox, and Pestilence: Disease in History*, ed. Kenneth Kiple et al. (New York: Marboro Books, 1997), p. 63; Leslie Bradley, "Some Medical Aspects of Plague," in *Plague Reconsidered: A New Look at Its Origins and Effects in Sixteenth and Seventeenth Century England* (Matlock, Derbs., England: Local Population Studies, 1977), pp. 11–23.

3. Hans Zinsser, *Rats, Lice and History* (original 1934; reprint New York: Black Dog and Leventhal, 1996), p. 69; Andrew Appleby, "Famine, Mortality and Epidemic Disease: A Comment," *Economic Historical Review* 2nd ser. 30 (1977), p. 510; also his "The Disappearance of the Plague: A Continuing Puzzle," *Economic History Review* 33 (1980), pp. 165, 170, 171; Stephen R. Ell, "Immunity as a Factor in the Epidemiology of Medieval Plague," *Review of Infectious Diseases* 6 (1984), pp. 869, 876; Bradley, "Medical Aspects," p. 20; Paul Slack, "The Disappearance of Plague: An Alternative View," *Economic History Review* 2nd ser. 34 (1981), pp. 469–76; Michael W. Flinn, "Plague in Europe and the Mediterranean Countries," *Journal of European Economic History* 8 (1979), p. 20; Carmichael, "Bubonic," p. 63; J. H. Bayliss, "The Extinction of Bubonic Plague in Britain," *Endeavour* 4 (1980), pp. 58–66; Porter, *Great Plague*, p. 172; V. N. Fyodorov, "The Question of the Existence of Natural Foci of Plague in Europe in the Past," *Journal of Hygiene, Epidemiology, Microbiology and Immunology* (Prague) 4 (1960), pp. 139–40.

4. Bayliss, "Extinction," p. 64; Slack, "Disappearance," p. 471; Ell, "Immunity," p. 869; Porter, *Great Plague*, p. 173.

5. Bayliss, "Extinction," p. 64; Scott and Duncan, *Return*, pp. 247–48; Bradley, "Medical Aspects," p. 20; see also Jean-Noël Biraben, *Les hommes et la peste en France et dans les pays européens et méditeranéens*, Vol. 2 (Paris: Mouton, 1976).

6. Scott and Duncan, *Return*, pp. 247–48; J. F. Shrewsbury, *History of Bubonic Plague in the British Isles* (New York: Cambridge University Press, 1970), p. 35; Flinn, "Plague," p. 139; Appleby, "Famine," pp. 166, 167; Henri Mollaret, "Introduzione," in *Venezia e la peste, 1348/1797. Comune di Venezia, Assessorato alla Culturale Belle Arti* (Venice: Marsilio Editori, 1979), p. 14; Bradley, "Medical Aspects," p. 21; Bayliss, "Extinction," pp. 59–60.

7. Kari Konkola, "More Than a Coincidence? The Arrival of Arsenic and the Disappearance of Plague in Early Modern Europe," *History of Medicine* 47 (1992), pp. 186–209; Carmichael, "Bubonic Plague," p. 63.

8. James C. Riley, *The Eighteenth-century Campaign to Avoid Disease* (London: Palgrave Macmillan, 1987), p. 135.

9. Flinn, "Plague," pp. 60–61; Gunther Rothenberg, "The Austrian Sanitary Cordon and the Control of Bubonic Plague: 1710–1871," *Journal of the History of Medicine and Allied Sciences* 28 (1973), pp. 15–23; Boris and Helga Velimirovic, "Plague in Vienna," *Review of Infectious Diseases* 2 (1989), pp. 822–23; Edward Eckert, "The Retreat of Plague from Central Europe, 1640–1720: A Geomedical Approach," *Bulletin of the History of Medicine* 74 (2000), pp. 1–28; Carmichael, "Bubonic Plague," p. 630.

10. On the plague in southern France in 1720–1722 see Jean Baptiste Bertrand, *A Historical Relation of the Plague at Marseille in the Year 1720*, trans. Anne Plumtre (New York: McGraw-Hill, 1973); Jean-Noël Biraben, "Certain Demographic Characteristics of the Plague Epidemic in France, 1720–22," *Daedalus* 97 (1968), pp. 536–45; Daniel Gordon, "Confrontations with Plague in Eighteenth-Century France," in *Dreadful Visitations*, ed. Alessa Johns (New York: Routledge, 1999), pp. 3–29; Shelby T. McCloy, *Government Assistance in Eighteenth-Century France* (Durham, NC: Duke University Press, 1946); T. F. Sheppard, *Lourmarin in the Eighteenth Century: A Study of a French Village* (Baltimore: Johns Hopkins University Press, 1971), pp. 117–120.

11. Bertrand, *Historical Relation*, pp. 49, 51, 55.

12. Ibid., p. 54.

13. Ibid., p. 85.

14. Ibid., p. 3.

15. Ibid., pp. 79, 65.

16. Sheppard, *Lourmarin*, p. 118.

17. On the English reaction to the Marseille plague see Porter, *Great Plague*, pp. 159–61; A. Zuckerman, "Plague and Contagionism in Eighteenth-century England: The Role of Richard Mead," *Bulletin of the History of Medicine* 78 (2004), pp. 273–308.

18. Paul Slack, "Responses to Plague in Early Modern England: Public Policies and Their Consequences" in *Famine, Disease and the Social Order in Early Modern Society*, ed. Walter R. Schofield (New York: Cambridge University Press, 1989), p. 167.

19. On the Russian plague of 1770–1772 see Charles De Mertens, *Account of the Plague Which Raged at Moscow, 1771* (Newtonville, MA: Oriental Research Partners, 1977); John T. Alexander, *Bubonic Plague in Early Modern Russia: Public Health and Urban Disaster* (Baltimore: Johns Hopkins University Press, 1980); N. K. Borodi, "The Activity of D. S. Samoilovich in the Ukraine," *Soviet Studies in History* 25 (1987), pp. 16–23; N. K. Borodi, "I. A. Poletika—an Outstanding Ukrainian Physician and Scholar of the Eighteenth Century," *Soviet Studies in History* 25 (1987), pp. 8–15; M. F. Prokhorov, "The Moscow Uprising of September 1771," *Soviet Studies in History* 25 (1987), pp. 44–78; S. R. Dolgova, "Notes of an Eyewitness of the Plague Riot in Moscow in 1771," *Soviet Studies in History* 25 (1987), pp. 79–90; N. K. Borodi "The History of the Plague Epidemic in the Ukraine in 1770–74," *Soviet Studies in History* 25 (1987), pp. 33–43.

20. De Mertens, *Account*, p. 23.

21. Ibid., p. 18.

22. Moscow had more doctors per capita than London in 1665.

23. Dolgova, "Notes," p. 81.

24. Bertrand, *Historical Relation*, p. xiv.

SELECTED READINGS

GENERAL WORKS ON THE PLAGUE

Aberth, John. *From the Brink of the Apocalypse: Crisis and Recovery in Late Medieval England*. New York: Routledge, 2000.

Alexander, John T. *Bubonic Plague in Early Modern Russia: Public Health and Urban Disaster*. Baltimore: Johns Hopkins University Press, 1980.

Bell, Walter George. *The Great Plague in London in 1665*. New York: AMS Press, 1976.

Benedictow, Ole. *The Black Death 1346–1353: The Complete History*. Boydell & Brewer, 2004.

———. *Plague in the Late Medieval Nordic Countries: Epidemiological Studies*. Oslo: Middelalderforlaget, 1992.

Borsch, Stuart. *The Black Death in Egypt and England*. Austin: University of Texas Press, 2005.

Bray, R. S. *Armies of Pestilence: The Effects of Pandemics on History*. Cambridge, UK: Lutterworth Press, 1998.

Byrne, Joseph P. *The Black Death*. Westport, CT: Greenwood Press, 2004.

Cantor, Norman. *In the Wake of the Plague: The Black Death and the World It Made*. New York: Harper, 2000.

Champion, Justin A. I., ed. *Epidemic Disease in London*. London: Centre for Metropolitan History Working Papers Series 1, 1993.

———. *London's Dreaded Visitation: The Social Geography of the Great Plague in 1665*. London: Historical Geography Research Paper Series 31, 1995.

Christakos, George, et al. *Interdisciplinary Public Health Reasoning and Epistemic Modeling: The Case of the Black Death*. New York: Springer, 2005.

Cohn, Samuel K., Jr. *The Black Death Transformed: Disease and Culture in Early Renaissance Europe*. New York: Oxford University Press, 2002.

Cunningham, Andrew, and Ole Peter Grell. *The Four Horsemen of the Apocalypse: Religion, War, Famine and Death in Reformation Europe.* New York: Cambridge University Press, 2000.

Dols, Michael W. *The Black Death in the Middle East.* Princeton: Princeton University Press, 1977.

Eckert, Edward A. *The Structure of Plagues and Pestilences in Early Modern Europe: Central Europe, 1560–1640.* New York: S. Karger Publishing, 1996.

Gottfried, Robert S. *The Black Death: Natural and Human Disaster in Medieval Europe.* New York: The Free Press, 1983.

Herlihy, David. *The Black Death and the Transformation of the West.* Cambridge, MA: Harvard University Press, 1997.

James, Tom Beaumont. *The Black Death in Hampshire.* Winchester: Hampshire County Council, 1999.

Jillings, Karen. *Scotland's Black Death: The Foul Death of the English.* stroud, Gloucs.: Tempus Publishing, 2003.

Karlen, Arno. *Man and Microbes: Disease and Plagues in History and Modern Times.* New York: Simon and Schuster, 1995.

Kelly, John. *The Great Mortality: An Intimate History of the Black Death.* New York: HarperCollins, 2005.

Kelly, Maria. *The Great Dying: The Black Death in Dublin.* Stroud, Gloucs.: Tempus, 2003.

———. *A History of the Black Death in Ireland.* Stroud, Gloucs.: Tempus, 2001.

Keys, David. *Catastrophe: An Investigation into the Origins of the Modern World.* New York: Ballantine Press, 2000.

Kiple, Kenneth, ed. *The Cambridge World History of Human Disease.* New York: Cambridge University Press, 1993.

Lee, Christopher. *1603: The Death of Queen Elizabeth I, the Return of the Black Plague, the Rise of Shakespeare, Piracy, Witchcraft, and the Birth of the Stuart Era.* New York: St. Martin's Press, 2004.

Lehfeldt, Elizabeth A. *The Black Death.* Boston: Houghton Mifflin, 2005.

Marriott, Edward. *Plague: A Story of Science, Rivalry, Scientific Breakthrough and the Scourge that Won't Go away.* New York: Holt, 2002.

McNeill, William. *Plagues and Peoples.* Garden City: Anchor Press, 1975.

Moote, A. Lloyd, and Dorothy C. Moote. *The Great Plague: The Story of London's Most Deadly Year.* Baltimore: Johns Hopkins University Press, 2004.

Mullett, Charles F. *The Bubonic Plague and England: An Essay in the History of Preventive Medicine.* Lexington: University of Kentucky Press, 1956.

Naphy, William G. *Plagues, Poisons and Potions: Plague Spreading Conspiracies in the Western Alps c. 1530–1640.* New York: Manchester University Press, 2002.

Naphy, William G. and Andrew Spicer. *The Black Death and the History of Plagues, 1345–1730.* Stroud, Gloucs.: Tempus, 2001.

Nohl, Johannes. *The Black Death.* Yardley, PA: Westholme Publishing, 2006.

Platt, Colin. *King Death: The Black Death and Its Aftermath in Late-medieval England.* Toronto: University of Toronto Press, 1996.

Porter, Stephen. *The Great Plague.* Stroud, Gloucs.: Sutton, 1999.

Rothenberg, Gunther. "The Austrian Sanitary Cordon and the Control of Bubonic Plague: 1710–1871." *Journal of the History of Medicine and Allied Sciences* 28 (1973): 15–23.

Slack, Paul. *The Impact of Plague in Tudor and Stuart England.* New York: Oxford University Press, 1990.

Van Andel, M. A. "Plague Regulations in the Netherlands." *Janus* 21 (1916): 410–44.

Walter, J. *Famine, Disease and Social Order in Early Modern Society.* New York: Cambridge University Press, 1989.

Wilson, F. P. *Plague in Shakespeare's London.* New York: Oxford University Press, 1999.

Ziegler, Philip. *The Black Death.* New York: Harper and Row, 1969.

SELECTED PRIMARY SOURCES

Ansari, B. M. "An Account of Bubonic Plague in Seventeenth Century India in an Autobiography of a Mughal Emperor." *Journal of Infection* 29 (1994): 351–52.

Backscheider, Paula R., ed. *A Journal of the Plague Year, Daniel Defoe* (Norton Critical Anthology). New York: Norton, 1992.

Barrett, W. P. *Present Remedies against the Plague.* London: Shakespeare Association, 1933.

Bartsocas, Christos. "Two Fourteenth Century Greek Descriptions of the 'Black Death.'" *Journal of the History of Medicine* 21 (1966): 394–400.

Bertrand, Jean Baptiste. *A Historical Relation of the Plague at Marseilles in the Year 1720.* New York: McGraw-Hill, 1973.

Boghurst, William. *Loimographia: An Account of the Great Plague of London in the Year 1665.* New York: AMS Press, 1976.

Brucker, Gene, ed. *Two Memoirs of Renaissance Florence: The Diaries of Buonaccorso Pitti and Gregorio Dati.* Prospect Heights, IL: Waveland Press, 1991.

Brunner, Karl. "Disputacioun Betwyx the Body and Worms," *Archiv für deutsche Studien der neueren Sprachen* 167 (1935): 30–35.

Bullein, William. *A dialogue against the fever pestilence.* London: Published for the Early English Text Society by H. Milford, Oxford University Press, 1888; Millwood, NY: Kraus Reprint, 1987.

Caraman, R. P. *Henry Morse: Priest of the Plague.* London: Longmans, Green and Co., 1957.

Dekker, Thomas. *The Plague Pamphlets of Thomas Dekker.* Washington, D.C.: Scholarly Press, 1994.

De Mertens, Charles. *Account of the Plague Which Raged at Moscow, 1771.* Newtonville, MA: Oriental Research Partners, 1977.

Dols, Michael W. "Ibn al-Wardī's 'Risālah al-naba' 'an al-waba,' A Translation of a Major Source for the History for the Black Death in the Middle East." In *Near Eastern Numismatics, Iconography, Epigraphy and History: Studies in Honor of George C. Miles,* edited by Dickran Kouymjian, 443–55. Beirut: American University of Beirut Press, 1974.

Duran-Reynals, M. L. and C.-E.A.Winslow "Jacme d'Agramont: *Regiment de preservacio a epidemia o pestilencia e mortaldats.*" *Bulletin of the History of Medicine* 23 (1949): 57–89.

Fealty, John, and Scott Rutherford. *Tears Against the Plague: A Seventeenth-century Woman's Devotional.* Cambridge, MA: Rhwymbooks, 2000.

Gyug, Richard F. *The Diocese of Barcelona during the Black Death: The Register Notule communium 15 (1348–1349).* Toronto: Pontifical Institute of Medieval Studies, 1994.

Hodges, Nathaniel. *Loimologia: Or, an Historical Account of the Plague in London in 1665.* New York: AMS Press, 1994.

Horrox, Rosemary, ed. *The Black Death.* New York: Manchester University Press, 1994.

Ibn Sasra. *A Chronicle of Damascus, 1389–1397.* 2 vols. Trans. William M. Brinner. Berkeley: University of California Press, 1963.

Ibn Taghri Birdi, Abu l-Ma·hasin. *An-Nujum az-Zahirah fi muluk Misr wal-Qahirah, History of Egypt 1382–1469 A.D..* Edited and trans. by William Popper. Berkeley: University of California Press, 1915–1964.

Landucci, Luca. *A Florentine Diary from 1450 to 1516.* Trans. Alice D. Jervis. London: J. M. Dent and Sons, 1927.

Latham, Robert, and William Matthews, eds. *The Diary of Samuel Pepys.* 11 vols. Berkeley: University of California Press, 2000.

Lydgate, John. "A diet and doctrine for pestilence." In *The Minor Poems of John Lydgate,* II, edited by Henry Noble McCracken, 702–707. London: Early English Text Society, 1934.

Manzoni, Alessandro. *The Column of Infamy.* Trans. Kenelm Foster and Jane Grigson. London: Oxford University Press, 1964.

Marcus, Jacob R. *The Jew in the Medieval World: A Source Book: 315–1791.* New York: Atheneum, 1979.

Martin, A. Lynn. *Plague?: Jesuit Accounts of Epidemic Disease in the Sixteenth Century* (Sixteenth Century Studies, Vol. 28). Kirksville, MO: Truman State University Press, 1996.

O'Hara-May, Jane. *Elizabethan Dyetary of Health.* Lawrence, KS: Coronado Press, 1977.

Parets, Miquel. *A Journal of the Plague Year: The Diary of the Barcelona Tanner Miquel Parets, 1651.* Trans. by James S. Amelang. New York: Oxford University Press, 1995.

Pickett, Joseph P. "A Translation of the *Canutus* Plague Treatise." In *Popular and Practical Science of Medieval England,* edited by Lister M. Matheson (Medieval Texts and Studies, 11), 263–282. East Lansing: Colleagues Press, 1994.

Sudhoff, Karl, ed. *The Fasciculus Medicinae of Johannes de Ketham.* Trans. by Charles Singer. Milan: 1924; reprinted Birmingham: Classics of Medical History, 1988.

Wither, George. *The History of the Pestilence (1625).* Edited by George Wither. Cambridge, MA: Harvard University Press, 1932.

MEDICAL AND EPIDEMIOLOGICAL MATTERS

Albury, W. R., and G. M. Weisz. "Erasmus of Rotterdam (1466–1536): Renaissance Advocate of the Public Role of Medicine." *Journal of Medical Biography* 11 (2003): 128–34.

Brockliss, Laurence and Colin Jones. *The Medical World of Early Modern France.* New York: Oxford University Press, 1997.

Bullough, Vern L. *Universities, Medicine, and Science in the Medieval West.* Burlington, VT.: Ashgate, 2004.

Cipolla, Carlo. *Cristofano and the Plague: A Study in the History of Public Health in the Age of Galileo.* Toronto: Collins, 1973.

————. *Faith, Reason, and the Plague in Seventeenth-Century Tuscany.* New York: W. W. Norton & Company, 1981.

————. *Fighting the Plague in Seventeenth-Century Italy.* Madison: University of Wisconsin Press, 1981.

————. *Miasmas and Disease: Public Health and the Environment in the Pre-industrial Age.* Translated by Elizabeth Potter. New Haven: Yale University Press, 1992.

————. *Public Health and the Medical Profession in Renaissance Florence.* New York: Cambridge University Press, 1976.

Drancourt M, Raoult D. "Molecular Detection of *Yersinia pestis* in Dental Pulp." *Microbiology* 150 (February 2004): 63–265.

Elmer, Peter, and Ole Peter Grell, eds. *Health, Disease, and Society in Europe, 1500–1800.* New York: Manchester University Press, 2004.

French, Roger K. *Medicine Before Science: The Business of Medicine from the Middle Ages to the Enlightenment.* New York: Cambridge University Press, 2003.

French, Roger K., and Andrew Wear, eds. *The Medical Revolution of the Seventeenth Century.* New York: Cambridge University Press, 1989.

Gambaccini, Piero. *Mountebanks and Medicasters: A History of Charlatans from the Middle Ages to the Present.* Jefferson, NC: McFarland and Co., 2004.

Goldrick, B. A. "Bubonic plague and HIV. The delta 32 connection." *American Journal of Nursing* 103 (2003): 26–27.

Granshaw, L. and Roy Porter, eds. *The Hospital in History.* London: Routledge, 1989.

Hendrickson, Robert. *More Cunning than Man: A Complete History of the Rat and Its Role in Human Civilization.* New York: Kensington Books, 1983.

Lindemann, Mary. *Medicine and Society in Early Modern Europe.* New York: Cambridge University Press, 1999.

Morgenstern, S. "Collection of Treatises on Plague Regimen and Remedies Published in the German Duchy of Swabia in the XVIIth Century." *Academy Bookman* 26 (1973): 3–20.

O'Boyle, Cornelius. *The Art of Medicine: Medical Teaching at the University of Paris, 1250–1400.* Boston: Brill, 1998.

Park, Katherine. *Doctors and Medicine in Early Renaissance Florence.* Princeton: Princeton University Press, 1985.

Pomata, Gianna. *Contracting a Cure: Patients, Healers, and the Law in Early Modern Bologna.* Baltimore: Johns Hopkins University Press, 1998.

Scott, Susan, and Christopher Duncan. *Biology of Plagues: Evidence from Historical Populations.* New York: Cambridge University Press, 2001.

————. *The Return of the Black Death: The World's Greatest Serial Killer.* Hoboken: Wiley, 2004.

Shrewsbury, J. F. *History of Bubonic Plague in the British Isles.* New York: Cambridge University Press, 1970.

Sotres, Pedro Gil. "The Regimens of Health." In *Western Medical Thought from Antiquity to the Middle Ages,* edited by Mirko Grmek, pp. 291–318. Cambridge, MA: Harvard University Press, 1998.

Twigg, Graham. *The Black Death: A Biological Reappraisal.* New York: Schocken Books, 1985.

Wear, Andrew. "Medicine in Early Modern Europe, 1500–1700." In *The Western Medical Tradition, 800 B.C. to A.D. 1800,* edited by Lawrence I. Conrad, pp. 215–361. New York: Cambridge University Press, 1995.

SOCIETY AND THE DISEASE

Calvi, Giulia. *Histories of a Plague Year: The Social and the Imaginary in Baroque Florence.* Berkeley: University of California Press, 1989.

Carmichael, Ann G. *Plague and the Poor in Renaissance Florence.* New York: Cambridge University Press, 1986.

Dohar, William J. *The Black Death and Pastoral Leadership: The Diocese of Hereford in the Fourteenth Century.* Philadelphia: University of Pennsylvania Press, 1995.

Dyer, Christopher. *Making a Living in the Middle Ages: The People of Britain 850–1520.* New Haven: Yale University Press, 2002.

Gottfried, Robert S. *Epidemic Disease in Fifteenth-Century England: The Medical Response and the Demographic Consequences.* New Brunswick, NJ: Rutgers University Press, 1978.

Harvey, Barbara. *Living and Dying in England, 1100–1540.* New York: Oxford University Press, 1993.

Hatcher, John. *Plague, Population, and the English Economy, 1348–1530.* London: Macmillan, 1977.

Palmer, R. C. *English Law in the Age of the Black Death, 1348–1381: A Transformation of Governance and Law.* Chapel Hill: University of North Carolina Press, 1993.

Poos, Larry. *A Rural Society after the Black Death: Essex, 1350–1525.* New York: Cambridge University Press, 1991.

CULTURAL STUDIES

Barroll, John Leeds. *Politics, Plague, and Shakespeare's Theater: The Stuart Years.* Ithaca: Cornell University Press, 1991.

Beaty, Nancy Lee. *The Craft of Dying: A Study in the Literary Tradition of the 'Ars Moriendi' in England.* New Haven: Yale University Press, 1970.

Boeckl, Christine. *Images of Plague and Pestilence: Iconography and Iconology.* Kirksville, MO: Truman State University Press, 2000.

Campbell, Anna Montgomery. *The Black Death and Men of Learning.* New York: Columbia University Press, 1931.

Cohen, Kathleen. *Metamorphosis of a Death Symbol: The Transi Tomb in the Late Middle Ages and the Renaissance.* Berkeley: University of California Press, 1973.

Cohen, Samuel K. *The Cult of Remembrance and the Black Death.* Baltimore: The Johns Hopkins University Press, 1992.

Crawfurd, Raymond. *The Plague and Pestilence in Literature and Art.* Oxford: Clarendon Press, 1914.

Eichenberg, Fritz. *The Dance of Death: A Graphic Commentary on the Danse Macabre through the Centuries.* New York: Abbeville Press, 1983.

Grigsby, Bryon Lee. *Pestilence in Medieval and Early Modern English Literature.* New York: Routledge, 2004.

Healy, Margaret. *Fictions of Disease in Early Modern England: Bodies, Plagues, and Politics.* New York: Palgrave, 2002.

Heyl, Christoph. "Deformity's Filthy Fingers: Cosmetics and the Plague in *Artificiall Embellishments, or Arts best Directions how to preserve Beauty or procure it* (Oxford, 1665)." In *Didactic Literature in England, 1500–1800,* edited by Natasha Glaisyer and Sara Pennell, pp. 137–51. Burlington, VT: Ashgate, 2003.

Images of the Plague: The Black Death in Biology, Arts, Literature and Learning. Binghamton, NY: The Gallery, 1977.

Koslofsky, C. M. *The Reformation and the Dead: Death and Ritual in Early Modern Germany, 1450–1700.* Basingstoke: Macmillan, 2000.

Leavy, Barbara Fass. *To Blight with Plague: Studies in a Literary Theme.* New York: New York University Press, 1992.

Meiss, Millard. *Painting in Florence and Siena after the Black Death: The Arts, Religion, and Society in the Mid-fourteenth Century.* Princeton: Princeton University Press, 1951.

Totaro, Rebecca. *Suffering In Paradise: The Bubonic Plague In English Literature From More To Milton.* Pittsburgh: Duquesne University Press, 2005.

MAJOR WORKS IN LANGUAGES OTHER THAN ENGLISH

Albini, G. *Guerra, fame, peste. Crisi di mortalità e sistema sanitario nella Lombardia tardomedioevale.* Bologna: Capelli, 1982.

Amasuno Sárraga, Marcelino V. *La peste en la corona de Castilla durante la Segunda mitad del siglo XIV.* Valladolid: Junta de Castilla y León, Consejería de Educación y Cultura, 1996.

Audoin-Rouzeau, Frédérique. *Les chemins de la peste: le rat, la puce et l'homme.* Rennes: Presses Universitaires de Rennes, 2003.

Ballesteros Rodríguez, Juan. *La peste en Córdoba.* Cordoba: Excma. Diputaciâon Provincial de Córdoba, Servicio de Publicaciones, 1982.

Bergdolt, Klaus. *Die Pest 1348 in Italien. 50 zeitgenössische Quellen.* Heidelberg: Manutius Verlag, 1989.

Betrán, José Luis. *La peste en la Barcelona de los Austrias.* Lleida: Milenio, 1996.

Biraben, Jean-Noel. *Les hommes et la peste en France et dans les pays européens et méditeranéens.* 2 vols. Paris: Mouton, 1975, 1976.

Borromeo, Federico. *La peste di Milano.* Milan: Rusconi, 1987.

Brossolet, Jacqueline, and Henri H. Mollaret. *Pourquoi la peste? Le rat, la puce, et la bubon.* Paris: Decouvertes Gallimard, 1994.

Cacciuttolo, Janine. *Chartres au debut du XVIIe siècle: une communaute urbaine face à la peste de 1628–1629.* Nanterre: Université de Paris, 1973.

Camps i Clemente. *La pesta del segle XV a Catalunya.* Lleida: Universitat de Lleida, 1998.

Carpentier, Elisabeth. *Une ville devant la peste: Orvieto et la Peste Noire de 1348.* Paris: S.E.V.P.E.N., 1962.

Carvalho, João Manuel Saraiva de. *Diário da peste de Coimbra (1599).* Lisbon: Fundação Calouste Gulbenkian: Junta Nacional de Investigação Científica e Tecnológica, 1994.

Chiapelli, Alberto. "Gli ordinamenti sanitari del commune di Pistoia contra la pestilenza del 1348." *Archivio Storico Italiano* 4th ser. 63 (1887): 3–24.

Esser, Thilo. *Pest, Heilsangst, und Frömmigkeit: Studien zur religiösen Bewältigung der Pest am Ausgang des Mittelalters.* Altenberge: Oros, 1999.

Favier, Jean, ed. *XIVe et XVe siècles: crises et geneses.* Paris: Presses Universitaires de France, 1996.

Guerry, Liliane. *La theme du "Triomphe de la Mort" dans le peinture italienne.* Paris: G. P. Maisonneuve, 1950.

Hatje, Frank. *Leben und Sterben im Zeitalter der Pest. Basel im 15. bis 17. Jahrhundert.* Basel: Helbing und Lichtenhahn, 1992.

Haye, Olivier de la. *Poeme sur la grande peste de 1348.* Edited by George Guigue. Lyon: n.p., 1888.

Höhl, Monika. *Die Pest in Hildesheim: Krankheit als Krisenfaktor im städtischen Leben des Mittelalters und der Frühen Neuzeit (1350–1750).* Hildesheim: Stadtarchiv, 2002.

Ibs, J. H. *Die Pest in Schleswig-Holstein von 1350 bis 1547/8.* Frankfurt-am-Main: Peter Lang, 1994.

Images de la maladie: la peste dans l'histoire. Paris: Association "Histoire au présent," 1990.

Livi-Bacci, Massimo. *La société italienne devant les crises de mortalité.* Florence: Dipartimento statistico, 1978.

Lucenet, Monique. *Les grandes pestes en France.* Paris: Aubier, 1985.

Marechal, G. "De Zwarte Dood te Brugge (1349–1351)." *Biekorf* 80 (1980): 377–392.

Monteano, Peio J. *La ira de Dios: Los navarros en la era de la peste (1348–1723).* Pamplona: Pamela, 2002.

Pasche, Véronique. *'Pour la salut de mon âme. Les Lausannois face à la mort (XIVe siècle).* Lausanne: Université de Lausanne, 1988.

Pastore, Alessandro. *Crimine e giustizia in tempo di peste nell'Europa moderna.* Bari: Laterza, 1991.

Persson, B. *Pestens gåta. Farsoter i det tidiga 1700–talets Skåne.* Lund: Historiska Institutionen vid Lunds Universitet, 2001.

Rubio, Augustin. *Peste negra, crisis y comportamientos sociales en la Espagne del siglo XIV. La ciudad de Valencia (1348–1401).* Granada: Universidad de Granada, 1979.

Schmölzer, Hilde. *Die Pest in Wien.* Vienna: Österreichischer Bundesverlag Gesellschaft, 1985.

Schwartz, Klaus. *Die Pest in Bremen: Epidemien und freier Handel in einer deutschen Hafenstadt, 1350–1713.* Bremen: Selbstverlag des Staatsarchivs, 1996.

Sies, Rudolf. *'Pariser Pestgutachten' von 1348 in altfranzosischen Fassung.* Würzburger Medizine historische Forschungen #7. Pattensen/Han: Wellm, 1977.

Villard, Pierre. "Constantinople et la peste (1467) (Critoboulos, V, 17)." *Histoire et société: Mélanges offerts à Georges Duby.* 4 vols. Aix-en-Provence: Publications de l'Université de Provence, 1992; IV, pp. 143–50.

Zeller, Michael. *Rochus: Die Pest und Ihr Patron.* Nuremberg: Verlag Hans Böckel, 1989.

INDEX

About the Author

JOSEPH P. BYRNE is a European historian and Associate Professor of Honors at Belmont University, Nashville, TN. He has conducted research and published articles on a wide variety of subjects, from Roman catacombs to American urbanization, though his area of expertise is Italy in the era of the Black Death. He is the author of *The Black Death* (Greenwood, 2004).